T0210563

Lecture Notes in Business Information Processing   **204**

More information about this series at http://www.springer.com/series/7911

Selmin Nurcan · Elias Pimenidis (Eds.)

Information Systems Engineering in Complex Environments

CAiSE Forum 2014
Thessaloniki, Greece, June 16–20, 2014
Selected Extended Papers

 Springer

Editors
Selmin Nurcan
Université Paris 1 Panthéon - Sorbonne
Paris
France

Elias Pimenidis
University of the West of England
Bristol
UK

ISSN 1865-1348   ISSN 1865-1356 (electronic)
Lecture Notes in Business Information Processing
ISBN 978-3-319-19269-7   ISBN 978-3-319-19270-3 (eBook)
DOI 10.1007/978-3-319-19270-3

Library of Congress Control Number: 2015939210

Springer Cham Heidelberg New York Dordrecht London

Printed on acid-free paper

Springer International Publishing AG Switzerland is part of Springer Science+Business Media
(www.springer.com)

CAISE 2014 Forum

Preface

CAISE is a well-established highly visible conference series on Information Systems Engineering. In 2014, the conference extended a special welcome to papers that address Information Systems Engineering in Times of Crisis.

The CAISE Forum was a place within the CAISE 2014 conference for presenting and discussing new ideas and tools related to information systems engineering. Intended to serve as an interactive platform, the forum aims at the presentation of fresh ideas, emerging new topics, controversial positions, as well as demonstration of innovative systems, tools, and applications. The Forum session at the CAISE conference facilitated the interaction, discussion, and exchange of ideas among presenters and participants.

Three types of submissions have been invited to the Forum:

(1) Visionary short papers that present innovative research projects, which are still at a relatively early stage and do not necessarily include a full-scale validation.
(2) Demo papers describing innovative tools and prototypes that implement the results of research efforts. The tools and prototypes will be presented as demos in the Forum.
(3) Case study reports using the STARR (Situation, Task, Approach, Results, Reflection) template.

The 17 papers presented in this volume were carefully reviewed and selected from 45 submissions.

CAISE 2014 Forum has received 45 submissions from 29 countries (Algeria, Austria, Belgium, Canada, China, Colombia, Czech Republic, Estonia, France, Germany, Greece, India, Israel, Italy, Japan, Latvia, Luxembourg, The Netherlands, Norway, Portugal, Saudi Arabia, Singapore, Spain, Sweden, Switzerland, Tunisia, Turkey, United Arab Emirates, Uruguay). Among the submissions, 27 are visionary papers, 14 are demo papers, and 4 are case study reports. Eleven papers have been redirected from the main conference. Thirty-four papers have been directly submitted to the Forum. The average acceptance rate of CAISE 2014 Forum is 35%.

The management of paper submission and reviews was supported by the EasyChair conference system. Selecting the papers to be accepted has been a worthwhile effort. All papers received three reviews from the members of the Forum Program Committee and the Program Board. Eventually, 26 high-quality papers have been selected; among them 16 visionary papers, a case study report and 9 demo papers. All of them have been presented during the Forum session in Thessaloniki.

After CAISE 2014 Forum, authors of the Forum papers have been invited to submit an extended version of their papers for post-proceedings that will be published as a

Springer LNBIP volume. Twenty-two full papers have been submitted. All papers received again three reviews from the members of the CAISE 2014 Forum LNBIP Proceedings Editorial Committee. At the end of a two-round review process supported by EasyChair, this LNBIP volume presents a collection of 17 extended papers; among them 12 visionary papers that present innovative research projects, which are still at a relatively early stage and do not necessarily include a full-scale validation; four demo papers describing innovative tools and prototypes that implement the results of research efforts; and one case study report.

As the CAISE 2014 Forum chairs, we would like to express again our gratitude to the Forum Program Board and the Program Committee for their efforts in providing very thorough evaluations of the submitted Forum papers.

As the Volume editors of the CAISE 2014 Forum LNBIP Proceedings, we would like to express our gratitude to the Proceedings Editorial Committee Members for their sustainable efforts in providing very thorough evaluations of the submitted extended Forum papers. We also wish to thank all authors who submitted papers to the CAISE 2014 Forum LNBIP Proceedings for having shared their work with us.

Last but not least, we would like to thank the CAISE 2014 Program Committee Chairs and the Local Organization Committee for their support.

March 2015   Selmin Nurcan
                                                                       Elias Pimenidis

Organization

CAISE 2014 Forum Chairs

Selmin Nurcan	Université Paris 1 Panthéon - Sorbonne, France
Elias Pimenidis	University of the West of England, UK

CAISE 2014 Forum LNBIP Proceedings - Editorial Committee Members

Saïd Assar	Télécom École de Management, France
Luciano Baresi	Politecnico di Milano, Italy
Judith Barrios	Universidad de Los Andes, Venezuela
Khalid Benali	Université de Lorraine, France
François Charoy	Université de Lorraine, France
Fabiano Dalpiaz	Utrecht University, The Netherlands
Maya Daneva	University of Twente, The Netherlands
Sergio España	Universidad Politécnica de Valencia, Spain
Xavier Franch	Universitat Politècnica de Catalunya, Spain
Christos Georgiadis	University of Macedonia, Greece
Johny Ghattas	University of Haifa, Israel
Chihab Hanachi	University Toulouse 1 Sciences Sociales, France
Charlotte Hug	University Paris 1 Panthéon Sorbonne, France
Evangelia Kavakli	University of the Aegean, Greece
Marite Kirikova	Riga Technical University, Latvia
Elena Kornyshova	CNAM, France
Agnes Koschmider	Karlsruhe Institute of Technology, Germany
Sai Peck Lee	University of Malaya, Kuala Lumpur, Malaysia
Raimundas Matulevicius	University of Tartu, Estonia
Naveen Prakash	GCET, India
Hajo Reijers	Eindhoven University of Technology, The Netherlands
Gustavo Rossi	Universidad Nacional de La Plata, Argentina
Motoshi Saeki	Tokyo Institute of Technology, Japan
Samira Si-Said Cherfi	CNAM, France
Jacques Simonin	Télécom Bretagne, France
Guttorm Sindre	Norwegian University of Science and Technology, Norway
Janis Stirna	University of Stockholm, Sweden
Arnon Sturm	Ben-Gurion University, Israel
Barbara Weber	University of Innsbruck, Austria
Jelena Zdravkovic	Stockholm University, Sweden

CAISE 2014 Forum Program Board Members

Xavier Franch	Universitat Politècnica de Catalunya, Spain
Marite Kirikova	Riga Technical University, Latvia
Barbara Weber	University of Innsbruck, Austria
Jelena Zdravkovic	Stockholm University, Sweden

CAISE 2014 Forum Program Committee Members

João Paulo A. Almeida	Federal University of Espírito Santo, Brazil
Saïd Assar	Télécom École de Management, France
Luciano Baresi	Politecnico di Milano, Italy
Judith Barrios	Universidad de Los Andes, Venezuela
Kahina Bessai	University Paris 1 Panthéon Sorbonne, France
François Charoy	Université de Lorraine, France
Fabiano Dalpiaz	Utrecht University, The Netherlands
Maya Daneva	University of Twente, The Netherlands
Sergio España	Universidad Politécnica de Valencia, Spain
Christos Georgiadis	University of Macedonia, Greece
Johny Ghattas	University of Haifa, Israel
Aditya Ghose	University of Wollongong, Australia
Chihab Hanachi	University Toulouse 1 Sciences Sociales, France
Charlotte Hug	University Paris 1 Panthéon Sorbonne, France
Evangelia Kavakli	University of the Aegean, Greece
Elena Kornyshova	CNAM, France
Agnes Koschmider	Karlsruhe Institute of Technology, Germany
Hui Ma	Victoria University of Wellington, New Zealand
Raimundas Matulevicius	University of Tartu, Estonia
Sai Peck Lee	University of Malaya, Kuala Lumpur, Malaysia
Naveen Prakash	GCET, India
Hajo Reijers	Eindhoven University of Technology, The Netherlands
Gustavo Rossi	Universidad Nacional de La Plata, Argentina
Motoshi Saeki	Tokyo Institute of Technology, Japan
Samira Si-Said Cherfi	CNAM, France
Jacques Simonin	Télécom Bretagne, France
Guttorm Sindre	Norwegian University of Science and Technology, Norway
Janis Stirna	University of Stockholm, Sweden
Arnon Sturm	Ben-Gurion University, Israel

Additional Reviewers

Carlos Azevedo	Federal University of Espírito Santo, Brazil
Evangelos Gongolidis	University of the Aegean, Greece
Christos Kalloniatis	University of the Aegean, Greece
Marcela Ruiz	Universidad Politécnica de Valencia, Spain

Contents

Visionary Papers

A Formal Broker Framework for Secure and Cost-Effective Business Process
Deployment on Multiple Clouds 3
 Elio Goettelmann, Karim Dahman, Benjamin Gateau, and Claude Godart

Presentation and Validation of Method for Security Requirements Elicitation
from Business Processes 20
 Naved Ahmed and Raimundas Matulevičius

An Explorative Study for Process Map Design 36
 Monika Malinova, Henrik Leopold, and Jan Mendling

Supporting Data Collection in Complex Scenarios with Dynamic Data
Collection Processes 52
 Gregor Grambow, Nicolas Mundbrod, Jens Kolb, and Manfred Reichert

A Method for Analyzing Time Series Data in Process Mining: Application
and Extension of Decision Point Analysis 68
 *Reinhold Dunkl, Stefanie Rinderle-Ma, Wilfried Grossmann,
 and Karl Anton Fröschl*

Extracting Data Manipulation Processes from SQL Execution Traces. 85
 Marco Mori, Nesrine Noughi, and Anthony Cleve

Mapping and Usage of Know-How Contributions 102
 Arnon Sturm, Daniel Gross, Jian Wang, Soroosh Nalchigar, and Eric Yu

Facilitating Effective Stakeholder Communication in Software
Development Processes 116
 Vladimir A. Shekhovtsov, Heinrich C. Mayr, and Christian Kop

Towards Path-Based Semantic Annotation for Web Service Discovery. 133
 Julius Köpke, Johann Eder, and Dominik Joham

A Semantic-Aware Framework for Composite Services Engineering Based
on Semantic Similarity and Concept Lattices 148
 *Ahmed Abid, Nizar Messai, Mohsen Rouached, Thomas Devogele,
 and Mohamed Abid*

Work Systems Paradigm and Frames for Fractal Architecture
of Information Systems   165
    Marite Kirikova

Towards Ontology-Based Information Systems and Performance
Management for Collaborative Enterprises   181
    Barbara Livieri and Mario Bochicchio

Innovative Tools and Prototypes

Conciliating Model-Driven Engineering with Technical Debt
Using a Quality Framework   199
    Fáber D. Giraldo, Sergio España, Manuel A. Pineda,
    William J. Giraldo, and Oscar Pastor

Towards Supporting the Analysis of Online Discussions in OSS Communities:
A Speech-Act Based Approach   215
    Itzel Morales-Ramirez, Anna Perini, and Mariano Ceccato

Visual and Ontological Modeling and Analysis Support for Extended
Enterprise Models   233
    Sagar Sunkle and Hemant Rathod

Unified Process Modeling with UPROM Tool   250
    Banu Aysolmaz and Onur Demirörs

Case Study Report

Requirements for IT Governance in Organizations Experiencing
Decentralization   269
    Jelena Zdravkovic, Irina Rychkova, and Thomas Speckert

Author Index   287

Visionary Papers

A Formal Broker Framework for Secure and Cost-Effective Business Process Deployment on Multiple Clouds

Elio Goettelmann[1,2]([✉]), Karim Dahman[3], Benjamin Gateau[2], and Claude Godart[1]

[1] LORIA - INRIA Grand Est, Université de Lorraine, Nancy, France
claude.godart@loria.fr
[2] CRP Henri Tudor, Kirchberg, Luxembourg, Luxembourg
{elio.goettelmann,benjamin.gateau}@tudor.lu
[3] Blu Age - Netfective Technology, Pessac, France
k.dahman@bluage.com

Abstract. Security risk management on information systems provides security guarantees while controlling costs. But security risk assessments can be very complex, especially in a cloud context where data is distributed over multiple environments. To prevent costs from becoming the only cloud selection factor, while disregarding security, we propose a method for performing multiple cloud security risk assessments. In this paper we present a broker framework for balancing costs against security risks. Our framework selects cloud offers and generates deployment-ready business processes in a multi-cloud environment.

Keywords: Business process · Security risk management · Cloud

1 Introduction

The Cloud business model proposes a multitude of services, at different prices, and with various quality levels. Cloud computing can reduce costs, but the selection of a solution adapted to one's needs is time consuming. For this purpose, cloud brokers have emerged; they propose to help cloud consumers for selecting adequate solutions. They compare existing offers, essentially against their prices. In this selection process, security still is an important factor. Since cloud computing presents new kinds of security risks [6,9], they need to be tamed before a wider adoption. Novel methods have to be defined in order to prevent potential losses on companies.

Distributing software over multiple locations increases the complexity of gathering sensitive business information. In this paper, we propose a framework for cloud brokers. We propose to help analyzing the security levels of different cloud offers by following standard risk assessment methodologies.

The paper is organized as follows. Section 2 presents a motivating example used to demonstrate the purpose and the scope of our framework. In Sect. 3

© Springer International Publishing Switzerland 2015
S. Nurcan and E. Pimenidis (Eds.): CAiSE Forum 2014, LNBIP 204, pp. 3–19, 2015.
DOI: 10.1007/978-3-319-19270-3_1

we present our model for assessing security risks in a cloud context. Section 5 applies our approach on the motivating example and gives our experimental results. Section 6 gives a brief description of our proof-of-concept implementation. Sections 7 and 8 discuss respectively related and future work.

2   Motivating Example and Overview

In this section, we introduce a motivating example to illustrate the concepts of our framework. We give an overview of our approach for selecting offers when deploying business processes on multiple clouds.

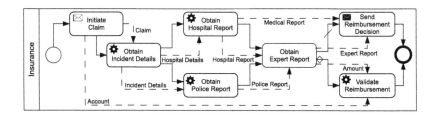

Fig. 1. Business process motivation example: Insurance Claim Recovery Chain.

Consider the *insurance claim recovery chain* [11] depicted in Fig. 1. This BPMN process is initiated when an *insurance* company receives a claim recovery declaration from a *beneficiary*. The emergency service is invoked to obtain details about the *incident*. The *hospital* and *police* reports are required by the *expert* to decide on the *reimbursement* decision. The *bank* is potentially requested and a notification is sent to the *beneficiary*.

In the figure, *data dependencies* between the different tasks are represented using dashed arrows. Additional requirements regarding the distribution of the process can be modeled. Examples of such requirements are described more precisely in [13].

Now suppose that this insurance company wants to outsource this process to the cloud. It has not necessarily the knowledge of moving it effectively on its own. A cloud broker could support the company by **evaluating the security risks** of a cloud outsourcing, **selecting the adequate offers** and **decomposing the process** to deploy it on multiple clouds. These three tasks are detailed below.

Our approach consists in a design-time tool and a model-driven approach for producing secure and cost-effective business processes on multiple clouds. It is illustrated in Fig. 2.

A cloud broker requests the *security needs* as non-functional requirements from the cloud consumer. It analyzes different *cloud offers* of cloud providers. In this paper we focus on the **risk assessment**. Our goal is to show how the risk can be assessed in a cloud context.

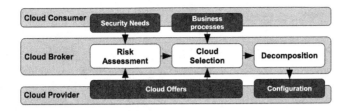

Fig. 2. Our design-time framework for multi-cloud business process deployment.

The broker uses *business processes* of the cloud consumer to **select** the adequate (secure and cost-effective) *cloud offers* based on the functional requirements, the costs and the previously calculated risk.

The broker **decomposes** the business process into smaller parts, as each task can be enacted on a different cloud site. The generated *configuration* is the assignment of these process fragments to cloud provider sites. The decomposition itself has already been addressed in [12].

In the next section we will define the different concepts of our approach.

3   A Formal Cloud Security Risk Assessment Model

In the following, we present our model (Fig. 3) for assessing security risks in a cloud context. We show examples of a formalization of each concept and their relations.

In traditional risk management methodologies, the risk is generally evaluated using the following formula: $risk = vulnerability \times impact \times threat$ [2,17]. The *threat* represents the event which would negatively affect the information system. The *impact* represents the loss (financial or other) which would occur for this event. The *vulnerabilities* represent the security flaws which could enable this event.

But in a cloud environment, the information system owner is separated from its user. In this context it is difficult to assess the risk in this way. Indeed, the cloud provider cannot determine the impact of a security breach on its consumer's system. The cloud consumer cannot identify easily the vulnerabilities of the cloud provider's infrastructure. Moreover, cloud providers often conceal their vulnerabilities to reduce their exposure to attacks.

Therefore, the cloud broker plays a crucial role. It is the sole stakeholder who can calculate a risk value by taking into account information from providers and consumers. Our model is divided into three packages:

- **Cloud Consumer Model**, for establishing the *impact* value of the risk.
- **Cloud Provider Model**, for establishing the *vulnerability* value.
- **Cloud Broker Model**, which combines these concepts with the *threats* to evaluate a final *risk* value.

In the following we furtherly investigate the model of each stakeholder.

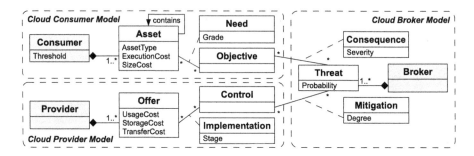

Fig. 3. Cloud security risk assessment model

Definition 1 (Cloud Consumer). *An entity which browses the offers from Cloud providers (or Cloud brokers) and uses the adequate service for its functional and non-functional requirements. It is formalized as follows:*

> **Asset** = *Process* ∪ *Task* ∪ *Data* ∪ *Message, defines business assets of the consumer information system,*
> **Objective** = {*Confidentiality, Integrity, Availability, Non-repudiation, Authenticity*}, *is a set of security objectives on the information system,*
> **Need** : *Asset* × *Objective* → *Grade, defines the security need of an asset and an objective,*
> **Threshold** : Ω → *Level, defines a global acceptable risk level,*
> *ExecutionCost* : *Task* → $\mathbb{N}^*$, *defines task execution costs (in seconds),*
> *SizeCost* : *Data* → $\mathbb{N}^*$, *defines data size costs (in bytes),*

A **Security Need** is defined as a **Grade** on an **Asset** for a **Security Objective**. For our approach we use the widespread CIANA security objectives (*Confidentiality, Integrity, Availability, Non-Repudiation* and *Authenticity*). For example, it is more important for some assets to be often available, whereas for other priority is more about confidentiality. Such security requirements can be described with these attributes. The grade defines "how much" of a security objective the asset needs. It can be adjusted regarding the use case but often corresponds to a qualitative or quantitative scale (see Table 1). Other reference frames can also be used as security objectives, for example STRIDE[1].

These needs can be annotated on the data elements of a business process and are then translated into task-centric needs, or they can be directly annotated on the tasks.

The **Threshold**, indicates the **Level** of acceptable risk for the information system.

Definition 2 (Cloud Provider). *An entity which can hold multiple cloud offers. It is responsible for the implementation of security controls, which protects its offers from attacks and complies with regulations. It is formalized as follows:*

---

[1] http://msdn.microsoft.com/en-us/magazine/cc163519.aspx.

Offer, *is a set of cloud offers,*
Control, *is a set of controls,*
Implementation: *Offer × Control → Stage, defines how a control is implemented for an offer,*
UsageCost, StorageCost, TransferCost : Offer → $\mathbb{N}^*$, defines offers' costs in terms of usage (in \$/second), storage (in \$/byte) and transfer (in \$/byte)

Security Controls are countermeasure reducing vulnerabilities of information systems. They may be given in guidelines or standards (as for example the CSA [6] or the ISO 27017 [1]). Providers can then audit the **implementation** of these controls for their **Offers**. Since some control implementations can be described by a fuzzy value, we add a **Stage** attribute. It expresses the fact that some controls are not fully implemented but only partially, which is still better than not at all. We consider that a cloud provider is more willing to publish such type of information than its vulnerabilities. It gives information about the security of their information system without directly revealing their vulnerabilities (e.g. the CSA Security, Trust and Assurance Registry: STAR [6]).

Definition 3 (Cloud Broker). *An entity that enhances existing services like security, combines multiple services or measures different providers and selects the best [18]. It is formalized as follows:*

Threat, *is a set of security threats, which can be weighted through a Probability,*
Control, *is the same set of controls as the Cloud provider,*
Objective, *is the same set of objectives as the Cloud consumer,*
Mitigation: *Threat × Control → Degree, is the mitigation of a threat by a control,*
Consequence: *Threat × Objective → Severity, is the consequence of a threat on an objective,*
Harm: *Threat × Asset → Rate, is the harm a threat could have on an asset,*
Coverage: *Threat × Offer → Score, is the coverage score of a threat for an offer,*
Risk: *Asset × Offer × Threat → Level, is the risk level of a threat for an asset on an offer,*

To stick to the previous risk definition, the broker defines a list of **Threats** the Cloud Consumer faces. The CSA regularly publishes an example of such a list [6]. As some threats are more likely to happen, we added a **Probability** of occurence. This ponderation depends on the context and on the type of cloud offer. For example, some companies are more exposed to hacking attacks than others or some threats may not be applicable for some cloud offers.

The **Mitigations** represent relations between controls and threats. Each control reduces one or more threats. But as some controls may have a bigger reduction effect, we introduce a **Degree** of mitigation. This value indicates how the control mitigates the given threat.

By combining this value with the **Implementation**, we calculate a **Score** that defines the threat **Coverage** for a provider. Basically, the more controls a provider implements, the more threat he will cover. But as some controls are "better" to mitigate some threats, the provider will have a different response for each threat. This is the value which allows the broker to differentiate the cloud providers.

Consequences represent the relation between objectives and threats. Each threat affects one or more security objectives. But as some objectives are more affected than others, we introduce the **Severity** of the consequence. It indicates how the objective is affected by the given threat. For example, a *Denial of Service* attack will affect the system's *Availability*, more than its *Confidentiality*.

We combine this value with the **Need** given by the consumer, to get the **Rate** of **Harm**. It represents the *impact* of previously given risk formula. For example, an asset that has an important need of *Availability* will have an important Harm in case of a *Denial of Service* attack.

Finally, we define the **Level** of **Risk** for an asset, an offer and a given threat. It can be calculated by the broker through a combination between the Harm, the Coverage and the Probability. In the next section we give an example of such a risk level.

4   Instantiation on the Motivating Example

This section instantiates our model on the motivating example. For this purpose, we specify the relations between the different concepts defined previously. To simplify relations and calculations we define all attributes on a $[0, 1]$ scale and work with a probabilistic approach.

4.1   Calculating the Harm

First, we calculate the Harm, which represents the *impact* in the commonly used risk formula. It is defined between the Cloud Consumer and the Cloud Broker.

Security Needs. As presented previously, the security needs are described using the five common CIANA attributes.

Table 1. Grades of need for each security objective

Confidentiality	Integrity	Availability	Non-repudiation	Authenticity	**Values**
Public	Passable	Sparse	Futile	Irrelevant	**0**
Restricted	Alterable	Usual	Tolerable	Common	**0.5**
Secret	Fixed	Continuous	Trusted	Verified	**1**

We define 3 grades for each objective and assign them a value in Table 1. A value of 0 means the objective is not needed at all and 1 that this objective is crucial.

Table 2. Annotations of the Security Needs on the motivation example's data.

Data Associations	Conf.	Integ.	Avail.	N.-rep.	Auth.
Claim	Public	Passable	Continuous	Tolerable	Irrelevant
Hospital details	Secret	Alterable	Usual	Futile	Common
Incident details	Public	Alterable	Usual	Futile	Common
Hospital report	Restricted	Fixed	Sparse	Tolerable	Common
Police report	Restricted	Fixed	Usual	Trusted	Verified
Medical report	Secret	Alterable	Usual	Tolerable	Verified
Expert report	Restricted	Fixed	Usual	Trusted	Verified
Account	Secret	Fixed	Sparse	Futile	Verified
Amount	Restricted	Fixed	Sparse	Trusted	Verified

For our motivating example, Table 2 shows the *security needs* on each data object. These security needs are negotiated by a risk manager with the cloud consumer. For example, the payment does not need a high *Availability* since it is sensible but not urgent. It will be not as much exposed to a *Denial of Service Attack* than another activity.

Business process deployment is task-centric, as tasks are assigned to cloud offers and not data objects. Therefore, these values need to be translated into security needs on tasks. We use the maximum values of the input and output objects of a task, similar to the approach presented by Watson in [22]. For example, *Obtain Incident Details* is associated to the data objects *Claim, Incident Details* and *Hospital Details*. We take the maximum of each data object's need to get the need of *Obtain Incident Details*: {*Secret, Passable, Continuous, Tolerable, Common*} for respectively {*Confidentiality, Integrity, Availability, Non-Repudiation, Authenticity*}. The security needs of all tasks are given in Table 3.

Consequences. We advocate a value for the **Severity** between 0 and 1. The minimum 0 means that the objective is not affected at all. The maximum 1 means that the objective is completely prevented by the given threat.

Table 3. Resulting Security Needs on the motivating example's tasks

Tasks	Conf.	Integ.	Avail.	N.-rep.	Auth.
Initiate Claim	Secret	Fixed	Continuous	Tolerable	Verified
Obtain Incident Details	Secret	Alterable	Continuous	Tolerable	Common
Obtain Hospital Report	Secret	Fixed	Usual	Tolerable	Verified
Obtain Police Report	Restricted	Fixed	Usual	Trusted	Verified
Obtain Expert Report	Restricted	Fixed	Usual	Trusted	Verified
Send Reimbursement Decision	Secret	Fixed	Usual	Trusted	Verified
Process Reimbursement	Secret	Fixed	Sparse	Trusted	Verified

Table 4. Severity of consequences for each security objective

	Conf.	Integ.	Avail.	Non-Rep.	Auth.
Data breaches	Significant	Negligible	Negligible	Negligible	Negligible
Data loss	Negligible	Negligible	Significant	Related	Negligible
Account hijacking	Significant	Significant	Related	Related	Related
Insecure interfaces	Significant	Significant	Related	Negligible	Significant
Denial of service	Negligible	Negligible	Significant	Negligible	Negligible
Malicious insiders	Significant	Significant	Significant	Significant	Significant
Abuse of Cloud Services	Negligible	Related	Negligible	Related	Related
Insufficient Due Diligence	Related	Related	Significant	Negligible	Negligible
Technology Vulnerabilities	Related	Related	Related	Related	Related

For our motivating example we define three levels ($\{Significant = 1, Related = 0.5, Negligible = 0\}$) and assign them in Table 4. These threats and relations are based on the CSA report [7].

Harm. To calculate the harm we use a probabilistic approach to remain in the $[0, 1]$ interval. We want to express that the harm is the union of the effects on all objectives. We define the formula:

Definition 4 (Harm). $\forall t \in Threat, \forall a \in Asset,$

$$Harm(t, a) = 1 - \left(\prod_{o_i \in Objective} 1 - (Need(a, o_i) \times Consequence(t, o_i)) \right) \quad (1)$$

Our framework also works with other types of combination strategies as weighted or mixed, which could be more adapted in other use cases. The result for all tasks of the process can be seen in Table 5.

4.2 Calculating the Coverage

Then, we calculate the Coverage, which represents the *vulnerability* in the commonly used risk formula. It is defined between the Cloud Provider and the Cloud Broker.

Implementation. In order to determine the response to cloud threats for each offer we use Security, Trust and Assurance Registry (STAR) [6] managaed by the CSA. The site publishes a list of major public cloud providers and the controls they implement. We define the **Stage** of **Implementation** over three levels: $\{Full = 1, Partial = 0.5, Ignored = 0\}$. As there are 197 implementable controls, we do not publish an exhaustive list for each provider in this paper.

Table 5. Harms on the process tasks and coverage of the providers for 5 cloud threats

	Initiate claim	Obt. incident det.	Obt hospital rep.	Obt. police rep.	Obt. expert rep.	Send reimb. dec.	Process reimb.	Softlayer	CloudSigma	FireHost	SHI Intern.	Terremark	Probability
	Harm							Coverage					
Data breaches	1.00	1.00	1.00	0.50	0.50	1.00	1.00	0.36	0.62	0.21	0.54	0.52	1.0
Data loss	1.00	1.00	0.63	0.75	0.75	0.75	0.50	0.49	0.59	0.42	0.59	0.67	1.0
Account Hijacking	1.00	1.00	1.00	1.00	1.00	1.00	1.00	0.55	0.64	0.46	0.59	0.46	1.0
Insecure interfaces	1.00	1.00	1.00	1.00	1.00	1.00	1.00	0.54	0.67	0.53	0.59	0.58	0.9
Denial of service	1.00	1.00	0.50	0.50	0.50	0.50	0.00	0.60	0.66	0.53	0.62	0.66	0.9
Malicious insiders	1.00	1.00	1.00	1.00	1.00	1.00	1.00	0.49	0.64	0.54	0.60	0.61	0.9
Abuse of Cloud Services	0.81	0.58	0.81	0.88	0.88	0.88	0.88	0.58	0.60	0.56	0.54	0.59	0.8
Insufficient Due Diligence	1.00	1.00	0.88	0.81	0.81	0.88	0.75	0.53	0.64	0.51	0.60	0.56	0.8
Technology Vulnerabilities	0.95	0.89	0.93	0.93	0.93	0.95	0.94	0.49	0.64	0.50	0.55	0.54	0.8

Mitigations. The CSA matrix recommends a list of security controls that a cloud provider should implement to reduce security risks. Each of these controls can be related to one or multiple threats. For example, the control "*IS-19.4 - Do you maintain key management procedures?*" mitigates the *Data Breaches* threat. We suggest a value for the **Degree** in the interval $[0, 1]$. The minimum 0 means that the control is completely ineffective for mitigating the given threat, the maximum 1 means that the control completely prevents the given threat. Optimally, the sum of all weightings for a given threat, should be equal to 1 (when following strictly the CSA guidelines the coverage should be maximal). Moreover, the broker can decide to assign the weightings differently. Indeed, some threats may not be completely coverable. There would always be a remaining risk residue even when implementing all controls. Or he can decide that some controls become useless when implementing other ones. As it would not be really relevant to our proposal and due to a lack of space, this mitigation matrix is not shown in this paper.

Coverage. We take a probabilistic approach to calculate the Coverage Score. We want to express that the coverage is the union of the effects of all controls. Thus, we remain in the same $[0, 1]$ interval. We defined the following formula:

Definition 5 (Coverage). $\forall t \in Threat, \forall o \in Offer$

$$Coverage(t, o) = 1 - \left(\prod_{c_i \in Control} 1 - (Implementation(o, c_i) \times Mitigation(t, c_i)) \right) \tag{2}$$

Note that, other types of combination strategies can be used without impacting our previously defined model. For example, in some use cases a mixed or a weighted strategy could be more adapted.

The results with this formula on 5 providers selected from the STA Registry are shown in Table 5 (*Softlayer*[2], *CloudSigma*[3], *FireHost*[4], *SHI Int.*[5] and *Terremark*[6]). It also indicates the probability we use for each threat. It follows the ranking given by the CSA [7].

4.3 Calculating the Security Risk

To assess the final risk value, **Harm**, **Coverage** and the Threat **Probability** are combined. We use the complementary of the coverage to comply to the commonly used risk formula (given in Sect. 3) which uses the *vulnerabilities*.

Definition 6 (Risk). $\forall a \in Asset, \forall o \in Offer, \forall t \in Threat,$

$$Risk(a, o, t) = Harm(t, a) \times (1 - Coverage(t, o)) \times Probability(t) \qquad (3)$$

Table 6. Maximum risk value of the tasks for each provider

	Softlayer	CloudSigma	FireHost	SHI Int.	Terremark
Initiate claim	0.64	0.41	0.79	0.46	0.54
Obt. incident det.	0.64	0.41	0.79	0.46	0.54
Obt. hospital rep.	0.64	0.38	0.79	0.46	0.54
Obt. police rep.	0.46	0.36	0.54	0.41	0.54
Obt. expert rep.	0.46	0.36	0.54	0.41	0.54
Send reimb. dec.	0.64	0.38	0.79	0.46	0.54
Process reimb.	0.64	0.38	0.79	0.46	0.54

With this formula, our security risk value remains in a $[0, 1]$ interval. It can then be brought to levels if needed, for example: $\{0 \leq Low \leq 0.3 < Medium < 0.7 \leq High \leq 1\}$. We select for each asset on each offer the highest risk value and present them in Table 6.

In accordance with the consumer, the broker defines the **Threshold**, the level of acceptable risk. For a given task, this value defines the providers with a too high risk and excludes these deployment options. In our example, we set the threshold to 0.5. In Table 6 the cells of eliminated providers are grayed out. Respectively a white cell means that the task can be deployed on the provider.

Note that two providers (FireHost and Terremark) are completely excluded, as they do not sufficiently cover threats in comparison to the other providers. Two other providers (CloudSigma and SHI Int.) can be used for enacting all tasks of the example process. They implement enough controls for presenting an acceptable security risk. The last provider (Softlayer) can only be used for

---

[2] http://www.softlayer.com.
[3] http://www.cloudsigma.com.
[4] http://www.firehost.com.
[5] http://www.shi.com.
[6] http://www.terremark.com.

deploying two tasks, as the others have to high security requirements for this provider.

The next section shows how the final configuration is chosen among the remaining offers.

5   Experimentation and Evaluation

In this section we go back to our global approach to deploy the example process in a secure and cost-effective way on multiple clouds. First we select the final configuration based on the costs, and then we deploy the process on the chosen offers.

5.1   Cloud Selection

We select the target cloud environments in two stages: different configurations evaluation and final clouds selection.

Configurations Evaluation. To evaluate the different possible deployment configurations, we introduce a cost model. It allows us to balance the risks against the costs.

Cost model - We consider three types of costs:

- **Usage costs**: the CPU power needed to execute the process (\$/GHz/month). The need is annotated on the tasks of the process.
- **Storage costs**, the space needed by the data of the process (\$/GB/month). The size is annotated on the data objects of the process.
- **Transfer costs**, the amount of incoming/outgoing messages (\$/GB). This size is calculated with the data exchanged between the process fragments.

When benchmarking different existing cloud providers we noticed that their pricing schemes generally match these types of costs. More complex pricing plans can often be brought to such a cost distinction.

Table 7 gives costs for the selected cloud offers of our motivating example.

Table 7. Costs of 5 Cloud offers

	Usage (\$/GHz/mo)	Storage (\$/GB/mo)	Transfer (\$/GB)
Softlayer	20.00	0.10	0.10
CloudSigma AG	13.86	0.18	0.06
FireHost	25.70	2.78	0.50
SHI International, Corp	11.56	0.29	0.01
Terremark	3.60	0.25	0.17

The motivating example presented in this paper is a quite simple case study, as there are only seven tasks to assign to a pool of five cloud providers. But in other use cases, this assignment problem can rapidly explode leading to a Quadratic Assignment Problem (QAP) (n tasks to p providers). Thus, to find a good solution in an acceptable time, we use an heuristic approach. It is not described in details in this paper, as it is not the goal of our proposal, but details can de found in [10]. Basically, it consists in finding an initial solution (a so-called *Greedy* solution) that we enhance using a *Tabu* search algorithm.

Table 8. Output for different runs

	First run					Second run					Third run					Fourth run				
	Softlayer	CloudSigma	FireHost	SHI Int.	Terremark	Softlayer	CloudSigma	FireHost	SHI Int.	Terremark	Softlayer	CloudSigma	FireHost	SHI Int.	Terremark	Softlayer	CloudSigma	FireHost	SHI Int.	Terremark
Initiate claim		x				x					x					x				
Obt. incident det.		x				x					x					x				
Obt. hospital rep.		x				x					x					x				
Obt. police rep.		x				x									x	x				
Obt. expert rep.		x				x									x	x				
Send reimb. dec.		x				x					x					x				
Process reimb.		x				x					x					x				
Risk	0.54					0.46					0.41					0.41				
Cost ($/mo)	67.65					203.38					232.28					275.13				

We experimented our algorithm on the motivating example in four different ways. The results are shown in Table 8.

First run has no restrictions regarding the security risk value, only the costs are taken into account. This gives us a "cheap" solution while leaving out security. In this run, the risk calculated in the previous section is completely disregarded and no providers are excluded. When compared to other possible solutions it can give an idea about the "costs of security".

Second run includes a global risk threshold of 0.5. The providers excluded in the previous section cannot be selected. The majority of the tasks are now located on a more expensive but also less "risky" offer.

Third run has a global risk threshold set to 0.45. By decreasing the acceptable risk value, the provider of the previous run can no longer be an option for some tasks. These tasks are moved to a more "secure" offer and thus increasing the global "security level". Obviously, the costs of the configuration are also increasing.

Fourth run presents a different approach, where we all tasks are moved to the "most secure" cloud. As this provider seems to be the best in terms of security (it has the lowest security risk values), it gives an idea about the "best" possible configuration when disregarding costs. But the risk value indicates that there is no real improvement in comparison to the previous run. Only the costs of the configuration increases, which makes this possible solution not really interesting.

We also notice that the **transfer costs** conduct to a regrouping of the tasks on one main offer to restrain the global costs.

Another point is that it is possible that no configuration is found if the threshold risk value is too low. In this case, either the user increases the threshold value, or he considers the Cloud context as too risky and decides not to move the process to the Cloud.

Final Configuration Selection. The cloud broker can analyze the deployment configurations our algorithm produces and select the most adequate one in conjunction with the cloud consumer. For our motivating example, we select the *Third run*. Indeed, in comparison to the **Second run** it brings a non-negligible improvement in terms of security and the increase of costs seems to us as acceptable. In the following we present briefly how the process can then be deployed on these two selected cloud offers.

5.2 Process Deployment in the Cloud

The process is deployed on the target environments in two steps: process decomposition and fragments deployment.

Process Decomposition. We decompose the process in two process fragments according to the selected configuration. A fragment is a business process enacted on one cloud and includes additional *synchronization tasks*. These tasks support the collaboration with the remote fragments to guarantee the control flow of the initial process. Please refer to [11,12] to see more details about that.

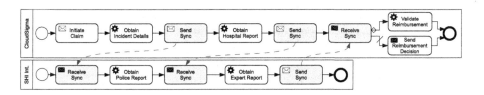

Fig. 4. The fragmented example process.

The decomposed motivating example according to the selected configuration is depicted in Fig. 4 (grey activities are *synchronization tasks*). The two tasks *Obtain Police Report* and *Obtain Expert Report* form an autonomous process located on a different cloud than the remaining process. This process fragment can execute when it receives the *synchronisation* message sent from the first fragment. These two fragments form a global process equivalent to the original centralized process. This global process ends when both fragments have reached their ending tasks.

Deployment in Clouds. The last step of our approach consists in deploying these fragments on the selected cloud offers. In [12] we presented how we deploy such service composition as BPEL programs on remote service orchestration engines (e.g., Apache ODE[7]). But as current Cloud offers do not support this kind of services, we selected offers providing infrastructure services and used them to deploy our own execution engines. We are confident that such type of platforms will rapidly emerge in the future, WSO2 Stratoslive[8] is such a PaaS even if still not available through web services. For some type of processes, tasks could be mapped to existing offers at the SaaS layer of the Cloud. For others, not service based, a development phase can be required before deploying them on the Cloud.

6   Proof of Concept Implementation

To show the feasibility of our approach we implemented our model in a web tool. It consists in a PHP application using the Laravel[9] framework and running on a web server with a MySQL database.

The user of the tool can add new assets, associate security objectives to them and assign the according **security needs** through a dropdown menu. Based on the given values the risk level for each provider is calculated and presented on a chart (see Fig. 5). The risk values a grouped by the type of threat and each provider is assigned to a specific color. The interface can also be adapted to group the values by providers and assign different colors to the different threats. In this case it becomes easy to see which providers are compliant to the given threshold. On this interface the user can also define a threshold which will filter out the offers with a too high risk value (the horizontal dotted line on Fig. 5).

Currently the risk is calculated through static database views, so, in order to add a new type of risk calculation or new levels for defining the security needs, a new view must be created manually. Even if it is sufficient for a prototype implementation and adapted for a demonstration purpose, we plan to extend our tool to support full customization from the user. Therefore, the user of the tool will be able to completely define how the risk will be calculated and re-adapt it "on-the-fly" to make it correspond to its needs.

7   Related Work

Fragmentation and multi-cloud deployment for increasing security is a hot topic in current research. Jensen [14] was one of the first to propose the decomposition of applications and their distribution on different cloud environments. AlZain confirmed later this trend in [4] and highlighted the importance of multi-cloud environments for increasing security.

---

[7] http://ode.apache.org/.

[8] WSO2 Business Process Server, http://wso2.com/products/business-process-server.

[9] http://laravel.com/docs/4.0.

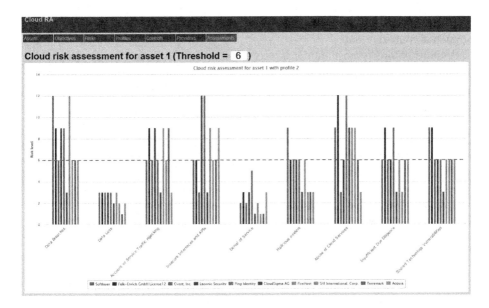

Fig. 5. Our proof-of-concept presenting the risk values for different cloud offers

In [15] the authors present methods to distribute applications on different cloud environments. The fragmentation can be done manually or use optimization algorithms. Similar to our approach the decomposition is considered in the early stages of business process modeling. However security aspects are not considered.

The authors of [3] are adapting processes through risk-reduction patterns, and in [23] processes are analyzed to decide if they are ready for a cloud deployment or not. But these two methods do not show the calculation of the risk value and do not consider process fragmentation.

Watson [22] decomposes workflows and deploys them on multiple clouds according to a cost model, but he defines arbitrary security levels for each provider. In our approach we take calculate these values with information obtained from real cloud providers. Another selection approach is presented in [5], where security requirements are matched with service capabilities. But it does not consider the business process globally and has not been designed for a cloud environment.

Otherwise, [8] provides a risk-prediction algorithm taking decisions during the execution of the process. We focus on design-time rather than on runtime, which changes slightly the kind of treated risks. This type of approach can be considered as complementary to our proposal.

The model presented in [20] allows to evaluate security vulnerabilities in a Service Oriented Architecture. Unfortunately, it does not take into account the cloud context. Our coverage approach is based on security controls from different standards specifically designed for the cloud [1,6]. It seems to us more adapted for such a context.

A more complete cost model is presented in [16]. It is not easily adaptable on business processes for an automated treatment, but could be used to refine our approach.

8   Conclusion and Future Work

In this paper we present a cloud broker framework for assessing security risks in a multiple-cloud deployment context. We assess security risks using standard-based and industry accepted security controls and risk listings. We focus on one use case to illustrate how these risk values, in combination with costs, can help cloud brokers to take decisions for the cloud provider selection. Our approach provides cost-effective and secure cloud deployment solutions. The paper demonstrates the feasibility of our approach with a motivating example and real cloud providers.

We define security needs with the five CIANA objectives and use the STAR Registry to calculate the threat coverage of cloud providers. However, as our approach is model driven, our tool can be extended to support other types of objectives, controls and threats.

Some limitations are not addressed in this paper. First, the shortage of empirical evaluation on real use cases, which will be realized in future works with domain experts and industrial partners. Another point is that our approach takes place at design-time, but as the Cloud is a very dynamic context, extending our framework to configuration at run-time would be an interesting improvement. We also argue that our security needs annotations on the business process could be furtherly explored. There are existing notations as BPMN extensions [19] or [21] that we could adapt to more precisely express the consumer's security requirements.

We are focusing our current work on the selection algorithm. Indeed, in this paper we select providers according to a single criterion, costs, while transforming the risk value in a constraint. However, multi-criteria optimization strategies could be more adapted, especially when taking into account more than two criteria. Quality of Service or response-time are also important parameters that need to be considered when outsourcing applications to the Cloud.

References

1. ISO/IEC 27017, Information tech., Security techniques, Code of practice for information security controls for cloud computing services based on ISO/IEC 27002
2. AS/NZS 4360 SET Risk Management, Australian/New Zealand Standards (2004)
3. Altuhhova, O., Matulevičius, R., Ahmed, N.: Towards definition of secure business processes. In: Bajec, M., Eder, J. (eds.) CAiSE 2012. LNBIP, vol. 112, pp. 1–15. Springer, Heidelberg (2012)
4. AlZain, M., Pardede, E., Soh, B., Thom, J.: Cloud computing security: from single to multi-clouds. In: HICSS 2012, pp. 5490–5499 (2012)

5. Carminati, B., Ferrari, E., Hung, P.C.K.: Security conscious web service composition. In: ICWS (2006)
6. Cloud Security Alliance. Cloud Control Matrix/Security, Trust & Assurance Registry/Consensus Assessments Initiative Questionnaire. Technical report
7. Cloud Security Alliance. The Notorious Nine - Cloud Computing Top Threats in 2013. Technical report (2013)
8. Conforti, R., de Leoni, M., La Rosa, M., van der Aalst, W.M.P.: Supporting risk-informed decisions during business process execution. In: Salinesi, C., Norrie, M.C., Pastor, Ó. (eds.) CAiSE 2013. LNCS, vol. 7908, pp. 116–132. Springer, Heidelberg (2013)
9. European Network and Information Security Agency. Benefits, risks and recommendations for information security. Technical report (2009)
10. Fdhila, W., Dumas, M., Godart, C.: Optimized decentralization of composite web services. In: CollaborateCom 2010, pp. 1–10 (2010)
11. Fdhila, W., Yildiz, U., Godart, C.: A flexible approach for automatic process decentralization using dependency tables. In: ICWS 2009, pp. 847–855. IEEE Computer Society, Washington, DC (2009)
12. Goettelmann, E., Fdhila, W., Godart, C.: Partitioning and cloud deployment of composite web services under security constraints. In: IC2E 2013 (2013)
13. Goettelmann, E., Mayer, N., Godart, C.: A general approach for a trusted deployment of a business process in clouds. In: MEDES 2013 (2013)
14. Jensen, M., Schwenk, J., Bohli, J., Gruschka, N., Iacono, L.: Security prospects through cloud computing by adopting multiple clouds. In: CLOUD 2011, pp. 565–572 (2011)
15. Leymann, F., Fehling, C., Mietzner, R., Nowak, A., Dustdar, S.: Moving applications to the cloud: an approach based on application model enrichment. IJCIS 20(3), 307–356 (2011)
16. Martens, B., Walterbusch, M., Teuteberg, F.: Costing of cloud computing services: a total cost of ownership approach. In: ICSS 2012, pp. 1563–1572 (2012)
17. National Institute of Standards and Technology. Information Security - Guide for Conducting Risk Assessments (2002)
18. National Institute of Standards and Technology. Cloud Computing Reference Architecture (2011)
19. Rodríguez, A., Caro, A., Cappiello, C., Caballero, I.: A BPMN extension for including data quality requirements in business process modeling. In: Mendling, J., Weidlich, M. (eds.) BPMN 2012. LNBIP, vol. 125, pp. 116–125. Springer, Heidelberg (2012)
20. Sackmann, S., Lowis, L., Kittel, K.: A risk based approach for selecting services in business process execution. Wirtschaftsinformatik 1, 357–366 (2009)
21. Turki, S.H., Bellaaj, F., Charfi, A., Bouaziz, R.: Modeling security requirements in service based business processes. In: Bider, I., Halpin, T., Krogstie, J., Nurcan, S., Proper, E., Schmidt, R., Soffer, P., Wrycza, S. (eds.) EMMSAD 2012 and BPMDS 2012. LNBIP, vol. 113, pp. 76–90. Springer, Heidelberg (2012)
22. Watson, P.: A multi-level security model for partitioning workflows over federated clouds. In: CloudCom, pp. 180–188 (2011)
23. Wenzel, S., Wessel, C., Humberg, T., Jürjens, J.: Securing processes for outsourcing into the cloud. In: CLOSER, pp. 675–680 (2012)

Presentation and Validation of Method for Security Requirements Elicitation from Business Processes

Naved Ahmed and Raimundas Matulevičius[✉]

Institute of Computer Science, University of Tartu,
J. Liivi 2, 50409 Tartu, Estonia
{naved,rma}@ut.ee

Abstract. In recent years, the business process modelling is matured towards expressing enterprise's organisational behaviour. This shows potential to perform early security analysis to capture enterprise security needs. Traditionally security in business processes is addressed either by representing security concepts graphically or by enforcing security constraints. But such security approaches miss the elicitation of security needs and their translation to security requirements for system-to-be. This paper proposes a method to elicit security objectives from business process models and translate them to security requirements. As a result, the method contributes to an alignment of business processes with the technology that supports the execution of business processes. The approach applicability is illustrated in few examples and its validity is reported in the comparative study.

Keywords: Security in business processes · Business process modelling · Requirements engineering

1 Introduction

There has been several attempts to engage the relatively matured security requirements engineering in business processes. However, the majority of studies either focusses on the graphical representation of security aspects in business process models [15,22] or enforces the security mechanisms [10] or both [23]. These studies analyse major problems when addressing security engineering in business process modelling. Firstly, security requirements are specified in terms of security architectural design (i.e., security control) and missing the rationale about the trade-offs of the security decision. Secondly, the requirement elicitation is either missing or haphazard: this leads to miss some critical security requirements. And finally, due to the dynamic and complicated nature of business processes, the studies only address varying aspects (i.e., authorisation, access control, separation of duty or binding of duty) but not the overall security of business processes. These problems can be overcome by eliciting security objectives from

© Springer International Publishing Switzerland 2015
S. Nurcan and E. Pimenidis (Eds.): CAiSE Forum 2014, LNBIP 204, pp. 20–35, 2015.
DOI: 10.1007/978-3-319-19270-3_2

business processes and by transforming them to the security requirements where the technology supports the business processes execution.

In this paper we analyse *how to determine security objectives from the business process models and to translate them to security requirements*. In a previous study [1] we have presented a method for security requirements elicitation from business processes (SREBP). The goal of this paper is to highlight what analysts need to do in order to define security models and to elicit security requirements using the SREBP method. In addition we present a comparative analysis of the coverage of security requirements sets elicited using the SREBP method and the security quality requirements engineering (a.k.a., SQUARE) approach. To show the generalisation of the SREBP application and to understand whether the results could be replicated, we briefly report on two SREBP (and SQUARE) application cases.

The rest of the paper is structured as follows. In Sect. 2 we presents the SREBP method using the land management example. In Sect. 3, validity of the proposal is analysed. Section 4 presents some related studies. Finally, Sect. 5 concludes the paper and presents some future work.

2   The SREBP Method

2.1   Illustrative Example: Land Management System

To perform the security requirements elicitation one needs to collect the knowledge of enterprise *value system* from the *value chain* and the *business functions*. Figure 1 illustrates a value chain for the land management system (LMS) example. It organises the enterprise business functions and relates them to each other (as enterprise cooperates to achieve the business goals). In Fig. 2 a detailed workflow of Prepare Plan process is given. The process has two business partners (Lodging Party and Planning Portal) expressed as *swimlanes*, while Registry is identified as an information system.

Fig. 1. Land management systems - value chain

Similarly to Prepare Plan, other sub-processes (e.g., Lodge Plan, Examine Plan, Approve Plan and Update Plan) are also expanded to the operational models. But in Sect. 2.2, we will present the SREBP method using the Prepare Plan process (as illustrated in Figs. 1 and 2).

2.2   Security Requirements Elicitation Method

In [2], we have presented a set of security risk-oriented patterns for securing business processes. Based on these patterns, the SREBP method helps deriving

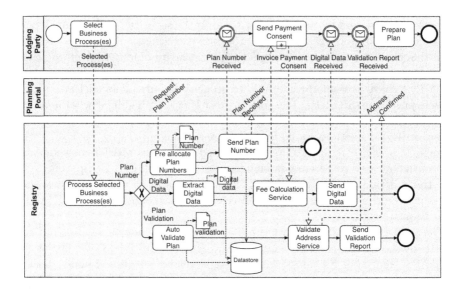

Fig. 2. Operational business process - prepare plan

security requirements as constraints that have to be respected when executing business processes. The first stage (see Fig. 3) is *business asset identification* and *security objective determination*. In the second stage, the *elicitation of security requirements* is done from the system's contextual areas.

2.3 Stage 1: Business Assets Identification & Security Objectives Determination

The first stage starts with the analysis of the *value chain* (see Fig. 1) from which the assets that must be protected against security risks are determined. The stage requires collaboration between security analysts and the stakeholders from the analysed enterprise. It consists of two activities:

(*i*) *Identify business assets:* During this activity the central artefact (or artefacts) considered in the value chain is identified. Typically, further details of this artefact are considered in the business process model, like Prepare Plan Process in Fig. 2. The enterprise's value chain can either have a single artefact used in all the processes or comprised of multiple artefacts in each operational business process. In the LMS case, Plan is identified as a protected asset, since, it is the central artefact used in all the business processes (see Figs. 1 and 2).

(*ii*) *Determine security objectives:* The activity addresses determining of key security objectives – confidentiality, integrity and availability – for identified business assets. In the LMS case, we define the following security objectives for business asset Plan: *i*) Plan should be confidential, i.e., no unauthorised individual should read it and its relevant data; *ii*) Plan should be integral, i.e., the Plan and its relevant data should not be tempered; and *iii*) Plan and its relevant data should be available to the business partners at anytime.

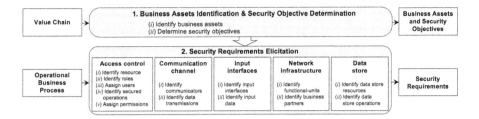

Fig. 3. Security requirements elicitation method

2.4 Stage 2: Security Requirement Elicitation

At the second stage, the security requirements elicitation is performed at five contextual areas: *access control, communication channel, input interfaces, network infrastructure,* and *data store.* It is important to note that each artefact– *data* or *process* – separately considered and protected at each area, contributes to the security of the business asset (i.e., Plan) identified at the first stage.

Access Control specifies how the business assets could be manipulated by individuals, applications or their groups. The major concern is to protect the confidentiality of identified business asset, in our example the Plan, when it is being manipulated by the IS asset, (i.e., the Registry). The security threat arises if the access to the Plan and its properties, like (Plan Number, Digital Data, and Plan Validation) is allowed to users without checking their access permissions. The risk event would: *i)* negate confidentiality of Plan, *ii)* lead to the Plan unintended use, and *iii)* harm the Registry's reliability. A way to mitigate the security risk is the introduction of access control mechanism, for example the Role-Based Access Control (RBAC) model. The RBAC model is elicited by performing the following activities:

(i) Identify resource: Hence, the business asset (i.e., Plan) is defined as a resource that needs to be protected from the unauthorised access. The protected resource is characterised by its attributes that add value to the asset. For example, in Fig. 4, Plan Number and Digital Data Number are attributes of Plan derived from the operational business process models.

(ii) Identify role: Roles are determined from the operational business process. The swimlanes are considered as outside role while the lanes of an information system corresponds to the internal role. We consider both outside and internal roles, since they both could access the secured business asset i.e., Plan. These roles (e.g., Lodging Party and Planning Portal) are modelled using ≪role≫ stereotype in RBAC security model (see Fig. 4).

(iii) Assign users: This activity assigns roles to users, which are instances of some role. Usually it is not possible to elicit concrete users from the operational business process. This, potentially, requires expertise of and collaboration with the domain experts.

(*iv*) *Identify secured operation:* An operation is an executable set of actions that can change the state of the protected resource. In this activity, any business activity (including both the task and sub-process) from the operational business processes that accesses the protective resource is identified as secured operation. For instance, Pre allocate Plan Numbers, Send Plan Number, Fee Calculation Service, and etc. are secured operations which manipulate properties Plan Number, Digital Data and Plan Validation (Fig. 4).

(*v*) *Assign permissions:* Permissions characterise role privileges to perform operations on the protected resource. In this activity, permissions specify the security actions –namely, *Create, Read* and *Update*– over secured operations that the role can perform to change the state of the protected resource. For example, Lodging Party role has the permission to create resource Plan.

By executing these activities, an RBAC security model (Fig. 4) is developed. Based on this model, the security requirement *check for the access rights* is evolved to the following context specific security requirements.

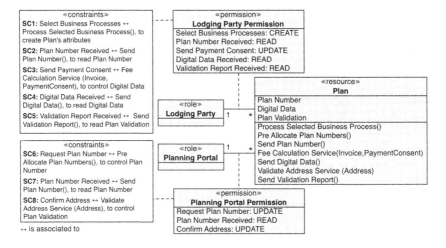

Fig. 4. RBAC Security model - prepare plan business process

RQ1. Lodging Party should be able to:
1. create or initialize the Plan Number, Digital Data and Plan Validation.
2. read the Plan Number, Digital Data and Plan Validation.
3. update the Digital Data.
RQ2. Planning Portal should be able to:
1. update the Plan Number and Plan Validation.
2. read the Plan Number.

The security model (i.e., Fig. 4) defines how authorised parties should access the protected resources. However, it does not support capturing scenarios like *entailment constraints* [11], *delegation constraints* [4] and *usage control* [19]. These requirements could be determined in collaboration between business and/or security analysts. For example, the following entailment constraints could be defined:

RQ3. Fee Calculation Service should be performed by different users assigned to the Lodging Party.
RQ4. Pre allocate Plan Numbers and Send Plan Number should be performed by the same user with Planning Portal's role.

RQ3 defines that there should exist at least two users in the Registry with the same role, to finish executing the task Fee Calculation Service: the first user issues the Invoice and the second user approves the Payment Consent. Requirement RQ4 highlights the concept binding of duties.

Communication Channel is used to exchange data between business partners (e.g., Lodging Party and Planning Portal) and system (e.g., Registry). Here, data, like Selected Business Process(es), Payment Consent and etc., need to be protected when they are transmitted over the (untrusted) communication channel, i.e., Internet. The communication channel could be intercepted by the threat agent and the captured data could be misused (i.e., read and kept for the later use or modified and passed over) by the threat agent. This could lead to the loss of the channel reliability, and could negate the confidentiality and integrity of the Plan. To mitigate the risk, in this contextual area one performs two activities:

(*i*) *Identify communicators:* Communicators are the entities that transmit or receive data. Operational business processes are considered to identify the information system of an enterprise and their business partners who exist outside of an enterprise but transmit/receive data to/from the enterprise. In Fig. 5, we illustrate a security model for communication channel between Registry and Lodging Party using a UML interaction diagram. Registry is modelled as LMS's information system that communicates with the Lodging Party identified as LMS's business partner.

(*ii*) *Identify data transmission:* One needs to determine the business asset and/or its relevant data transmitted or received between the identified communicators over the untrusted communication channels, i.e., Internet. For example, Selected Process(es) and Plan Number are communicated between Registry and Lodging Party, thus, they require to be protection.

In order to ensure the secure transmission of business assets or its relevant data, the above activities results in the following security requirements for the Lodging Party and Registry and correspondingly for other entities that communicates with Registry:

RQ5. Registry should have unique identity in the form of key pairs (public key, private key) certified by a certification authority.
RQ6. Lodging Party and Planning Portal should encrypt and sign Selected Process(es), Plan Number, and other using keys before sending it to Registry.

A security requirements implementation could be fulfilled by the standard transport layer security (a.k.a., TLS) protocol [3] as illustrated in Fig. 5. As the first contact, the Lodging Party sends Registry a handshake message, which includes

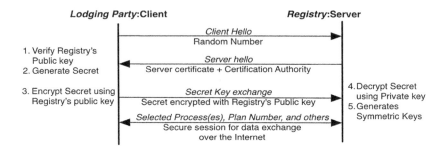

Fig. 5. TLS Protocol implementation, adapted from [3]

a random number. Following RQ6, the Registry responds with its public key and the information about the certification authority. After verification of the Registry's public key, the Lodging Party generates the secret and sends it to the Registry encrypted with the Registry's public key. The Registry then decrypt the secret using the private key and generates symmetric session keys. The keys enable Lodging party and Registry to establish a secure session for data exchange. Following RQ7, encryption keeps the transmitted data (e.g., Selected Business Process(es), Payment Consent and etc.) confidential and signing it ensures that the received data is not tempered. The secure communication continues until it is not explicitly terminated by Lodging Party or Registry.

Input interfaces ensure that the input data submitted by business partners are correct and complete. In this contextual area two activities are suggested:

(*i*) *Identify input interfaces:* The activity identifies the input interfaces of information system from the operational business processes that has incoming message flows. The input interfaces are those activities of information system that receives input from the enterprise stakeholders.

(*ii*) *Identify input data:* The activity identifies the input data received by the input interfaces from the enterprise's business partners.

In LMS (see Fig. 2), we identify Process Selected Business Process(es) and Fee Calculation Service as input interfaces of Registry that receives the Selected Process(es) and Payment Consent from Lodging Party. The threat agent can exploit the vulnerability of the input interfaces by submitting the data with a malicious scripts. If happening so the availability and integrity of any activity (e.g., Send Digital Data) after the input interface (e.g., Fee Calculation Service) may be negated. To avoid this risk the following security requirements must be implemented for the identified input interface:

> **RQ7.** Fee Calculation Service should filter Payment Consent.
> **RQ8.** Fee Calculation Service should sanitize Payment Consent to transform it to the required format.
> **RQ9.** Fee Calculation Service should canonicalize Payment Consent to verify against its canonical representation.

Input filtration [6] (RQ8) validates the input data against the secure and correct syntax. The string input should potentially be checked for length and character set validity (e.g., allowed and blacklisted characters). The numerical input should be validated against their upper and lower value boundaries. *Input sanitization* (RQ9) should check for common encoding methods used (e.g., HTML entity encoding, URL encoding, etc.). The *input canonicalization* [6] (RQ10) verifies the input against its canonical representation.

Network infrastructure secures the infrastructure where the information system is deployed and where it executes its tasks. The enterprise's information system is composed of several small functional units, which can either be deployed at single location or multiple locations connected through internet. The goal of this contextual area is to guarantee availability of these functional units to the enterprise user or their partners. Two activities are performed within this contextual area:

(*i*) *Identify functional-unit:* A functional-unit is an activity or sub-process implemented on independent network infrastructure to provide certain functionality of an enterprise's information system. An information system can comprised of one or more functional-units. In LMS case, their information system (i.e., Registry) illustrated in Fig. 2 is consists of three functional-units (i.e., Pre allocate Plan Numbers, Fee Calculation Service and Validate Address Service) deployed on three independent network infrastructure connected through internet to form a single information system (i.e., Registry) for LMS. Later, we demonstrate the security requirements elicitation of Pre allocate Plan Numbers functional-unit using a UML security model (see Fig. 6).

(*ii*) *Identify business partner:* Business partners are the external entities that can access the network infrastructure in order to communicate with the enterprise information system. The access includes any request type necessary to receive or send data. In LMS, we identify Lodging Party and Planning Portal as external entities that communicate with Registry in Prepare Plan process.

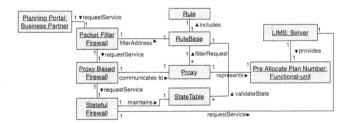

Fig. 6. Firewall architecture, adapted from [24]

In Fig. 2, Registry has a functional-unit Pre allocate Plan Numbers offered to Planning Portal through the communication channel. The threat agent may exploit the hosts in the channel and hack them because of the protocol (e.g., TCP, ICMP or DNS [5]) vulnerability; i.e., the ability to handle an unlimited number of requests for service. When receiving simultaneously multiple requests, the server i.e., Registry, will not be able to handle them, thus, the services become unavailable.

The successful denial of service attacks could also provoke the loss of partner's (e.g., Planning Portal) confidence on Registry. The above activities helps to develop a UML security model (see Fig. 6) that defines three types of firewalls [24] – Packet Filter Firewall, Proxy Based Firewall and Stateful Firewall. The security model introduce the following requirements to mitigate the risks to the functional-units of Registry:

> **RQ10.** Pre allocate Plan Numbers should establish a rule base (i.e., a collection of enterprise' constraints used by different firewalls) to communicate with Lodging Party and Planning Portal.
> **RQ11.** Packet Filter Firewall should filter the Planning Portal's address to determine if it is not a host used by the threat agent.
> **RQ12.** Proxy Based Firewall should communicate to the proxy which represents Pre allocate Plan Number to determine the validity of request received from Planning Portal.
> **RQ13.** State Firewall should maintain the state table to check the Planning Portal's request for additional conditions of established communication.

It is important to notice that the communication between the Planning Portal (and also Lodging Party) and the Registry is bidirectional. The similar requirements must be taken into account when Registry sends messages (e.g., Fee Calculation Service sends Invoice) back to the business party.

Data Store is used to define how data are stored and retrieved to/from the associated databases (e.g., Data store in Fig. 2). If the threat agent is capable of accessing and retrieving the data, their confidentiality and integrity would potentially be negated, thus, resulting in the harm of the business asset (i.e., the Plan) and its supporting IS assets (i.e., the Registry). To avoid unauthorised access to the datastore we introduce a RBAC model. In this contextual area, the RBAC model is developed using the following activities:

(*i*) *Identify Datastore resource:* In this context, Datastore is identified as a single collective resource. The identified business assets and their related data in the operational process models are modelled as the resource attributes. In Fig. 7, the attributes Plan Number, Digital Data and Plan Validation, actually, represents the attributes of business asset Plan.

(*ii*)*Identify Datastore's operations:* The activity identifies operations that save or retrieve the data, identified in previous activity, from Datastore. These operations are modelled as operations of Datastore's resource in the RBAC model as illustrated in Fig. 7.

Once the resource and operations are modelled, the activities *identify role* and *assign permissions* are performed as described in the *access control* contextual area. This results in a security RBAC model for enterprise's Datastore given in Fig. 7. The security model helps to elicit the following Datastore's requirements that ensure the integrity and confidentiality of stored business assets.

> **RQ14.** The Registry should audit the operations after the retrieval, storage or any other manipulation of data in the Data store.

Auditing (supported by the access control policy) is the process of monitoring and recording selected events and activities [18]. It determines who performed what operations on what data and when. This is useful to detect and trace security violations performed on the Plan Number, Digital Data and Plan Validation.

> **RQ15.** The Registry should perform operations to hide/unhide data when they are stored/retrieved to/from the Data store.

A possible RQ15 implementation is cryptographic algorithms. The encryption offers two-fold benefits: (*i*) the data would not be seen by the Data store users (e.g., database administrator) where the circumstances do not allow one to revoke their permissions; (*ii*) due to any reasons if someone gets physical access to the Data store (s)he would not be able to see the confidential data stored.

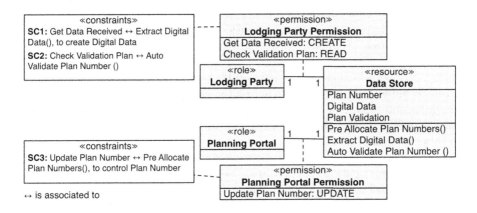

Fig. 7. RBAC security model - data store auditing

3 Validation

3.1 Validation Design

The research question of this validation is to determine which method – SREBP or SQUARE– results in a higher *coverage* of resulting security requirements. We have consequently applied both method on the business processes modelled using BPMN. These models were used as the input for both methods. The business process models included the activities whose execution is supported by the information system or its architecture. Hence we have received the results after applying the methods on the same set of business process models. Both methods were applied by two persons, but these were different in the studied cases.

The SQUARE method [14] is developed as a systematic and flexible approach to elicit security requirements from various sources. Its major steps are: agreement on definition, identification of security goals, selection of elicitation techniques, development of artefacts, risk assessment, elicitation of security requirements,

requirements categorisation, prioritisation, and inspection. We selected SQUARE with the purpose to compare it to SREBP. The SQUARE input was limited to the value chain and process models. We note that if applying the SQUARE in the broader context, the outcome potentially would be different.

The received sets of security requirements were confronted to the security requirements categories (see Sect. 3.2) in order to identify their coverage regarding these categories. The received results were compared to answer the validation research question.

3.2   Coverage of Security Requirements

In this study coverage of the security requirements is estimated as the aggregation of the different security requirements categories, defined following the existing literature [9,24]. *Identification* requirements are security requirements that associate an individual or application with its unique identity before any interaction with the information system. *Authentication* requirements are security requirements that recognise and validate the individual's identity before interacting with the information system. *Authorisation* requirements are the security requirements that describe the role or individual authorised to access the business assets or its related data in the information system. *Accounting* requirements are security requirements to record security related actions or events (e.g., unauthorised access or communication to an information system or its datastore) and make the information available about these actions or events. *Audit* requirements are security requirements to analyse the information captured using security accounting requirements and verify against a set of valid rules to indicate if there is any security violations happened. *Non-repudiation* requirements are security requirements that capture and maintain the evidence to identify the individuals participated in an activity (e.g., transaction or interaction) to provide protection if they deny their involvement. *Immunity* requirements are the security requirements to specify the ability of an information systems to protect itself from unauthorized access undesirable programs (e.g., viruses or application-specific attacks). *Data exchange* requirements are security requirements to protect the confidential business data from unauthorised access during transmission over internet. We assume that these categories mutually covers the 100 % of security requirements – therefore, each category contributes 12,5 % coverage to the total.

In this study we apply both SQUARE and SREBP to elicit security requirements from two business processes. In order to assess the coverage of each category, we use a 5-grade scale (0, 25, 50, 75 and 100 %). The coverage is assessed by analysing how many of the asset's attributes was addressed by the security requirements. If none of the asset's attributes had been addressed, it was given the value 0 % and if all attributes were addressed, the value 100 % was assigned. Similarly, the values 25 % (few attributes addressed), 50 % (half of the attributes addressed), 75 % (more than half but not all attributes addressed), were assigned for each criterion.

3.3 Laboratory Information Management System

Analysis of laboratory information management system (LiMS) was executed by two researchers, including the first author of this paper. The value chain (see Fig. 8) comprised of 7 business processes –namely Offer Quote Process, Project Registration Process, Quality Check Process, Check Inventory Process, Prepare Samples Process, Process Samples Process, and Deliver Samples Process. The business processes are expanded to business process models. Once the security requirements are derived using SREBP and SQUARE, their *coverage* is compared as illustrated in Fig. 9. It is important to note that although the SREBP resulted in higher number of security requirements than SQUARE, we do not take this numbers into account when comparing the security requirements coverage, because our goal is to understand the coverage regarding each requirements category.

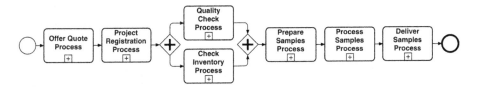

Fig. 8. LiMS Value chain

Business Assets	Categories	\<SREBP\> Identification	Authentication	Authorization	Accounting	Audit	Non-repudiation	Immunity	Data exchange	TOTAL	\<SQUARE\> Identification	Authentication	Authorization	Accounting	Audit	Non-repudiation	Immunity	Data exchange	TOTAL	DIFFERENCE
		12.5	12.5	12.5	12.5	12.5	12.5	12.5	12.5	100	12.5	12.5	12.5	12.5	12.5	12.5	12.5	12.5	100	
Offer Quote	Reqs.	2	40	14	18	12	2	59	6	153	2	2	10	6	0	0	13	4	37	116
	%age	75%	100%	58%	100%	67%	100%	100%	67%	83%	75%	33%	58%	75%	0%	0%	75%	33%	44%	40%
	Coverage	9.38	12.50	7.29	12.50	8.33	12.50	12.50	8.33	83.33	9.38	4.17	7.29	9.38	0.00	0.00	9.38	4.17	43.77	39.56
Project	Reqs.	2	46	22	29	18	1	66	10	194	2	2	12	6	0	0	13	4	39	155
	%age	75%	100%	58%	100%	67%	100%	100%	67%	83%	75%	33%	58%	75%	0%	0%	75%	33%	44%	40%
	Coverage	9.38	12.50	7.29	12.50	8.33	12.50	12.50	8.33	83.33	9.38	4.17	7.29	9.38	0.00	0.00	9.38	4.17	43.77	39.56
Sample Quality	Reqs.	2	50	7	18	12	0	75	2	166	2	2	11	6	0	0	15	4	40	126
	%age	75%	100%	58%	100%	67%	0%	100%	67%	71%	75%	33%	58%	75%	0%	0%	75%	33%	44%	27%
	Coverage	9.38	12.50	7.29	12.50	8.33	0.00	12.50	8.33	70.83	9.38	4.17	7.29	9.38	0.00	0.00	9.38	4.17	43.77	27.06
Purchase Order	Reqs.	2	46	14	15	10	1	66	4	158	2	2	13	6	0	0	15	4	42	116
	%age	75%	100%	58%	100%	67%	100%	100%	67%	83%	75%	33%	58%	75%	0%	0%	75%	33%	44%	40%
	Coverage	9.38	12.50	7.29	12.50	8.33	12.50	12.50	8.33	83.33	9.38	4.17	7.29	9.38	0.00	0.00	9.38	4.17	43.77	39.56
Sample Plate	Reqs.	2	40	11	29	18	1	57	2	160	2	2	11	6	0	0	15	4	40	120
	%age	75%	100%	58%	100%	67%	100%	100%	67%	83%	75%	33%	58%	75%	0%	0%	75%	33%	44%	40%
	Coverage	9.38	12.50	7.29	12.50	8.33	12.50	12.50	8.33	83.33	9.38	4.17	7.29	9.38	0.00	0.00	9.38	4.17	43.77	39.56
Process Sample Sheet	Reqs.	2	46	18	36	24	1	66	2	195	4	4	22	12	0	0	27	8	77	118
	%age	75%	100%	58%	100%	67%	100%	100%	67%	83%	75%	33%	58%	75%	0%	0%	75%	33%	44%	40%
	Coverage	9.38	12.50	7.29	12.50	8.33	12.50	12.50	8.33	83.33	9.38	4.17	7.29	9.38	0.00	0.00	9.38	4.17	43.77	39.56
Sample Result	Reqs.	2	42	16	21	14	0	57	8	160	6	6	35	18	0	0	39	12	116	44
	%age	75%	100%	50%	100%	67%	0%	100%	67%	70%	75%	33%	58%	75%	0%	0%	75%	33%	44%	25%
	Coverage	9.38	12.50	6.25	12.50	8.33	0.00	12.50	8.33	69.79	9.38	4.17	8.33	9.38	0.00	0.00	9.38	4.17	44.81	24.98
TOTAL	%age	75%	100%	57%	100%	67%	71%	100%	67%	80%	75%	33%	59%	75%	0%	0%	75%	33%	44%	36%
	Coverage	9.38	12.50	7.14	12.50	8.33	8.93	12.50	8.33	79.61	9.38	4.17	7.44	9.38	0.00	0.00	9.38	4.17	43.92	35.69

Fig. 9. Coverage of the LiMS security requirements

The comparison illustrates that SREBP method reaches a coverage of almost 80 % of coverage in addressing security of the LiMS business assets; whereas the coverage achieved using SQUARE is close to 44 %. The differences are mainly due to different target audience of these methods, SREBP facilitates business analysts while SQUARE targets security analysts. Hence, SQUARE independently addresses the security comprehensively although its integration with business processes require more efforts to elicit security requirements. SREBP is asset-driven and security requirements are specified in details satisfying the majority of their security objectives. Instead, SQUARE focusses on the technology that supports the execution of business processes and represents security requirements at general level. This shifts the priority from acquiring the security objectives towards implementing security controls.

3.4   Football Federation Information Management System

When considering the football federation (FF) case we wanted to understand whether the result received in LIMS can be repeated. It is important to note that the FF case was also executed by two different persons than LiMS (the second author of the paper acted only as the supervisor during this case execution).

The value chain illustrated in Fig. 10 suggested five business assets (i.e., Player, Team, Umpire, Game and Timetable). The further security requirements elicitation was performed using SREBP and SQUARE. As illustrated in Fig. 11 the comparison illustrates that SREBP method reaches a coverage of almost 82 % in addressing security of the FF business assets; whereas the coverage achieved using SQUARE is close to 47 %. This results highly corresponds to the results of the LiMS analysis.

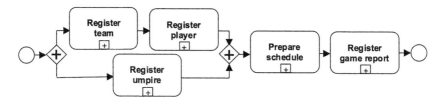

Fig. 10. FF Value chain

3.5   Threats to Validity

The validity of results may be affected by few threats. Firstly, the risk of researchers' familiarity with the concepts (e.g., BPMN, attack trees, UML and etc.) affects the results. The researchers personal interpretation of the problem and constructed models has an impact on the objectivity of results. Therefore, we adapted principles of: i) data triangulation [21], where several sources are used to collect data (i.e., threats and vulnerabilities), and this limits the effects of the interpretation of one single data source; ii) peer debriefing [21], where peer having different expertise allows avoiding the risk of being biased during the application of both methods. Similarly, peer debriefing helped reducing the risk of construct validity where peer focusing on what the researchers has in mind and that the actual problem has been investigated.

Business Assets	Categories	SREBP Identification	Authentication	Authorization	Accounting	Audit	Non-repudiation	Immunity	Data exchange	TOTAL	SQUARE Identification	Authentication	Authorization	Accounting	Audit	Non-repudiation	Immunity	Data exchange	TOTAL	DIFFERENCE
		12.5	12.5	12.5	12.5	12.5	12.5	12.5	12.5	100	12.5	12.5	12.5	12.5	12.5	12.5	12.5	12.5	100	
Player	Reqs.	2	12	12	15	3	1	33	12	90	1	4	5	5	1	0	6	5	27	63
	%age	75%	100%	83%	75%	75%	75%	100%	67%	81%	25%	58%	58%	92%	8%	0%	75%	50%	46%	36%
	Coverage	9.38	12.50	10.35	9.38	9.38	9.38	12.50	8.33	81.20	3.13	7.31	7.31	11.47	1.04	0.00	9.38	6.25	45.89	35.31
Team	Reqs.	2	18	18	21	6	2	44	22	133	1	5	5	5	1	0	6	5	28	105
	%age	75%	100%	83%	75%	75%	75%	67%	67%	77%	25%	58%	58%	92%	8%	0%	75%	50%	46%	31%
	Coverage	9.38	12.50	10.35	9.38	9.38	9.38	8.33	8.33	77.03	3.13	7.31	7.31	11.47	1.04	0.00	9.38	6.25	45.89	31.14
Umpire	Reqs.	2	12	14	15	6	2	51	14	116	1	5	5	5	1	0	6	5	28	88
	%age	75%	100%	83%	100%	75%	75%	100%	67%	84%	25%	58%	58%	92%	8%	0%	75%	50%	46%	39%
	Coverage	9.38	12.50	10.35	12.50	9.38	9.38	12.50	8.33	84.32	3.13	7.31	7.31	11.47	1.04	0.00	9.38	6.25	45.89	38.43
Game	Reqs.	4	24	14	30	3	1	86	24	166	1	4	5	5	0	1	6	4	26	140
	%age	75%	100%	83%	100%	75%	75%	100%	67%	84%	25%	58%	58%	92%	0%	25%	75%	50%	48%	37%
	Coverage	9.38	12.50	10.35	12.50	9.38	9.38	12.50	8.33	84.32	3.13	7.31	7.31	11.47	0.00	3.13	9.38	6.25	47.98	36.34
Timetable	Reqs.	2	20	12	21	3	1	48	18	125	1	4	5	5	2	1	6	4	28	97
	%age	75%	100%	67%	100%	75%	75%	100%	67%	82%	25%	58%	58%	92%	25%	25%	75%	50%	51%	31%
	Coverage	9.38	12.50	8.33	12.50	9.38	9.38	12.50	8.33	82.30	3.13	7.31	7.31	11.47	3.13	3.13	9.38	6.25	51.11	31.19
TOTAL	%age	75%	100%	80%	90%	75%	75%	93%	67%	82%	25%	58%	58%	92%	10%	10%	75%	50%	47%	35%
	Coverage	9.38	12.50	10.35	10.94	9.38	9.38	11.46	8.33	81.72	3.13	7.31	7.31	11.47	0.78	0.78	9.38	6.25	46.41	35.31

Fig. 11. Coverage of the FF security requirements

Concerning external validity, the findings are independent of their application and the results are largely overlapping. Potentially, the methods could be generalised and repeated on other case studies. However, different organisations have their specific security goals, which need to be considered separately.

We started by applying SREBP method to reduce learning effects. There are no carry-over effects to SREBP application as participants were not familiar with the process models. However, the SQUARE method benefitted carry-over effects as participants became familiar with the domain. We have adapted similar approach in verifying security requirements, by verifying SREBP requirements first; this avoids any carry-overs to SREBP but SQUARE requirements are verified later therefore any carry-over benefitted SQUARE.

4   Related Work

Fabian et al. [8] conducted a thorough study comparing the security requirements engineering methods. For instance *goal-oriented approaches*, such as Knowledge Acquisition in Automated Specification (KAOS) [12], Secure $i*$ [7], and Secure Tropos [16], facilitate the requirements elicitation and specification by providing the rationale for a particular requirement. *UML based approaches*, like Misuse cases [25] or SecureUML [13], focus on the system design. In the SREBP method SecureUML is used to define security requirements of *access control* and *data store* contextual areas, UMLsec is applied to create requirements models within *communication channel* and *business service* contextual areas.

Security in business processes is integrated in several ways: security objective elicitation, security requirements modelling, security risk-driven approaches and security requirements conformance checking. In [26] a generic security model specifies security goals, policies, and constraints based on a set of basic entities, attributes, interactions, and effects. In [10] business process elements are used to expresses the common security requirements. These studies guarantee that security constraints are not violated by achieving the security goals. However, they do not define graphical notations and do not guide elicitation.

A formal descriptive language [23] is used to derive security requirements that assign security level to business process components. In [22] BPMN is extended with a specific padlock symbols to annotate business processes with early security requirements. Similarly, in [20] two new artefacts – operating condition and control case – are proposed to express the constraints, which help mitigate risk and facilitate the early discovery of security requirements. An annotation language [17] embedded in business process models is proposed to express security requirements as structured text annotations. In comparison to this related work where the focus is placed on representing security requirements (graphically) on the process models, SREBP suggests a novel approach to elicit these requirements and define them as the business rules.

5   Conclusion and Future Work

In this paper, we presented the SREBP method for eliciting security requirements from the business processes. Its strength lies in its general description of security goals and the systematic analysis of the contextual areas. We have defined the application guidelines and compared it to the SQUARE method. The study illustrates that SREBP is rather generalisable to different problems. We could also conclude that the method contributes with a relatively complete (with respect to the security requirements categories) set of security requirements. We also illustrate that the achieved result is rather repeatable in different cases.

As the future work, SREBP has to be strengthened with analyses of threat likelihood, vulnerability and impact levels. This would help prioritise the security requirements and support business analyst in deciding, which security requirements should be implemented in case of limited time, resources, or finances. It is also important to continue the SREBP validation regarding its correctness (i.e., proving that some formally defined criteria are satisfied) and usability (i.e., investigating method acceptance in practical settings).

References

1. Ahmed, N., Matulevičius, R.: A method for eliciting security requirements from the business process models. In: CAiSE Forum and Doctoral Consortium **2014**, 57–64 (2014)
2. Ahmed, N., Matulevičius, R.: Securing business processes using security risk-oriented patterns. Comput. Stan. Interfaces **36**(4), 723–733 (2014)
3. Apostolopoulos, G., Peris, V., Saha, D.: Transport layer security: how much does it really cost? In: Proceedings IEEE INFOCOM 1999 The Conference on Computer Communications, vol. 2, pp. 717–725 (1999)
4. Atluri, V., Warner, J.: Security for workflow systems. In: Gertz, M., Jajodia, S. (eds.) Handbook of Database Security, pp. 213–230. Springer, US (2008)
5. Chang, R.: Defending against flooding-based distributed denial-of-service attacks: a tutorial. Commun. Magazine, IEEE **40**(10), 42–51 (2002)

6. Clarke, J., Fowler, K., Oftedal, E., Alvarez, R.M., Hartley, D., Kornbrust, A., O'Leary-Steele, G., Revelli, A., Siddharth, S., Slaviero, M.: SQL Injection Attacks and Defense, 2nd edn. Syngress Publishing, Burlington (2012)
7. Elahi, G., Yu, E.: A goal oriented approach for modeling and analyzing security trade-offs. In: Parent, C., Schewe, K.-D., Storey, V.C., Thalheim, B. (eds.) ER 2007. LNCS, vol. 4801, pp. 375–390. Springer, Heidelberg (2007)
8. Fabian, B., Gürses, S., Heisel, M., Santen, T., Schmidt, H.: A comparison of security requirements engineering methods. Requirements Eng. 15(1), 7–40 (2010)
9. Firesmith, D.G.: Engineering security requirements. J. Object Technol. 2(1), 53–68 (2003)
10. Herrmann, P., Herrmann, G.: Security requirement analysis of business processes. Electronic Commerce Research 6(3–4), 305–335 (2006)
11. Hummer, W., Gaubatz, P., Strembeck, M., Zdun, U., Dustdar, S.: Enforcement of entailment constraints in distributed service-based business processes. Inf. Softw. Technol. 55(11), 1884–1903 (2013)
12. van Lamsweerde, A.: Engineering requirements for system reliability and security. In: Broy, M., Grunbauer, J., Hoare, C.A.R. (eds.) Software System Reliability and Security, vol. 9, pp. 196–238. IOS Press, Amsterdam (2007)
13. Lodderstedt, T., Basin, D., Doser, J.: SecureUML: a UML-based modeling language for model-driven security. In: Jézéquel, J.-M., Hussmann, H., Cook, S. (eds.) UML 2002. LNCS, vol. 2460, pp. 426–441. Springer, Heidelberg (2002)
14. Mead, N.: identifying security requirements using the security quality requirements engineering (SQUARE) method. In: Mouratidis, H., Giorgini, P. (eds.) Integrating Security and Software Engineering, pp. 44–69. Idea Publishing Group, Hershey (2006)
15. Menzel, M., Thomas, I., Meinel, C.: Security requirements specification in service-oriented business process management. In: ARES, pp. 41–48 (2009)
16. Mouratidis, H., Giorgini, P.: Secure tropos: a security-oriented extension of the tropos methodology. Int. J. Soft. Eng. Knowl. Eng. 17(02), 285–309 (2007)
17. Müllle, J., von Stackelberg, S., Bohm, K.: Modelling and transforming security constraints in privacy-aware business processes. In: SOCA, pp. 1–4 (2011)
18. Natan, R.B.: Implementing Database Security and Auditing: Includes Examples for Oracle, SQL Server, DB2 UDB Sybase. Digital Press, Newton (2005)
19. Park, J., Sandhu, R.: The UCON-ABC usage control model. ACM Trans. Inf. Syst. Secur. 7(1), 128–174 (2004)
20. Pavlovski, C.J., Zou, J.: Non-functional requirements in business process modeling. In: APCCM, pp. 103–112. Australian Computer Society, Inc. (2008)
21. Robson, C.: RealWorld Research - A Resource for Social Scientists and Practitioners-Researchers. Blackwell Publishing, Oxford (2002)
22. Rodríguez, A., Fernández, M.E., Piattini, M.: A BPMN extension for the modeling of security requirements in business processes. IEICE-TIS E90–D(4), 745–752 (2007)
23. Röhrig, S., Knorr, K.: Security analysis of electronic business processes. Electron. Commer. Res. 4(1–2), 59–81 (2004)
24. Schumacher, M., Fernandez, E.B., Hybertson, D., Buschmann, F., Sommerlad, P.: Security Patterns: Integrating Security and Systems Engineering. Wiley, New York (2006)
25. Sindre, G., Opdahl, A.L.: Eliciting Security Requirements with Misuse Cases. Requirements Eng. 10(1), 34–44 (2005)
26. Wolter, C., Menzel, M., Schaad, A., Miseldine, P., Meinel, C.: Model-driven business process security requirement specification. JSA. 55(4), 211–223 (2009)

An Explorative Study for Process Map Design

Monika Malinova[(✉)], Henrik Leopold, and Jan Mendling

WU Vienna, Welthandelsplatz 1, 1020 Vienna, Austria
{monika.malinova,henrik.leopold,jan.mendling}@wu.ac.at

Abstract. Process maps provide a holistic view of all processes of an organization and the essential relationships between them. The design of a process map is of central importance as many organizations create them at the start of a business process management (BPM) initiative to serve as a framework. Despite this importance, the design of process maps is still more art than science, essentially because there is no standardized modeling language available for process map design. In this paper, we address the research question of which concepts are currently used in process maps in practice. To this end, we investigate a collection of 67 process maps from industry. Our contribution is a meta-model for process map design which is grounded in actual usage. Furthermore, we discuss the importance of different concepts for process map design.

Keywords: Process map · Process architecture · Process category

1 Introduction

Process maps are a key concept for providing an overview of a company's business processes [1]. They visualize the main relationships between processes and facilitate a basic understanding of how the company operates. The importance of process maps is illustrated by the growing extent of process modeling initiatives in practice. Often companies maintain process model repositories with thousands of process models [2]. Typically, creating a process map is the first task when introducing Business Process Management (BPM) into an organization as it provides an abstract view of all processes [3]. The process map is then used as a foundation for conducting the subsequent steps of the BPM lifecycle [4].

To date, a lot of research has focused on the quality and the design of singular process models [5–7]. Due to the increasing size of process model repositories in practice, many frameworks for the successful management of large repositories were introduced [8–10]. Also, some techniques have been developed for automatically deriving process categories from process model collections [11]. In this context, process architectures turned out to be a particularly useful strategy. Process architecture serves to systematically organize a collection of process models into different categories and store the details of each process model in the appropriate architecture level [12]. A process map is considered as the top most abstract level of the corresponding process architecture, hence, it represents the entrance to the different levels. While there is some initial research on abstraction

© Springer International Publishing Switzerland 2015
S. Nurcan and E. Pimenidis (Eds.): CAiSE Forum 2014, LNBIP 204, pp. 36–51, 2015.
DOI: 10.1007/978-3-319-19270-3_3

and categorization of model collections [11,13,14], there is notable insecurity on how to capture such process-related information on the most abstract level i.e. the process map [1].

In practice, process maps are used for that purpose, however, without a standard modeling language being available. The major challenge in this context remains the specification of a language for process map design that integrates insights from actual usage in practice. Despite the importance of process maps for a BPM initiative and the management of process model repositories, there is only little research on process map design. For instance, prior research demonstrated that the design of process maps may have negative effects on the business process management success if due to incompleteness and incorrectness the maps cannot be understood intuitively [1]. One of the major challenges is that there are no standards available for creating process maps. Hence, companies freely define and visualize their process maps based on their own creativity. As a result, the meaning of the introduced symbols is often not well defined, and important aspects are subject to misinterpretation [1].

In this paper, we address this research gap by conducting an explorative study in order to better comprehend the nature of existing process maps. More specifically, we investigate the included concepts of 67 process maps from practice. As a result, we present a process map meta-model which integrates the concepts and relationships represented in these maps. Furthermore, we investigate patterns of usage of these concepts. In this way, we aim to provide a foundation for the standardization of a language for process map design.

The rest of the paper is structured as follows. Section 2 gives an overview of BPM and process maps. Section 3 introduces the collection of process maps we used for analysis along with the methods we used to derive our findings. Section 4 presents the results of our study. This includes a process map meta-model, as well as statistical analysis of the usage of process map concepts. Section 5 points to implications for practice and research. Section 6 concludes the paper.

2 Background

In this section, we discuss the background of our research. We first give insights into the organization of business processes within a company and the available techniques for doing so. Then, we present an overview of the current state of the art of process maps and highlight the motivation for our study.

2.1 Organizing business processes

Organizations operate through business processes which consist of activities performed in a particular order. Typically, a sequence of such business processes is performed in order to create a value for the customer [3]. However, processes may differ in their importance for value creation. Thus, they are commonly categorized based on the degree of their proximity to the end-user. To manage interrelations between the processes and to systematically document how the firm operates as a whole, organizations often adopt the BPM approach and start modeling their processes in form of process models. A process model visualizes the process steps by providing a diagrammatic representation of a business process. As a result of such modeling initiatives, organizations often end up with a large collection of process models, which may have limited value, if not organized properly. In this case, a process architecture helps to store all detailed process models and the relations between them in a systematic manner [12]. A process map is typically used as the top-level and most abstract model in a process architecture. It visualizes all processes and their relationships in a compact way [1].

In prior work, a rich stream of research has proposed guidelines for modeling singular processes [6–8] and for process architecture design [12,15–22]. Frameworks such as SCOR [23], eTom [24], Handels-H model [25], ARIS [26], DoD architecture framework [27], or the BPTrends pyramid [28] provide guidance for structuring process models on the different architecture levels. Some apply only to specific industry domains (SCOR, eTom, etc.), while others are more domain-neutral (ARIS, BPTrends Pyramid, etc.). In contrast to all these efforts, hardly any guidelines for designing process maps on the most abstract level of the process architecture exists. Existing process modeling languages (e.g. BPMN, EPC) are being used by practitioners for depicting singular business processes in details, however hardly any process map from practice has been designed using the rich pallette of symbols these modeling languages offer. Practitioners typically use their own creative capabilities and software not primarily developed for process modeling purposes (e.g. PowerPoint) when designing their process maps. As a result we are faced with a vast amount of heterogeneous process map designs, despite the fact that they all serve a similar purpose. Hence, up until now a modeling language for process map design is missing.

2.2 Process Maps

We can trace back the concept of process maps to the early 1980s when Porter introduced the value-chain model. The value chain provides a process view of an organization and represents it as a set of core activities a company has to conduct in order to create value for the customer [29]. Support activities are also required for value creation, but of less strategic importance. In order to understand their mutual dependence, linkages between activities have to be identified [30]. Scheer adopts the concept of a value-added chain [26]. He introduces a diagram that represents those processes that create value for the company. These processes are shown in a sequence, and each could be hierarchically decomposed into subprocesses that a super-ordinate process needs in order to be executed [26]. SIPOC is another frequently used approach, especially in Six Sigma and Lean manufacturing, stemming from the late 1980s [28,31]. It stands for supplier, inputs, process, outputs, and customer and is used as a guide for analyzing these five aspects with main focus on the customer [28].

Beyond the process view of an organization, there are additional (external and internal) parties that influence the value creation. A framework encompassing

all these is referred to as the business model. An example of such a model is
the e3-value business model, which integrates three different value viewpoints,
namely the business value viewpoint, i.e. the way economic value is created
and consumed by the actors, the process viewpoint, i.e. the value viewpoint in
terms of business processes, and the system architecture viewpoint, i.e. the information systems that enable and support business processes [32,33]. Nine perspectives are distinguished by the business model canvas [34]. For an overview
see [35].

Examples of concrete process maps can also be found in literature [3, 28, 36–
41]; however, all studies refer to process maps coming from practice. Most are
based upon the value-chain concept, while some include additional information
as being used in business models. One thing all process maps have in common is
that they all provide means of identifying typical process categories and the role
each type of process plays for the company. Most of these process maps depict
processes belonging to three different categories. An example of such a process
map can be seen in Fig. 1.

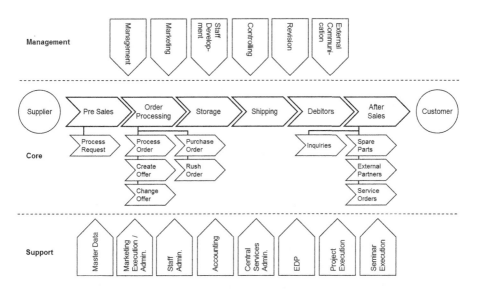

Fig. 1. Example process map, adapted from [36]

As illustrated in Fig. 1, generally, those processes that directly create value
for the customer and generate revenue are called *core processes* [1,37]. In a
process map, these processes are usually related to each other in a sequential
manner. Hence they are represented as end-to-end processes because they have
a customer request as an input, and contain all those processes that lead to the
request being served [42]. An end-to-end process is commonly a cross-functional
process, i.e. a process that goes through more than one organizational unit
[42]. In Fig. 1, the six core processes constitute an end-to-end process, with an

indicated input (Supplier) and output (Customer). While an end-to-end process is build up of a number of core processes, a core process is a singular process that contains activities. A large-scale enterprise deals with core processes that contain even hundreds to thousands of such activities [8]. Therefore, in order to avoid a process model becoming too complex, it is usually hierarchically decomposed into subprocesses [12,37]. For example, in Fig. 1 the core process "Order Processing" is hierarchically decomposed into five subprocesses (Process Order, Create Offer, etc.). Accordingly, this set of subprocesses build up to the initial core process.

In addition to the core process category, there are also processes that indirectly influence the value creation. These are clustered as support and management processes. *Support processes* provide resources to the core processes and enable them to operate in the most effective and efficient way, such as human resource management, information technology, etc. [37,43]. Whereas, *management processes* include those processes that develop strategic plans, measure and analyse the performance of the core processes, and ensure that their execution is aligned with the company's strategy [1,37]. Thus, management processes are present throughout the entire core process flow, whereas support processes are called only when necessary. For example, the end-to-end process in Fig. 1 is triggered by a "Supplier" providing input, and all core processes are executed up until the customer has received the order. During the process execution the support process "Accounting" may be called in case some payment done by the customer needs to be handled. Similarly, a management process takes care that throughout the entire process flow all activities carried out are in compliance with the company's strategy, such as high quality product, customer satisfaction, etc.

In addition to process categories, a process map also depicts relationships between the processes. According to [1], a relationship between processes coming from both same and different process categories, can be implicitly or explicitly shown. An explicit relationship occurs in case of a directed arrow or a close proximity between two processes, such as the end-to-end process in the core process category in Fig. 1. Also, most process maps explicitly portray a process decomposition into subprocesses [1]. The notion of input/output can as well be very often observed in process maps from practice. Same applies for resources, which serve as intermediate supply during process execution.

Whereas all these components are depicted in most process maps, hardly any research has been conducted on the extent to which these elements serve all the representational needs of process map designers. Therefore, we identify a metamodel on the basis of existing process maps from practice. In this way, we aim to consolidate the current practice of process map design in order to provide a foundation for developing a language that helps practitioners to design process maps in a standardized manner.

3   Research Design

The objective of this study is to understand the current practice of process map design. To this end, we analyze process maps from practice. In this context, we focus on the following goals:

1. Elicit meaning and develop knowledge of the concepts used within a single process map and the relations between them.
2. Find patterns of the combined usage of concepts and their frequency.

3.1   Methods

To address the first point, we gather process maps and analyze each of them for the concepts being used and any means by which the identified concepts were related to each other. We do this by examining each process map and identifying all concepts that are included within them. For example, the process map in Fig. 1 exhibits the notion of processes (e.g. Controlling, Pre Sales, Storage, Process Request, Accounting, etc.) belonging to three different process categories (Management, Core and Support). The processes in the core process category are represented as a value-chain diagram, hence we identify the sequential relation between the core processes. We can also observe the decomposition relation, because almost all of the core processes are decomposed into subprocesses. Due to the pentagon-shaped symbol used for the management processes pointing to the core processes, we assume an implicit manage relation between these two process categories. We observe the same behaviour between the support and core processes, thus assume the relation between these two categories is support coming from the support processes towards the core processes. Last, this process map also includes the notion of Supplier and Customer, which are instances of the concepts input/output, as they are positioned right before the first core process of the value-chain and directly after the last core process of the value-chain, respectively, showing that a core process starts with a trigger from a supplier, while the outcome of a core process goes to a customer.

Therefore, for identifying the concepts included in all process maps under investigation we rely on both the visual representation (e.g. symbols used) and the semantics of each represented concept (e.g. Customer after a value-chain of core processes indicates a consumer of a process output). As a result, we generate a process map meta-model which encapsulates all concepts and relations we observed. In this way, we generalize from a set of instance models towards their underlying meta-model. A similar research approach has been used in [44], however, with the goal of building hypotheses. In our research, we are interested in uncovering the implicitly used meta-model. We use UML (Unified Modeling Language) as a language to design the meta-model.

For identifying the frequency and combinations of concepts, we adopt the approach of [45]. First, we created an Excel spread sheet and recorded each concept, relation between the concepts, whether these relations occur between singular processes or a set of processes, etc. For example, in the process map from Fig. 1 we observed and recorded the following concepts: process, category (core, support and management), input, output, and relation (sequential trigger, decompositional trigger, support, manage). We treated each process map as a single unit of observation, and denoted each concept occurrence with a binary value. Consequently, we derived a chart depicting the most often used concepts in process maps from practice. As we encode usage of each concept with 1 and 0, we can apply hierarchical clustering using the Euclidean distance measure which finds the co-occurrence relationship between concepts, based on how many concepts the process maps have in common. In this way, we identify concepts that most frequently occur in a specific combination, and also those that rarely occur together within a single map.

3.2 Data Collection

Although we analyze process maps coming from both practice and literature, we refer to all as process maps from practice, because process maps from literature are typically slightly adapted maps taken as example from practice. As there are only very few research articles that discuss process maps, we browsed the following BPM books, which all cover process architecture as a topic [36–41, 46–50]. We ended up with a total of 21 adapted practice process maps from literature. In addition, we used three sources to collect the process maps we use for analysis. First, we conducted interviews with companies and 13 of them provided us with a print of their process map. Also, we used 5 process maps that were part of published case studies [51]. In order to reach saturation, thus make sure we cover all concepts used in existing process maps, we searched for additional process maps using an Internet search engine. For this we used two key words, namely "process map" and "process landscape". Besides the many search results, we chose 23 process maps that seemed to be somewhat different than the ones we already had (e.g. the concepts within these process maps had a slightly different visual representation of the concepts, or we spotted new concept combinations within single process maps, etc.). Altogether, we use 67 process maps in the analysis.

4   Findings

In this section, we discuss the findings of our study. In Sect. 4.1, we present the meta-model that we derived from the process map analysis and explain the included concepts. In Sect. 4.2 we give insights into the use of process map concepts, and we present the results of the hierarchical cluster analysis.

4.1 Process Map Meta-Model

The results of the process map analysis are summarized in the meta-model depicted in Fig. 2. The model provides a generic way to deal with process map design by depicting all unique concepts we found in the 67 process maps. In the following paragraphs, we describe the meta-model concepts in detail.

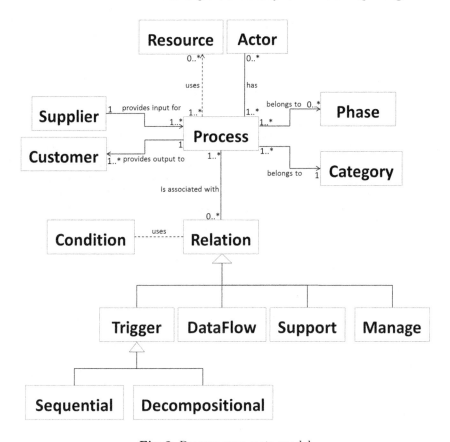

Fig. 2. Process map meta-model

Process. The key component of process maps is a business process. A process is triggered by an input from the supplier. A process is usually clustered in a category with other processes that serve a similar purpose. A process could also belong to one or more phases depending on the time of execution. Processes can be conducted by actors and could eventually use a resource during their execution. It can be related to other processes in order to produce an output for the customer.

Supplier. A supplier is a party that provides inputs that triggers the execution of an end-to-end process, i.e. a sequence of core processes. The types of input provided by a supplier may include:

○ An order (e.g. product, service, requirement, problem, etc.)
○ A by-product (e.g. outcome of other processes within the same organization)
○ A communication channel (e.g. telephone, email, etc.)
○ A document (e.g. invoice, research data, etc.)
○ A raw material (e.g. an unprocessed item used to create an end product)
○ etc.

Customer. A customer is the one who receives outputs resulting from the execution of a process. An output consumed by a customer may include:

○ A consummated order (e.g. ordered products, service, support, etc.)
○ A document (e.g. invoice, process data, etc.)
○ A finished good (e.g. product, etc.)
○ etc.

Resource. A resource is a source of supply or support that can be drawn upon when needed by any process or an instance of a process. As example, consider the resource *water*, which is required during the production of energy. If necessary, one process uses one or more resources throughout its execution. However, a process does not necessarily need to use a resource in order to produce an output.

Actor. One process can have one or more actors (e.g. process owners) that are responsible for its performance. However, a process could also be executed without having an assigned actor.

Category. A category is a group of processes that have a particular role within one company. One process can belong to only one category. Processes that are clustered in one category serve a similar purpose. For example, the core process category typically holds all value-creation processes, while those processes that analyse and measure the performance of the core processes are usually placed in the management process category.

Phase. A phase is a temporal cluster of processes that contains a subset of processes coming from one or more process categories. It is temporal because a certain number of processes need to be performed in order for an intermediate outcome to be produced. This intermediate outcome is used as a trigger for the processes that belong to the next phase. The intermediate outcome could also be kept in the database for later usage, thus it does not necessarily need to trigger the next phase of processes. For example, manufacturing a product is commonly done in different phases. The first phase will deal with supplying all material needed for the product to be manufactured. The second phase would keep all those processes that handle the actual production. Finally, the third phase contains the processes that market or sale the finished goods.

Condition. The condition constraints or guards the relation that is used between two or more processes. For instance, if process C can only start after processes A and B have been executed, than the condition will rule-out all those relations that do not capture this behavior.

Relation. One process can be related to other processes through one or more relation types. There are four main process relations: trigger relation, data flow relation, support relation, and manage relation.

Trigger relations could be used between processes that belong to the same or to different process categories. There are two types of trigger relations:

○ *Sequential* trigger is a control-flow relation used between processes to indicate order of performance. Thus, if two processes are related by a sequential trigger, then only when the first process finishes, the second process can start with execution. Alternative variations of process order are also possible. For instance, when one process is finished with execution, it could trigger more than one process. Accordingly, processes could also be executed in parallel. There could also exist process loops, which means that one single process, if necessary, could be triggered several times in a row until the desired outcome is produced.

○ *Decompositional* trigger involves abstraction. It relates a core process with its subprocesses. Thus, if a process is hierarchically decomposed, it automatically has one or more subprocesses that need to be executed in order for the core process to finish. For example, for the core process "Pre Sales" from Fig. 1 to be performed, the subprocess "Process Request"need to be executed. On the other hand, the core process "Order Processing" can finish its execution if only the subprocess "Process Order" has been done. Typically after a decompositional trigger has been used, the next process to be performed is related with a sequential trigger. Otherwise, the process ends.

Data flow could be used between processes that belong to the same or different categories. This relation, when used, does not necessarily trigger another process. Instead, it only passes information from one process to another without interrupting its performance. For example, if process A produces some type of a document, and this document is one of many documents needed by process B, then process A passes the document to process B. However, even after receiving the document from process A, process B is still in an idle state and starts only when it has received all necessary documents.

Support relation is used only between processes that belong to different categories. This relation exists between the core and support process category. The direction of support goes from the support processes to the core processes. It is an implicit relation, thus no direct explicit relation is shown between two particular processes, as it is typically the case of using an arrow to indicate sequential trigger relation. Instead, all support processes are there to serve any immediate need by all of the core processes.

Manage relation, similarly like the support relation, is used only between processes that belong to different categories. However, this relation exists only between the management and core processes. The management processes manage the core processes by governing the entire process during its execution and by taking care that the process is performed according to the rules defined by the management processes.

4.2   Use of Process Map Concepts

The presented meta-model from Fig. 2 summarizes process map concepts in a compact fashion, whereas Fig. 3 gives an overview of the process map concepts and their use in the investigated maps.

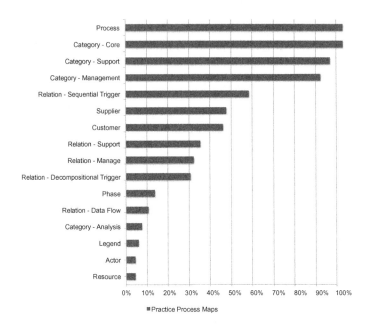

Fig. 3. Occurrence frequency of process map concepts

The numbers from Fig. 3 illustrate that the three category types *core*, *management*, and *support* are the most frequently used concepts. In fact, there is not a single process map without a core process category. However, also the management and support category are used by more than 85 % of the investigated maps. On the other hand, while sequential trigger is used by more than 50 % of the process maps, the remaining concepts included in process maps are significantly lower. About 40 % of the process maps are using inputs (Supplier) and outputs (Customer). Interestingly, the support and manage relations can be seen in only about 30 % of the process maps. This is quite unexpected considering the high usage of the corresponding categories. Apparently, the explicit inclusion of relations is only done by a few maps. Nevertheless, also other concepts are used by only some of the process maps. Particularly, the actor and the resource concept is rarely included. Also legends for explaining the illustrated concepts can only be found in a few cases.

In order to gain a deeper understanding of how the various process map concepts are utilized, we conducted a hierarchical cluster analysis using the Euclidean distance measure. As a result, we obtained a hierarchical classification of process map concepts that indicates which concepts are used alternatively and which concepts are used in combination.

Figure 4 illustrates the result of the hierarchical cluster analysis. The Figure gives us insights into the design of process maps, namely, it shows us which concepts are most frequently used together in a combination within one process

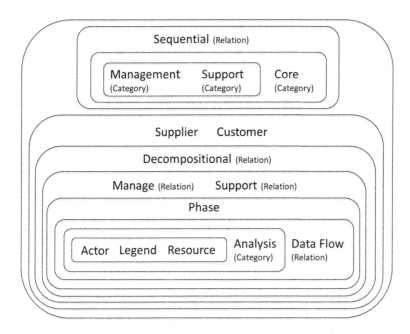

Fig. 4. Hierarchical clusters of process map concepts

map. On first glance we see that apparently there is a connection between the four most frequently used concepts as seen in Fig. 3 and the most frequent combination of concepts that usually appear in a single process map as seen in the upper part of Fig. 4. Thus, in most process maps we can expect to see the three process categories, and a sequential relation between the processes.

Concerning the *categories*, we learn that the management and the support category typically occur together. This indicates that organizations either focus on core processes (which are included in all investigated process maps), or they provide a broader view. In case they aim at providing a broader view, they tend to include both, the management and the support category.

With the *relations* we can also identify a clear pattern. While the sequential relation is often used in connection with the previously discussed categories, this does not apply to the other relations such as data flow or the manage and support relations. It appears that there are organizations with varying opinions about the level of detail they include in their process maps. While some organizations have process maps that provide many details including several types of relations, other organizations' process maps aim at providing a broad overview and omit relations other than the sequential trigger. As for the *supplier* and the *customer*, we observe that both are part of one cluster. This indicates that these concepts are very likely to occur together. So, organizations tend to either show both or none of them.

Concerning the less frequently used concepts as seen in Fig. 3, we observe two aspects. First, actors, resources, and legends are part of one cluster. Hence, their occurrence is positively correlated. This can be explained by the phenomenon we already discussed in the context of relations. Either an organization provides all in their process map or they include none. Apparently, this tendency also applies to actors and resources. Moreover, if these two are used, they are likely to also be accompanied by a legend. The second point relates to the co-occurrence of actors, resources, and data flow. As indicated by the clusters, there is a tendency for these concepts to occur together. This illustrates that maps containing actors and resources are also more likely to illustrate how these resources are used during the entire process flow, until the point an output is produced.

The hierarchical cluster analysis points to the fact that process maps might be used with differing intentions. While some maps provide extensive detail such as actors, resources, and triggers, other are rather inclined to provide an abstract picture of the company's processes. The latter category tends to omit concepts like data flow relations and other details such as actors and resources.

5 Implications

The findings from this paper have several implications for research and practice. In relation to implications for practice, we emphasize the importance of process map design. We argue that a well-designed process map should be able to elicit basic understanding over the company's operations. This is particularly important because of the heterogeneous nature of currently used process maps due to the lack of a standardized modeling language for process map design. As such they might not be readily readable to people who were not involved in the creation of the process map. Therefore, in order to assure that the process map will be correctly interpreted and understood by all concerned parties, besides depicting the company's processes in process categories, the process map designer should in addition include all concepts that aid in transmitting the knowledge the process map should convey. Hence, using a wide range of concepts makes a process map self-explanatory i.e. a person could interpret how the company operates without necessarily going into process details [1]. Beyond this, and also a topic for future research, despite the formal concepts included in all process maps, the creation of a process map should incorporate additional visual variables, such as color, shape, size, etc. [52], that will assist in transferring the knowledge in a cognitively effective manner [1]. The study [1] has shown that the inclusion of more concepts and visual variables in a process map does indeed have an effect on the underlying BPM success in a company. Also, taking into account that a process map design is considered as a strategic step and as such the foundation for the consequent BPM implementation [4,53], a process map design could strongly influence the subsequent detailed process modeling.

In terms of implications for research, the analysis we present, along with the meta-model, provides solid basis for consolidation of concepts and represents a step towards a standardized language for process map design. Thus, this paper sets a starting point for their design by summarizing all used concepts in currently existing process maps from practice. This particularly assists in establishing a body of knowledge on current process map design.

This paper is also related to a stream of research that aims to improve conceptual modeling by investigating actual usage. In this way, it complements papers that investigate UML usage [54], BPMN usage [45], as well as the usage of models versus text [44].

6   Conclusion

In this paper, we investigated the concepts used in 67 process maps from practice. Based on this analysis, we derived a process map meta-model that covers all concepts these process maps use, as well as the relations between them. We presented the occurrence frequency of process map concepts. In addition, by using a hierarchical clustering method we showed the most frequent combinations of concepts used within a single process map.

We found that the core process category is used in all process maps, while those maps that include a support category also have a tendency to include the management process category. The sequential relation is frequently used by most maps to relate processes. In addition, our findings showed that those process maps that include additional information beyond process categories and relations, such as an actor, are also likely to include even more extra concepts, such as a resource, and show how all this information flows throughout the process execution with the use of a data flow relation.

References

1. Malinova, M., Mendling, J.: The effect of process map design quality on process management success. In: Proceedings of the 21st European Conference on Information Systems (2013)
2. Rosemann, M.: Potential pitfalls of process modeling: part A. Bus. Process Manage. J. **12**(2), 249–254 (2006)
3. Dumas, M., Rosa, M., Mendling, J., Reijers, H.: Fundamentals of Business Process Management. Springer, Heidelberg (2013)
4. Malinova, M., Hribar, B., Mendling, J.: A framework for assessing BPM success. In: Proceedings of the 22nd European Conference on Information Systems (2014)
5. Kock, N.: Systems analysis & design fundamentals: a business process redesign approach. SAGE, Thousand Oaks (2006)
6. Mendling, J., Reijers, H.A., van der Aalst, W.M.P.: Seven process modeling guidelines (7PMG). Inf. Softw. Technol. **52**(2), 127–136 (2010)
7. Becker, J., Rosemann, M., von Uthmann, C.: Guidelines of business process modeling. In: van der Aalst, W.M.P., Desel, J., Oberweis, A. (eds.) Business Process Management. LNCS, vol. 1806, pp. 30–49. Springer, Heidelberg (2000)
8. Dijkman, R.M., La Rosa, M., Reijers, H.A.: Managing large collections of business process models-current techniques and challenges. Comput. Ind. **63**(2), 91–97 (2012)

9. Bandara, W., Jayaganesh, M., Lippe, S., Raduescu, C., Tan, H., Zur Muehlen, M.: A framework of issues in large process modelling projects. In: ECIS (2006)
10. Yan, Z., Dijkman, R., Grefen, P.: Business process model repositories-framework and survey. Inf. Softw. Technol. **54**(4), 380–395 (2012)
11. Malinova, M., Dijkman, R., Mendling, J.: Automatic extraction of process categories from process model collections. In: Lohmann, N., Song, M., Wohed, P. (eds.) BPM 2013 Workshops. LNBIP, vol. 171, pp. 430–441. Springer, Heidelberg (2014)
12. Malinova, M., Leopold, H., Mendling, J.: An empirical investigation on the design of process architectures. Wirtschaftsinformatik **75** (2013)
13. Leopold, H., Mendling, J., Reijers, H.A., Rosa, M.L.: Simplifying process model abstraction: techniques for generating model names. Inf. Syst. **39**, 134–151 (2014)
14. Smirnov, S., Reijers, H.A., Weske, M., Nugteren, T.: Business process model abstraction: a definition, catalog, and survey. Distrib. Parallel Databases **30**(1), 63–99 (2012)
15. Frolov, V., Mengel, D., Bandara, W., Sun, Y., Ma, L.: Building an ontology and process architecture for engineering asset management. In: Kiritsis, D., Emmanouilidis, C., Koronios, A., Mathew, J. (eds.) Engineering Asset Lifecycle Management, pp. 86–97. Springer, London (2010)
16. Zur Muehlen, M., Wisnosky, D., Kindrick, J.: Primitives: design guidelines and architecture for bpmn models. In: 2010 Australasian Conference on Information Systems (ACIS 2010) Australasian Computer Society (2010)
17. Pritchard, J.P., Armistead, C.: Business process management-lessons from european business. Bus. Process Manage. J. **5**(1), 10–35 (1999)
18. Armistead, C.: Principles of business process management. Manage. Serv. Qual. **6**(6), 48–52 (1996)
19. Green, S., Ould, M.A.: The primacy of process architecture. In: CAiSE Workshops (2), pp. 154–159. Citeseer (2004)
20. Armistead, C., Machin, S.: Implications of business process management for operations management. Int. J. Oper. Prod. Manage. **17**(9), 886–898 (1997)
21. Grady, J.O.: System Management: Planning, Enterprise Identity, and Deployment. CRC Press/Taylor & Francis, London (2010)
22. Green, S., Ould, M.: A framework for classifying and evaluating process architecture methods. Softw. Process: Improv. Pract. **10**(4), 415–425 (2005)
23. Stewart, G.: Supply-chain operations reference model (SCOR): the first cross-industry framework for integrated supply-chain management. Logistics Inf. Manage. **10**(2), 62–67 (1997)
24. Kelly, M.B.: Report: the telemanagement forum's enhanced telecom operations map (eTOM). J. Netw. Syst. Manage. **11**(1), 109–119 (2003)
25. Becker, J., Hansmann, H., Rieke, T.: Architekturen von informationssystemen. Ein Sektor mit Zukunft, Informationswirtschaft (2008)
26. Scheer, A.: Aris: Business Process Modeling. Springer, Heidelberg (2000)
27. Of Defense Architecture Framework Working Group, D., et al.: Dod architecture framework, version 1.5. Department of Defense, USA (2007)
28. Harmon, P.: Business process change: a guide for business managers and BPM and six sigma professionals. Morgan Kaufmann, San Francisco (2010)
29. Porter, M.E.: Competitive Advantage: Creating and Sustaining Superior Performance. SimonandSchuster, New York (2008)
30. Porter, M.E., Millar, V.E.: How information gives you competitive advantage. Harvard Bus. Rev. **63**(4), 149–160 (1985)
31. Eckes, G.: The Six Sigma revolution: How General Electric and others turned Process into Profits. Wiley, New York (2002)

32. Gordijn, J., Akkermans, H., Van Vliet, J.: Designing and evaluating e-business models. IEEE Intell. Syst. **16**(4), 11–17 (2001)
33. Gordijn, J., Akkermans, H.: Ontology-based operators for e-business model de-and reconstruction. In: Proceedings of the 1st international conference on Knowledge capture, pp. 60–67 ACM (2001)
34. Osterwalder, A., Pigneur, Y.: Business Model Generation: A Handbook for Visionaries, Game Changers, and Challengers. Wiley, New Jersey (2010)
35. Zott, C., Amit, R., Massa, L.: The business model: recent developments and future research. J. Manage. **37**(4), 1019–1042 (2011)
36. Fischermanns, G.: Praxishandbuch Prozessmanagement. Schmidt, Wettenberg (2006)
37. Mahal, A.: How Work Gets Done: Business Process Management Basics and Beyond. Technics Publications, LLC, USA (2010)
38. Jeston, J., Nelis, J.: Business Process Management: Practical Guidelines to Successful Implementations. Routledge, New York (2008)
39. Becker, J., Kugeler, M., Rosemann, M.: Process management: a guide for the design of business processes: with 83 figures and 34 tables. Springer Verlag, New York (2003)
40. Weske, M.: Business Process Management: Concepts, Languages, Architectures, 2nd edn. Springer, New York (2012)
41. Franz, P., Kirchmer, M.: Value-Driven Business Process Management: The Value-switch for Lasting Competitive Advantage. McGraw-Hill, New York (2012)
42. Maddern, H., Smart, P.A., Maull, R.S., Childe, S.: End-to-end process management: implications for theory and practice. Prod. Plan. Control **25**(16), 1–19 (2013)
43. Kiraka, R.N., Manning, K.: Managing organisations through a process-based perspective: its challenges and benefits. Knowl. Process Manage. **12**(4), 288–298 (2005)
44. Recker, J., Safrudin, N., Rosemann, M.: How novices design business processes. Inf. Syst. **37**(6), 557–573 (2012)
45. zur Muehlen, M., Recker, J.: How much language is enough? theoretical and practical use of the business process modeling notation. In: Bellahsène, Z., Léonard, M. (eds.) CAiSE 2008. LNCS, vol. 5074, pp. 465–479. Springer, Heidelberg (2008)
46. Bergsmann, S.: End-To-End-Geschäftsprozessmanagement: Organisationselement-Integrationsinstrument-Managementansatz. Springer DE, New York (2011)
47. Komus, A.: BPM Best Practice. Springer DE, Heidelberg (2011)
48. Slama, D., Nelius, R.: Enterprise BPM: Erfolgsrezepte für unternehmensweites Prozessmanagement. Dpunkt verlag, Heidelberg (2011)
49. Hanschke, I.: Enterprise Architecture Management-einfach und effektiv. Carl Hanser Verlag GmbH & Co., Munich (2011)
50. Snabe, J.H., Rosenberg, A., Mller, C., Scavillo, M.: Business Process Management: The SAP Roadmap. SAP Press, WALLDORF (2008)
51. Kern, E.M.: Prozessmanagement individuell umgesetzt: Erfolgsbeispiele aus 15 privatwirtschaftlichen und öffentlichen Organisationen. Springer, Heidelberg (2012)
52. Bertin, J.: Semiology of graphics. Diagrams, networks, maps **16**(1), 416 (1983)
53. Rosemann, M., vom Brocke, J.: The six core elements of business process management. In: Handbook on Business Process Management 1. 107–122 Springer (2010)
54. Dobing, B., Parsons, J.: How UML is used. Commun. ACM **49**(5), 109–113 (2006)

Supporting Data Collection in Complex Scenarios with Dynamic Data Collection Processes

Gregor Grambow[✉], Nicolas Mundbrod, Jens Kolb, and Manfred Reichert

Institute of Databases and Information Systems, Ulm University, Ulm, Germany
{gregor.grambow,nicolas.mundbrod,jens.kolb,manfred.reichert}@uni-ulm.de
http://www.uni-ulm.de/dbis

Abstract. Nowadays, companies have to report a large number of data sets (e.g., sustainability data) regarding their products to different legal authorities. However, in today's complex supply chains products are the outcome of the collaboration of many companies. To gather the needed data sets, companies have to employ cross-organizational and long-running data collection processes that imply great variability. To support such scenarios, we have designed a lightweight, automated approach for contextual process configuration. That approach can capture the contextual properties of the respective situations and, based on them, automatically configure a process instance accordingly, even without human involvement. Finally, we implemented our approach and started an industrial evaluation.

Keywords: Process configuration · Business process variability · Data collection · Sustainability · Supply chain

1 Introduction

In todays' industry many products are the result of the collaboration of various companies working together in complex supply chains. Cross-organizational communication in such areas can be quite challenging due to the fact that different companies have different information systems, data formats, and approaches to such communication. These days, state authorities, customers and public opinion demand sustainability compliance from companies, especially in the electronics and automotive sector. Therefore, companies must report certain sustainability indicators such as, their greenhouse gas (GHG) emissions or the amount of lead contained in their products. Such reports usually involve data from suppliers of the reporting company. Therefore, companies launch a sustainability data collection process along their supply chain. In turn, this might involve the suppliers of the suppliers, and so on. Figure 1 illustrates this scenario with three exemplified tiers of suppliers of a company. While having only two direct suppliers on tier one, the company also has eight indirect suppliers on the tiers two and three.

© Springer International Publishing Switzerland 2015
S. Nurcan and E. Pimenidis (Eds.): CAiSE Forum 2014, LNBIP 204, pp. 52–67, 2015.
DOI: 10.1007/978-3-319-19270-3_4

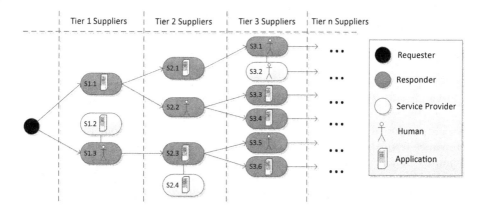

Fig. 1. Supply chain scenario

As sustainability data collection is a relatively new and complicated issue, service providers (e.g., for data validation or lab tests) are involved in such data collection as well. This fact is exemplified in Fig. 1, where three service providers in different tiers are involved. Another property that makes these data collection processes even more complex and problematic is the heterogeneity in the supply chain: companies use different information systems, data formats, and overall approaches to sustainability data collection. Many of them even do not have any information system or approach in place for this and answer with low quality data or not at all. Therefore, no federated system or database could be applied to cope with such problems and each request involves an often long-running, manual, and error-prone data collection process. The following simplified scenario illustrates issues with the data collection process on a small scale.

Scenario: Sustainability Data Collection
An automotive company wants to collect sustainability data relating to the quantity of lead contained in a specific part. This concerns two of the company's suppliers. One of them has an IHS (In House Solution) in place, the other has no system and no dedicated responsible for sustainability. For the smaller company, a service provider is needed to validate the manually collected data in order to ensure that it complies with legal regulations. The IHS of the other company has its own data format that must be converted before it can be used. This simple scenario already shows how much complexity results even from simple requests and indicates how this can look like in bigger scenarios involving hundreds or thousands of companies with different systems and properties.

In the SustainHub[1] project, we develop a centralized information exchange platform that supports sustainability data collection along the entire supply chain. We have already thoroughly investigated the properties of such data

---

[1] SustainHub (Project No.283130) is a collaborative project within the 7th Framework Programme of the European Commission (Topic ENV.2011.3.1.9-1, Eco-innovation).

collection in the automotive and electronics sectors and reported on the challenges and state-of-the-art regarding this topic [1]. This paper, proposes an approach that enables an inter-organizational data collection process. Thereby, the main focus is the capability of this process to automatically configure itself in alignment with the context of its concrete execution.

To guarantee the utility of our approach as well as its general applicability, we have started with collecting problems and requirements directly from the industry. This included telephone interviews with representatives from 15 European companies from the automotive and electronics sectors, a survey with 124 valid responses from companies of these sectors, and continuous communication with a smaller focus group to gather more precise information. Among the most valuable information gathered there was a set of core challenges for such a system: as most coordination for sustainability data exchange between companies is done manually, it can be problematic to find the right companies, departments, and persons to get data from as well as to determine, in which cases service providers must be involved (the first Data Collection Challenge - DCC1). Moreover, this is aggravated by the different systems and approaches different companies apply. Even if the right entity or person has been selected, it might still be difficult to access the data and to get it in a usable format (DCC2). Furthermore, the data requests rely on a myriad of contextual factors that are only managed implicitly (DCC3). Thus, a request is not reusable since an arbitrary number of variants may exist for it (DCC4). A system aiming at the support of such data collection must explicitly manage and store various data sets: the requests, their variants, all related context data, and data about the different companies and support manual and automated data collection.

The remainder of this paper is organized as follows: Sect. 2 shows our general approach for a process-driven data collection. Section 3 extends this approach with additional features regarding context and variability. Section 4 presents the implementation for our concept. This is followed by a discussion of a preliminary practical application in Sect. 5, a comprehensive discussion of related work in Sect. 6, and the conclusion.

2   Data Collection Governed by Processes

The basic idea behind our approach for supporting data collection in complex environments is governing the entire data collection procedure by explicitly specified processes. Furthermore, these processes are automatically enacted by a Process-Aware Information System (PAIS) integrated into the SustainHub platform. This way, the process of data collection for a specific issue as a sustainability indicator can be explicitly specified through a process type while process instances derived from that type govern concrete data collections regarding that issue (cf. Fig. 2).

Activities in such a process represent the manual and automatic tasks to be executed as part of the data collection by different companies. This approach already covers a number of the elicited requirements. It enables a centralized

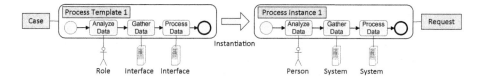

Fig. 2. Utilizing processes for data requests

and consistent request handling (cf. DCC1) and supports manual as well as automated data collection (cf. DCC2). One big advantage is the modularity of the processes. If a new external system shall be integrated, a new activity component can be developed while the overall data collection process does not need to be adapted. Finally, the realisation in a PAIS also enables the explicit specification of the data collection process (cf. DCC4). Through visual modeling, the creation and maintenance of such processes is facilitated.

However, the process-driven realization can only be the basis for comprehensive and consistent data collection support. To be able to satisfy the requirements regarding contextual influences, various types of important data and data request variants, we propose an extended process-driven approach for data collection as illustrated in Fig. 3.

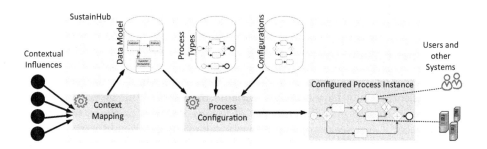

Fig. 3. SustainHub configurable data collection approach

To generate an awareness of contextual influences (e.g. the concrete approach to data collection in a company, cf. DCC3) and to make them usable for the data collection process, we define an explicit context mapping approach (as discussed in Sect. 3.1). This data is required for enabling the central component of our approach, i.e., the automatic and context-aware process configuration (as discussed in Sect. 3.2). That component uses pre-defined process types and configuration options to automatically generate a process instance containing all necessary activities to match the properties of the current requests situation (cf. DCC4). As basis for this step, we include a comprehensive data model where contextual influences are stored (cf. DCC3) alongside different kinds of content-related data. This data model integrates process-related data with customer-related data as well as contextual information.

We now briefly introduce the different kinds of incorporated data by different sections of our data model. At first, such a system must manage data about its customers. Therefore, a customer data section comprises data about the companies, like organizational units or products. Another basic component of industrial production, which is important for topics like sustainability, are substances and (sustainability) indicators. As these are not specific for one company, they are integrated as part of a master data section. In addition, the data concretely exchanged between the companies is represented within a separate section (exchange data). To support this data exchange, in turn, the system must manage certain data relating to the exchange itself (cf. DCC1): For whom is the data accessible? What are the properties of the requests and responses? Such data is captured in a runtime data section in the data model. Finally, to be able to consistently manage the data request process, concepts for the process and its variants as well as for the contextual meta data influencing the process have been integrated with the other data. More detailed descriptions of these concepts and their utilization will follow in the succeeding sections.

3   Variability Aspects of Data Collection

This section deals with the necessary areas for automated process configuration: The mapping of contextual influences into the system to be used for configuration and the modeling of the latter.

3.1   Context Mapping

As stated in Sect. 1, a request regarding the same topic (in this case, a sustainability indicator) may have multiple variants influenced by a myriad of possible contextual factors (e.g. the number of involved parties or the data formats used). Hence, if one seeks to implement any kind of automated variant management, a consistent manageable way of dealing with these factors becomes crucial. However, the decisions on how to apply process configuration and variant management often cannot be mapped directly to certain facts existing in the environment of a system. Moreover, situations might occur, in which different contextual factors will lead to the same decision(s) according to variant management. For example, a company could integrate a special four-eyes-principle approval process for the release of data due to different reasons, e.g., if the data is intended for a specific customer group or relates to a specific law or regulation. Nevertheless, it would be cumbersome to enable automatic variant management by creating a huge number of rules for each and every possible contextual factor. In the following, therefore, we propose a more generic mapping approach for making contextual factors usable for decisions regarding the data collection process.

In our approach, contextual factors are abstracted by introducing two separate concepts in a lightweight and easily configurable way: The *Context Factor* captures different possible contextual facts existing in the systems' environment.

Opposed to this, the *Process Parameter* is used to model a stable set of parameters directly relevant to the process of data collection. Both concepts are connected by simple logical rules as illustrated on the left side of Fig. 4. In this example, a simple mapping is shown. If a contact person is configured for a company (CF1), parameter 'Manual Data Collection' will be derived. If the company is connected via a tool connector (CF2), automatic data collection will be applied (P3). If the company misses a certain certification (CF3), an additional validation is needed (P2).

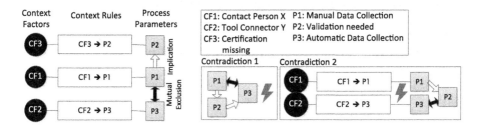

Fig. 4. Context mapping

When exchanging data between companies, various situations might occur, in which different decisions regarding the process might have implications on each other. For example, it would make no sense to collect data both automatically and manually for the same indicator at the same time. To express that, we also include the two simple constraints 'implication' and 'mutual exclusion' for the parameters. For an example, we refer to Fig. 4, where manual and automatic data collection are mutually exclusive.

Though we put emphasis on keeping the applied rules and constraints simple and maintainable, there still exist situations, in which these lead to contradictions. One case (Contradiction 1 in Fig. 4) involves a contradiction only created by the constraints, where one activity requires and permits the occurrence of another activity at the same time. A second case (Contradiction 2 in Fig. 4) occurs when combining certain rules with certain constraints, in which a contradicting set of parameters is produced. To avoid such situations, we integrate a set of simple correctness checks for constraints and rules.

3.2 Process Configuration

In this section, we will introduce our approach for process configuration. We have not only considered the aforementioned challenges, but also want to keep the approach as easy and lightweight as possible to enable users of the Sustain-Hub platform to configure and manage the approach. Furthermore, our findings include data about the actual activities of data collection as well as their relation to contextual data. Data collection often contains a set of basic activities that are part of each data collection process. Other activities appear mutually exclusive, e.g. manual or automatic data collection, and no standard activity can be determined here. In most cases, one or more context factors impose the application of a set of additional coherent activities rather than one single activity.

In the light of these facts, we opt for the following approach for automatic process configuration: For one case (e.g. a sustainability indicator) a process family is created. That process family contains a *base process* with all basic activities for that case. Additional activities, added to this base process, are encapsulated in *process fragments*. These are automatically added to the process on account of the parameters of the current situation represented in the system by the already introduced *process parameters* and *context factors*. Thus, we only rely on one single change pattern applicable to the processes, an insert operation. This operation has already been described in literature, for its formal semantics, see [2]. Thus our approach avoids problems with other operations as described in the context of other approaches like Provop [3].

To keep the approach lightweight and simple, we model both the base process and the fragments in a PAIS that will be integrated into our approach. Thus, we can rely on the abilities of the PAIS for modeling and enacting the processes as well as for checking their correctness.

To enable the system to automatically extend the base process at the right points with the chosen fragments, we add the concept of the *extension point (EP)*. Both EPs and fragments have parameters the system can match to find the right EP for a fragment (see Fig. 5 for an example with two EPs and three fragments with matching parameters). Regarding the connection of the EPs to the base processes, we have evaluated multiple options as, for example, connecting them directly to activities. Most options introduce limitations to the approach or impose a fair amount of additional complexity (see [3] for a detailed discussion). For these reasons we have selected an approach involving two *connection points* of an EP with a base process. These points are connected with nodes in the process as shown in Fig. 5. Taking the nodes as connection points allows us to reference the nodes' id for the connection point because this id is stable and only changes in case of more complicated configuration actions [3]. If the base process contains nodes between the connection points of one EP, an insertion will be applied in parallel to these, otherwise sequentially. Furthermore, if more than one fragment shall be inserted at one EP, they will be inserted in parallel to each other.

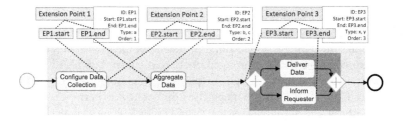

Fig. 5. Process annotation

The example from Fig. 5 illustrates this approach refining the aforementioned scenario. It comprises four basic activities for configuring the data collection, aggregating the data, and delivering the collected data. To insert further activities for data collection and processing, three EPs are defined. These have different connection points to the nodes in the process. Figure 5 further shows properties for the EPs including the connection points and an EP type (e.g. 'review' or 'approval') that will be used to determine which extension(s) may be applied at that point during configuration. A particular EP may be applicable for multiple fragments, but multiple EPs for the same fragment are not possible as it would be ambiguous, for which point to apply it. This is automatically checked during modeling. Another property, called 'Order', governs in which order extensions will be applied. It will also be checked that the ordering is not ambiguous.

However, to correctly insert fragments into a base process other facts must be considered as well: First, it must be determined whether a fragment, inserted in a LOOP, shall be executed multiple times. Second, it must be defined how the activities of a fragment are exactly inserted into the base process. Therefore, we extend the process fragment with a number of parameters. The first parameter, 'Insert', governs, if the fragment shall be inserted directly into the base process or as sub-process. The latter could be considered, i.e., when the fragment comprises a bigger number of activities with a complicated structure. The second is the 'Type' that relates to the EP type and is used to match both of them. The third, 'Exec' governs, if a fragment might be executed multiple times.

Figure 6 illustrates process fragments and their parameters utilizing the scenario presented in Sect. 1. It contains five fragments: Fragments 1 and 2 comprise the activities for data collection of the two suppliers. They are integrated at the same position in parallel. Fragments 3 and 4 comprise the activities for data processing, integrated in parallel as well. Fragment 3 further demonstrates the insertion as sub-process if the base process shall not be bloated with many activities from large fragments. As both EP1 and EP2 are at the same position the 'Order' parameter comes into play governing the insertion of the data

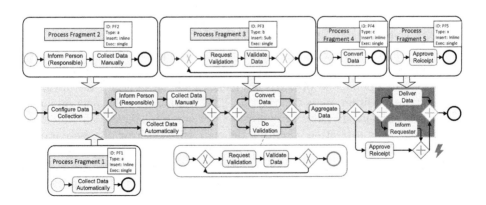

Fig. 6. Process fragments insertion

processing activities after the data collection activities. Finally, Fragment 5 contains an activity for demonstrating the insertion at the erroneously defined EP3. This would cause a violation to the regular nesting of the patterns (as XOR and AND) in the process called block structure. This is recommended for understandable modeling [4] and required by many PAIS for correct execution. As aforementioned, such definitions are prevented by automatic checks.

By relying on the capabilities of the PAIS, we keep the number of additional correctness checks small. However, connection points are not checked by the PAIS and could impose erroneous configurations. To keep correctness checks on them simple we rely on two things: The relation of two connection points of one EP and block-structured processes [4]. The first fact avoids the need to check all mutual connections of all connection points as two always belong together. The second one implies certain guarantees regarding the structuring of the process models. That way, we only have to check a small set of cases, as e.g., an erroneous definition of an extension point, as EP3 in Fig. 5 that would cause a violation to the block structure when inserting a fragment as shown in Fig. 6.

4   Implementation

This section elaborates on the concrete realization of the concepts presented in Sect. 3. It shows how the abstract context mapping and process configuration concepts can be transformed into a concrete implementation. At first, we discuss the classes we created to implement our approach. Thereafter, we elaborate on the components we apply to concretely conduct the process configurations.

To illustrate the relations of the concepts crucial for our concept, Fig. 7 shows a simplified class diagram. The latter indicates a separation between the classes defining the configuration concepts (build-time) and classes managing their execution (runtime). To be able to reuse a process family easily in different contexts, we separate the concepts into a process family (class `ProcessFamily`) and a so-called context application (class `ContextApplication`). The process family comprises the concepts for representing the base process as well as the process fragments (classes `AdaptableProcessTemplate` and `AdaptableProcess` `-TemplateFragment`). These classes hold references to concrete process templates of the PAIS. In addition, the base process has an arbitrary number of extension points (class `ExtensionPoint`) that mark the points where process fragments may be inserted. In order to be able to determine, when and at which extension point one of these fragments shall be inserted, we integrate an activation condition (class `Condition`). This condition implements an interface we use to unite all rules or expressions of our implementation (interface `Expression`). The activation condition depends on the set of process parameters connected to the process template (class `ProcessParameter`). As discussed, the process parameters may be associated with constraints. These are realized by the class `ProcessParamterConstraint`, which implements the `Expression` interface as well.

To be able to use a process family for a certain situation, we must map existing contextual factors into SustainHub. That way, they become usable for the process parameters. This is done by the context application (class `Context-Application`) that encapsulates process parameters as well as context rules (class `ContextRule`). A context rule, in turn, refers to context factors and process parameters. The rule itself is implemented as a JavaScript expression (class `JavaScriptExpression`) that also implements the expression interface.

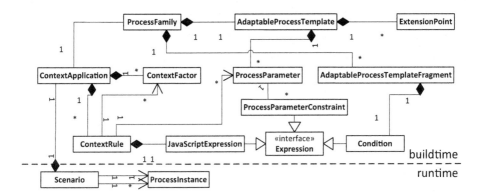

Fig. 7. Class diagram

At runtime, we apply a so-called scenario (class `Scenario`) that models a current situation. It comprises all concepts of a process family and a context application via an included context application. Besides that, the scenario also refers to multiple process instances (class `ProcessInstance`), which represent the base process and potential sub-processes executed in the PAIS.

We proceed with a discussion of the concrete components and procedure at runtime. First of all, we have implemented the process configuration as an adaptation operation on the running process instances instead of configuring the process templates. Otherwise we would have created a high number of additional configured process templates for each possible configuration. Therefore, we have created an additional automatic adaptation component that interacts with the PAIS and the process instance. This is illustrated in Fig. 8.

In the following, we introduce the different steps performed for the execution of a scenario. The first action is to start a process instance (cf. Fig. 8 (1)) that corresponds to a base process of a process family. This action also registers the automatic adaptation component as observer on this process instance so the former can interact with the latter. This is necessary due to a specific property of adaptable PAIS: For adapting a running process instance, instance execution must be temporarily suspended. This can only be done when no activity is active. Being registered as observer, the automatic adaptation component may apply adaptations directly when the instance gets suspended. The first action of the automatic adaptation component is to setup the scenario for the current process instance (2). After that, the first activity of the process instance gets executed (3). For every base process, this activity is a so-called 'analyse and adapt' activity we apply to gather context information from both the user and

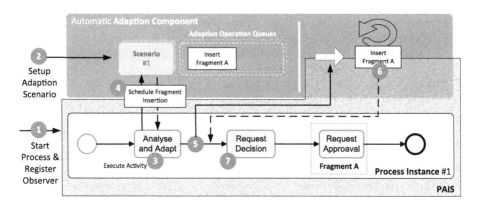

Fig. 8. Configuration procedure

the environment. This data is then stored as context factors and passed to the automatic adaptation component (4). The latter then starts a scenario engine that determines the adaptation actions from the context factors. After that it schedules a suspension of the process instance, which is applied right after the termination of the 'analyse and adapt' activity.

When the 'anaylse and adapt' activity is finished, the process instance is suspended and the automatic adaptation component is triggered (5). The latter then uses the API of the PAIS to apply the scheduled adaptations (6). Following this, the instance is reactivated and proceeds with its execution (7). This approach bears the advantage that the running process instance can be adapted at any position after the 'analyse and adapt' activity, while the user is not impeded from the adaptation.

Having explained our adaptation approach abstractly, we now go into detail about the interaction between the components. This is illustrated as a sequence diagram (cf. Fig. 9).

After being activated by the PAIS, the 'analyse and adapt' activity determines the context factors values. Then, it calls the automatic adaptation component via a REST interface passing the id of the process instance and the context values to it. The adaptation component uses the ID to determine the right scenario and calls the engine to execute the scenario with the received context values. In turn, the engine uses this data to determine the concrete adaptation operations. In particular, it runs the context rules to obtain the process parameters and the activation conditions to determine which fragments are to be inserted for the current situation. After that, the engine applies these operations meaning it signals the adaptation component and the activity to signal the suspension of the process instance.

When the 'analyse and adapt' activity finishes, the instance gets suspended automatically and the adaptation component gets triggered to apply the adaptations. The latter then checks, which operations are scheduled and applies them to the instance. Finally, the adaptation component returns control to the process instance that proceeds with its execution.

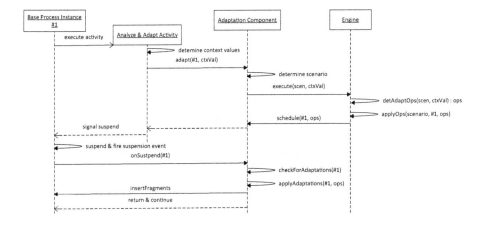

Fig. 9. Sequence diagram

5   Preliminary Practical Application

We already implemented a set of indicator use cases and, based on that, we have had a first feedback loop with our industry partners in the SustainHub project. As our partner companies could confirm the practical applicability of our approach, we will now continue to implement a bigger set of indicators for further evaluations. In the following, we show one use case dealing with energy consumption that is rather simple. It involves three context factors based on the following questions: Can the responder distinguish between own and bought energy, between consumption categories, and energy sources? The context factors are mapped to one process parameter. In Fig. 10, we show this mapping, the base process and an example fragment modeled in the PAIS we used for our implementation (AristaFlow [5]), and the SustainHub web-GUI while executing this process. In addition to this, we have recently started to implement a use case from the educational domain: the management of theses at a university. Our approach shows promise to also suit this domain well.

6   Related Work

The the area of sustainable supply chain communication is relatively new. Despite this fact, a set of approaches exist in this area (e.g., [6] or [7]). However, instead of proposing technical solutions, they focus on analyzing the importance of corporate sustainability reporting or evaluating sustainability indicators. Therefore, we will focus on the technical aspects in the rest of this section.

Regarding the topic of process configuration, various approaches exist. Most of them focus on the modeling of configuration aspects of processes. One example is C-EPC [8], which enables behavior-based configurations by integrating configurable elements into a process model. Another approach with the same

Fig. 10. Application use case

focus is ADOM [9]. It allows for the specification of constraints and guidelines on a process model to support variability modeling. Such approaches focus on the extension of available process modeling notations and produce maximized models containing all possible activities. Such models might be difficult to comprehend and maintain.

In [10], a comprehensive meta-model for process variability is proposed. It incorporates a set of different perspectives, as e.g., a functional as well as a resource perspective. Therefore, it allows specifying a rich set of process information as well as necessary configurations and changes to it. Compared to our approach, this meta model is rather complicated and heavyweight and therefore difficult to understand. Moreover, it lacks adequate facilities for context modeling.

The approach presented in [11] features a meta model for process fragments as well as also a definition for actions on these fragments (e.g., composition). However, it strongly focuses on this topic and neglects the modeling of contextual facts that trigger such operations. Another meta model is proposed by [12]. Its intend is to extend process models to incorporate aspects that have been neglected so far, i.e., the data and resource perspectives. The authors therefore introduce role-task and object-task associations for EPCs. This, however, provides no additional support for easier automated or contextual configurations.

Besides the approaches just discussed, which focus on the configurability topic in general, there exist other approaches focusing on specific aspects like correctness or recovery. For example, [13] provides a concept for enabling recovery strategies for workflows incorporating dynamically inserted fragments. This is achieved by introducing transactional behaviour for the fragments, which enables two different recovery strategies: a forward recovery and a backward recovery strategy. The former repairs a faulted process fragment by executing additional process logic. This is achieved by inserting a new fragment into the faulted one that is capable of repairing it. The backward recovery strategy, in turn, is applied if the problem is too severe to repair the fragment. Therefore, it is compensated or removed to enable another way of achieving the business goal of the process. The approach presented in [14] aims at presenting correctness for process configuration. In particular, it enables verification of configurable process models intended for execution. This verification is executed at design time and imposes no additional constraints on the model. The authors have further implemented their approach concretely for the C-YAWL language. Both of these approaches offer solutions for specific aspects of process configuration. None of them, however, provides means to support automated and contextual configuration abilities as out approach does.

All modeling approaches share the same drawbacks: First, they strongly focus on the modeling of process configuration aspects and neglect its execution. Second, process configuration must be manually applied by humans, which might be complicated and time-consuming. Two approaches, which take the automatic composition of processes out of a set of fragments into account are presented in [15] and [16]. The former addresses the issue of incorporating new run-time knowledge in pervasive computing. It employs pervasive process fragments and allows modeling incomplete and contextual knowledge. To be able to reach the process goal and include dynamic contextual knowledge, all relevant data is encoded as AI planning problem. In [16], however, an approach for dynamically composing fragments at run-time is presented. It is applied it to a logistics scenario and includes an explicit variation model as addition to a base process model and process fragments. At run-time a solver creates a solution using the specified models and context data implying the insertion of fragments matching the specified situation.

Both approaches focus strongly on the automatic selection of potentially concurring fragments. In contrast, our approach targets user support as well: we emphasize keeping the model simple and apply correctness checks for the user-modeled concepts. An approach, more closely related to ours, is Provop [3]. It allows storing a base process and corresponding pre-configured configurations. As opposed to Provop, SustainHub provides a framework for completely automatic, context-aware configuration of processes without need for any human interaction. Furthermore, Provop is more fine-grained, complicated, and heavyweight.

Another approach having many similarities to ours is Corepro [17]. It enables modeling and automated generation of large process structures. Furthermore, it comprises features for dynamic runtime adaptation as well as exception handling. However, it has one major drawback: context data utilized to generate the processes is limited to product data. Processes get generated solely relating to the product for whose production they intended. Further reading regarding other configuration approaches can be found in [18] and [19] as well as our predecessor paper for SustainHub [1].

7   Conclusion

In this paper, we have introduced a lightweight approach for automatic and contextual process configuration as required in complex scenarios. We have investigated concrete issues relating to sustainability data collection in supply chains. Our approach centralizes data and process management uniting many different factors in one data model and supporting the entire data collection procedure based on process templates executable in a PAIS. Moreover, we enable this approach to apply automated process configurations conforming to different situations by applying a simple model allowing for mapping contextual factors to parameters for the configuration. However, our approach is not only theoretical but is applicable in a real information system to support supply chain communication. Therefore, we have shown specifics of the implementation of our concepts. In future work, we plan to continue the evaluation of our work with our industrial partners and also in the educational domain. Further, we plan to extend our approach to cover further aspects regarding runtime variability, automated monitoring, and automated data quality management.

Acknowledgement. The project SustainHub (Project No.283130) is sponsored by the EU in the 7th Framework Programme of the European Commission (Topic ENV. 2011.3.1.9-1, Eco-innovation).

References

1. Grambow, G., Mundbrod, N., Steller, V., Reichert, M.: Challenges of applying adaptive processes to enable variability in sustainability data collection. In: 3rd International Symposium on Data-Driven Process Discovery and Analysis, pp. 74–88 (2013)
2. Rinderle-Ma, S., Reichert, M., Weber, B.: On the formal semantics of change patterns in process-aware information systems. In: Li, Q., Spaccapietra, S., Yu, E., Olivé, A. (eds.) ER 2008. LNCS, vol. 5231, pp. 279–293. Springer, Heidelberg (2008)
3. Hallerbach, A., Bauer, T., Reichert, M.: Configuration and management of process variants. In: vom Brocke, J., Rosemann, M. (eds.) International Handbook on Business Process Management I, pp. 237–255. Springer, Heidelberg (2010)
4. Mendling, J., Reijers, H.A., van der Aalst, W.M.: Seven process modeling guidelines (7pmg). Inf. Softw. Technol. **52**(2), 127–136 (2010)
5. Dadam, P., Reichert, M.: The adept project: a decade of research and development for robust and flexible process support - challenges and achievements. Comput. Sci. Res. Dev. **23**(2), 81–97 (2009)
6. Pagell, M., Wu, Z.: Building a more complete theory of sustainable supply chain management using case studies of 10 exemplars. J. Supply Chain Manage. **45**(2), 37–56 (2009)
7. Singh, R.K., Murty, H.R., Gupta, S.K., Dikshit, A.K.: An overview of sustainability assessment methodologies. Ecol. Ind. **9**(2), 189–212 (2009)
8. Rosemann, M., van der Aalst, W.M.P.: A configurable reference modelling language. Inf. Syst. **32**(1), 1–23 (2005)

9. Reinhartz-Berger, I., Soffer, P., Sturm, A.: Extending the adaptability of reference models. IEEE Trans. Syst. Man Cyber. Part A **40**(5), 1045–1056 (2010)
10. Saidani, O., Nurcan, S.: Business process modeling: a multi-perspective approach integrating variability. In: Bider, I., Gaaloul, K., Krogstie, J., Nurcan, S., Proper, H.A., Schmidt, R., Soffer, P. (eds.) BPMDS 2014 and EMMSAD 2014. LNBIP, vol. 175, pp. 169–183. Springer, Heidelberg (2014)
11. Eberle, H., Leymann, F., Schleicher, D., Schumm, D., Unger, T.: Process fragment composition operations. In: Proceedings of APSCC 2010, IEEE Xplore, pp. 1–7, December 2010
12. La Rosa, M., Dumas, M., ter Hofstede, A.H.M., Mendling, J., Gottschalk, F.: Beyond control-flow: extending business process configuration to roles and objects. In: Li, Q., Spaccapietra, S., Yu, E., Olivé, A. (eds.) ER 2008. LNCS, vol. 5231, pp. 199–215. Springer, Heidelberg (2008)
13. Eberle, H., Leymann, F., Unger, T.: Transactional process fragments - recovery strategies for flexible workflows with process fragments. In: APSCC 2010, pp. 250–257 (2010)
14. van der Aalst, W., Lohmann, N., La Rosa, M., Xu, J.: Correctness ensuring process configuration: an approach based on partner synthesis. In: Hull, R., Mendling, J., Tai, S. (eds.) BPM 2010. LNCS, vol. 6336, pp. 95–111. Springer, Heidelberg (2010)
15. Sirbu, A., Marconi, A., Pistore, M., Eberle, H., Leymann, F., Unger, T.: Dynamic composition of pervasive process fragments. In: ICWS 2011, pp. 73–80 (2011)
16. Murguzur, A., De Carlos, X., Trujillo, S., Sagardui, G.: Dynamic composition of pervasive process fragments. In: CAiSE 2014, pp. 241–255 (2014)
17. Müller, D., Reichert, M., Herbst, J.: A new paradigm for the enactment and dynamic adaptation of data-driven process structures. In: Bellahsène, Z., Léonard, M. (eds.) CAiSE 2008. LNCS, vol. 5074, pp. 48–63. Springer, Heidelberg (2008)
18. Torres, V., Zugal, S., Weber, B., Reichert, M., Ayora, C., Pelechano, V.: A qualitative comparison of approaches supporting business process variability. In: Rosa, M.L., Soffer, P. (eds.) BPM 2012 Workshops. LNBIP, pp. 560–572. Springer, Heidelberg (2012)
19. Ayora, C., Torres, V., Weber, B., Reichert, M., Pelechano, V.: VIVACE: a framework for the systematic evaluation of variability support in process-aware information systems. Inf. Softw. Technol. **57**, 248–276 (2014)

A Method for Analyzing Time Series Data in Process Mining: Application and Extension of Decision Point Analysis

Reinhold Dunkl$^{(\boxtimes)}$, Stefanie Rinderle-Ma, Wilfried Grossmann,
and Karl Anton Fröschl

Faculty of Computer Science, University of Vienna, Vienna, Austria
{reinhold.dunkl,stefanie.rinderle-ma,
wilfried.grossmann,karl-anton.froeschl}@univie.ac.at

Abstract. The majority of process mining techniques focuses on control flow. Decision Point Analysis (DPA) exploits additional data attachments within log files to determine attributes decisive for branching of process paths within discovered process models. DPA considers only single attribute values. However, in many applications, the process environment provides additional data in form of consecutive measurement values such as blood pressure or container temperature. We introduce the DPATS method as an iterative process for exploiting time series data by combining process and data mining techniques. The latter ranges from visual mining to temporal data mining techniques such as dynamic time warping and response feature analysis. The method also offers different approaches for incorporating time series data into log files in order to enable existing process mining techniques to be applied. Finally, we provide the simulation environment DPATSSim to produce log files and time series data. The DPATS method is evaluated based on application scenarios from the logistics and medical domain.

Keywords: Process mining · Decision mining · Data mining · Time series data

1 Introduction

The interest of research and practice in process mining has dramatically increased during the last years. Process mining has different objectives, ranging from discovering process models from event log data to comparing events logs and existing process models (conformance checking) [1]. Event logs can be described as time-stamped event data (so-called log files) gathered from or produced by process instances executed in some process environment. Example event logs might stem from higher education processes [2] or skin cancer treatment processes [3].

The work presented in this paper has been partly conducted within the EBMC^2 project funded by the University of Vienna and the Medical University of Vienna.

S. Nurcan and E. Pimenidis (Eds.): CAiSE Forum 2014, LNBIP 204, pp. 68–84, 2015.
DOI: 10.1007/978-3-319-19270-3_5

This paper focuses on process discovery. So far, process discovery techniques have emphasized the control flow, i.e., discovering the process activities and the control structures of the process models from the event logs. The minimum information required for control flow discovery is information about the process task connected with the event (`WorkflowModelElement`) and a `Timestamp` as contained in the following event log fragment (in MXML format [4]).

```
<AuditTrailEntry>
    <WorkflowModelElement>Move to D</WorkflowModelElement>
    ...
    <Timestamp>2013-02-27T10:29:06.404+01:00</Timestamp>
</AuditTrailEntry>
```

An extension towards the branching logic of processes is provided by Decision Point Analysis (DPA) [5]. DPA is based on enriching log file entries with additional information about process environments or other process-relevant data and aims at deriving decision rules at alternative branching in process models. Basically, DPA works as follows: in a first step, the underlying process model is discovered based on the event log entries. If the resulting process model contains decision points (and additionally data relevant for the decisions is present in the event logs), the corresponding decision rules are determined using decision trees. Assuming that task `Move to D` marks a decision point in the process, the following log fragment could be basis for DPA:

```
<AuditTrailEntry>
    <WorkflowModelElement>Move to D</WorkflowModelElement>
    <Data>
        Attribute name="ContainerTemperature">37.2</Attribute>
    </Data>
    <Timestamp>2013-02-27T10:29:06.404+01:00</Timestamp>
    ...
</AuditTrailEntry>
```

Figure 1 depicts the container transportation example associated with the two log fragments above. It is based on the real-world case provided in [6], where some temperature-sensitive cargo is transported and cargo temperature is measured repeatedly. On the left, the application of DPA [5] is illustrated: depending on the temperature value for each transport monitored (at task `Move to D`), DPA concludes that for a temperature over 37°C, the vehicle has to return to its home base. Otherwise, it unloads the goods at the destination. As this example illustrates, i) DPA takes into consideration single-valued attributes; ii) DPA is able to derive decision rules of type "x OP value" where x is the decision variable and OP is a comparison operator; iii) DPA relies on values that are stored within the event log of a process.

However, in many application domains, not only single values of data attributes are collected, but *time series data*. Examples comprise the logistics, health care, and the manufacturing domain where container temperature, blood pressure, or sensor data are measured in a continuous way. Such continuously updated data [7] can be stored as time series data. The main question of this

Fig. 1. Process applications with time series data

paper is whether it is possible to extend DPA from single value analysis to adequately incorporating time series data. By doing so, it shall also become possible to determine more complex decision rules than "x OP value", for example, "temperature exceeds a certain threshold for a given time frame" (cf. right side in Fig. 1).

In this paper, we will present such an extension of DPA by means of a novel method DPATS that enables (a) a joint consideration of event log data and time series data, (b) iterative application of process and data/visual mining techniques, and (c) derivation of complex decision rules. Note that this paper is an extended version of [8]. The general method has been detailed and extended, e.g., incorporating further techniques such as time warping and a second evaluation example for multivariate data has been added.

Section 2 discusses different ways how time series attributes can affect the business process. This leads to two separable challenges within the problem setting, data preparation itself as well as data and visual mining aspects and how those integrate in the overall DPATS method (Sect. 3). The method uses as essential part approaches towards temporal data mining. The ensuing process mining method is evaluated based on a real-world examples of process analysis (Sect. 4). After reflecting our contribution against the state of the art in process, data, and visual mining (Sect. 5), some concluding remarks (Sect. 6) finish this presentation.

2   Business Processes and Time Series Attributes

Process mining uses event logs that consist of a minimal data set of case ids, activity names, and timestamps. It is also possible to store data values that were produced during process execution, e.g., the age of a patient. These single-valued attributes are exploited by, for example, DPA. In case of attributes defined as time series the situation is more complex because the measurement of the time series defines an additional process. This so called *measurement process* produces time series attributes which might cause effects on the execution of the business process of interest. The following two types of effects can be distinguished:

- *Separable effects* control the decision about activities in the business process. Depending on the results of the measurement process a decision about the execution of different activities in the business process is made. Take as example a treatment process in medical applications. The decision about different options for further therapy usually depends on the status of the patient

documented by time series for some medical parameters such as blood pressure recorded in the past. Looking at the development of these parameters, the doctor decides about future therapy, for example, choice of medication.
– *Intermingled effects* control the execution of activities in the business process. This means that the results of the measurement process influence the execution of the activities in business process. Take as example the transportation process of a container with temperature-sensitive cargo. During the transport, a measurement process continuously records the temperature of the container. In case of abnormal behavior of the temperature, the affected activity `transport` is interrupted (see e.g., [7]) and a new activity called the `return` starts.

Usage of time series data in modeling business processes depends not only on the above described types of effects, but also on the structure of the time series data. The simple case is based on the assumption that the effects of the time series data on the process depend only on the actual value of the time series. We call this effects *Markov-like effects*. The rationale behind this denotation is that the effect can be compared with the Markov property in processes, which states that all information about the process at a certain time is captured in the actual value. In the examples mentioned above, this would be the actual blood pressure of the patient or the actual temperature in the container.

In many applications such an assumption cannot be justified. For example, in case of container transport a short period of high temperature is not critical and return is only advisable in case of high temperature over a certain time period. Such cases need additional analysis about properties of the time series. We call such effects *non-Markov-like effects*.

The above elaboration makes clear that usage of time series data in DPA needs additional considerations. Basically, DPA is designed for applications with non temporal attributes. In case of temporal attributes, it can be applied, but only provided that the time series measurements generate separated effects and the effects depend only on the actual measurements, i.e., have a Markov like property. It is the aim of DPATS to develop an analysis framework which can handle also more complex cases. As explained in the following section, the framework is based on a combination of methods for process analysis, methods for temporal data mining, and appropriate representation of data.

3   DPATS Method

The DPATS method is illustrated in Fig. 2 and describes the process of analyzing time series data as basis for decision point analysis in business processes. The proposed method does not depend on a particular domain. The only precondition for its application is the existence of time series data collected at decision points in the process. In the following, we will motivate the design of the DPATS method by shortly explaining its steps. A more detailed discussion is following in the subsequent sections.

The DPATS method constitutes and extension of DPA which consists of the steps *classification* and *data mining* [5]. In order to be able to consider time series data, the DPATS method has to introduce a prior step of *data preparation* as the storage of time series data is not foreseen in existing log formats (cf. XES as standard log format [4]). The data preparation step is elaborated in Sect. 3.1.

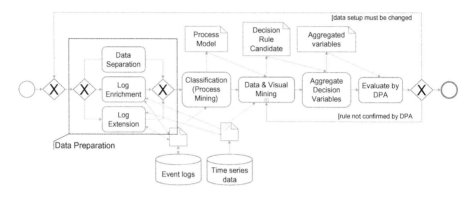

Fig. 2. DPATS method (in BPMN notation)

As we operate on time series data, various techniques for temporal data mining can be used in the *Data & Visual Mining* step (cf. Fig. 3 and Sect. 3.2) in order to explain the decisions in the observed process instances. This step follows the model set out by Keim et al. [9] which generates knowledge (in DPATS the decision rules) based on the data and a tightly integrated data visualization and mining approach. This more experimental mode of analysis, utilizing continuously improved understanding of (perhaps not yet) available process and environment data seems more appropriate at this stage of the analysis than a mechanical brute-force exploration.

As a result of the *Data & Visual Mining* step, candidates for decision rules can be identified and transformed into aggregated variables (*Aggregate Decision Variables*). These variables can then be used to employ DPA in order to evaluate the decision rule candidate (*Evaluate by DPA*). Depending on the result, the inspection by both, data and temporal data mining techniques has to be repeated. It is also possible that the way the time series data was reflected inside or outside the logs has to be modified. For that reason as well as for the possible change of decision rule candidates, the *Evaluate by DPA* step can differ significantly from one iteration to the next one.

3.1 Data Preparation

As existing log files do not offer means to capture time series data, the question is how to provide such data for DPA. Intuitively, time series data can be offered within or outside the event logs. The first option is followed by *data separation*.

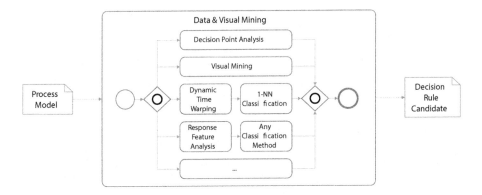

Fig. 3. Subprocess data and visual mining of the DPATS method

Integrating time series data within logs can be done in two ways: either by introducing a time series variable (enrichment) or simulating the production of time series data by extending the log with an (artificial) recurring measurement event. In detail:

1. *Data Separation:* We can prepare an analytical data set consisting of recurring measurements with sufficient temporally information to enable a matching with event data and provide this data separated from the log files.
2. *Log Enrichment:* This analytical data set can also be incorporated into the log by adding an attribute to the corresponding event within the log (e.g., a XES extension that allows such recurring measurement data structures).
3. *Log Extension:* Another approach is to dissemble the recurring measurement data and interlacing it into the log file as recurring events with single-valued attributes.

In the following we discuss first the pros and cons of each option from a technical point of view and afterwards the application in DPATS.

Data separation does not modify the original event log data and therefore contributes to the maintenance of both data sets, an advantage if the event log data is used by other applications as well. The obvious disadvantage is that the connection between the event log data and the time series data is not explicitly stored and every analysis tool has to load and match the data by itself. Log enrichment and extension leads to an explication of this relation with the disadvantage of an additional preprocessing step to do so. Log enrichment does not change the number or kind of log entries as log extension does. Thus, process mining algorithms are not affected and, in turn, the resulting process models do not become more complex. Hence, the integration is, in principle, easier than for log extension. Log extension pushes the time series data into the event log what might be intended depending on the application and can therefore be an advantage as well as a disadvantage. This approach changes the log effectively, but makes format extensions and extra files dispensable.

In practical application, the choice between the options depends on the *Data & Visual Mining* techniques applied in DPATS (cf. Fig. 3), on the possible effects of the time series on the process, and on the structure of the time series. In the first step of DPATS, data separation is usually a good choice. After performing the *Classification (Process Mining)* step of DPATS, one can identify the decision points in the process and obtain a first understanding whether the time series has separable effects or intermingled effects (cf. Sect. 2).

In case of separable effects, the best choice for further analysis is log enrichment. Whether the log enrichment allows immediate application of standard DPA depends on the structure of the time series. If the effects of the time series are Markov-like (cf. Sect. 2), one can immediately use the actual values of the time series at the decision points for DPA in the *Data & Visual Mining* step. If the time series causes non-Markov-like effects the *Data & Visual Mining* step comprises different applications of temporal mining for finding candidates for the decision rule base on separated data.

In case of intermingled effects, a good starting point for the *Data & Visual Mining* step is what we call *post-mortem analysis*; i.e., we assume that all measured values of the observed process instances are known and an analysis after observation of the entire process instance is conducted. All values of the time series are considered as one entity and are input for extraction of decision rules candidates. By doing so the intermingled effect becomes a separable effect at the decision point at the price that the decision uses probably not only actual values of the time series, but also future values. The candidates for decision variables are usually derived by temporal mining techniques for separated data (step *Aggregate Decision Variables*). The rule can be evaluated afterwards. Note that a post-mortem analysis can only be used for decision rules of completed process instances, but not as decision rules for new process instances at runtime.

For development of decision rules at runtime, the best choice is usually to envisage a model with log extension. This means that whenever a new value of the time series occurs one has to make a decision about interruption of the involved activities. In best case, the decision variables for the different decision points can be derived in step *Aggregate Decision Variables* from the decision rules of the post-mortem analysis by applying the rule to the segment of the time series from the beginning up to the actual observation time. In more complicated cases new analyses for each possible decision point may be necessary.

3.2   Temporal and Visual Data Mining

Two frequently used approaches towards classification and clustering of temporal data are based on *dynamic time warping* and on *response feature analysis* [10].

The basic idea behind dynamic time warping is that observations of time series may have the same structural characteristics, for example, number of peaks and relation between peaks, but the position may be blurred due to external effects. In order to find the similarity between such time series, dynamic time warping stretches and compresses the time scale of the series in such a way that the distance between the time series is minimized. A side condition for these transformations is that the order of the measurements in both series is preserved. The approach can be applied for time series of different length. Moreover, exact information of the time stamps in the observations is not necessary. Details may be found in for example in [11].

As a result of dynamic time warping, one obtains a matrix showing the similarity between different time series. This similarity matrix can be used later on for classification or clustering. In case of clustering, any method based on distances can be applied, in case of classification the straightforward approach is using the similarity matrix with 1-NN classification. As reported in [10], this rather simple classification method has been shown successful in many applications.

Response feature analysis reduces the problem of clustering and classification of time series to problems for non-temporal data. Response features can be obtained in different ways, depending on the problem. In business applications, typical response features can be based on defining regression or time series models for each observed time series. As a result, one obtains a number of time-independent parameters. Another approach is to look at characteristic of the frequency distribution of the individual time series, for example, means, variances, or quantiles of the values of the time series. As a third method, one can find structural properties of the time series, for example, change points in the behavior of the time series. The response features can be used afterwards as input for classical classification and clustering algorithms.

Dynamic time warping and response feature analysis transform the problem of classification and clustering of time series into problems without temporal structure. Another interesting and more experimental approach is *visual data mining*. By plotting different time series it may become possible to detect interesting features of the time series which allow also interpretation in terms of the problem. In Sect. 4, we will show applications of all three approaches.

4 Evaluation

For the generation of process log data as well as time series data produced by recurring events within the iterations we implemented the simulation environment DPATSSim. Using a programming language like Java instead of a model interpreting tool like CPN-Tools [12] for simulation purpose gives us the flexibility to implement more complex rules. The time series data was integrated into the event data in various ways and exported in the log file format MXML to be used in ProM 5.2. Additionally, the time series data were exported in a simple CSV file to be used for data mining independent of the ProM framework. We used various mining algorithms from the ProM 5.2 framework to mine the process models as a basis for DPATS. To avoid misinterpretation of event names the keyword "complete" – signifying a point in time event in ProM – was removed from the screen shots (Figs. 4 and 6). Both Figues show the basic mined modells depicting the scenarios as well as the decsison points found, with gray background the decision point that was selected while the screenshot was taken.

After that we analyzed the log by integrating recurring measurement data using the proposed DPATS method and compared the found decision rules with the original ones.

The rationale behind the selection of the scenarios is to illustrate the analysis of time series data. The first example was chosen simple with one variable as this is sufficient to explain the challenges of time series data. The second example illustrates the more complex case, i.e., the multivariate case. The choice is independent of the application domain.

4.1   Univariate Scenario: Container Transportation

We start our evaluation by simulating the process of a container transport example adapted from [6] with exact knowledge of the (complex) decision rules. The basic idea of the container transport example is that a temperature-sensitive cargo is moved, implying that there is some temperature threshold not to be exceeded during the handling; otherwise, if this threshold is violated for a certain duration, the carriage is interrupted, and the transporting vehicle returns to its home base. Apparently, the decision whether to continue or interrupt the carriage depends on the monitored cargo temperature, measured by some sensor, for instance every 10 min as long as the vehicle moves towards its destination. 100 process instances are generated synthetically with up to 12 temperature measurements, such that in 30 % of the cases the pre-set temperature threshold of 37°C is exceeded at least twice consecutively – in which case the carriage has to interrupt – whereas in 20 % of the cases the threshold value exceeds 37°C only at one time point. In the remaining 50 % of the process instances the threshold value is not overshot at all. Hence, in 70 % of the process instances the haulage continues until the destination is reached. For the instances where the transport was interrupted the time series are usually shorter taking into account only time for reaching the parking lot.

In the first step we decide to start with separated data and use in the second step for finding the first process model only the transportation events without consideration of the time series data. Using the alpha algorithm of ProM 5.2[1] we develop the model shown in Fig. 4 (first model). Obviously the decision point generates an interruption of the transportation activity. We identify the measurement process of temperature as useful candidate for the decision mining activity. This process has intermingled effects on the transportation process. Hence, we decide to use in the third step post-mortem analysis for learning the effect of the time series. Because we have to consider her the complete time series it is not reasonable to think about a Markov-like effect on the transport process and we use again separated data for temporal data mining. The time series data are augmented with the observed decisions "normal" and "return".

We start the temporal mining activity with dynamic time warping for the observed time series. Using 1-NN classification for the time series we obtain a correct classification of all cases which return to the parking lot but 11 cases

---

[1] http://promtools.org/prom5/.

which completed the transport were wrongly classified as cases which had to return to the parking lot. In order to understand the reasons for misclassification we decide to use visual mining using plots of the time series. The plots of correctly classified and misclassified cases are shown in Fig. 5. The misclassified cases are labelled as "normal-critical". From visual inspection it is quite obvious that the normal-critical cases are characterized by isolated spikes with high temperature, whereas all return cases show high temperature for at least two consecutive measurements. Hence, we conclude that a decision rule candidate could be: measurement at two consecutive measurement time point is above 37°C. Using this rule in the decision point of the post-mortem analysis we obtain 100 % correctly classified instances.

Now we start with a new analysis round and decide to use the time series data with log extension. In that case the decision rule from post-mortem analysis can be immediately transferred into a rule at runtime by the attribute "minimum of the actual and previous measurement". The decision rule is whether the attribute is above 37°C or not. Evaluating this rule in the process model with log extension shown in the lower part of Fig. 4 gives us a correct classification.

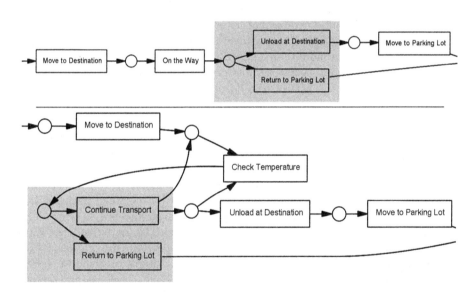

Fig. 4. Univariate scenario: derived models, based on log enrichment and log extension (using ProM 5.2)

4.2   Multivariate Scenario: Hypertension in Pregnancy

The second example we want to use for evaluating the DPATS method is from the medical field where certain diagnostic values are measured recurrently. Elevated blood pressure during the pregnancy is an important sign for illnesses like preeclampsia or general hypertension. Additionally, the weight and the proteinuria are measured as second indicators. In this case blood pressure and

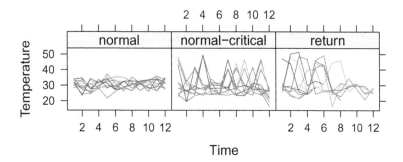

Fig. 5. Univariate scenario: correctly and misclassified time series

weight are measured by the patient herself, additionally to that proteinuria at the patient's regular visit at the doctor. We have to consider four data elements *BodyWeight*, *SystolicBloodPressure*, *DiastolicBloodPressure* and *Proteinuria* during the pregnancy. If the *SystolicBloodPressure* reaches more that 160 mmHg or the *DiastolicBloodPressure* more than 100 mmHg, the patient has to be admitted to a hospital. Additional criteria are a *SystolicBloodPressure* over 140 mmHg or a *DiastolicBloodPressure* over 90 mmHg in combination with *Proteinuria* over 0.3 g/l or a more than 1 kg weight gain in a week. Epiphenomenon like sight disorder, cerebral symptoms and pain in the epigastrum are also criteria that leads to admit the patient to a hospital but are skipped to simplify the example.

Like in the container scenario, we produced synthetic data using a simulation tool. 300 cases were generated where in 27 cases the patient had to be admitted to a hospital. The recurring measurements start after the 20th week of gestation until the patient is hospitalized because of the violation of one of the three rules or giving birth. The measurements are recurring but, opposed to the container scenario, missing values can occur. Randomly distributed, some patients are more often measuring than others, some patients weigh themselves every day while measuring their blood pressure much less frequently and the other way round. If the blood pressure is elevated (higher than 140/90) through four days, the regular check for proteinuria is brought forward. After a proteinuria check, weight and blood pressure is always checked, too. Each check is represented by an event with attributes attached. We started with data using recurrent measurement events.

In a first attempt of process mining using the alpha and heuristic miner no fitting model (according to our understanding) was identified. Parallel checking of three different values in a loop overcharges these algorithms. We changed to a genetic mining algorithm [13] and got a fitting model (cf. Fig. 6 as Petri Net) that can be used for DPA. DPA was not able to find any rules for any of the three relevant decision points.

For a new iteration of the DPATS method, we inserted a decision event comprising all four attributes thus consolidating the model's decision point we

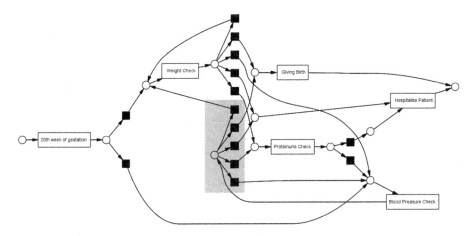

Fig. 6. Multivariate scenario: derived petri net model as basis for DPA

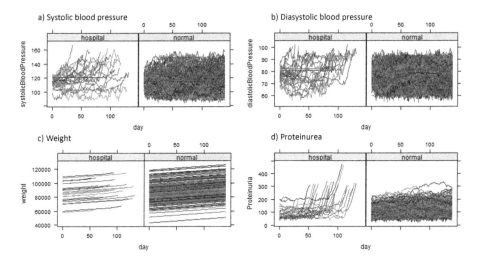

Fig. 7. Multivariate scenario: evaluation of variables a) - d)

want to analyze. DPA was not able to find any rule, most likely due to the already stated fact that loops present a challenge to DPA.

After that we turned to data mining to improve our data understanding. For the next iteration of the DPATS method we defined a second analysis round with a data mining goal for learning the decision. Because the time series have different length and probably also monitoring times we treat them as vector of time series data, i.e. four measurements at each time point, and group the data according to the case ID characterizing the subject and classify the entire series as normal or hospital. We started with trend analysis of the series and produce plots in the four variables as shown in Fig. 7(a) – (d). Plots (a) – (c) lead to the conjecture that going to hospital may be explained by increase in at least one of the attributes systolic, diastolic and proteinuria. At least for proteinuria the results are striking. The plots indicate that there is a change point in the proteinuria series in case of hospitalization. With respect to weight such a conjecture is not so obvious. Hence we have to think about more complex models. One option is modeling the intercept of weight increase as a personal parameter and the slope as a group specific parameter. Another option is to transform the time series.

Using the second approach we learn that first differences are not sufficient, mainly because of random fluctuation of the measurements. Hence, we look at weight increase in longer time periods and find that a period of seven days could be a good candidate for discrimination of the two groups from a practical point of view as decision rule for the patients. The behavior of the two groups with respect to this new attribute is shown in Fig. 8. Also in this case a change point in the behavior of the series seems to be a good indicator for the groups.

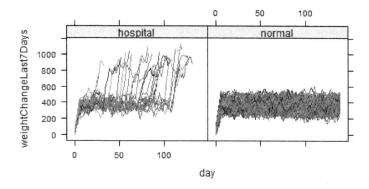

Fig. 8. Multivariate scenario: weight change of the last 7 days

Putting all these results together, we attempt to formulate a classification model with the following response features attributes (i) 0.95 quantiles for weight, proteinuria, systolic, and diastolic blood pressure; (ii) change points for weight change in the last seven days, and proteinuria; (iii) slopes of the weight series. We used not the maximum but the 0.95 quantile for getting more robustness against single extreme values. For these variables we applied tree classification, support vector machines and AdaBoost. All classifications were done with R and 10 fold cross validation was used. Classification trees with 10 fold cross validation generated a simple decision tree using only the change points of the variable `weightChangeLast7Days`. Alternatives for the splits were the slopes of the weight variable. All patients with hospitalization were correctly classified. From the 275 time series of persons with normal pregnancy three were misclassified. An application of boosting and support vector machines produced better results. However, explanation of the decision from practical point of view is difficult. Note that in this case we are not in position to learn the classification rule applied in data generation. In particular, the influence of blood pressure measurements on the decision is not visible, mainly because there are no cases with only blood pressure effects in the data. Also missing values in blood pressure hamper the use of that series in the analysis.

As a last iteration we now can use all the gathered information from our data mining approaches and translate that into aggregated variables to be evaluated with DPA. For this multivariate application it is possible – but was not necessary – to aggregate all variables into one decision variable for evaluation like in the transportation example. But in this case it is advantageous to keep variables separated as different rules are dependent on combinations of different variables. As shown before not all rules could be found with the data set at hand, which was also reflected by the last evaluation step with DPA.

5   Related Work

The DPATS method can be located at the interface of three areas, i.e., process mining (e.g., [1]), data mining (e.g., [10]), and visual mining (e.g., [9]) as depicted in Fig. 9. Clearly, for all these areas several approaches exist, also at the interfaces between the different areas. A combination of process mining and visual mining is proposed by [14] where mined process models can be compared using difference graphs as a visual means. DPATS is to the best of our knowledge the first method to combine all three areas in order to be able to tackle the analysis of time series data in the context of process mining.

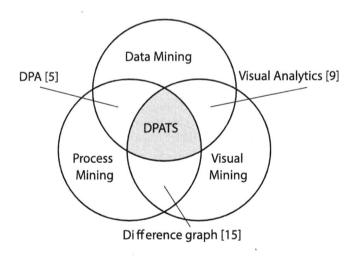

Fig. 9. Related research areas

DPA [5] is based on the combined application of process and data mining, more precisely, decision trees. In [15], DPA was improved and generalized using algebraically-oriented procedures for finding complex decision rules with more than one variable. By contrast, the DPATS method aims at finding new rules using statistically-oriented empirical methods, augmenting the space of possible decision functions with attributes through a data-driven search among empirical models. [16] overcomes other difficulties of DPA like invisible transitions and therefore certain kinds of loops within the process model or deviating behavior by control-flow alignment. Our approach differs from that in dealing with time series data and therefore recurring events that might not be found within existing log files. Our approach also resolves problems with loops through extending DPA with data mining techniques to identify aggregation value attributes and defining new events within the business processes these attributes can be attached to. Another interesting approach is [17] that addresses the clustering of health care processes. The DPATS method, by contrast, focuses on the classification of temporal data occurring in connection with processes.

Log preparation tools cover the extraction and integration of data from different sources as well as data quality improvement, e.g., [18,19]. Log enrichment is one possibility to deal with the latter, e.g. in [20] it is proposed to make more complex time data usable.

6 Conclusions

In this paper, we proposed the DPATS method for analyzing time series data and process logs by a combined and iterative application of process and data mining techniques. For equipping and analyzing the logs with time series data, we discussed the possibilities of log enrichment and extension as well as of keeping log and time series data in a separated way. Log preparation might be more challenging with real world data, particularly at the presence of complex logs that are further extended by recurring measurement events reflecting the production of time series data. Then the aspect of analyzing expressive constructs, i.e., time series data, has to be balanced with complexity of the analysis. We will expand our studies in this direction by applying DPATS in real-world settings. Candidates are the $EBMC^2$ project (ebmc2.univie.ac,at) on patient treatment or FP7 project ADVENTURE (http://www.fp7-adventure.eu/) from the manufacturing domain.

The DPATS method features data and visual mining techniques such as dynamic time warping as main analysis step and is implemented and evaluated based on use cases from the logistic and medical domain. Several future research directions such as the inclusion of time sequences and application of the DPATS method for monitoring process execution during runtime have been discussed. We will follow up along this line of research.

References

1. van der Aalst, W.M.P.: Process Mining – Discovery, Conformance and Enhancement of Business Processes. Springer, Ber (2011)

2. Ly, L.T., Indiono, C., Mangler, J., Rinderle-Ma, S.: Data transformation and semantic log purging for process mining. In: Ralyté, J., Franch, X., Brinkkemper, S., Wrycza, S. (eds.) CAiSE 2012. LNCS, vol. 7328, pp. 238–253. Springer, Heidelberg (2012)

3. Binder, M., Dorda, W., Duftschmid, G., Dunkl, R., Fröschl, K.A., Gall, W., Grossmann, W., Harmankaya, K., Hronsky, M., Rinderle-Ma, S., Rinner, C., Weber, S.: On analyzing process compliance in skin cancer treatment: an experience report from the evidence-based medical compliance cluster (EBMC^2). In: Brinkkemper, S., Franch, X., Ralyté, J., Wrycza, S. (eds.) CAiSE 2012. LNCS, vol. 7328, pp. 398–413. Springer, Heidelberg (2012)

4. Verbeek, H.M.W., Buijs, J.C.A.M., van Dongen, B.F., van der Aalst, W.M.P.: XES, XESame, and ProM 6. In: Soffer, P., Proper, E. (eds.) CAiSE Forum 2010. LNBIP, vol. 72, pp. 60–75. Springer, Heidelberg (2011)

5. Rozinat, A., van der Aalst, W.M.P.: Decision mining in ProM. In: Dustdar, S., Fiadeiro, J.L., Sheth, A.P. (eds.) BPM 2006. LNCS, vol. 4102, pp. 420–425. Springer, Heidelberg (2006)

6. Rinderle, S., Bassil, S., Reichert, M.: A framework for semantic recovery strategies in case of process activity failures. In: ICEIS 2006, vol. 1, pp. 136–143 (2006)

7. Bassil, S., Rinderle, S., Keller, R., Kropf, P., Reichert, M.: Preserving the context of interrupted business process activities. In: Chen, C.-S., Filipe, J., Seruca, I., Cordeiro, J. (eds.) Enterprise Information Systems VII, pp. 149–156. Springer, The Netherlands (2006)

8. Dunkl, R., Rinderle-Ma, S., Grossmann, W., Fröschl, K.A.: Decision point analysis of time series data in process-aware information systems. In: CAISE Forum 2014, pp. 33–40. ceur-ws.org (2014)

9. Keim, D.A., Andrienko, G., Fekete, J.-D., Görg, C., Kohlhammer, J., Melançon, G.: Visual analytics: definition, process, and challenges. In: Kerren, A., Stasko, J.T., Fekete, J.-D., North, C. (eds.) Information Visualization. LNCS, vol. 4950, pp. 154–175. Springer, Heidelberg (2008)

10. Mitsa, T.: Temporal Data Mining. CRC Press, Boca Raton (2010)

11. Giorgino, T.: Computing and visualizing dynamic time warping alignments in R: The dtw package. J. Stat. Softw. **31**(7), 1–24 (2009)

12. Jensen, K., Kristensen, L.M., Wells, L.: Coloured petri nets and CPN tools for modelling and validation of concurrent systems. Int. J. Softw. Tools Technol. Tran sf. **9**(3), 213–254 (2007)

13. van der Aalst, W.M.P., de Medellin, A.K.A., Weijters, A.J.M.M.T.: Genetic process mining. In: Cardozo, G., Darondeau, P. (eds.) ICAHN 2005. LNCS, vol. 3536, pp. 48–69. Springer, Heidelberg (2005)

14. Kriglstein, S., Wallner, G., Rinderle-Ma, S.: A visualization approach for difference analysis of process models and instance traffic. In: Daniel, F., Wang, J., Weber, B. (eds.) BPM 2013. LNCS, vol. 8094, pp. 219–226. Springer, Heidelberg (2013)

15. de Leoni, M., Dumas, M., García-Bañuelos, L.: Discovering branching conditions from business process execution logs. In: Cortellessa, V., Varró, D. (eds.) FASE 2013 (ETAPS 2013). LNCS, vol. 7793, pp. 114–129. Springer, Heidelberg (2013)

16. de Leoni, M., van der Aalst, W.M.: Data-aware process mining: discovering decisions in processes using alignments. In: Proceedings of the 28th Annual ACM Symposium on Applied Computing, pp. 1454–1461. ACM (2013)

17. Rebuge, Á., Ferreira, D.R.: Business process analysis in healthcare environments: a methodology based on process mining. Inf. Syst. **37**(2), 99–116 (2012)

18. Rodriguez, C., Engel, R., Kostoska, G., Daniel, F., Casati, F., Aimar, M.: Eventifier: extracting process execution logs from operational databases. In: BPM 2012 Demo Track (2012)
19. Nooijen, E.H.J., van Dongen, B.F., Fahland, D.: Automatic discovery of data-centric and artifact-centric processes. In: La Rosa, M., Soffer, P. (eds.) BPM Workshops 2012. LNBIP, vol. 132, pp. 316–327. Springer, Heidelberg (2013)
20. Dunkl, R.: Data improvement to enable process mining on integrated non-log data sources. In: Moreno-Díaz, R., Pichler, F., Quesada-Arencibia, A. (eds.) EUROCAST. LNCS, vol. 8111, pp. 491–498. Springer, Heidelberg (2013)

Extracting Data Manipulation Processes
from SQL Execution Traces

Marco Mori[⊠], Nesrine Noughi, and Anthony Cleve

Precise Research Center, University of Namur,
Rue Grandgagnage 21, 5000 Namur, Belgium
{marco.mori,nesrine.noughi,anthony.cleve}@unamur.be

Abstract. Modern data-intensive software systems manipulate an increasing amount of data in order to support users in various execution contexts. Maintaining and evolving activities of such systems rely on an accurate documentation of their behavior which is often missing or outdated. Unfortunately, standard program analysis techniques are not always suitable for extracting the behavior of data-intensive systems which rely on more and more dynamic data access mechanisms which mainly consist in run-time interactions with a database. This paper proposes a framework to extract behavioral models from data-intensive program executions. The framework makes use of dynamic analysis techniques to capture and analyze SQL execution traces. It applies clustering techniques to identify data manipulation functions from such traces. Process mining techniques are then used to synthesize behavioral models.

Keywords: Data-manipulation behavior recovery · Data-oriented process mining · Data-manipulation functions

1 Introduction

Data-intensive systems typically consists of a set of applications performing frequent and continuous interactions with a database. Maintaining and evolving data-intensive systems can be performed only after the system has been sufficiently understood, in terms of structure and behavior. In particular, it is necessary to recover missing documentation (models) about the data manipulation behavior of the applications, by analyzing their interactions with the database. In modern systems, such interactions usually rely on dynamic SQL, where automatically generated SQL queries are sent to the database server. In this context, our paper aims at answering the following research question: *To what extent can we extract the data-manipulation behavior of a data-intensive system starting from its traces of database access?*

M. Mori—beneficiary of an FSR Incoming Post-doctoral Fellowship of the *Académie universitaire 'Louvain'*, co-funded by the Marie Curie Actions of the European Commission.

S. Nurcan and E. Pimenidis (Eds.): CAiSE Forum 2014, LNBIP 204, pp. 85–101, 2015.
DOI: 10.1007/978-3-319-19270-3_6

The literature includes various static and dynamic program analysis techniques to extract behavioral models from traditional software systems. Existing *static* analysis techniques [1–5], analyzing program *source code*, typically fail in producing complete behavioral models in presence of dynamic SQL. They cannot capture the dynamic aspects of the program-database interactions, influenced by context-dependent factors, user inputs and results of preceding data accesses. Existing *dynamic* analysis techniques [6], analyzing program *executions*, have been designed for other purposes than data manipulation behavior extraction. Several authors have considered the analysis of SQL execution traces in support to data reverse engineering, service identification or performance monitoring [7–11]. Such techniques look very promising for recovering an approximation of data-intensive application behavior.

In this paper, we propose a framework to recover the data manipulation behavior of programs, starting from SQL execution traces. Our approach uses clustering to group the SQL queries that implement the same high-level data manipulation function, i.e., that are syntactically equal but with different input or output values. We then adopt classical process mining techniques [12] to recover data manipulation processes. Our approach operates at the level of a *feature*, i.e., a software functionality as it can be perceived by the user. A feature corresponds to a *process* enabling different instances, i.e., *traces*, each performing possibly different interactions with a database.

This paper is structured as follows. Section 2 presents the basic elements of our framework in terms of artifacts and components and how to integrate those elements to recover the data manipulation behavior of a data-intensive system. Section 3 presents a validation based on a tool integrated with current practice technologies and a set of experiments showing completeness and noise of mined processes depending on the input log coverage. Section 4 discusses related work and Sect. 5 ends the paper showing possible future directions.

Motivating Example. We consider an e-commerce web store for selling products in a world-wide area. The system provides a set of features requiring frequent and continuous interactions with the database by means of executing SQL statements. For instance, the feature for retrieving products (*view_products*) accesses information about categories, manufacturers and detailed product information. Which data are accessed at runtime depends on dynamic aspects of the system. For example, given that a certain feature instance retrieves the categories of products before accessing product information we can derive that it corresponds to a category-driven search. If a certain instance accesses manufacturer information before product information we analogously derive that it corresponds to a manufacturer-driven search. By capturing and mining the database interactions of multiple feature instances, it is possible to recover the actual data manipulation behavior of the feature, e.g., a process model with a variability point among two search criteria.

2   Data Manipulation Behavior Recovery

Our framework supports the extraction of the data manipulation behavior of programs by exploiting several artifacts (see Fig. 1). We assume the existence

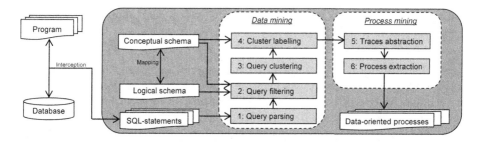

Fig. 1. Basics models: artifacts and components

of a *logical* and possibly of a *conceptual schema* with a mapping between them. The *conceptual schema* is a platform-independent specification of the application domain concepts, their attributes and relationships. The *logical schema* contains objects (tables, columns and foreign keys) implementing abstract concepts over which queries are defined. The conceptual schema and the mapping to the logical schema can be either available, or they can be obtained via database reverse engineering techniques [13,14]. *SQL statements* defined over the logical schema materialize the interactions occurring between multiple executions (traces) of a feature and the underlying *database*. Once the source code related to a feature has been identified [15], different techniques can capture SQL execution traces. Those techniques, compared in [8], range from using the DBMS log to sophisticated source code transformation. Among others, the approaches presented in [16,17] recover the link between SQL executions and source code locations through automated program instrumentation, while [18] makes use of tracing aspects to capture SQL execution traces without source code alteration. Once a sequence of queries is captured, it is necessary to identify the different traces, each corresponding to a feature instance. This problem has been tackled in the literature of specification mining by analyzing value-based dependencies of methods calls [19].

Our approach is independent from the adopted trace capturing techniques. For each feature, it requires as minimal input a set of execution traces, each trace consisting of a sequence of SQL queries. A *query parsing* component assignees to each query a set of data-oriented properties each describing its data-manipulation behavior. A *query filtering* component removes queries that do not refer to concepts and relationships of the input conceptual schema. A *query clustering* component clusters together queries that have the same set of properties thus implementing the same data-manipulation function. Consequently, a *cluster labeling* component identifies the signature representing the data-manipulation function (i.e., cluster) in terms of a label and a set of Input/Output (I/O) parameters. The *traces abstraction* component replaces traces of queries with the corresponding signatures and the *process extraction* component generates the *data-oriented process* corresponding to the input traces of a feature.

Noteworthy, our approach is applicable to any system for which a query interception phase is possible. It could, for instance, be applied to legacy Cobol systems, Java systems with or without Object-Relational-Mapping technologies, or web applications written in PHP.

Query Parsing (1). We characterize SQL queries according to (1) the information they recover or modify and (2) the related selection criteria. To this end, for each query we record a set of data-oriented properties according to the query type. For a *select* query we record a property with the *select* clause while for *delete*, *update*, *replace* or *insert* queries we record a property with the name of the table. If the query is either *update*, *replace* or *insert* we also record a property with the *set* clause and all its attributes. Finally for all query types but the *insert* we add a property for the *where* clauses along with their attributes. By means of these properties we ignore the actual values taken as input and produced as output by each query. Figure 2 shows three SQL traces along with their corresponding properties. These queries are created starting from the logical schema represented in Fig. 3. Among others query q_1 is a select query over attribute *Password* of *Customer* table (property p_1) and it contains a *where* clause with an equality condition over Id attribute (p_2); query q_2 is a *select* query over attributes

```
Trace 1:

q1:  SELECT Customer.Password FROM Customer WHERE Customer.Id = 'Mark27'; [p1,p2]
q2:  SELECT Category.Id, Category.Image FROM Category; -> [p3]
q3:  SELECT Product.Id, Product.Price FROM Product, PCategory WHERE Product.Id=PCategory.Product_Id AND
     PCategory.Category_Id='1'; -> [p4,p5,p6]
q4:  SELECT PLang.Description FROM PLang, Language WHERE PLang.Language_Id=Language.Code AND PLang.Product_Id
     ='1A23' AND Language.Name='Italian'; -> [p7,p8,p9,p10]
q5:  SELECT SpecialProduct.NewPrice FROM SpecialProduct,Product WHERE SpecialProduct.Product_Id=Product.Id
     AND Product.Id='1A23'; -> [p11,p12,p13]
q6:  SELECT Manufacturer.Name FROM Manufacturer,Product WHERE Manufacturer.Id=Product.Manufacturer_Id AND
     Product.Id='1A23'; -> [p14,p15,p13]
q7:  SELECT PLang.Description FROM PLang, Language WHERE PLang.Language_Id=Language.Code AND PLang.Product_Id
     ='1F32' AND Language.Name='Italian'; -> [p7,p8,p9,p10]
q8:  SELECT SpecialProduct.NewPrice FROM SpecialProduct,Product WHERE SpecialProduct.Product_Id=Product.Id
     AND Product.Id='1F32'; -> [p11,p12,p13]
q9:  SELECT Manufacturer.Name FROM Manufacturer,Product WHERE Manufacturer.Id=Product.Manufacturer_Id AND
     Product.Id='1F32'; -> [p14,p15,p13]
q10: INSERT INTO Log(IdEvent,Event,Date,Time) VALUES ('021','PrAcc1A23-1F32','2013-02-22','12:21:00'); -> [
     p16]

Trace 2:

q11: SELECT Customer.Password FROM Customer WHERE Customer.Id = 'JennyMa'; [p1,p2]
q12: SELECT Category.Id, Category.Image FROM Category; -> [p3]
q13: SELECT Product.Id, Product.Price FROM Product, PCategory WHERE Product.Id=PCategory.Product_Id AND
     PCategory.Category_Id='2'; -> [p4,p5,p6]

Trace 3:

q14: SELECT Customer.Password FROM Customer WHERE Customer.Id = 'DanWer'; [p1,p2]
q15: SELECT Manufacturer.Id, Manufacturer.Name FROM Manufacturer -> [p17]
q16: SELECT Product.Id, Product.Price FROM Product WHERE Product.Manufacturer_Id='AppleNamur01' -> [p4,p18]
q17: SELECT PLang.Description FROM PLang, Language WHERE PLang.Language_Id=Language.Code AND PLang.
     Product_Id='2D11' AND Language.Name='Italian'; -> [p7,p8,p9,p10]
q18: SELECT SpecialProduct.NewPrice FROM SpecialProduct,Product WHERE SpecialProduct.Product_Id=Product.Id
     AND Product.Id='2D11'; -> [p11,p12,p13]
q19: SELECT Manufacturer.Name FROM Manufacturer,Product WHERE Manufacturer.Id=Product.Manufacturer_Id AND
     Product.Id='2D11'; -> [p14,p15,p13]
q20: INSERT INTO Log(IdEvent,Event,Date,Time) VALUES ('022','PrAcc2D11','2013-02-28','14:00:03'); -> [p16]

SQL-statements properties:

p1="SELECT Customer.Password", p2="Customer.Id.EQ_VALUE", p3="SELECT Category.Id Category.Image",
p4="SELECT Product.Id Product.Price", p5="Product.Id=PCategory.Product_Id",
p6="PCategory.Category_Id.EQ_VALUE", p7="SELECT PLang.Description", p8="PLang.Language_Id=Language.Code",
p9="PLang.Product_Id.EQ_VALUE", p10="Language.Name.EQ_VALUE", p11="SELECT SpecialProduct.NewPrice",
p12="SpecialProduct.Product_Id=Product.Id", p13="Product.Id.EQ_VALUE", p14="SELECT Manufacturer.Name",
p15="Product.Manufacturer_Id=Manufacturer.Id",  p16="INSERT INTO Log",
p17="SELECT Manufacturer.Id Manufacturer.Name", p18="Product.Manufacturer_Id.EQ_VALUE"
```

Fig. 2. Web Store: Traces of SQL statements with data-oriented properties

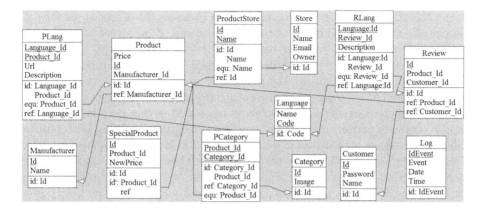

Fig. 3. Web-store case study: logical schema.

Id and *Image* of *Category* and it corresponds to property p_3; query q_3 is a *select* over attributes *Id* and *Price* of *Product* (property p_4), it contains two where clauses, i.e., a natural join between *Product.Id* and *PCategory.Product_Id* (p_5) and an equality condition over *PCategory.Category_Id* attribute (p_6).

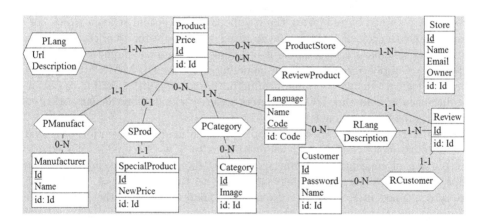

Fig. 4. Web-store case study: conceptual schema.

Query Filtering (2). We remove from the input traces the queries that do not express end-user concepts, i.e., the ones referring to database system tables or log tables appearing only in the logical schema. In our example we remove q_{10} and q_{20} accessing table *Log* without a counterpart in the conceptual schema (see Figs. 3 and 4).

Query Clustering (3). Starting from the traces of SQL statements we apply the Formal Concepts Analysis (FCA) [20] in order to cluster together queries having the same data-oriented properties. FCA provides the definition for formal context $C = (O, A, R)$ where O is the set of objects, A is the set of attributes and $R \subseteq O \times A$ is the relation between objects and attributes. In our case objects are SQL queries while attributes are their data-oriented properties. For the formal context, a formal concept c is defined as a pair (O_i, A_i) where $O_i \subseteq O$ and $A_i \subseteq A$ and every object in O_i has each attribute in A_i. In our case we assign each query to the concept with the same set of properties thus dividing queries in disjoint sets each performing different operations over the database. We report in Table 1 the clusters obtained from queries in Fig. 2. It is worth noticing that FCA is much more powerful than how we used it; indeed we did not consider objects (queries) having only subsets of equal properties. Nevertheless, we automatize the clustering of queries having the same set of data-oriented properties.

Table 1. Web Store: Clusters of SQL queries.

C1	C2	C3	C4	C5	C6	C7	C8
$\{q_1, q_{11}, q_{14}\}$	$\{q_2, q_{12}\}$	$\{q_3, q_{13}\}$	$\{q_4, q_7, q_{17}\}$	$\{q_5, q_8, q_{18}\}$	$\{q_6, q_9, q_{19}\}$	$\{q_{15}\}$	$\{q_{16}\}$
$\{p_1, p_2\}$	$\{p_3\}$		$\{p_4, p_5, p_6\}$	$\{p_7, p_8, p_9, p_{10}\}$	$\{p_{11}, p_{12}, p_{13}\}$	$\{p_{13}, p_{14}, p_{15}\}$	$\{p_{17}\}$	$\{p_4, p_{18}\}$

Cluster Labeling (4). We identify the data manipulation function implemented by each cluster in term of a label and a set of I/O parameters. First, labels are obtained by analyzing the fragment of conceptual schema which corresponds to the logical subschema accessed by the cluster queries. In case a conceptual schema is not available it is sufficient to reverse engineer the logical schema by simply adopting a data-modeling tool like DB-MAIN[1]; thus given that the logical schema contains meaningful names it is still possible to obtain significant labels. Second, I/O parameters are created based on the data-oriented properties belonging to each cluster.

For determining the labels we adopt the same naming convention proposed in [21] to associate conceptual level operations to SQL query code. We extract the portion of conceptual schema accessed by the queries of a cluster and we apply a different labeling strategy according to the query types. Concerning the query types *insert, replace, delete* and *update*, we create the label of the data-manipulation functions starting from the unique entity E of the conceptual schema accessed by each of these query types, i.e., *InsertIntoE, ReplaceIntoE, DeleteFromE* and *UpdateE* respectively. In case of a *select* query we distinguish four cases according to the portion of the conceptual schema involved in the cluster queries (refer to Table 1 and Fig. 4 for the given examples):

a. One entity E. In this case we proposed two possible mapping names based on the presence of an equality condition over the primary key of E. If such condition is present, we map the cluster with the label *getEById*. Conversely, we simply map the cluster with the label *getAllE*. In our example we translate

---

[1] DB-MAIN official website, http://www.db-main.be.

cluster $C1$ to $getCustomerById$ since queries in $C1$ retrieve information contained within entity $Customer$ by taking as input its primary key. Concerning cluster $C2$, since its queries retrieve all tuples of entity $Category$ without considering any condition over its primary key, it translates to $getAllCategory$.

b. Two entities E_1, E_2 related by a many-to-many relationship R. In this case, the adopted label is $getAllE_1OfE_2ViaR$ providing that the queries give as result the attributes of all the instances of E_1 associated with a given instance of E_2 through R. Concerning our example we translate clusters $C3$ to $getAllProductOfCategoryViaPCategory$ since it extracts all the products of a certain category and we translate $C4$ to $getAllLanguageOfProductViaPLang$ provided that it extracts all language descriptions of a product.

c. Two entities E_1, E_2 related by a one-to-one relationship R. In this case, we map the cluster with the label $getE_1OfE_2ViaR$ provided that the queries retrieve the instance of E_1 associated to a certain input instance of E_2. In the web-store example, we map cluster $C5$ to label $getSpecialProductOfProductViaSProd$ in order to extract the occurrence of $SpecialProduct$ related to a certain product via the one-to-one relationship $SProd$.

d. Two entities E_1, E_2 related by a one-to-many relationship R. In this case, we distinguish two cases. If the queries return the instance of E_1 that participates to the relationship R with multiplicity N, we translate the query with the function $getE_1OfE_2ViaR$. Conversely, if the query returns the set of instances of E_2 that participate to R with multiplicity 1 we translate the query with the label $getAllE_2OfE_1ViaR$. In our web-store example we translate cluster $C6$ to $getManufacturerOfProductViaPManufact$ since it retrieves the single occurrence of $Manufacturer$ participating to the relationship $PManufact$ with $Product$. We translate cluster $C8$ to $getAllProductOfManufacturerViaPManufact$ since it retrieves the multiple occurrences of $Product$ related to $Manufacturer$ via $PManufact$.

As far as I/O parameters are concerned, input parameters are the attributes involved in equality or inequality conditions that appear in the data-oriented properties of the queries, while output parameters are the set of attributes appearing within the *select* query property. Table 2 shows labels and I/O parameters for the clusters of the Web Store example.

It is worth noticing that in our approach it is enough to translate just one arbitrary query within the same cluster and to evaluate its input and output parameters; indeed all queries belonging to a cluster have the same set of properties and they consequently access the same portion of the conceptual schema. In defining signatures we have not considered the complete SQL grammar, e.g., we ignored *group by* operators that add more fined-grained information at the attribute level and we ignored the *where* clauses without value-based equality and inequality conditions. Nevertheless, we plan to adopt the latter for providing more detailed definitions of the data manipulation functions.

Process Mining (5–6). We generate a process starting from a set of SQL traces of a single feature. The *traces abstraction* phase replaces SQL traces with

Table 2. Web Store: Clusters with data manipulation functions and I/O parameters.

Cluster	Input	Output
C1:*getCustomerById*	{*Id*}	{*Password*}
C2:*getAllCategory*	–	{*Id, Image*}
C3:*getAllProductOfCategoryViaPCategory*	{*Category_Id*}	{*Id, Price*}
C4:*getAllLanguageOfProductViaPLang*	{*Product_Id, Name*}	{*Description*}
C5:*getSpecialProductOfProductViaSProd*	{*Product.Id*}	{*NewPrice*}
C6:*getManufacturerOfProductViaPManufact*	{*Product.Id*}	{*Name*}
C7:*getAllManufacturer*	–	{*Id, Name*}
C8:*getAllProductOfManufacturerViaPManufact*	{*Manufacturer_Id*}	{*Id, Price*}

the corresponding traces of data manipulation functions. The *process extraction*
phase exploits a process mining algorithm to extract the feature behavior as a
sequence of function executions with sequential, parallel and choice operators.

In the following we show how to recover the data manipulation behavior of
the *view_products* web-store feature starting from the traces of data manipulation functions in Table 3 (obtained by replacing the queries in Fig. 2 with their
corresponding cluster labels of Table 2).

Table 3. Web Store: Traces of data manipulation functions

Trace 1	*getCustomerById*(**C1**) - *getAllCategory*(**C2**) - *getAllProductOfCategoryViaPCategory*(**C3**) -
	getAllLanguageOfProductViaPLang(**C4**) - *getSpecialProductOfProductViaSProd*(**C5**) -
	getManufacturerOfProductViaPManufact(**C6**) - *getAllLanguageOfProductViaPLang*(**C4**) -
	getSpecialProductOfProductViaSProd(**C5**) - *getManufacturerOfProductViaPManufact*(**C6**)
Trace 2	*getCustomerById*(**C1**) - *getAllCategory*(**C2**) - *getAllProductOfCategoryViaPCategory*(**C3**)
Trace 3	*getCustomerById*(**C1**) - *getAllManufacturer*(**C7**) - *getAllProductOfManufacturerViaPManufact*(**C8**) -
	getAllLanguageOfProductViaPLang(**C4**) - *getSpecialProductOfProductViaSProd*(**C5**) -
	getManufacturerOfProductViaPManufact(**C6**)

Trace 1 gets customer information (*C1*), it performs a category-driven search
of products by means of getting all the product categories (*C2*) and all the
products of a certain selected category (*C3*). For each retrieved product, three
functions are iterated: *C4* retrieves product description, *C5* extracts special

product information and *C6* extracts related manufacturer information. *Trace 2* is different from *Trace 1* because after function C3 no products are retrieved and the process ends. If we apply a mining algorithm to *Trace 1* and *2* we obtain a process (Fig. 5(a)) which performs consecutively functions *C1*, *C2* and *C3* before entering in the loop iterating *C4*, *C5*, and *C6*. The process ends after zero, one or more iterations of the loop. Let us now assume to include into the process *Trace 3* which is equal to *Trace 1* except that it searches products based on their manufacturer (functions *C7* and *C8*) instead of searching by category (*C2* and *C3*). If we mine the process model by considering as input all the traces (Fig. 5(b)), we end up with a new alternative branch: the customer can now perform either a manufacturer-driven search or a category-driven search.

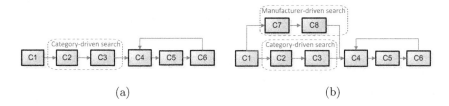

(a) (b)

Fig. 5. Web Store: process mined with (a) *Trace 1* and *2* and (b) *Trace 1*, *2* and *3*.

3 Validation

We validated our approach to data-manipulation behavior recovery by means of *(i)* a tool integrated with current practice technologies and *(ii)* a set of experiments showing the sensitivity of our technique in producing correct processes depending on the traces log coverage.

3.1 Tool Support

The presented framework is implemented into an integrated tool which takes as input a set of SQL traces (each representing an instance of the same feature), the logical schema and optionally the conceptual schema and the conceptual-to-logical schema mapping. The tool relies on a set of implemented and third-party components. The former do not require any additional user inputs while the latter may require the intervention of the designer. Among the implemented components, a *SQL parser* extracts the data-oriented properties while a *filtering* component filters out the ones referring to concepts and relationships not in the input conceptual schema. A *clustering* component exploits the *colibri-Java* Formal Concept Analysis tool[2] to cluster queries according to their properties. A *labeling* component generates data manipulation functions (i.e., cluster signatures) while a *traces abstraction* component uses a Java library[3] to create standardized event logs.

---

[2] http://code.google.com/p/colibri-java/.
[3] http://www.xes-standard.org/openxes/start.

Starting from the event logs obtained with our implemented components, we rely on the de-facto standard process mining tool (*ProM* tool[4]) to mine data manipulation processes. *ProM* supports different process mining algorithms providing different trade-offs between completeness and noise [22,23] to be chosen according to specific application needs. In our case, we chose as miner algorithm the Integer Linear Programming (ILP) miner [24] since it is able to produce complete process models *(i.e., Petri Nets[5]* [25]*)* with a low level of noise[6]. Petri nets, which results from ILP miner, are well-semantically defined models enabling different types of analysis among which a precise comparison of different model instances. Once a process has been created, we exploit the ProM tool to export the Petri Net as a PMNL[7] file which can be given as input to a Petri Net editor tool, e.g., *WoPeD*[8] allowing reading and editing operations. ProM provides user-friendly graphical interfaces which support designers in easily loading standardized event logs, mining Petri Nets through ILP miner and exporting such models for editing purposes enabled by WoPeD.

3.2   Experiment Inputs

For our experiments we collected a set of database access traces from an e-restaurant web application developed by one of our bachelor students at our university. This data-intensive system provides different features each accessing a different portion of an underlying database to support the activities of taxi drivers, restaurant owners and clients. Clients consult menu information (*MenuInfo* feature), information about special offers (*DailySpecials* feature) and general information about restaurants (*RestaurantInfo* feature). They can reserve a table for a meal (*Reservation* feature) and they can issue orders of meals with two possible options, they either pick-up the meal at the restaurant or they

---

[4] http://www.promtools.org/.

[5] A Petri Net consists of a set of places, transitions, directed arcs and tokens. Transitions are represented with boxes and they indicate a certain event/task, places are represented with circles, directed arcs link together transitions and places in a bipartite manner, while tokens are represented as black dots which can move from one place to another trough a transition.

[6] In the literature of process mining two main metrics have been proposed to evaluate how good is an algorithm in mining models conforming to an input set of traces. The *fitness* measure expresses to what extent the model is able to produce the input traces (completeness), while the *appropriateness* measure expresses to what extent the model is able to represent the exact set of input traces (noise). Mining a process model which is both complete and without noise is not always possible unless we accept to obtain a model with too low level of abstraction (i.e., too specific) which does not help user readability. Therefore, between completeness and noise we give more importance to the first since we prefer to have a model which is able to reproduce all the input traces (fitness=1) even if we introduce a certain level of noise in it (appropriateness< 1).

[7] http://www.pnml.org/ - (Petri Net Markup Language) is a proposal of an XML-based interchange format for Petri nets (de-facto standard).

[8] www.woped.org.

ask for a taxi service to deliver them the booked meal (*IssueOrders* feature). Restaurant owners prepare the meal to be delivered to clients (*RestaurantOrders* feature) while taxi drivers check delivery requests and they carry out the delivering process (*TaxiDelivery* feature). Among a wide set of implemented features we chose a subset of features whose data manipulation processes covered execution patterns of different nature, e.g., sequential execution, cycles and decision points. Since we played the role of the designer, we were able to select the most interesting features i.e., *DailySpecials*, *RestaurantInfo*, *MenuInfo*, *Reservation* and *IssueOrders*. Consequently we collected the corresponding sequences of SQL queries to give as input to the tool. The complete list of SQL statements grouped by feature with different traces and extracted data-manipulation functions are available at [26] along with conceptual and logical database schema accessible through DB-MAIN. We assume that for each feature, its input set of extracted traces corresponds to 100 % of coverage ratio of the process and it contains exactly 6 different traces.

3.3   Experiments

Starting from the inputs data we conducted a set of experiments aiming at answering the following research question: *What is the quality of the processes extracted through the integrated tool with a variable traces coverages, with respect to their correct versions identified by the designer?* In answering this research question, we organized the experiment in two different phases: the *start-up* phase creates for each feature the correct processes starting from its complete set of traces (traces coverage = 100 %) with the support of the integrated tool and the intervention of the designer; the *core* phase mines processes with a variable traces coverage ($\leq$ 100 %) and it evaluates the quality of such processes with respect to the correct ones previously identified with the support of ProM tool plug-ins.

Start-Up. For each feature we adopted the tool for creating the data-manipulation processes with the complete set of traces. Consequently, since these models could either contain noise or they could be not complete, we asked the designer to derive a correct version from it. Designers have a deep knowledge and understanding of the processes and they can easily assess if a certain process is correct or not. In our case, as designers, we adopted the WoPeD tool for visualizing the processes as Petri Nets and to perform the possible required modifications, i.e., addition/deletion of places and arcs. For instance, Fig. 6(a) shows the feature *DailySpecial* mined with our technique while Fig. 6(b) shows the version of the same feature as it has been corrected by the designer. The correct version of this feature mainly consists of retrieving a certain set of restaurants (A), checking if they provide special dishes (B) and for each of those dishes it retrieves the corresponding information (C) along with the category to which the dish belongs (D). The mined process contains all valid traces in the corrected process but, as a consequence of the noise introduced by the mining algorithm, it enables more traces than the correct one, e.g., the traces that retrieve a certain

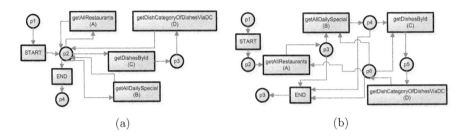

Fig. 6. *DailySpecial*: mined process (a) and process corrected by the designer (b).

dish (C) without first retrieving the special dishes (B). These traces are not considered admissible by the designer, who modifies the links among transitions to disable the former traces and forcing the process to perform C only after B.

Core. Once the designer has determined the correct versions of the processes of the input features, we performed a set of experiments in order to compare them with the models produced by our approach with a different ratio of the coverage of the input traces. We define P_{tool} as the Petri Net produced by our approach, P_{exp} as the correct Petri Net and their corresponding set of valid traces as $T(P_{tool})$ and $T(P_{exp})$. Then we define $recall = \frac{|tp|}{|tp+fn|} = \frac{|T(P_{tool}) \cap T(P_{exp})|}{|T(P_{exp})|}$ and $precision = \frac{|tp|}{|tp+fp|} = \frac{|T(P_{tool}) \cap T(P_{exp})|}{|T(P_{tool})|}$ metrics where tp (true positive) is the set of traces identified by our technique that are also included into the correct model, fp (false positive) is the set of traces identified by our technique that are not included into the correct model, while fn (false negative) is the set of traces not identified by our technique but included into the correct model. Given that the set of traces for a Petri Net could be infinite, we consider as an approximation the minimum number of traces that covers the Petri Net where loops are iterated at most once. Since ProM tool already provides a plug-in for evaluating precision and recall between two Heuristic Net's and to translate a Petri Net to a Heuristic Net, we adopted both for evaluating mined models.

For each feature we have mined different processes starting from a variable set of input traces. We have considered as input all the combinations of $1, ..., t$ traces from the global set of t traces (in our experiments $t=6$). For each combination of traces we have mined the corresponding process model and we have measured precision and recall values of this model with respect to the correct one [26]. Finally, we have evaluated the average precision and recall obtained with all the combinations of 1 trace from the t traces, all the combinations of 2 traces from t traces, ..., and all the combinations of t traces from t traces. Then we repeated the same set of experiments for all features.

Figure 7(a) and (b) show the averages recall and precision values obtained for the input features. Figure 7(a) shows that for all processes the averages recall measure increases if we consider a greater set of traces as input. In case we consider all the traces, we have a recall equal to 1 meaning that all the traces

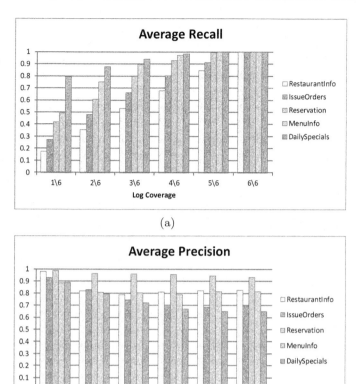

(a)

(b)

Fig. 7. e-Restaurant case study: average recall measure (a) and average precision measure (b) of the mined process models depending on log coverage (1-trace logs, 2-trace logs, ..., 6-trace logs).

within the correct model have been identified by our approach. On average, if the number of traces decreases, the recall decreases as well. As shown in Fig. 7(b), averages precision measure increases with the reductions of traces considered as input, meaning that on average with a lower number of traces the noise introduced by our approach is lower than with a greater number of traces. We claim that the trend of precision and recall averages do not depend on the nature of processes, indeed they all follow the same behavior which depends on the coverage of the input log.

3.4 Threats to Validity

Our technique extracts data-manipulation process models that may suffer of two different types of noise. The first belongs to the adopted mining algorithm and it results in non-correct mined models having possibly additional traces. To mitigate this noise we asked designers to perform a correction to the models mined by our technique. In this way we were able to create models that were 100 % correct which have been exploited as input to evaluate the sensivitity of our technique depending on the log coverage. The second type of noise belongs to the input SQL statements that refer to technical implementation details not relevant for the application logic. To mitigate this problem, we have introduced a pre-processing phase to filter out queries that do not refer to a certain subset of the conceptual schema as selected by the designer. Our technique may also have threats to the scalability depending on the increasing input of SQL statements. Indeed, even once the non-relevant queries have been pruned out, we could mine a non-readable process due to the large space of extracted data-manipulation functions. To mitigate this problem, we advice designers to prune iteratively the conceptual schema until they obtain a readable process (by iteratively applying our technique to the input set of queries).

Recall and precision values obtained for the different features depend on the adopted mining algorithm. In [23] different mining algorithms have been compared to identify the one that better fits the application needs. In our experiments we exploited the ILP miner algorithm which is able to create models with 100 % of fitness (precision) and an acceptable level of appropriateness (recall) with respect to the input set of traces. By adopting mining algorithms with different fitness and appropriateness, we would have obtained different precision and recall values. Nevertheless, we claim that we expect to obtain similar trends of precision and recall depending on the log coverage. Indeed, we expect that by increasing the log coverage, we consequently increase the recall while lowering the precision.

The e-restaurant system adopted in the experiments can be considered a good representative for data-intensive systems i,.e., systems where most of the complexity is hidden into its interactions with a database. Indeed, the e-restaurant consists of numerous interactions with a database where data are the basis for supporting the core business activities. Even though the experimented system is of limited size and complexity, it sufficiently evidenced the capability of the proposed approach in revealing heterogeneous data-manipulation processes in real environments. With this aim, we have also mitigated the quality of the input traces by analyzing features of different nature.

4   Related Work

In the literature different approaches use dynamic analysis of SQL queries with a different goal than data manipulation behavior understanding. The approaches presented in [7,8] analyze SQL statements in support to database reverse engineering, e.g., detecting implicit schema constructs [8] and implicit foreign keys [7]. The approach presented by Di Penta et al. [9] identifies services from SQL traces. The authors apply FCA techniques to name services I/O parameters thus supporting the migration towards Service Oriented Architecture. Debusmann et al. [10]

present a dynamic analysis method for system performance monitoring, i.e., measuring the response time of queries sent to a remote database server. Yang et al. [11] support the recovery of a feature model by means of analyzing SQL traces. Although the former approaches analyze (particular aspects of) the data access behavior of running programs, none of the former approaches [7–11] is able to produce process models expressing such a behavior at a high abstraction level, as we do in this paper.

Other approaches (e.g., [27,28]) extract business processes by exploiting/ combining static and dynamic analysis techniques, but they are not designed to deal with dynamically generated SQL queries. The most related approach, by Alalfi et al. [29], extracts scenario diagrams and UML security models by considering runtime database interactions and the state of the PHP program. These models are used for verifying security properties but they do not describe the generic data manipulation behavior of the program, they only analyze web-interface interactions. In addition they have not considered different possible instances of a given scenario as we claim it is necessary to extract a complete and meaningful model. Understanding processes starting from a set of execution traces is at the core of process mining. This paper does not make any additional contributions as far as process mining is concerned, but it is the first to apply such techniques to analyze program-database interactions.

5   Conclusions and Future Work

Our paper presented a tool-supported approach to recover the data manipulation behavior of data-intensive systems. The approach makes use of clustering, conceptualization and process mining techniques starting from SQL execution traces captured at runtime. We discussed how we exploited current practice technologies to implement our approach and we carried out a set of experiments to assess the quality of the mined processes depending on the coverage of the input traces. We assumed that designers were able to produce correct models based on which we measured precision and recall metrics with respect to models produced with our approach. Results showed that average precision and recall depend on the log coverage almost independently from the extracted process. As for future work we plan to enrich the input traces with multiple sources of information like user input, source code and query results with the aim of identifying the conditions that characterize decision points within process models.

References

1. Silva, J.C., Campos, J.C., Saraiva, J.: Gui inspection from source code analysis. ECEASST **33** (2010)
2. Petit, J.M., Kouloumdjian, J., Boulicaut, J.F., Toumani, F.: Using queries to improve database reverse engineering. In: Loucopoulos, P. (ed.) ER 1994. LNCS, vol. 881, pp. 369–386. Springer, Heidelberg (1994)
3. Willmor, D., Embury, S.M., Shao, J.: Program slicing in the presence of a database state. In: ICSM 2004, pp. 448–452 (2004)

4. Cleve, A., Henrard, J., Hainaut, J.L.: Data reverse engineering using system dependency graphs. In: WCRE 2006, 157–166 (2006)
5. van den Brink, H., van der Leek, R., Visser, J.: Quality assessment for embedded sql. In: SCAM, pp. 163–170 (2007)
6. Cornelissen, B., Zaidman, A., van Deursen, A., Moonen, L., Koschke, R.: A systematic survey of program comprehension through dynamic analysis. IEEE Trans. Softw. Eng. **35**(5), 684–702 (2009)
7. Cleve, A., Meurisse, J.R., Hainaut, J.L.: Database semantics recovery through analysis of dynamic sql statements. J. Data Semant. **15**, 130–157 (2011)
8. Cleve, A., Noughi, N., Hainaut, J.-L.: Dynamic program analysis for database reverse engineering. In: Lämmel, R., Saraiva, J., Visser, J. (eds.) GTTSE 2011. LNCS, vol. 7680, pp. 297–321. Springer, Heidelberg (2013)
9. Grosso, C.D., Penta, M.D., de Guzmán, I.G.R.: An approach for mining services in database oriented applications. In: CSMR. pp. 287–296 (2007)
10. Debusmann, M., Geihs, K.: Efficient and transparent instrumentation of application components using an aspect-oriented approach. In: Brunner, M., Keller, A. (eds.) DSOM 2003. LNCS, vol. 2867, pp. 209–220. Springer, Heidelberg (2003)
11. Yang, Y., Peng, X., Zhao, W.: Domain feature model recovery from multiple applications using data access semantics and formal concept analysis. In: WCRE, pp. 215–224 (2009)
12. van der Aalst, W.M.P.: Process mining: overview and opportunities. ACM Trans. Manage. Inf. Syst. **3**(2), 7 (2012)
13. Hainaut, J.L., Henrard, J., Englebert, V., Roland, D., Hick, J.M.: Database reverse engineering. In: Liu, L., Ozhu, M.T. (eds.) Encyclopedia of Database Systems, pp. 723–728. Springer, US (2009)
14. Cleve, A., Hainaut, J.L.: What do foreign keys actually mean? In: 2012 19th Working Conference on Reverse Engineering (WCRE), pp. 299–307 (2012)
15. Kazato, H., Hayashi, S., Kobayashi, T., Oshima, T., Okada, S., Miyata, S., Hoshino, T., Saeki, M.: Incremental feature location and identification in source code. In: CSMR, pp. 371–374 (2013)
16. Alalfi, M., Cordy, J., Dean, T.: WAFA: fine-grained dynamic analysis of web applications. In: WSE 2009, pp. 41–50 (2009)
17. Ngo, M.N., Tan, H.B.K.: Applying static analysis for automated extraction of database interactions in web applications. Inf. Softw. Technol. **50**(3), 160–175 (2008)
18. Cleve, A., Hainaut, J.L.: Dynamic analysis of SQL statements for data-intensive applications reverse engineering. In: WCRE 2008, 192–196 (2008)
19. Ammons, G., Bodík, R., Larus, J.R.: Mining specifications. In: ACM Sigplan Notices, vol. 37, pp. 4–16 (2002)
20. Ganter, B., Wille, R., Wille, R.: Formal Concept Analysis. Springer, Heidelberg (1999)
21. Cleve, A., Brogneaux, A.F., Hainaut, J.L.: A conceptual approach to database applications evolution. In: ER, pp. 132–145 (2010)
22. Rozinat, A., van der Aalst, W.M.P.: Conformance checking of processes based on monitoring real behavior. Inf. Syst. **33**(1), 64–95 (2008)
23. Buijs, J.C.A.M., van Dongen, B.F., van der Aalst, W.M.P.: On the role of fitness, precision, generalization and simplicity in process discovery. In: Meersman, R., Panetto, H., Dillon, T., Rinderle-Ma, S., Dadam, P., Zhou, X., Pearson, S., Ferscha, A., Bergamaschi, S., Cruz, I.F. (eds.) OTM 2012, Part I. LNCS, vol. 7565, pp. 305–322. Springer, Heidelberg (2012)

24. van derWerf, J.M.E., van Dongen, B.F., Hurkens, C.A., Serebrenik, A.: Process discovery using integer linear programming. Fundamenta Informaticae **94**(3), 387–412 (2009)
25. Peterson, J.L.: Petri Net Theory and the Modeling of Systems. Prentice Hall PTR, Upper Saddle River, NJ (1981)
26. Mori, M., Noughi, N., Cleve, A.: Experiment artifacts: database schemas, sql-statements traces, data-manipulation traces and processes. http://info.fundp.ac.be/~mmo/MiningSQLTraces/
27. Nezhad, H.R.M., Saint-Paul, R., Casati, F., Benatallah, B.: Event correlation for process discovery from web service interaction logs. VLDB **20**(3), 417–444 (2011)
28. Labiche, Y., Kolbah, B., Mehrfard, H.: Combining static and dynamic analyses to reverse-engineer scenario diagrams. In: ICSM, pp. 130–139 (2013)
29. Alalfi, M.H., Cordy, J.R., Dean, T.R.: Recovering Role-Based Access Control Security Models from Dynamic Web Applications. In: Brambilla, M., Tokuda, T., Tolksdorf, R. (eds.) ICWE 2012. LNCS, vol. 7387, pp. 121–136. Springer, Heidelberg (2012)

Mapping and Usage of Know-How Contributions

Arnon Sturm[1,2(✉)], Daniel Gross[1], Jian Wang[1,3],
Soroosh Nalchigar[1], and Eric Yu[1]

[1] University of Toronto, Toronto, Canada
{daniel.gross,eric.yu}@utoronto.ca,
soroosh@cs.toronto.edu
[2] Ben-Gurion University of the Negev, Beer–Sheva, Israel
sturm@bgu.ac.il
[3] Wuhan University, Wuhan, China
jianwang@whu.edu.cn

Abstract. Mapping know-how, which is knowledge of how to achieve specific goals, is important as the creation pace and amount of knowledge is tremendously increasing. Thus, such knowledge needs to be managed to better understand tradeoffs among solutions and identify knowledge gaps. Drawing from goal-oriented requirements engineering, in this paper we propose a specialized (and light weight) use of concept maps to map out contributions to problem-solving knowledge in specific domains. In particular, we leverage on the means-end relationship which plays a major role in such domains and further extend it to be able to depict alternatives and tradeoffs among possible solutions. We illustrate the approach using problems and solutions drawn from two domains and discuss the usefulness and usability of the know-how maps. The proposed mapping approach allows for a condensed representation of the knowledge within a domain including the contributions made and the open challenges.

Keywords: Knowledge mapping · Requirement engineering · Concept map

1 Introduction

The state of the art in fields is a fast moving target. With innovation occurring globally at a fast pace, researchers and practitioners who are pushing the boundaries to better deal with new problems and needs, expend significant efforts to keep up with the current state of the art. To stay up-to-date and to make new contributions to bodies of knowledge, researchers and practitioners must continuously maintain an overview of a field, understand the problems addressed and solutions proposed, as well as identify the outstanding issues that should receive further attention. Given the fast pace of new developments, keeping such an overview up-to-date is challenging. Researchers and practitioners typically make use of, or produce, literature reviews to better understand and map out specific domains. Some use informal literature maps to map out fields of research, indicating with overlapping circles, or boxes with lines in between them,

© Springer International Publishing Switzerland 2015
S. Nurcan and E. Pimenidis (Eds.): CAiSE Forum 2014, LNBIP 204, pp. 102–115, 2015.
DOI: 10.1007/978-3-319-19270-3_7

sub-topics or themes and relationships between them. Some also use their own accumulated list of scholarly references typically included in bibliographic software, as their main personal "knowledge" database which is then tagged and labeled to cue of the existing and expanding works in their fields of interest.

While such approaches are commonly used, they much depend on the researchers and practitioners capability to identify means-end relationships details, which are not guided by the following questions: how problems are characterized, what problems are already addressed, how proposed solutions are making significant contributions to problems, what proposed solutions fail to address, and where further contributions and improvements can be sought.

We observe that problems and solutions in fields of study, and the contribution relationships between problems and solutions can be characterized as *means* that come to address specific *ends* in some better way. We observed a lack of exploiting such a conceptual relationship in current approaches to mapping out engineering domains. Means-ends relationships that are made use of relationships between problems and solutions are such conceptual relationships that are used only to a limited extent in the context of knowledge mapping. Nevertheless, these are widely used within goal-oriented requirements engineering (GORE) approaches [27], in general, and the i* (pronounced i-star) goal-oriented modeling framework approach, in particular [27]. The i* approach, for example, has at its center the means-ends relationship, and the capability to differentiate alternate means towards some end by indicating their differing contributions towards desired quality objectives (by use of additional contribution links). Following the i* notions and based on [9, 23], we propose a knowledge mapping approach to represent and map out problems and solutions in domains which relies on the means-end relationships. We envision that using such an approach would better support researchers and practitioners in representing, capturing and reasoning about research advancements in such domains.

In this paper, we describe a means-end oriented approach for knowledge mapping, and illustrate its use for various domains of technology-oriented (such as the data mining domain) and business-oriented (such as the customer relationship management domain). In addition, as we are aiming at mapping out relationships among domains we further define the cross relationships among domain maps. In particular, we demonstrate how the data mining domain is used to solve problems in the domain of Customer Relationship Management (CRM), which can indicate ways communities working in those different domains could collaborate to better solve existing problems. Furthermore, in this paper we stress the notion of context and quantitative contribution. In addition, we present an initial evaluation of the approach and further discuss our vision of future developments along the lines of the proposed approach.

The paper is organized as follows. Section 2 discusses related work. Section 3 introduces the mapping approach and demonstrates it using examples from the two domains. Section 4 introduces the evaluations we performed to assess the usefulness of the proposed approach. Section 5 further discusses the proposed approach. Finally, Sect. 6 concludes and further elaborates on our vision regarding the usage of such knowledge maps in the future.

2 Related Work

To date, little work has been done to offer a conceptual approach to mapping out domain knowledge within one or more fields. Researchers mainly use literature reviews, including systematic reviews [14], tagging and classifications approaches[1] to accumulate and organize literature in one or more domains [16]. Such approaches help cluster literature along themes or viewpoints of interest, however, offer little insights into the structure of domain knowledge itself, such as to characterize problems, solutions and innovative contributions. Some works aim at mapping out inter-disciplinary research using approaches to visualizing domains knowledge and kinds of relationships between domains knowledge. This includes, for example, citation graphs, subject heading and terminology clustering [4, 5, 17], as well as work toward output indicators for interdisciplinary science and engineering research, which give insight into social dynamics that lead to knowledge integration [24].

While these approaches offer important sign-posts for researchers to orient themselves in disciplinary and cross-disciplinary fields of research, such approaches typically use quantitative measures and descriptive statistic approaches, including novel multi-dimensional networking graphics, to indicate citation structures and interconnections between topics across disciplines, without, however relating the conceptual structuring of the knowledge and evolution of such knowledge in domains.

Some research has been done to offer a conceptual view of literature in a domain and to support a conceptual consolidating of scholarly works. This includes concept maps [19], cause maps [7], and claim-oriented argumentation [21, 22]. One particularly noteworthy line of research is VIVO, a semantic approach to scholarly networking and discovery. VIVO provides a semantic-web based infrastructure and ontologies to represent, capture and make discoverable conceptual linkages that define scholars, and their scholarly work [2].

While these offer useful structuring of domain knowledge, they do not specifically focus on linking problem and solution knowledge within and across domains, in general, and during knowledge innovation and evolution, in particular.

As researchers and practitioners are looking for innovation, they would benefit from supporting tools that would help them in clustering related topics (clustering), as well as explicate problems and solutions (expressiveness), to represent and reason about differences between existing solutions (reasoning), and to be able to adjust the mapping as the domain evolves over time (dynamic evolution). Indeed, the aforementioned approaches offer different kinds of textual, conceptual and visual mapping over domains. However, as mentioned, they lack essential capabilities to evaluate or compare state-of-the-art studies at an engineering knowledge level. Table 1 presents a comparison of the approaches with respect to the needed capabilities.

In addition to mapping specific domains, both researchers and practitioners have a need to explore the possibilities of adopting or adjusting existing solution in one

---

[1] There are also reference management systems like EndNote and Mendeley that support classification using folders and tagging.

Table 1. Comparing mapping techniques

Approach	Advantages	Drawbacks
Literature survey	Literature review enables clustering and since it uses natural language its expressiveness is extensive	As a literature review provides mapping by textual means, a direct reasoning on it is challenging. Furthermore, as such review is done once in a while its relevance is limited. In addition, usually such reviews are taking an a priory point of view and thus might be leaning towards specific directions
Classification	Classification aims at clustering existing work and also facilitates the addition of related knowledge into existing clusters	Classification has limited expressiveness as it indicates only the association to specific categories and not the reason for that. Also, classification does not allow for clear differentiation among works within each category. Usually, classification is done at high level of abstraction and thus provides limited reasoning capabilities. Also, changing clusters requires re-assignment of the already categories work, so the support for dynamic evaluation is limited
Cause map	Cause maps do provide some kind of clustering, though it is not explicated. It allows for some reasoning on various alternatives to achieve an end and also support dynamic evolution of domains as alternatives can be easily be incorporated in such map	Cause maps focuses on means-ends relationships in a conservative manner, usually, without explicit differentiation among alternatives to achieve an end
Concept maps	Concept map has an extensive expressiveness as they can be used to specify any kind of claims	Concept maps are similar to literature review, but add the identification of key concepts. Thus, reasoning remains a challenge. Clustering also should be explicated as it is not clear in such maps
Argumentation	Argumentation approaches can be easily be equipped with extended expressiveness. Being formal in nature reasoning with such approaches is easy. Also, by various arguments differentiations among various works can be explicated	By simply looking at the set of arguments it would be difficult to identify clustering. Yet, this can be achieved through a reasoning procedure

domain to problems in other domains. This exploration would increase collaboration among different research communities.

3   Specializing Concept Maps for Specific Domains

In this section we introduce an approach to map out domains that are characterized by the means-end relationship. To address this need we extend concept map by the means-end relationships to enable reasoning and evolution of existing maps. We begin with briefly presenting the domains that are used in this paper for demonstrating the approach. Then, we present the concepts used within the approach and demonstrate these on the introduced domains.

3.1   Two Examples of Know-How Domains

In this paper, we refer to two domains, namely, the business domain of customer relationship management and the technical domain of data mining. For each domain, some of the content and problems they address are briefly discussed.

3.1.1   The Customer Relationship Management Domain

Customer Relationship Management (CRM) is a comprehensive process of building long term and profitable relationships with customers. It includes four dimensions: customer identification, customer attraction, customer retention, and customer development [16]. Customer retention aims to keep loyal customers by reducing their defections. To this end, approaches to predicting customer churn were developed [11, 23]. Churn prediction is a well-studied domain with various proposed techniques. Moreover, various experiments have been undertaken to compare those techniques (e.g., [26]). Those experiments further asked the following questions: How to examine the existing techniques and to identify opportunities for new contributions in that specific domain for improving customer relationship management practices? How to find techniques from other disciplines and use them for churn prediction? We show how the knowledge mapping approach helps in answering such questions.

3.1.2   The Data Mining Domain

Data mining, the process of extracting interesting patterns and trends from large amounts of data, has gained much attention and success in many scientific and business areas [9]. The main goal is to build a model from data [7]. Major classes of data mining tasks are: predictive modeling, clustering, pattern discovery, and probability distribution estimation [18]. Predictive modeling deals with the problem of performing induction over the dataset in order to make predictions. One of the ways of predictive modeling is classification which builds a concise model or classifier that represents distribution of class labels in terms of predictor features.

Data mining is a domain of rapidly growing interest in which various algorithms and techniques are being proposed. For example, to support data classification different algorithms were proposed, including Support Vector Machines (SVM), Naïve Bayes, and Decision Trees. Also for the other data mining tasks, several algorithms exist and new ones appear continually, making it hard to keep track over time, as well as choose one over another. This problem is further complicated by the fact that various algorithms have different performance rates over different datasets and there is no single algorithms that outperforms all the others for all datasets. Furthermore, even specialists lack comprehensive knowledge about the full range of algorithms and techniques along with their performances. As a result, understanding the strengths and weaknesses of various algorithms and choosing the right one is a challenging task and a critical step both during the design and implementation of data mining applications, as well as when researching novel solutions. In the next sections we illustrate how a knowledge mapping approach can partially alleviate these challenges.

3.2   The Knowledge Mapping Approach

This section presents an approach to conceptually map domains that has at its center means-end relationships. We applied the approach to map out portions of engineering domains including agent-oriented software engineering, geo-engineering, web mining, and documentation of software architecture. We adopted a minimal set of modeling constructs to two types of nodes and a number of types of links. By convention, the map is laid out with problems or objectives at the top and solutions at the bottom.

Figures 1 and 2, respectively illustrate parts of the knowledge maps of the data mining and the customer relationship management domain. Note the maps purpose is to illustrate the concepts used in the proposed mapping approach rather to demonstrate comprehensive maps. For our modeling needs we used the concept mapping toolset

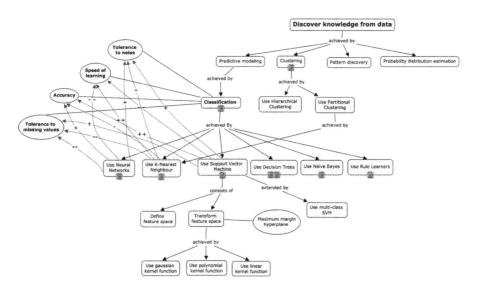

Fig. 1. A partial knowledge map of the data mining domain

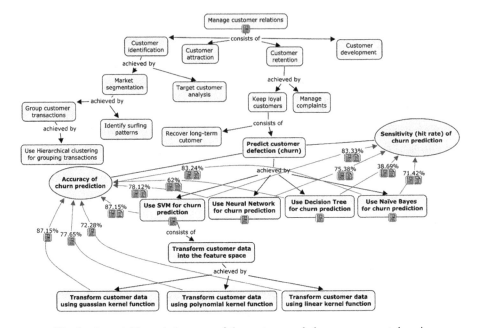

Fig. 2. A partial knowledge map of the customer relation management domain

cmap tools[2] to draw the knowledge maps. Using the cmap tool allows us to benefit from all implemented features of the platform, including collaborative modeling and sharing of concept maps. It also provides a modeling mechanism to support the connections among several domains.

In the following we explain and demonstrate the constructs used in the proposed mapping approach.

- The **task** is the main element used to define means-ends relationship, and when chained together, means-ends hierarchies. A task can be interpreted either as a problem or a solution. Typically, it is named with a verb phrase, and is graphically depicted as a rectangular shape with rounded corners. For example, in Fig. 1, the task "*Discover knowledge from data*" is a typical problem in the data mining domain that needs to be addressed. It can be addressed by tasks such as "*Predictive modeling*", "*Clustering*", "*Pattern discovery*", and "*Probability distribution estimation*". Each of these solutions can in turn be viewed as sub-problems that need further addressing. For example, the "*Predictive modeling*" problem can be addressed by "*Classification*".
- A **quality** element is used to express quality attributes that are desired to sufficiently hold when addressing tasks. A quality is depicted as an ellipse, and is typically named with adverbial or adjectival phrases or quality nouns (e.g., "-ilities").

---

[2] http://cmap.ihmc.us/.

Example qualities in Fig. 1 are *"Accuracy"*, *"Tolerance to noise"*, and *"Speed of learning"*.

- Links connect tasks and qualities. We propose the use of following link types:
  - The **achieved by** link represents a means-end relationship. The arrow points from the "end" to the "means". Figure 1 indicates that *"Classification"* is one way to achieve *"Predictive modeling"*. *"Use Neural Networks"*, *"Use K-Nearest Neighbour"*, *"Use Support Vector Machine"*, *"Use Decision Trees"*, *"Use Naive Bayes"* and *"Use Rule Learners"* are alternative ways of achieving *"Classification"*. While in Fig. 2, *"Keep loyal customers"* and *"Manage complaints"* are solutions to achieve the task (in this case the problem of) *"Customer retention"*.
  - The **consists of** link indicates that a task has several sub-parts, all of which should be addressed for the parent task to be addressed. In Fig. 1, *"Use Support Vector Machine"* consists of *"Define feature space"*, and *"Transform feature space"*, among other problems that need to be addressed. While in Fig. 2, *"Manage customer relations"* consists of *"Customer identification"*, *"Customer attraction"*, *"Customer retention"*, and *"Customer development"*.
  - The **association link** (an unlabeled and non-directional link) indicates the desirable qualities that should sufficiently hold for a given task, once addressed. These qualities are later also to be taken into account when evaluating alternative ways for addressing the task. For example, in Fig. 1 *"Accuracy"* and *"Speed of learning"* are qualities that could serve as criteria when evaluating different ways to address *"Classification"*. In Fig. 2, *"Sensitivity (hit rate) of churn prediction"* and *"Accuracy of churn prediction"* are two qualities to evaluate different solutions for task *"Predict customer defection (churn)"*.
  - The **extended by** link indicates that the target task is an extension of the source task. For example, in Fig. 1, *"Use multi-class SVM"* is an extension of *"Use Support Vector Machine"*. All qualities that hold for the parent task also hold for its extensions.
  - The **contribution link** (a curved arrow) indicates a contribution towards a quality, which can be directed either from a task or another quality. Following the i* guidelines, the contribution is subjective and can range from positive to negative contribution. For example, in Fig. 1, *"Use Neural Networks"* contributes positively ("+") to *"Accuracy"* and *"Tolerance to noise"*, but negatively ("−") to *"Tolerance to missing values"* and *"Speed of learning"*. However, in the case of the knowledge map, where an objective scale measure can be associated with a solution that addresses a particular quality, these measures can also be associated with the link. For example, as shown in Fig. 2, the *"accuracy of churn prediction"*, according to [28] if it is addressed by *"Use SVM for churn prediction"* is 87.15 %, by *"Use Neural Network for churn prediction"* is 78.12 %, by *"Use Decision Tree for churn prediction"* is 62 %, and, finally, by *"Use Naive Bayes for churn prediction"* is 83.24 %.

Each element in the knowledge map can have a context associated, such as a conditions, datasets, experimental settings, and so on, and must have a set of references, which are the knowledge sources. These help justifying the existence of the element within the map. To avoid cluttering we have omitted such contexts or references elements in Figs. 1 and 2. Instead we included them in the attached note icons and reference icons of the tasks in the figures, which are displayed when clicking the icons in the tool. For example, the attached reference icon of "*Classification*" in Fig. 1 shows that the knowledge source of the task is from [15]; the attached note icon of the number "78.12 %" in Fig. 2 shows that the experiment is conducted on a subscriber dataset consisting of 100,000 customers with 171 potential predictor variable, and the attached reference icon shows that the experiment is reported in [28].

It is important to note that a map is essentially an index to the actual knowledge. The purpose of a map is not to represent the entire knowledge but rather organize the knowledge to increase its accessibility.

To construct the knowledge map in Fig. 1, we referred to the definitions of data mining, classification and support vector machine in Wikipedia and analyzed a survey paper on classification techniques [15], as well as a tutorial paper on support vector machines [3]. Similarly, to construct the knowledge map in Fig. 2, we analyzed a survey paper on the application of data mining to customer relationship management [18], as well as a paper on customer churn prediction using SVM [28]. Following these resources, we were able to construct the map while having supporting evidences for the claims implied by nodes and links included in the map.

As we further identify innovation in a domain (by identifying papers reporting the innovation), we make additions to the maps. For example, Fig. 2 shows results of our analysis of another paper on customer churn prediction based on SVM [25], which compares several classification techniques by considering not only the accuracy which is compared in [28], but also the sensitivity (hit rate) of churn prediction. Note that the work of Xia and Jin [25] adopted a different dataset (the machine learning UCI database of University of California). We then further analyzed a survey paper on clustering [12] and a paper on grouping customer transactions based on hierarchical pattern-based clustering [26]. All the model elements and the links in the knowledge map are derived from contents reported in the above mentioned knowledge sources. However, due to space limitations, we only show a small part of the knowledge on clustering in Figs. 1 and 2.

To demonstrate the mapping work procedure, in the following we use Fig. 2 to illustrate the construction process of a knowledge map. The first step is to identify tasks. For example, in Fig. 2, the problems of the CRM dimensions, the CRM elements, and the solutions such as data mining functions and specific data mining techniques, are identified and recorded as tasks. Afterwards, we link the identified tasks by *consists-of* or *achieved-by* links according to their relations. For example, the CRM dimensions such as "*Customer identification*" and "*Customer attraction*" are linked with "*Manage customer relations*" by *consists-of* links.

The next step is to identify qualities related to tasks and use association links to associate them with their respective tasks. For example, as shown in Fig. 2, the "*Accuracy of churn prediction*", a criteria used in the comparison among different solutions, is identified as a quality of the task "*Predict customer defection (churn)*". Finally, we need to link the alternative solutions with qualities by contribution links. In Fig. 2, the numbers on the contribution links originated from the comparison tables in [28].

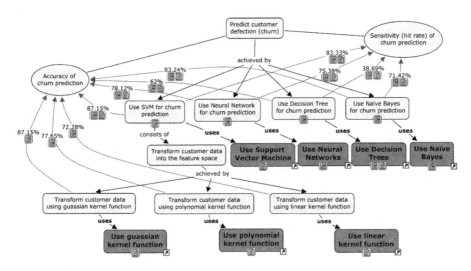

Fig. 3. Connecting the knowledge of the two domains

As noted, one of the approach objectives is to reveal and map out relationships across different but related domains. Some technologies in one domain may be applied in other domains. For example, techniques in the data mining domain have been applied in the CRM domain. Since a knowledge map mainly embodies the knowledge within a specific domain, we introduce a new link type named "uses" to connect tasks in different domains. For example Fig. 3 illustrates a connection between the knowledge in data mining domain and the CRM domain, by linking the task "*Use SVM for churn prediction*" via a *uses* link to the technology "*Use Support Vector Machine*" of the data mining domain included in Fig. 1. In this case, the CRM domain is named as the problem domain while the data mining domain is the solution domain. Including the knowledge of one domainin in another domain can contribute to discover heuristic solutions for the problems in other domains.

Referring to the questions raised in Sect. 3.1, the knowledge map in Fig. 2 can be used to map out the existing techniques in the CRM domain. Furthermore, it is easy to the add new contributions to the existing knowledge map based on the problems they address and compare them with existing contributions using the contribution links. New techniques from other disciplines can be identified from the "uses" links. As illustrated in Fig. 3, considering such links can assist in finding appropriate solutions by leveraging the knowledge in other domains. These can help answer questions such as what techniques from other disciplines have been used for churn prediction. Also, our approach can help users to examine and compare existing techniques and find opportunities for new contributions. For example, if the "speed of learning" is a major concern for the churn prediction in a certain context, Fig. 1 can facilitate identifying that "Use K-Nearest Neighbour" will be the best choice for the problem at hand. Finally, regarding the question about selecting the right data mining algorithm raised in

Sect. 3.1.2, we believe that adding contexts and references for contribution links can help gaining a better understanding about the comparisons of various algorithms.

4 Evaluation of the Know-How Mapping Approach

In order to evaluate the approach, we have performed several evaluation steps during its development. The evaluation consists of two main themes: comprehension of maps and construction of maps.

For the comprehension theme we compared the understanding of a knowhow map versus a literature review[1]. In that evaluation, we used a preliminary notation which was a sub-set of the i* framework (that represents tasks and qualities along with the related relationships). We had twelve subjects of which four were familiar with i* and eight which were not familiar with that framework. The four subjects who were familiar with i* got the knowledge map of a web mining domain along with other four subjects. The other four subjects got the literature review of the same domain. We further made sure that information in both the map and the literature is equivalent. Upon getting the domain knowledge (either as a map or as a text) we ask the subjects to answer a questions related to problems, solutions, properties, and tradeoffs in the domain at hand. The results indicated that having the knowledge map better allowed the subjects to understand the domain and in less time than was required by the literature review, even by those subjects who were unfamiliar with i*.

For the construction theme, we recruited four graduate students and after training them with the proposed approach, we ask them to map out their own research domain. The mapping was performed in a few stages, so we were able to control and give feedback on their mapping. We then the reviewed the resulted maps and ask them to fill out a questionnaire indicating the usability of the proposed approach. Analyzing their responses we concluded the following:

- The approach is easy to use for the purpose of mapping a literature review.
- The approach helps in organizing the knowledge in a way that facilitates grouping of similar studies, as well as, differentiating among related studies.
- The approach facilitates identification of research gaps and possible contributions from other domains.
- The approach helps in positioning own research.
- The approach encourages critical thinking with respect to literature reviews.

Although further validation is required, the results obtained so far indicated that the approach does provide meaningful benefits.

5 Discussion

Using the specialized concept maps to connect between a conceptual representation of problems and solutions in domains of interest supports researchers and practitioners in quickly gaining insights into the problems they deal with and solution practices available to them, within and across domains. A key advantage that such an overview offers is the systematic overview of solution approaches that could fit problems thereby reducing the risk of missing relevant techniques to address specific challenges. However, while the proposed approach facilitates representing problems and solutions in existing state-of-the-art, we encountered a number of challenges:

Conceptual Mismatch: Identifying problems, solutions, qualities, and the relationships among them is often non-trivial. Researchers and stakeholders often present needs and benefits in solution-oriented terminology and languages and neglect the connection with the problem-oriented aspects.

Naming Decompositions: During the construction of a knowledge map elements are decomposed into lower level elements. Decomposition is the main mechanism to unearth variation and differences in approach details (solution features) that matter with respect to qualities. However, in some domains it appears difficult to identify and name those solution feature "components" that differentiate among alternative approaches. This suggests that more holistic representations of solution approaches, or, finer-grained concept map based analysis guidelines are needed to help make explicit in what way proposed solutions differ in their details.

Multiple Vantage Points and Terminology Use: Because of different viewpoints map creators might take, they may develop maps differently, both in terminology and in the abstraction level. Furthermore, it is in the purview of the map creator to decide which level of abstraction is the most fitting to express problems and solution approaches. When constructing larger maps out of contributions from different map authors, aligning the levels of abstraction is non-trivial.

Scalable Tool Support: Better tool support is needed. Using concept maps we took advantage of existing tools, and their "scalability" features such as: element expanding/collapsing and map referencing.

Domain Knowledge Extraction: Currently, knowledge extraction and its mapping are done manually. This introduces a burden on adopting the approach. Nevertheless, we envision crowd-mapping as an approach that distributes the burden across interested participants, who benefit from mutual contributions, and approaches to automated concept extraction from bodies of text guided by the proposed concepts that link needs with solutions.

6 Conclusion and Future Work

We propose an approach to map out problem-solution oriented fields using a light-weight modeling technique, based on concepts borrowed from the area of goal-oriented requirements engineering. We argue for benefits that such an approach would offer, such as the ability to represent and facilitate the analysis for novel solution approaches in light of their quality properties and to identify gaps of un-addressed problems. We also illustrated the ability to represent the use of solutions drawn from more than one domain, and how these contribute to improve the ability to address problems at hand, whilst also having relevant problem qualities in mind. We believe that the approach is applicable to any domains which aim to identify better solutions to well defined problems, and hence its characterizations fits with the problem-solution means-end chains the proposed approach represents. We also note that benefits for such domains vary and depend on the domain maturity, such as, whether problems are already well understood and solutions already worked out. In particular, the approach works best in cases where domains are mature enough and a large body of knowledge and terminology has been established. In such cases, the mapping would be helped by existing domain resources (i.e., the research literature, such as papers and textbooks), which would likely already have established a common and unified terminology. On the other hand, domains which are evolving would probably use various sets of terminology which would make the mapping difficult. To further explore and facilitate the use of knowledge mapping we plan to expand knowledge map capabilities in a number of directions. We aim to further develop guidelines for map creators to support extracting knowledge from research domains and including them in knowledge maps; to support scalability by developing a framework for mapping and searching knowledge maps; to support a crowd-mapping approach where different stakeholders contribute to creating, arguing about and improving a collaborative created knowledge map; to support for trust mechanisms, as well as, evidence based augmentations of knowledge maps that offer further validity insights; to develop semi-automated reasoning support to identify gaps or even possible solution approaches to already identified gaps, with searches across different knowledge maps; and develop automated extraction of knowledge mappings from bodies of engineering texts, guided by core concepts proposed in this paper. We are also planning further evaluations for testing the benefits of the proposed approach.

Acknowledgement. This research is partially supported by the Israel Science Foundation (Grant No. 495/14) and by the Natural Sciences and Engineering Research Council of Canada.

References

1. Abrishamkar, S.: Goal-Oriented Know-How Mapping- Modelling Process Documentation, a Prototype, and Empirical Studies, M.I. thesis, University of Toronto (2013)
2. Börner, K., Conlon, M., Corson-Rikert, J., Ding, Y. (eds.): VIVO: A Semantic Approach to Scholarly Networking and Discovery. Morgan & Claypool Publishers LLC, San Rafael (2012)
3. Burges, C.J.C.: A tutorial on support vector machines for pattern recognition. Data Min. Knowl. Disc. **2**(2), 121–167 (1998)
4. Chen, C.M., Paul, R.J.: Visualizing a knowledge domain's intellectual structure. Comput. **34** (3), 65–71 (2001)
5. Chen, C.M., Paul, R.J., O'Keefe, B.: Fitting the jigsaw of citation: information visualization in domain analysis. J. Am. Soc. Inform. Sci. Technol. **52**(4), 315–330 (2001)
6. Eden, C., Ackermann, F., Cropper, S.: The analysis of cause maps. J. Manage. Stud. **29**(3), 309–324 (1992)
7. Giraud-Carrier, C., Povel, O.: Characterising data mining software. Intell. Data Anal. **7**(3), 181–192 (2003)
8. Gross, D., Sturm, A., Yu, E.: Towards know-how mapping using goal modeling. In: International iStar Workshop, pp. 115–120 (2013)

9. Han, J., Kamber, M., Pei, J.: Data Mining: Concepts and Techniques. Data Management Systems, 3rd edn. Morgan Kaufmann, Waltham (2012)
10. Jain, A.K., Murty, M.N., Flynn, P.J.: Data clustering: a review. ACM Comput. Surv. (CSUR) **31**(3), 264–323 (1999)
11. Kawale, J., Pal, A., Srivastava, J.: Churn prediction in MMORPGs: a social influence based approach. In: International Conference on Computational Science and Engineering, vol. 4, pp. 423–428 (2009)
12. Kitchenham, B., Brereton, P., Budgen, D., Turner, M., Bailey, J., Linkman, S.: Systematic literature reviews in software engineering - a systematic literature review. Inf. Softw. Technol. **51**(1), 7–15 (2009)
13. Kotsiantis, S.B.: Supervised machine learning: a review of classification techniques. Informatica **31**, 249–268 (2007)
14. Kwasnik, B.: The role of classification in knowledge representation and discovery. Libr. Trends **48**, 22–47 (1999)
15. Leydesdorff, L., Rafols, I.: A global map of science based on the ISI subject categories. J. Am. Soc. Inf. Sci. Technol. **60**(2), 348–362 (2009)
16. Ngai, E.W.T., Xiu, L., Chau, D.C.K.: Application of data mining techniques in customer relationship management: a literature review and classification. Expert Syst. Appl. **36**, 2592–2602 (2009)
17. Novak, J. D., Cañas, Al. J.: The Theory Underlying Concept Maps and How To Construct and Use Them, Institute for Human and Machine Cognition (2006)
18. Panov, P., Soldatova, L.N., Džeroski, S.: Towards an ontology of data mining investigations. In: Gama, J., Costa, V.S., Jorge, A.M., Brazdil, P.B. (eds.) DS 2009. LNCS (LNAI), vol. 5808, pp. 257–271. Springer, Heidelberg (2009)
19. Shum, S.B., Motta, E., Domingue, J.: ScholOnto: An ontology-based digital library server for research documents and discourse. Int. J. Digit. Libr. **3**(3), 237–248 (2000)
20. Simsek, D., Buckingham Shum, S., Sandor, A., De Liddo, A., Ferguson, R.: XIP Dashboard: visual analytics from automated rhetorical parsing of scientific metadiscourse. In: Proceedings of 1st International Workshop on Discourse-Centric Learning Analytics (2013)
21. Sturm, A., Gross, D., Wang, J., Yu, E.: Analyzing engineering contributions using a specialized concept map. In: CAiSE (Forum/Doctoral Consortium), pp. 89–96 (2014)
22. Wagner, C.S., Roessner, J.D., Bobb, K., Klein, J.T., Boyack, K.W., Keyton, J., Rafols, I., Börner, K.: Approaches to understanding and measuring interdisciplinary scientific research (IDR): a review of the literature. J. Informetr. **5**(1), 14–26 (2001)
23. Xia, G., Jin, W.: Model of customer churn prediction on support vector machine. Syst. Eng. Theory Pract. **28**(1), 71–77 (2008)
24. Yang, Y., Padmanabhan, B.: GHIC: A hierarchical pattern-based clustering algorithm for grouping Web transactions. IEEE Trans. Knowl. Data Eng. **17**(9), 1300–1304 (2005)
25. Yu, E., Giorgini, P., Maiden, N., Mylopoulos, J.: Social Modeling for Requirements Engineering. MIT Press, Cambridge (2011)
26. Zhao, Y., Li, B., Li, X., Liu, W., Ren, S.: Customer churn prediction using improved one-class support vector machine. In: Li, X., Wang, S., Dong, Z.Y. (eds.) ADMA 2005. LNCS (LNAI), vol. 3584, pp. 300–306. Springer, Heidelberg (2005)

Facilitating Effective Stakeholder Communication in Software Development Processes

Vladimir A. Shekhovtsov[✉], Heinrich C. Mayr, and Christian Kop

Institute for Applied Informatics, Alpen-Adria-Universität Klagenfurt, Klagenfurt, Austria
{Volodymyr.Shekhovtsov,Heinrich.Mayr,Christian.Kop}@aau.at

Abstract. Effective communication in software development is impaired when parties perceive communicated information differently. To address this problem, the project QuASE has been established. It aims at a solution that supports understandability and reusability of communicated information as well as the quality of decisions based on such information. In this paper, we focus on the architectural aspects of the QuASE system and on its knowledge base which consists of two ontologies: a site ontology defining the site-specific communication environment, and a "quality ontology" that incorporates all knowledge necessary for supporting communication. We describe the overall architecture of the system, introduce the ontologies as well as their interplay, and outline the approach for gathering knowledge necessary to form the QuASE site ontology.

Keywords: Stakeholders · View harmonization · Software development process · Software quality · Communicated information · Communication environment

1 Introduction

Software development processes require a continuous involvement of the affected business stakeholders in order to be successful (this requirement, in particular, is reflected by the ISO/IEC standard for software life cycle processes [9]). A prerequisite of such involvement is establishing an appropriate communication basis for the different parties. In particular, such a basis is needed for coming to terms and agreements on the quality of the software under development. Without this, quality defects are often detected only when the software is made available for acceptance testing.

Clearly, besides of enabling effective communication, the communicated quality-related information has to be managed properly and made available during the software development lifecycle; moreover, as past-experience may help to take the right decisions, such information should be provided in a way that allows for easy access and analysis.

The QuASE project[1] [22–29] aims at a comprehensive solution for these issues (Fig. 1). In particular, this solution will provide support for managing (1) the

---

[1] QuASE: Quality Aware Software Engineering is a project sponsored by the Austrian Research Promotion Agency (FFG) in the framework of the Bridge 1 program; Project ID: 3215531.

© Springer International Publishing Switzerland 2015
S. Nurcan and E. Pimenidis (Eds.): CAiSE Forum 2014, LNBIP 204, pp. 116–132, 2015.
DOI: 10.1007/978-3-319-19270-3_8

understandability of quality-related *communicated information*, (2) the **reusability** of that information, and (3) the **quality of decisions** based on that information.

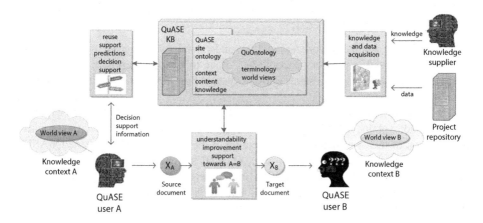

Fig. 1. General activities of the QuASE approach

Figure 1 presents different support scenarios.

1. User A and B use the *QuASE tool* to achieve a common understanding of some aspects of a software under development (SUD) that are described in a document X. In this scenario, the *QuASE knowledge base* (QuASE KB) provides the means of improving the understandability [25] of the document by translating or explaining its content where needed. Figure 1 shows the case where a source document X_A of user A is transformed into a version X_B that can be understood by B. Clearly, the translations/transformations can act in both directions.
2. User A uses the QuASE tool for decision support. As a means of such support, QuASE KB facilitates analysis of previous communications and the parties involved there-in; such information may be reused to improve the future communications, for predicting particular attributes, or for supporting decisions on the strategy of communication with the given party in the given context.

For supporting such scenarios, fundamental knowledge related to the communication domain has to be gathered and stored in the QuASE KB. There are two strategies: (1) knowledge supplier enters the data into the KB; (2) it is filled automatically from the project repositories e.g., the JIRA issue tracking database.

In the QuASE KB, the information about the given communication environment (who communicates, which documents store the communicated information etc.) has to be separated from the information about the knowledge being communicated; the latter can contain the set of core notions acting as a glue between the knowledge specific to different parties. This assures that the views of communicating parties can be harmonized [22].

The QuASE KB, therefore, consists of two parts:

1. *QuASE site ontology:* defines the site-specific communication environment;
2. *QuOntology:* contains knowledge about/around the communicated information (both common and site-specific).

The QuASE data acquisition process and the understandability management activities have been presented in previous papers [24, 25]. In this paper, therefore, we focus on the architectural aspects of the whole QuASE system, the QuASE KB and its knowledge structures.

The paper is structured as follows. Section 2 introduces the QuASE KB with its two parts and explains their features as well as their interplay. Section 3 continues with a description of the overall generic architecture of the QuASE system and the QuASE KB. It explains how other modules (e.g., QuASE site ontology generator, QuASE QuOntology generator, data acquisition engine etc.) work together. Furthermore Sect. 3 explains two alternative QuASE KB implementation strategies. Section 4 focuses on the support for gathering knowledge necessary to form the QuASE site ontology. After a short discussion of related work in Sect. 5, the paper concludes with a summary and an outlook on future research (Sect. 6).

2   Knowledge Structures for Representing the Communication Environment and the Communicated Information

We distinguish the structures representing (1) the knowledge about the communication environment (such as the communicating parties, the documents containing communicated information etc.) and (2) the communicated knowledge itself (concepts and facts being communicated, related information). In establishing such structures, we aimed at the following goals: (a) flexibility: the permitted structures have to be easily adapted to the particular deployment site; (b) support for understandability management and analysis activities.

2.1   Project Repositories

Prior to defining the knowledge structures, it is necessary to enumerate the possible sources of data corresponding to these structures. Software development projects, as a rule, keep communicated information within *project repositories* such as (1) *project databases* controlled by issue management systems (IMS), e.g., JIRA [11], MantisBT [6] and others; such databases contain communicated information in form of issues (generalizing bug reports or feature requests) and related discussions; (2) *file-based repositories* containing meeting minutes, requirement and design specifications etc.; these files are usually kept in some kind of a directory tree; (3) *wiki-based systems*.

Consequently, QuASE considers these types of repositories as sources of information and therefore provides data acquisition interfaces to them.

2.2 QuASE Site Ontology

The data collected from project repositories are interpreted and mapped into the QuASE KB. Figure 2 depicts the high-level structure of the QuASE site ontology (in UML-like notation) which consists of the following key concepts:

1. *site:* owner of the given QuASE installation, e.g. a software provider.
2. *context:* units having particular views on communicated information, e.g. projects, organizations and their departments, involved people (stakeholders) etc. Context units are characterized by context attributes and can be connected to other units; a context configuration, for example, could include the representation of the whole organizational hierarchy or the whole portfolio of projects defined for a particular IT company. In addition, the set of context units can include the categories of such units (i.e. "IT company", "Business stakeholder") as it is possible to define the views on communicated information belonging to such categories (i.e. the view on quality belonging to IT companies).
3. *content:* units shaping communicated information originated from project repositories: they serve as containers for such information or organize such containers. Examples of content units are issues and their sets, issue attribute values, and requirement specifications. Content units can be related to context units.
4. *knowledge:* units encapsulating quality and domain knowledge that is subject of communication and harmonization. Every QuASE knowledge unit is a triple (o, v, r) composed of the following components:
   (a) *ontological foundation:* a reference to the conceptualization of the particular piece of quality or domain knowledge through ontological means: such conceptualizations form a modular ontology (*QuOntology*) providing a framework for translating between world views.
   (b) *representation:* the representation of the knowledge unit in a format that could be perceived by the communicating parties (e.g. plain text). Representation units are contained in content units and can be connected to each other.
   (c) *resolution means:* the means of resolving understandability conflicts related to the particular knowledge unit (such as explanations or external references).

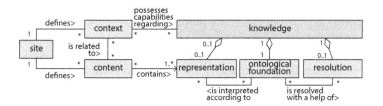

Fig. 2. Base structure of the QuASE site ontology

Context units possess *capabilities* to deal with knowledge units; in particular, these capabilities could refer to the ability of understanding a given knowledge unit at hand (i.e. its representation); or of explaining a knowledge unit using resolution means.

2.3   QuOntology

QuOntology covers all knowledge that has/can be communicated in the respective environment. Initial research on QuOntology has been published in [28], whereas the current version of the relevant conceptualizations is presented in [22]. Figure 3 shows the key components of that ontology as well as its relation to the site ontology.

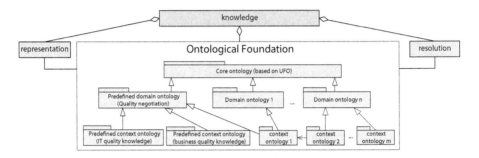

Fig. 3. Organization of QuOntology

QuOntology is organized in three layers [see also Fig. 3]:

1. *QuOntology core* represents a stable subset of the knowledge available from research and industrial practice; it does not depend on the particular problem domain. We use the Unified Foundational Ontology (UFO) [7, 8] as a foundation for QuOntology core; the motivation for this selection is provided in [22].
2. *Domain ontologies* [8] represent the specifics of the particular problem domain which is addressed by the given software under development (finance, oil and gas etc.); as a part of the project, we implement for this layer a Domain Ontology for software quality [22].
3. *Context ontologies* represent the knowledge related to particular components of the QuASE context: they contain organization-specific, project-specific etc. concepts. As a part of the project, we implement for this layer ontologies for business-specific and IT-specific views on quality.

As both QuASE site ontology and QuOntology are specialized ontologies supporting only the concepts depicted in Fig. 3, we propose to allow knowledge suppliers to use for their definition domain-specific visual modeling languages with limited set of constructs which are easier to understand and learn than ontology languages such as OWL. The models defined by means of these languages are then transformed into specific ontology instantiations. The process of specifying such models and transforming them into ontological format is described in the following section.

3   QuASE System Architecture

Figure 4 gives an overview of the QuASE system architecture. The components are described one by one in the following sections.

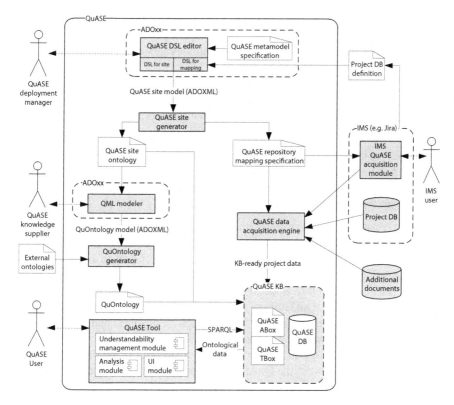

Fig. 4. Generic QuASE system architecture

3.1 Architectural Components and Their Interaction

The site-specific configuration of the communication environment is interactively defined as a *site model* in the domain-specific visual modeling language *site DSL* supported by a *site editor* tool. Such model can be also predefined by the supplier of the system based on the information collected on site. The site editor provides the DSL support based on the QuASE *site metamodel*; this support also uses the definition of the source project repository to enable defining the correspondence between QuASE concepts and this repository.

Obtained as a result of the above activities, the site model contains the description of the permitted structure of the site-specific set of concepts related to the communication environment (context and content configuration together with the knowledge elements) and their correspondence to the project repository structures (e.g. JIRA tables). This model, by the means of *QuASE site generator*, is transformed into the QuASE site ontology (introduced in Sect. 2) and the *QuASE repository mapping specification*. The site DSL and the corresponding editor are described in Sect. 4 together with a partial example of the site model.

The representation of the site ontology obtained as an output of the site generator describes the site-specific set of environment concepts by means of OWL 2. The transformation between the site model and the site ontology again is described in detail in Sect. 4.

QuASE repository mapping specification controls the execution of the *QuASE data acquisition engine*. The process of data acquisition is described in detail in [24]. In particular, this engine is responsible for the following functionality:

1. acquiring the raw project data directly from the project repositories (both IMS-controlled project databases and file-based repositories)
2. obtaining the non-repository data (e.g. the values of a content unit or context unit attributes not represented in project repositories) interactively from the users of these repositories through the extended IMS interface.

QuOntology construction is performed similarly to the construction of the QuASE site ontology. A knowledge supplier interacts with the *QML editor* tool supporting a visual modeling DSL (*Quality Modeling Language, QML*); QML is based on a metamodel that reflects knowledge unit configuration from the QuASE site model. By means of this tool, the supplier creates a *QML model* which is then transformed into an OWL 2 representation of QuOntology. QuOntology could also reuse the existing knowledge by importing external domain ontologies. The description of QML and the process of constructing QuOntology will be presented in a separate publication.

Both QuASE site ontology and QuOntology are combined to form the structural part (TBox in description logics) of the QuASE KB. The individuals comprising the ABox of this KB are provided by the QuASE data acquisition engine based on the raw project data. An approach to defining QuASE KB architecture is described in Sect. 3.2.

QuASE tool includes components responsible for providing understandability and decision support to the end users. All interaction between this tool and the KB is performed through an internal API referring only to the information from the QuASE metamodel; these API calls transparently form and execute SPARQL queries to KB and return the data based on their results. By providing this API, it is guaranteed that the code of the tool is decoupled from the particular site definition; this definition is used as the set of ontology individuals treated as the data structures by the tool code.

3.2   Defining QuASE KB Architecture

We used an architectural approach to define QuASE KB (Fig. 5) based on transparent ontology storage: the ontology ABox is explicitly formed by the QuASE data acquisition engine as a set of individuals corresponding to the classes defined in the QuASE TBox. Together TBox and ABox form an OWL 2 ontology which is then transparently stored into the triple store; we are using the capabilities of the Jena framework (Jena TDB triple store, http://jena.apache.org/documentation/tdb/) to implement this storage; all queries are handled by the SPARQL engine.

The advantage of this approach is the simplicity of the architecture: only the ontology has to be formed; the mapping between this ontology and the permanent storage is provided by TDB transparently. Another advantage is the maturity of the supporting

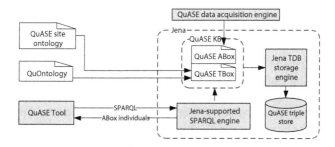

Fig. 5. Knowledge base architecture based on transparent ontology storage

technology (Apache Jena, and, in particular, TDB storage solution, are currently widely used in both academia and industry).

While considering this approach, the performance and scalability of such configuration were under question, as achieving the optimal performance of ontological reasoning over the database-backed ontology is still an open research challenge. But we ultimately decided in favor of it after achieving an acceptable performance of the QuASE site KB populated from the industrial-size project repository of one of the consortium partners (collected since 2008: over 8000 issues resulting in OWL 2 KB containing 1.8 million axioms).

The rejected alternative was based on using the OBDA (Ontology-Based Data Access) techniques [15] where the OBDA reasoner hides the independently configured relational database (QuASE DB) behind the ontological interface: this approach was rejected as (1) the OBDA solution turned out to be more difficult to configure and less capable (e.g. the available OBDA reasoners are restricted in OWL support with OWL2 QL which is not sufficient for expressing QuASE site ontology and KB), and (2) acceptable performance was achieved using the transparent storage approach.

3.3   QuASE System Usage Scenarios

In this section, we provide examples of using the proposed architecture to facilitate communication between stakeholders in a software project. We distinguish site definition, knowledge acquisition, and QuASE tool usage scenarios.

1. *Site and knowledge definition scenario:*
    (a) The knowledge supplier *K* (an employee of the company *E*) creates the *E*'s site model using the QuASE site modeler tool. Then he/she initiates the site ontology generation for *E* based on the specified model.
    (b) *K* extends the *E*'s site model adding the repository mapping specification referring to *E*'s JIRA installation.
    (c) *K* provides QuOntology concepts, representations, and explanations using QML editor and initiates the generation of QuOntology.
    (d) As a result, the *E*'s site ontology, QuOntology, and repository mapping specification are created; the system becomes ready to acquire knowledge.

2. *Knowledge acquisition scenario – incremental case:*
   (a) The Jira user U creates the new issue X_U and adds extra information (e.g. attributes and related decisions with preferred alternatives) to X_U based on E's site model and mapping information, the information is stored in E's local QuASE database (by QuASE Jira plug-in) and E's project repository (by Jira).
   (b) K initiates the process of populating the site KB based on the site ontology and QuOntology specifications, the repository mapping specification, X_U data from the project repository, and X_U extra data contained in the QuASE internal DB.
   (c) As a result, the QuASE site KB becomes synchronized with the current state of the project repository and the extra information specified by U.
3. *QuASE tool usage scenarios.* A complete set of usage scenarios for the QuASE tool is defined in [29], so here we limit ourselves only with a short outline of the instantiation of two basic scenarios presented in Sect. 1:
   (a) *Understandability support:* Users A and B use the QuASE tool to achieve common understanding of a new issue X_A. The issue is transferred into the QuASE tool, where the target context is set to B. After that, X_A's text is parsed by the tool and the problematic terms are looked up in the QuASE KB via SPARQL queries. B-specific representations and/or explanations for these terms are obtained as a result of these queries and shown to B forming a resolved issue X_B.
   (b) *Decision support:* User A uses the QuASE tool for decision support concerning his/her future communication with the stakeholder B. He/she selects the subset of B's metrics and asks QuASE tool to look for all similar stakeholders (similarity search), for recommendations related to B, and for predicted values of the selected metrics. The tool queries the QuASE KB using SPARQL and provides the requested information to A based on the existing knowledge.

4 Defining QuASE Site Model and QuASE Site Ontology

In this section, we define the QuASE site DSL through its metamodel, and show how QuASE site models are created by means of this DSL. We also describe an approach to transforming these models into the instances of QuASE site ontology.

4.1 Metamodel for QuASE Site DSL

We define the metamodel for the QuASE site DSL on two levels: foundational level shown in Fig. 6; and QuASE site level shown on Fig. 7.

On the foundational level (shown using an UML-like notation), we restricted ourselves with a very lean set of concepts: *Modeling Element* consisting of *Attributes* forms the top of the hierarchy; it specializes to *Structural Modeling Element* and *Descriptional Modeling Element*; *Entity* and *Relation* are specializations of Structural Modeling Element; Entities can again consist of entities. Relations consists of *Perspectives* connecting them to Entities; in turn, Entities are related through Relations. *Attribute* and *Perspective* are Descriptional Modeling Elements.

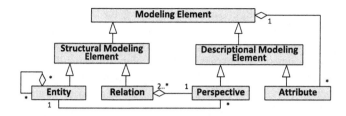

Fig. 6. Foundational concepts for the metamodel of the QuASE site DSL

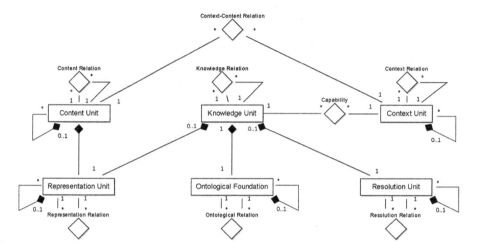

Fig. 7. Metamodel for the QuASE site DSL (the notation uses notions from ER)

On the QuASE site level, we instantiate the foundational concepts as metaclasses. In this level's metamodel:

1. Separate entity metaclasses are defined to specify modeling constructs corresponding to context units (*Context Unit*), content units (*Content Unit*), and knowledge units (*Knowledge Unit*). The Knowledge Unit is composed of a triple of *Representation Unit*, *Ontological Foundation*, and *Resolution Unit* metaclasses.

2. For every entity metaclass, the corresponding "relation to itself" metaclass is defined which can be instantiated to connect modeling constructs belonging to this metaclass (e.g. the instances of *Content Unit Relation* metaclass can connect model elements which are the instances of Content Unit; a model level example of such relation could define that Issue Versions are related to Issues).

3. Part-whole composition meta-relations are defined for entity metaclasses.

4. Two relation metaclasses are defined that can be instantiated to connect instances of different entity metaclasses: the instances of *Context-Content Relation* connect Context Units and Content Units (defining e.g. that the Persons are able to provide their knowledge while forming Issues), whereas the instances of *Capability* connect Context Units and Knowledge Units (defining e.g. that the Persons are able to understand Notions).

5. Context Units can contain Representation Units (e.g. the Description of the particular Issue can contain a set of Plain Text Fragments).
6. For every relation and entity metaclass, the *type* is defined as an additional meta-attribute (not shown on a diagram); in particular, for capabilities the following predefined relation types are available: "is able to understand", "is able to understand with explanation", "is able to explain", and "is able to perform". Such types are not defined as separate metaclasses to restrict the number of metamodel elements; it allows keeping it stable while allowing defining additional types for the particular instance of the QuASE site model.

4.2   Defining the QuASE Site Model by Means of the QuASE Site DSL

The QuASE site DSL editor tool is produced by implementing the QuASE site meta-model in the ADOxx meta-modeling framework (http://www.adoxx.org). Figure 8 shows a snapshot of its user interface displaying an instance of the QuASE site model.

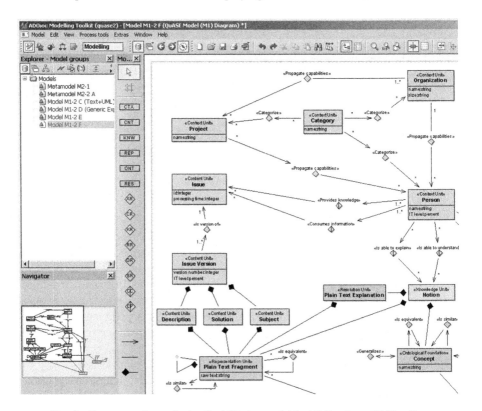

Fig. 8. Fragment of a particular QuASE site model in ADOxx-based DSL editor

On the current stage of the project, we restricted ourselves with a limited set of notational elements; the notation is going to evolve alongside the progress of the project.

Entity-based and relation-based constructs are respectively denoted with colored boxes and colored diamonds; relations have incoming and outgoing connectors with associated cardinalities. Categories of constructs are distinguished by their background color; for context-content relations and capabilities, two colors are used separated by the vertical line. The names of categories are also shown in angle brackets similarly to the names of stereotypes in UML class diagrams. In addition, the UML-inspired composition connectors can be defined between elements if allowed by the metamodel.

Attributes are specified using a notation similar to the one used in UML class diagrams. The attributes for relations can also be specified (not shown on the diagram).

In Fig. 8, the QuASE site model includes the following context units as elements of the site-specific context configuration: Category, Organization, Project, and Person. Individual context units are connected by the relation of type "propagate capabilities" which denote that the capabilities belonging to the source unit are inherited by the target unit unless it overrides them, e.g. the capabilities of the particular project are inherited by the persons involved in the project.

The configuration of content units reflects the JIRA-like structure of the project database; it includes Issue and Issue Version as higher-level content units; in a project repository (e.g. a JIRA database), such units can correspond to interrelated tables. Description, Solution, and Subject are lower-level units (representation holders); their instances contain Plain Text Fragments (instances of representation units); in a project repository, these units can correspond to the attributes able to hold communicated information. The container for these units is Issue Version.

The only knowledge unit shown in Fig. 8 is Notion; it contains Plain Text Fragment as a representation unit, Concept as ontological foundation, and Plain Text Explanation as a resolution unit. I.e., the site model defines that the notions are represented and explained using plain text. Concepts can be connected to each other with "generalize", "is similar" and "is equivalent" relations; this fragment of the model is intended to define the means of specifying QuOntology.

The instances of Plain Text Fragments can be also connected to the other instances of this concept via "is equivalent" and "is similar" relations. This models the configuration where the means of representation can be compared and checked for similarity.

4.3   Generating QuASE Site Ontology

The QuASE site model defines a conceptual configuration of the communication environment as a set of interrelated entities. To incorporate this configuration into the structure of the QuASE KB, it has to be transformed into computational ontology representation; we propose to target OWL 2 representation in this transformation.

We have implemented Java-based a *QuASE site generator* tool aimed at this purpose. It obtains the serialized QuASE site model from the QuASE site editor and applies a set of rules to generate OWL 2 constructs corresponding to the QuASE site DSL constructs. These rules are based on a set of rules published in [3] to control the conversion of the generic conceptual modeling language OntoUML into OWL:

1. The set of *metamodel-based OWL classes* is included in the resulting ontology prior to processing the model elements; it is stable across conversions. Such classes represent metaclasses defined on both, foundational and QuASE site levels: *Context Unit ⊑ Entity ⊑ ModelingElement, Capability ⊑ Relation ⊑ ModelingElement*;

2. An entity model element is transformed into an OWL class as a subclass of the class which represents the entity's meta-class: e.g. the rule activated on arriving of a Context Unit model element named *Person* forms the following OWL class hierarchy: *Person ⊑ ContextUnit ⊑ Entity ⊑ ModelingElement*.

3. A relation model element is transformed into

   (a) an OWL class for the element (named based on the value of its *type* attribute and the names of connected entities: e.g. *Person_IsAbleToExplain_Notion*); this class becomes a subclass of a class that represents a particular value of its *type* attribute which in turn becomes a subclass of the relation's meta-class: *Person_IsAbleToExplain_Notion ⊑ IsAbleToExplain ⊑ Capability ⊑ Relation ⊑ ModelingElement*

   (b) a set of object properties for perspectives and for the relation itself named by prefixing the relation name with *[SOURCE_FOR]* or *[TARGET_FOR]* for perspective-based properties or with *[PROPERTY_FOR]* for the relation-based properties: *[SOURCE_FOR] Person_IsAbleToExplain_Notion ⊑ [SOURCE_FOR]Capability ⊑ [SOURCE_FOR] Relation ⊑ topObjectProperty*; inverse properties are additionally prefixed with *[INV]*.

   (c) a set of axioms connecting the resulting class and its target entity classes through perspective properties; following [3], we made these axioms depend on the cardinalities specified for the perspectives in the site model:

       (i) for the cardinality of 0..* (optional perspective) no axiom is added, only domain and range restrictions are specified for the particular property:

       $$\top \sqsubseteq \forall\, [SOURCE\_FOR]\, Person\_IsAbleToUnderstand\_Notion.$$
       $$Person\_IsAbleToUnderstand\_Notion$$
       $$\top \sqsubseteq \forall\, [SOURCE\_FOR]\, Person\_IsAbleToUnderstand\_Notion.Person$$

       (ii) for the cardinality of 1..* (mandatory perspective) existence axioms are added as equivalent classes to both the relation and the target classes:

       $$Person\_IsAbleToExplain\_Notion \equiv$$
       $$[SOURCE\_FOR]\, Person\_IsAbleToExplain\_Notion.Person$$
       $$Person \equiv [INV]\, [SOURCE\_FOR]\, Person\_IsAbleToExplain\_Notion.$$
       $$Person\_IsAbleToExplain\_Notion$$

       (iii) for quantity-based cardinalities (0..n, n, n..m, and n..*) cardinality axioms are added; e.g. if every issue must have at least 2 versions the axiom defining the relation class will be as follows: *IssueVersion_IsAVersionOf_Issue ≡ ⩾2 [SOURCE_FOR]IssueVersion_IsAVersionOf_Issue. IssueVersion*

4. Attributes are transformed into data properties and the corresponding axioms connecting these properties to the possessing classes.

On the technical level, as ADOxx-based modeling tools serialize models using XML-based ADOXML format, these transformation rules are applied to the units of data obtained from ADOXML stream. According to ADOXML specification, these units uniformly represent instances of the modeling elements defined on diagrams. The matching conditions are based on the values of attributes of these instance units.

The tool can be extended with plugins encapsulating new type-level rules (additional types defined as new values for the type meta-attribute).

5 Related Work

In this section, we discuss several categories of the related work: (1) addressing the complete set of goals for QuASE, (2) addressing particular goals of QuASE, (3) addressing collecting knowledge about communication environment and communicated information and obtaining the data from project repositories for analytical purposes.

The approaches addressing the complete set of QuASE goals belong to the category of solutions that facilitate reusing, adapting, and analyzing the development knowledge. In particular they apply the existing body of research on knowledge management to the field of software engineering [2, 4]. A more specific category of solutions is related to managing past software engineering experience; they are known as experience management solutions [21]. With respect to our aims, such solutions bear the following shortcomings: (1) they do not specifically address quality-related issues, it is true especially for those issues that are available from existing repositories; (2) they collect the experience only as viewed from the developer side; the business stakeholder's view is mostly ignored, understandability management is not supported.

Current research *addressing understandability of the information in the software process* mainly deals with this quality characteristic defined for the following software process artifacts (we group these artifacts by the stage of the development process): (1) *requirement engineering-related artifacts*: in particular, understandability of the requirement specifications is addressed in [14], whereas [1] deals with understandability of the use case models; (2) *design-related artifacts*: in particular, the set of metrics for measuring understandability of the conceptual models is defined in [18], understandability of entity-relationships diagrams is introduced in [6], and the set of factors influencing understandability of the business process models is outlined in [20]; (3) *implementation-related artifacts*: in particular, the set of metrics for source code understandability is defined in [10, 16];

The differences between our approach and the above techniques are as follows: (1) most state-of-the-art techniques address understandability of the particular categories of development-related artifacts (such as requirements, source code, or conceptual models); our research, to the contrary, addresses understandability of the generic fragments of communicated information which could be contained in documents belonging to different categories; in this paper, these documents are exemplified by issues; (2) these techniques, as a rule, do not specifically address understandability of quality-related information; (3) they do not employ ontology-based approach for establishing common understanding between parties in the software process.

The approaches to obtaining information from project repositories for analytical purposes typically belong to the research area of mining software repositories [12]. Particular examples include automatic categorization of defects [30], building software fault prediction models based on repository data [31], and using repositories to reveal traceability links [13]. Other approaches use repository information to analyze the applicability of specific development practices [5].

Repository mining solutions use software repositories as sources of quantitative code- and coding process-related information (such as the frequency of bugs, the time spent on various tasks, information about commits into repositories etc.). In contrast to that, QuASE uses repositories as sources for communicated information by looking into issue descriptions, negotiation opinions, wikis, and requirements documents. In addition to the difference in the general goals, our approach differs from these solutions as it is based on an established set of conceptual structures that represent communication environment and communicated knowledge.

6   Conclusions and Future Work

In this paper, we outlined a solution that is intended to support understandability and reusability of quality-related information, and thus may help to improve the quality of decisions in the software development process. The QuASE provides a knowledge-oriented interface to information that is communicated and collected in the course of software development projects. For this purpose, we introduced a set of knowledge structures representing both communication environment and the communicated information and described how they are incorporated into QuASE site ontology and QuOntology to form QuASE KB. We also defined the architecture of the QuASE system and introduced the techniques for creating QuASE site ontology by the knowledge suppliers.

Ongoing research within the framework of the QuASE project in the short term aims at implementing understandability and analysis scenarios in a QuASE tool based on the defined conceptual structures. It has to be achieved through implementing and testing the QuASE solution on top of establishing site models for all partner companies, generating QuASE site ontology instances based on these models, and collecting project data corresponding to the established site models.

We also aim at the following long-term research goals:

1. Establishing *QuASE process support* by elaborating the means of integration of the QuASE-specific activities into different software development process models (by implementing the scenarios implementing "QuASE for agile" etc.)
2. Generalizing QuASE as a means of implementing generic understandability management and issue-based analysis support:
   (a) through handling different representation formats (not only plain text): in particular to manage understandability of conceptual schemas or other artifacts;
   (b) by establishing generic process support to be specialized for different processes not limited to software development; the case study for this generalization can

be integrating QuASE capabilities into the HBMS framework [17, 19] for managing understandability in the Ambient Assisted Living domain.

References

1. Anda, B., Sjøberg, D., Jørgensen, M.: Quality and understandability of use case models. In: Lindskov Knudsen, J. (ed.) ECOOP 2001. LNCS, vol. 2072, pp. 402–428. Springer, Heidelberg (2001)
2. Aurum, A., Jeffery, R., Wohlin, C., Handzic, M. (eds.): Managing Software Engineering Knowledge. Springer, Heidelberg (2003)
3. Barcelos, P.P.F., dos Santos, V.A., Silva, F.B., Monteiro, M.E., Garcia, A.S.: An automated transformation from OntoUML to OWL and SWRL. In: ONTOBRAS 2013. CEUR Workshop Proceedings, vol. 1041, pp. 130–141. CEUR-WS.org (2013)
4. Bjørnson, F.O., Dingsøyr, T.: Knowledge management in software engineering: a systematic review of studied concepts, findings and research methods used. Inf. Softw. Technol. **50**, 1055–1068 (2008)
5. Ernst, N.A., Murphy, G.C.: Case studies in just-in-time requirements analysis. In: 2012 IEEE Second International Workshop on Empirical Requirements Engineering (EmpiRE), pp. 25–32. IEEE (2012)
6. Genero, M., Poels, G., Piattini, M.: Defining and validating metrics for assessing the understandability of entity–relationship diagrams. Data Knowl. Eng. **64**, 534–557 (2008)
7. Guizzardi, G.: Ontological foundations for structural conceptual models. Twente (2005)
8. Guizzardi, G., Falbo, R., Guizzardi, R.S.: Grounding software domain ontologies in the unified foundational ontology (UFO): the case of the ODE software process ontology. In: RESE 2008, pp. 244–251 (2008)
9. ISO: ISO/IEC 12207:2008, Information technology – software life cycle processes. International Organization for Standardization, Geneva (2008)
10. Jin-Cherng, L., Kuo-Chiang, W.: A model for measuring software understandability. In: Proceedings of CIT 2006, pp. 192–192 (2006)
11. JIRA Issue Tracking System. http://www.atlassian.com/software/jira. Accessed 8 May 2014
12. Kagdi, H., Collard, M.L., Maletic, J.I.: A survey and taxonomy of approaches for mining software repositories in the context of software evolution. J. Softw. Maint. Evol. Res. Pract. **19**, 77–131 (2007)
13. Kagdi, H., Maletic, J.I., Sharif, B.: Mining software repositories for traceability links. In: ICPC 2007. pp. 145–154. IEEE (2007)
14. Kamsties, E., von Knethen, A., Reussner, R.: A controlled experiment to evaluate how styles affect the understandability of requirements specifications. Inf. Softw. Technol. **45**, 955–965 (2003)
15. Kontchakov, R., Rodríguez-Muro, M., Zakharyaschev, M.: Ontology-based data access with databases: a short course. In: Rudolph, S., Gottlob, G., Horrocks, I., van Harmelen, F. (eds.) Reasoning Weg 2013. LNCS, vol. 8067, pp. 194–229. Springer, Heidelberg (2013)
16. Lin, J.-C., Wu, K.-C.: Evaluation of software understandability based on fuzzy matrix. In: Fuzzy Systems, (IEEE World Congress on Computational Intelligence), IEEE International Conference on FUZZ-IEEE 2008, pp. 887–892. IEEE (2008)
17. Machot, F.A., Mayr, H.C., Michael, J.: Behavior modeling and reasoning for ambient support: HCM-L modeler. In: Ali, M., Pan, J.-S., Chen, S.-M., Horng, M.-F. (eds.) IEA/AIE 2014, Part II. LNCS, vol. 8482, pp. 388–397. Springer, Heidelberg (2014)

18. Mehmood, K., Cherfi, S.S.: Data quality through model quality: a quality model for measuring and improving the understandability of conceptual models. In: MDSEDQS 2009, pp. 29–32. ACM (2009)

19. Michael, J., Mayr, H.C.: Conceptual modeling for ambient assistance. In: Ng, W., Storey, V.C., Trujillo, J.C. (eds.) ER 2013. LNCS, vol. 8217, pp. 403–413. Springer, Heidelberg (2013)

20. Reijers, H.A., Mendling, J.: A study into the factors that influence the understandability of business process models. IEEE Trans. Syst. Man Cybern. A Syst. Hum. **41**, 449–462 (2011)

21. Schneider, K.: Experience and Knowledge Management in Software Engineering. Springer, Heidelberg (2009)

22. Shekhovtsov, V., Mayr, H.C., Kop, C.: Harmonizing the quality view of stakeholders. In: Mistrik, I., Bahsoon, R., Eeles, R., Roshandel, R., Stal, M. (eds.) Relating System Quality and Software Architecture, pp. 41–73. Morgan-Kaufmann, Waltham (2014)

23. Shekhovtsov, V.A., Mayr, H.C.: Let stakeholders define quality: a model-based approach. In: Linssen, O., Kuhrmann, M. (eds.) Qualitätsmanagement und Vorgehensmodelle - 19. Workshop der GI-Fachgruppe Vorgehensmodelle, pp. 101–110. Shaker Verlag GmbH (2012)

24. Shekhovtsov, V.A., Mayr, H.C.: Managing quality related information in software development processes. In: CAiSE-Forum-DC 2014. CEUR Workshop Proceedings, vol. 1164, pp. 73–80. CEUR-WS.org (2014)

25. Shekhovtsov, V.A., Mayr, H.C.: Towards managing understandability of quality-related information in software development processes. In: Murgante, B., Misra, S., Rocha, A.M.A., Torre, C., Rocha, J.G., Falcão, M.I., Taniar, D., Apduhan, B.O., Gervasi, O. (eds.) ICCSA 2014, Part V. LNCS, vol. 8583, pp. 572–585. Springer, Heidelberg (2014)

26. Shekhovtsov, V.A., Mayr, H.C., Kop, C.: Acquiring empirical knowledge to support intelligent analysis of quality-related issues in software development. In: Faria, J.P., Silva, A., Machado, R.J. (eds.) QUATIC 2012, pp. 153–156. IEEE Press (2012)

27. Shekhovtsov, V.A., Mayr, H.C., Kop, C.: Stakeholder involvement into quality definition and evaluation for service-oriented systems. In: USER 2012 Workshop at ICSE 2012, pp. 49–52. IEEE (2012)

28. Shekhovtsov, V.A., Mayr, H.C., Kop, C.: Towards conceptualizing quality-related stakeholder interactions in software development. In: Kop, C. (ed.) UNISON 2012. LNBIP, vol. 137, pp. 73–86. Springer, Heidelberg (2013)

29. Shekhovtsov, V.A., Mayr, H.C., Lubenskyi, V.: QuASE: A tool supported approach to facilitating quality-related communication in software development. In: da Silva, A.R., Silva, A.R., Brito, M.A., Machado, R.J. (eds.) QUATIC 2014, pp. 162–165. IEEE (2014)

30. Thung, F., Lo, D., Jiang, L.: Automatic defect categorization. In: WCRE 2012, pp. 205–214. IEEE (2012)

31. Vandecruys, O., Martens, D., Baesens, B., Mues, C., De Backer, M., Haesen, R.: Mining software repositories for comprehensible software fault prediction models. J. Syst. Softw. **81**, 823–839 (2008)

Towards Path-Based Semantic Annotation for Web Service Discovery

Julius Köpke[✉], Johann Eder, and Dominik Joham

Department of Informatics-Systems, Alpen-Adria-Universität Klagenfurt,
Klagenfurt, Austria
{julius.koepke,johann.eder}@aau.at, dominik.joham@gmail.com
http://www.aau.at/isys

Abstract. Annotation paths are a new method for semantic annotation, which overcomes the limited expressiveness of concept references as defined in the SAWSDL standard. We introduce annotation paths and show how annotation paths can be applied for service matching capturing the semantics of XML schemas and web service descriptions more precisely. We report some experimental evaluation of the feasibility of annotation paths for web service discovery. The experiments suggest that annotation paths appears as a promising approach for improving web service discovery.

Keywords: Web service matching · Service discovery · Semantic annotation · SAWSDL · Annotation paths · XML schema matching · Semantic matching

1 Introduction

Web service discovery aims at (semi-)automating the search for suitable web services [14]. A web service discovery systems accepts a service request (a specification of the needed web service) and a set of web service descriptions (advertisements) as input and returns a list of web service descriptions ranked by relevance for the request. There are many different approaches ranging from the structural or lexical comparison of requests and advertisements to approaches based on the explicit definition of the semantics using ontologies [14]. We specifically address the usage of external knowledge provided by semantic annotations with a reference ontology using SAWSDL [7] annotations. The W3C recommendation SWASDL (Semantic Annotations for WSDL and XML Schema) specifies a lightweight approach for the annotation of web services with arbitrary semantic models (e.g. ontologies). SAWSDL introduces additional attributes for XML Schema and WSDL documents: *ModelReferences* and *Lifting-* and *Lowering-Mappings*. *ModelReferences* refer to ontology concepts and *Lifting-* and *Lowering-Mappings* refer to arbitrary scripts that transform the inputs and output XML-data to and from instances of some semantic model (ontology). *ModelReferences* are proposed for service discovery, while *Lifting-* and *Lowering-Mappings* are proposed

S. Nurcan and E. Pimenidis (Eds.): CAiSE Forum 2014, LNBIP 204, pp. 133–147, 2015.
DOI: 10.1007/978-3-319-19270-3_9

for service invocation and only apply to the annotation of inputs and outputs formulated as XML Schemas.

Our previous work focused on the annotation of XML Schemas with reference ontologies in order to automate the generation of executable schema mappings for document transformations [8–11,15]. We could show that the expressiveness of the SAWSDL *ModelReferences* annotation is not sufficient for the generation of schema mappings when as usual in interoperability scenarios general reference ontologies are directly used for the annotation. *Lifting-* and *Lowering-Mappings*, on the other hand, suffer from their procedural rather than declarative semantics. Therefore, we have proposed an extended annotation method based on annotation paths rather than single concept annotations. Since this method already showed its usefulness for XML-document transformations [8] we expect that annotation paths can also improve web service discovery. The general hypothesis for this research is that if the annotation method allows a more precise definition of the semantics, then the precision of service matching for service discovery can be improved. More concretely we state as hypothesis that the annotation path method leads to better results in service discovery.Existing approaches for SAWSDL based service discovery such as [4,6] can partly solve the problem of non precise semantic annotations by using additional dimensions such as structure or textual similarity.

To give a first answer on this hypothesis we discusses the usage of annotation paths for web service discovery and report some experimental results. This paper is an extended version of our previous work [12].

2   Annotation Path Method

The SAWSDL [7] standard addresses semantic annotations for both web service descriptions and for XML Schemas. They are related since WSDL descriptions use XML Schema to define the inputs and outputs of operations. Therefore, whenever we refer to an XML Schema, schema annotation or schema matching, this also applies for annotated WSDL documents and requests.

2.1   Example and Motivation

In order to motivate the need for a more expressive annotation method we will first discuss some examples. The XML Schema document shown in Fig. 2 is annotated using simple concept references referring to the ontology shown in Fig. 1 using the *sawsdl* : *ModelReference* attribute.

The annotated document in Fig. 1 exhibits the following problems:

- The elements *BuyerZipcode* and *BuyerStreet* cannot be annotated because the *zip-code* is modeled in form of a data-type property and not by a concept in the ontology.
- The *BuyerCountry* element is annotated with the concept *country*. This does not fully express the semantics because we do not know that the element should contain the country of the buying-party. In addition, the *SellerCountry* element has exactly the same annotation and can therefore not be distinguished.

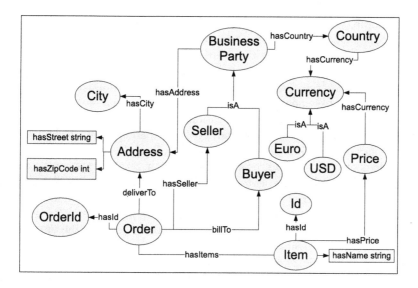

Fig. 1. Example reference ontology [9]

```
<xs:schema xmlns:xs="http://www.w3.org/2001/XMLSchema" xmlns:sawsdl="http://www.w3.org/
  <xs:element name="order" sawsdl:modelReference="/order">
    <xs:complexType>
      <xs:sequence>
        <xs:element name="BuyerZipcode"/>
        <xs:element name="BuyerStreet"/>
        <xs:element name="BuyerCity" sawsdl:modelReference="City"/>
        <xs:element name="BuyerCountry" sawsdl:modelReference="Country"/>
        <xs:element name="SellerCountry" sawsdl:modelReference="Country"/>
        <xs:element name="Item" maxOccurs="unbounded" sawsdl:modelReference="Item">
          <xs:complexType>
            <xs:attribute name="ID" use="required" sawsdl:modelReference="Id"/>
            <xs:attribute name="Name" use="required"/>
            <xs:attribute name="Price" use="required" sawsdl:modelReference="Price"/>
          </xs:complexType>
        </xs:element>
      </xs:sequence>
    </xs:complexType>
  </xs:element>
</xs:schema>
```

Fig. 2. Sample XML Schema with model-references [9]

– The attribute *Price* is annotated with the concept *Price*. Unfortunately, this does not capture the semantics. We do not know the subject of the price (an item) and we do not know the currency.

In the example, we have always used exactly one concept for the annotation. However, SAWSDL supports lists of concepts in the *modelReference* attribute but it does not allow specifying the relations between the concepts in this list. Therefore, this does not help to solve the shown problems. In the examples above, we have only annotated data-carrying elements. If we would in addition also annotate the parent elements in this case the *order* element we could add a bit more semantic information as the annotations of the child-elements of the order-element can be seen in the context of an order. Such an approach has limitations and drawbacks, e.g. the ambiguities between the *BuyerCountry*- and the *Seller-Country* element could not be resolved. In addition, such an approach requires a strong structural similarity between the ontology and the annotated XML Schema or service description, which we cannot assume when many different schemas or services are annotated with a single reference ontology. In addition, SAWSDL does not define that there are any relations between the annotations of parent and child elements. A solution for these non-precise annotations is the usage of a more specific reference ontology, which contains concepts that fully match the semantics of each annotated element. For example, it would need to contain the concept *InvoiceBuyerCountry* and *InvoiceBuyerZipCode*. However, enhancing a general reference ontology with all possible combinations of concepts leads to a combinatorial explosion.

2.2 Examples for Annotation Paths

Our annotation method [9] that solves the discussed problems is based on so-called annotation paths. An annotation paths consists of a sequence of steps, where one step can refer to a concept, an object-property or a data-type property of the reference ontology. Steps referring to concepts may have additional constraints, which are denoted in square brackets. Each such annotation path expression can automatically be transformed to an OWL concept. Therefore, matchers can exploit the more precise OWL concepts for matching. The example schema document in Fig. 3 is annotated with the proposed path expressions. We will discuss some examples and introduce the annotation paths formally in Sect. 2.3. The element *BuyerZipcode* is annotated with */ **Order**/deliverTo/ **Address**/ hasZipCode*. The annotation of the *BuyerCountry* element is */ **Order**/billTo/ **Buyer**/has Country/ **Country***. The steps that are marked bold refer to concepts. The other steps refer to object-properties or datatype-properties of the reference ontology. Now the *BuyerCountry* element can clearly be distinguished from the *SellerCountry* element and the elements *BuyerZipcode* and *BuyerStreet* can be annotated. The shown paths refer to concepts, object properties and datatype properties. Another requirement is to address instances of the ontology. For example, the path */ **Order**/billTo/ **Buyer** [Mr_Smith]/hasCountry/ **Country*** defines that the Buyer is restricted to one specific buyer with the URI *Mr_Smith*.

   In most cases, we assume that a simple annotation path as shown in the examples above is sufficient for an annotation. Nevertheless, there can be cases where additional restrictions are required: When using a simple path expressions as shown above the *Price* attribute of the example schema can be annotated

```
<xs:schema xmlns:xs="http://www.w3.org/2001/XMLSchema" xmlns:sawsdl="http://www.w3.org/ns/sawsdl" elementFormDefault="qualified" attrl
  <xs:element name="order" sawsdl:modelReference="/Order">
    <xs:complexType>
      <xs:sequence>
        <xs:element name="BuyerZipcode" sawsdl:modelReference="/Order/deliverTo/Address/hasZipCode"/>
        <xs:element name="BuyerStreet" sawsdl:modelReference="/Order/deliverTo/Address/hasStreet"/>
        <xs:element name="BuyerCity" sawsdl:modelReference="/Order/deliverTo/Address/hasCity/City"/>
        <xs:element name="BuyerCountry" sawsdl:modelReference="/Order/billTo/Buyer/hasCountry/Country"/>
        <xs:element name="SellerCountry" sawsdl:modelReference="/Order/hasSeller/Seller/hasCountry/Country"/>
        <xs:element name="Item" maxOccurs="unbounded" sawsdl:modelReference="/order/hasItems/Item">
          <xs:complexType>
            <xs:attribute name="ID" use="required" sawsdl:modelReference="/Order/hasItems/Item/hasId/Id"/>
            <xs:attribute name="Name" use="required" sawsdl:modelReference="/Order/hasItems/Item/hasName"/>
            <xs:attribute name="Price" use="required" sawsdl:modelReference="/Order/hasItems/Item/hasPrice/Price[hasCurrency/Euro]"/>
          </xs:complexType>
        </xs:element>
      </xs:sequence>
    </xs:complexType>
  </xs:element>
</xs:schema>
```

Fig. 3. Sample XML Schema document with annotation-path method [9]

with /*Order*/hasitems/*Item*/hasPrice/*Price*. Unfortunately, this does not express the currency of the price. Since the ontology in the example has no specialized price-concept for each currency, we need to define the currency within the annotation. The correct currency of a price can be defined by a restriction on the price concept. This restriction is denoted in square brackets and expresses that the price must have a *hasCurrency* property that points to the concept *Euro*. This leads to the full annotation of the *Price* attribute: /*Order*/hasitems/*Item*/hasPrice/ *Price*[hasCurrency/*Euro*].

2.3   Formal Definition

In order to define the annotation path method we will first define the structure of the reference ontology.

Definition 1. *Ontology:* An ontology O is a tuple $O = (C, DP, OP, I, A)$, where C is a set of concepts, DP is a set of datatype-properties, OP a set of object-properties, I a set of individuals and A a set of axioms over C, DP, OP, and I. Each element in C, DP, OP, and I is a string that represents the URI of the specific element. The sets C, DP, I, and OP are disjoint.

We have already shown the string representation of annotation paths in the examples. The string representation is just a sequence of steps delimited by a slash, where each step refers to a concept or property from the reference ontology. In general, an annotation path is defined as:

Definition 2. *Annotation Path:* An annotation path p of length n is valid for some specific ontology O. It is a tuple $p = (S, t, c)$, where $p.S$ is a sequence of n steps: $p.S = \{s_1, \ldots, s_n\}$, $p.t$ represents the type of the annotation path and $p.c$ refers to the representation of p in form of an ontology concept (see Sect. 2.4).

Each step $s \in p.S$ is a tuple of the form $(uri, type, res)$, where $s.uri$ is an URI defined in the reference ontology: $s.uri \in O.C \bigcup O.OP \bigcup O.DP$. The type of the step $s.type$ can be cs (concept-step), op (object-property) step or dp (datatype-property-step). It is defined by the type of the referenced element in O:

$s.uri \in O.C \Rightarrow s.type = cs$;
$s.uri \in O.OP \Rightarrow s.type = op$;
$s.uri \in O.DP \Rightarrow s.type = dp$.

Concept-steps $(s.type = cs)$ can have an optional set of restrictions $s.res$. A restriction $r \in s.res$ can restrict the concept to a specific individual $(r \in O.I)$ or it can restrict the concept with an annotation path. Such a path must not contain concept-steps with restrictions in form of annotation paths itself. The first step of such a restricting path is always the restricted concept $s.uri$ (This is omitted in the string representation of the examples). If $s.res$ contains multiple restrictions they all apply to the corresponding step s (logical and). The type $p.t$ of an annotation path can be either $ConceptAnnotation$, or $DataTypeProperyAnnotation$. It is defined by the last step of $p.S$:

$p.S_n.type = cs \Rightarrow p.t = ConceptAnnotation$
$p.S_n.type = dp \Rightarrow p.t = DataTypeProperyAnnotation$

Definition 3. *An annotation path p of length n is structurally valid iff:*

- $p.S_1.type = cs$ - The first step must refer to a concept.
- $p.S_n.type \in \{dp, cs\}$ - The last step must refer to a concept or a datatype-property.
- $\forall i \in \{1..n-1\} : p.S_i.type = cs \Rightarrow p.S_{i+1}.type \in \{dp, op\}$ - The successor of a concept-step must be an object-property or datatype-property-step.
- $\forall i \in \{1..n-1\} : p.S_i.type = op \Rightarrow p.S_{i+1}.type = cs$ - An object-property step must be followed by a concept-step.
- $\forall i \in \{2..n\} : p.S_i.type = op \Rightarrow p.S_{i-1}.type = cs$ - The previous step of an object-property step must be a concept-step.
- $\forall i \in \{1..n-1\} : p.S_i.type = dp \Rightarrow p.S_i = p.S_n$ - Only the last step can refer to a datatype-property.

2.4   Representing Annotation Paths as Ontology Concepts

We specify the semantics of annotation paths by representing them in form of ontology concepts that we call annotation concepts. This allows concept-level reasoning over the annotations and can consequently be used to match the annotated elements of different schemas/SAWSDL documents. Given a sequence of steps of an annotation path $p.S$, p, we show, how the corresponding annotation concept $p.c$ can be represented in OWL. The URI of the annotation concept is equivalent to the string representation of the sequence of steps $p.S$. Therefore, it can directly be used as a SAWSDL *Model Reference*. We illustrate the representation of annotation paths with one example of a concept annotation.

```
1  Class:  Order/billTo/Buyer[Mr_Smith]/hasCountry/Country
2  EquivalentClasses(
3       ConceptAnnotation  and  Country  and  inv
4       (hasCountry)  some
5            (Buyer  and  {Mr_Smith}  and  inv  (billTo)  some  (Order)
6       )
7  )
```

Listing 1. Representation of a concept annotation path in OWL [9]

In listing 1 the OWL representation of the path */Order/billTo/Buyer [Mr_Smith]/hasCountry/Country* is shown. The annotation path has the type *ConceptAnnotation* because the last step refers to a concept. It defines a specialization of a *country* concept. In particular a *country*, that has an inverse *hasCountry* object-property to a *Buyer*. This buyer must be an individual of the enumerated class *{Mr_Smith}* and must have an inverse *billTo* relation to an *Order*.

Obviously, such a translation can be achieved fully automatically by iterating over the steps of the path. It is required to semantically separate annotations of the type *ConceptAnnotation* from those of the type *DataTypeProperyAnnotation*. This is achieved by defining each annotation concept as a subconcept of the corresponding type.

In general, annotation concepts are constructed using qualified existential restrictions on the inverse of the connecting properties. In contrast, annotation paths that occur in restrictions on concepts are created in the opposite direction without using the inverse of the connecting properties. Qualified existential restrictions are a standard feature of OWL/OWL2 [1] and are consequently supported by current OWL reasoners.

3   Service Matching Based on Annotation-Paths

After introducing the annotation method, we can discuss how the annotation paths can be used for service matching. We first provide some preliminaries and then present our service-matching prototype.

3.1   Preliminaries

XML Schema allows reusing types and elements. This has also influence on the matching of annotated schemas. We base the matching on Expanded Schemas.

Definition 4. *Expanded Schema:* An Expanded Schema *ES* of an annotated XML Schema *S* is an annotated schema, where all references and type definitions of *S* have been expanded with their definitions (targets of the references or types) and the annotations are rewritten if elements and referenced types are annotated. The result is a set of nodes that form a tree structure. Since an XML Schema can potentially have multiple root nodes there are possibly multiple Expanded Schemas for one XML Schema.

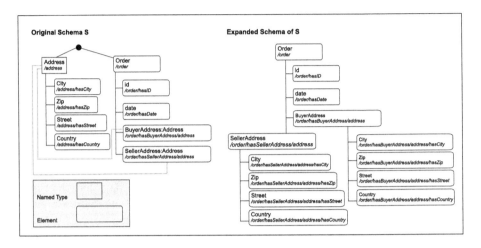

Fig. 4. Example of annotated XML Schema and corresponding Expanded Schema

For recursive definitions of elements and types in XML Schema the Expanded Schema would be infinite. In the current prototype we, therefore, do not support recursive definitions.

In Fig. 4, an example of an original XML Schema (left side) and its corresponding Expanded Schema is shown. The original schema has one globally defined type *address* that is referenced by the two elements *SellerAddress* and *BuyerAddress*. This requires the rewriting of the annotation paths for *address*, *SellerAddress* and *BuyerAddress*. In general, if the annotated XML Schema reuses types or elements (via type or ref properties) and both the element and the referenced element or type are annotated then the annotation needs to be constructed from the annotation path of the element and the annotation path of the referenced element. Due to the hierarchical structure of XML, this needs to be applied recursively.

Let *e* be an element with the annotation *e.annotation* and the XML-Type *e.type*. Let *s* be an annotated sub-element of the XML-Type *e.type*, then the complete annotation of *s* is defined as the path resulting from replacing the last step of *e.annotation* with *s.annotation*.

In the example, the *country* element of the *sellerAddress* is annotated with */order/hasSellerAddress/address/hasCountry*. This is constructed from the annotation */address/hasCountry* of the *country* element that is a child of the *SellerAddress* element and the annotation */order/hasSellerAddress/address* of the *SellerAddress* element. This path combination adds structural dependencies between the schema and the reference ontology. Therefore, XML-Types should only be reused for semantically related entities, which is in accordance with good modeling practice.

In order to match the SAWSDL advertisements and requests the annotations of the corresponding Expanded Schema are added to the reference ontology. We call the resulting ontology the extended reference ontology:

Definition 5. *Extended Reference Ontology:* Given two Expanded Schemas S and T and the corresponding reference ontology O. The extended reference ontology O' is defined as $O \cup S.A \cup T.A$, where $S.A$ is the set of all annotation concepts of annotations from S and $T.A$ is the set of all annotation concepts from T. The annotation concepts are created based on the annotation path expressions as shown in Sect. 2.4. In order to separate source and target annotations different prefixes are used for the URIs of S.A and T.A.

The extended reference ontology must not contain logically invalid annotation concepts (see [11]). Therefore, as a precondition for matching all annotation concepts must be satisfiable.

3.2   Path-Based Service Matching Prototype

We have implemented a logics based service matcher [2] to apply the annotation path method to web service discovery. The matcher operates only on path-based annotations of the inputs and outputs of operations. No other dimensions of the service descriptions are used for matching. We assume that matching services/requests have semantically matching input and output parameters. We do not address the annotation of operations themselves. In order to rank the suitability of different web services for a request we automatically generate one XML Schema for the inputs and one XML Schema for the outputs of each operation of the advertisements and the request. These schemas are then matched and an overall confidence value for the service match in the interval $[0..1]$ is computed. The ranking is then based on the confidence values. The matching process of the schemas operates in 4 phases:

- *Annotation Path Extraction:* The input and output schemas of each operation are transformed to an Expanded Schema where no types are reused using the COMA3 [13] library. The annotation paths are rewritten as described in Sect. 3.1.
- *Extended Ontology Generation:* The annotations are extracted from the expanded source and expanded target schema and are transformed to OWL concepts and the extended reference ontology O' is created.
- *Matching and Mapping:* The XML Schemas of the request and of each advertisement are matched based on the annotations using a standard OWL reasoner (pellet). The matching function is shown is Fig. 5. Two schema elements s from the source schema and t from the target schema match if the annotation concept (the corresponding annotation path represented as an OWL concept) of s is equivalent to the annotation concept of t or if there is a subclass or superclass relation between s and t. In case of equivalence, the confidence value of the match is defined by α. In case of the subclass match the confidence value of the match is defined by β weighted by the distance between the annotation concept of s and t in the extended reference ontology. Superclass to subclass matches are defined by γ also weighted by the distance in the ontology. For our experiments, we used the following values

$$sm(s, t, O') = \begin{cases} \alpha & \text{if } semEqual(s.a, t.a, O') \\ \beta * / \frac{1}{ConceptDistance(s.a, t.a, O')} & \text{else if } isSubConcept(s.a, t.a, O') \\ \gamma * / \frac{1}{ConceptDistance(s.a, t.a, O')} & \text{else if } isSubConcept(t.a, s.a, O') \\ 0 & \text{else} \end{cases}$$

Fig. 5. Semantic matching function [8].

for the parameters: $\alpha = 1$, $\beta = 0.8$, $\gamma = 0.6$. After the confidence values are computed for each combination of elements of the source and target schema, a schema mapping is created based on the best matching elements.

– *Ranking:* Finally, an overall confidence value of each schema mapping is computed by aggregating the confidence values of the mapping elements using either min, max or avg. strategies and the advertisements are ordered descending by the overall confidence values.

4   Evaluation

The goal of the evaluation is to check the feasibility of the hypothesis that the annotation path method leads to better results in service discovery. Therefore, we have evaluated [2] our simple service matcher that exploits only path based semantic annotations against existing SAWSDL-based service matchers. We expect that if this simple service matcher can compete with state of the art service matchers that exploit far more aspects of a service and use advanced techniques like machine learning, then the application of annotation paths can improve service discovery.

We have annotated a subset of the SAWSDL-TC3[1] data set with our annotation path method and have evaluated our matcher against service matchers that took part in the *International Semantic Service Selection Contests*[2]. We have evaluated two scenarios. We will first discuss both scenarios and the results of our matcher in Sects. 4.1 and 4.2 and then discuss the results in comparison to state of the art matchers in Sect. 4.3.

4.1   Scenario 1

The goal of this scenario was to evaluate how, our simple matcher can compete against current state of the art matchers based on existing requests and advertisements of the SAWSDL-TC-3 data set. Since our approach requires different annotations, we have annotated a subset of the SAWSDL-TC3 data set with our annotation method and have evaluated our matcher using our matching method against other matchers using the original SAWSDL annotations.

---

[1] http://projects.semwebcentral.org/projects/sawsdl-tc/.
[2] http://www-ags.dfki.uni-sb.de/%7Eklusch/s3/index.html.

```
<xsd:complexType name="BookType" sawsdl:modelReference="/Book">
  <xsd:sequence>
    <xsd:element name="isTitled" type="Title" sawsdl:modelReference="/Book/isTitled/Title"/>
    <xsd:element name="hasType" type="Book-Type" sawsdl:modelReference="/Book/hasType/Book-Type"/>
    <xsd:element name="writtenBy" type="Author" sawsdl:modelReference="/Book/writtenBy/Author"/>
    <xsd:element name="publishedBy" type="Publisher" sawsdl:modelReference="/Book/publishedBy/Publisher
      "/>
    <xsd:element name="datePublished" type="Date" sawsdl:modelReference="/Book/datePublished/Date"/>
    <xsd:element name="timePublished" type="Once" sawsdl:modelReference="/Book/timePublished/Once"/>
  </xsd:sequence>
</xsd:complexType>
```

Fig. 6. Annotated Booktype fragment of the request of Scenario 1

Request: We have selected the *book_price_service* request from the *SAWSDL-TC3* data set. It describes one operation in its interface. This operation has an input *BookType* and an output *PriceType*. The *BookType* consists of several elements that describe a title, a book type, an author, a publisher and a publishing date. The resulting output *PriceType* consists of an amount and a currency. The book type annotated with our annotation path method as a fragment of the *book_price_service* is shown in Fig. 6.

Advertisements and Ranking: We have annotated a subset of the *SAWSDL-TC3* service advertisements with our annotation paths method. The *SAWSDL-TC3* contains relevance grades for each advertisement and each request. The relevance grades are 0 (not relevant), 1 (partially relevant), 2 (relevant) and 3 (highly relevant). We have annotated 5 random advertisements of each relevance grade. The selected advertisements, their defined relevance grades and the ranking computed by our simple matcher (SAPM-WS) are shown in Table 1. The 3 best ranked services of our approach also have the highest relevance grade of 3. The other two services with a relevance grade of 3 are the *monograph_price_service* - rank 6 in our result and the *printedmaterial_price_service* (rank 7). The advertisement *bookpersoncreditcardaccount_price_service* has been ranked to position 4 with a confidence value of 0.9412, while it has an expert rating of 2. The reason for this is that the input of the advertisement consists of a *book*, a *person* and a *creditcardaccount* type. While the *book* type consists of several other subtypes, *person* and *creditcardaccount* are single types and have not as much weight as the book type with its 6 sub elements in our basic aggregation function. Finally, the advertisement *sciencefictionbookuser_price_service*, ranked to rank 14 has a confidence value of 0.5000 with a predefined rating of 2. This low rating results from the *ScienceFictionBook* concept, which is only a sub concept of the *Book* concept. Furthermore, there is additionally a *User* concept in the input of the advertisement, which cannot be found in the request. Overall, we suppose that our simple matcher that operates only on annotation paths with a very simple aggregation method and static parameters already achieves good results. Tuning and more sophisticated aggregation and weighting methods will help achieve even better results.

Table 1. Scenario 1: SAPM-WS

Rank	CV	Advertisement	Relevance grade
1	1.0000	book_authorprice_Novelservice	3
2	1.0000	book_reviewprice_service	3
3	1.0000	book_taxedpriceprice_service	3
4	0.9412	bookpersoncreditcardaccount_price_service	2
5	0.9000	sciencefictionbook_authorprice_service	2
6	0.8000	monograph_price_service	3
7	0.6667	printedmaterial_price_service	3
8	0.6500	novel_authorrecommendedprice_service	1
9	0.5833	printedmaterialpersoncreditcardaccount_price_service	2
10	0.5500	author_monographmaxprice_service	1
11	0.5417	romanticnovel_authorprice_service	2
12	0.5000	carbicycle_price_service	0
13	0.5000	expensivecar_price_service	0
14	0.5000	sciencefictionbookuser_price_service	2
15	0.5000	userscience-fiction-novel_price_Bestservice	1
16	0.5000	book_person_Publisherservice	0
17	0.5000	coconut_price_service	0
18	0.4000	sciencefictionbook_author_service	1
19	0.3750	SFNovelReview_service	1
20	0.3333	autocycle_price_service	0

4.2 Scenario 2

The goal of the second scenario was to assess how our matcher competes against other matchers if the semantics cannot be expressed by simple concept annotations. In this case, matchers operating on simple concept annotations can only infer the missing semantics by exploiting other dimensions such as the structure or naming of elements. We have created a new request for this Scenario. We now search for the EURO prices of science fiction comics excluding VAT. The request consists of one operation with an input type *ScienceFictionComic* (annotated with the path */ScienceFictionBook*) and an output type *EuroPriceExcluding-VAT* (annotated with the path */TaxFreePrice* but including a sub element with a path *TaxFreePrice/hasCurrency/Euro*). While *ScienceFictionBook* and *EuroPriceExcludingVAT* can also be expressed with standard concept references, the annotation *TaxFreePrice/hasCurrency/Euro* requires annotation paths.

For the second experiment, we have annotated 15 advertisements of the SAWSDL TC3 data set. Since we now use a request that is not part of the SAWSDL TC3 data set, we asked an independent expert to provide the relevance

Table 2. Scenario 2: SAPM-WS

Rank	CV	Advertisement	Relevance Grade
1	1.000	sciencefictioncomic_europricetaxfree_request	3
2	0.667	author_sciencefictionbooktaxfreeprice_service_20	2
3	0.667	author_monographtaxfreeprice_service_20	1
4	0.567	book_pricereviewbook_service_20	2
5	0.567	book_price_service_20	2
6	0.567	book_Cheapestprice_service_20	2
7	0.529	bookperson_price_service_20	2
8	0.300	book_taxedprice_service_20	2
9	0.267	book_reviewprice_service_20	2
10	0.267	author_bookprice_service_20	1
11	0.167	author_sciencefictionbooktaxedprice_service_20	2
12	0.167	author_sciencefictionbookmaxprice_service_20	2
13	0.167	author_noveltaxedprice_service_20	1
14	0.000	author_sciencefictionbookrecommendedprice_service_20	2
15	0.000	author_bookrecommendedprice_service_20	1

grades of each advertisement for our new request. The selected advertisements, the ranking according to our matcher and the relevance grades assigned by an independent expert are shown in Table 2. The perfectly matching request was found and the ranking of the non-fully matching services is mostly in accordance to their relevance grades. However, there are some outliers: First *author_monographtaxfreeprice_service_20* with a rank of 3 and with a confidence value of 0.667 but only a relevance grade of 1 and second *author_sciencefiction bookrecommendedprice_service_20* with a rank of 14 but a relevance grade of 2 with a confidence value of 0.0. The low confidence value of *author_sciencefiction bookrecommendedprice_service_20* is the result of a processing failure of our matcher. The high confidence value of *author_monographtaxfreeprice _service_20* is due to a superclass match. Further improvements of our matcher especially tuning the parameters of the matching function should allow achieving even better results.

4.3   Results and Comparison

We have executed the evaluation of both scenarios with the Service Matchmaker and Execution Environment (SME2[3]), which is also used for the International Semantic Service Selection Contests. Due to the partial TC3 data set we were not able to execute all matchers. However, we could execute two major representatives iSem [4,5] and SAWSDL-MX [6]. The *iSem* matcher when applied for

---

[3] http://projects.semwebcentral.org/projects/sme2/.

Table 3. Result comparison

Matcher	NDCG Scenario 1	NDCG Senario 2
Path-based matcher	0.977	0.970
iSem hybrid	0.990	0.886
SAWSDL-MX	0.937	0.867

SAWSDL is a hybrid service matcher exploiting inputs and outputs and service names that employs strict and approximated logical matching, text-similarity-based matching and structural matching and automatically adjusts its aggregation and ranking parameters using machine learning. It reached the best binary precision in the contest of 2012. SAWSDL-MX is a typical representative of a hybrid matcher using logics and syntax-based matching. We have assessed the overall performance of each matcher based on the reached Normalized Discounted Cumulative Gain [3] (NDCG) which is also used in the International Semantic Service Selection Contests. The results of both scenarios are shown in Table 3. Our matcher performed more than 4 percent better than the *SAWSDL-MX* matcher. In comparison to the nearly perfect *iSEM iSEM* matcher we have achieved around 1 percent less precise matches. In the second scenario our matcher performed around 9 percent better than *iSem* and around 12 percent better than *SAWSDL-MX*.

While these preliminary results do not yet allow to draw final conclusions the annotation paths approach is promising for improving web service discovery. Our simple path-based matcher could clearly show its advantage in Scenario 2 and in Scenario 1 it could compete well with existing state of the art matchers which use far more advanced matching methods and additional aspects of service descriptions and advertisements.

5   Conclusions and Future Work

The annotation path method for semantic annotation was developed to overcome limitations in the expressiveness of simple concept references. We showed in some feasibility tests that already a simple implementation of an annotation path based XML Schema matcher used for comparing web service advertisements with service requests can successfully compete with state-of the art web service discovery systems. We therefore conclude that annotation paths are well suited for capturing the semantics of objects in much finer detail and that the annotation path method and matchers based on it are promising approaches to improve web service discovery. Encouraged by the promising results we plan to evaluate our annotation path based matcher with a larger data set and against additional existing matchers. Other future work is to integrate our matcher into existing state of the art matchers to gain even better results. Another direction of future work is to evaluate not only the matching precision but also the minimum amount of manual work to semi-automatically create annotation path annotations in comparison to simple concept references.

References

1. Hitzler, P., Krötzsch, M., Parsia, B., Patel-Schneider, P.F., Rudolph, S. (eds.): OWL 2 Web Ontology Language: Primer. W3C Recommendation, 27 October 2009. http://www.w3.org/TR/owl2-primer/
2. Joham, D.: Path-based semantic annotation of web service descriptions for improved web service discovery. Master thesis, Alpen Adria Universitaet Klagenfurt, Universitaetsstrasse 65–67, 9020 Klagenfurt, February 2014
3. Kekäläinen, J.: Binary and graded relevance in IR evaluations-comparison of the effects on ranking of IR systems. Inf. Process. Manage. **41**(5), 1019–1033 (2005)
4. Klusch, M., Kapahnke, P.: iSeM: approximated reasoning for adaptive hybrid selection of semantic services. In: 2010 IEEE Fourth International Conference on Semantic Computing (ICSC), pp. 184–191, September 2010
5. Klusch, M., Kapahnke, P.: The iSeM matchmaker: a flexible approach for adaptive hybrid semantic service selection. Web Semant. Sci. Serv. Agents World Wide Web **15**(3), 1–14 (2012)
6. Klusch, M., Kapahnke, P., Zinnikus, I.: Hybrid adaptive web service selection with SAWSDL-MX and WSDL-analyzer. In: Aroyo, L., Traverso, P., Ciravegna, F., Cimiano, P., Heath, T., Hyvönen, E., Mizoguchi, R., Oren, E., Sabou, M., Simperl, E. (eds.) ESWC 2009. LNCS, vol. 5554, pp. 550–564. Springer, Heidelberg (2009)
7. Kopecký, J., Vitvar, T., Bournez, C., Farrell, J.: Sawsdl: semantic annotations for WSDL and XML schema. IEEE Internet Comput. **11**(6), 60–67 (2007)
8. Köpke, J.: Declarative semantic annotations for XML document transformations and their maintenance. Ph.D. thesis, Alpen Adria Universitaet Klagenfurt (2012)
9. Köpke, J., Eder, J.: Semantic annotation of XML-schema for document transformations. In: Meersman, R., Dillon, T., Herrero, P. (eds.) OTM 2010. LNCS, vol. 6428, pp. 219–228. Springer, Heidelberg (2010)
10. Köpke, J., Eder, J.: Semantic invalidation of annotations due to ontology evolution. In: Meersman, R., Dillon, T., Herrero, P., Kumar, A., Reichert, M., Qing, L., Ooi, B.-C., Damiani, E., Schmidt, D.C., White, J., Hauswirth, M., Hitzler, P., Mohania, M. (eds.) OTM 2011, Part II. LNCS, vol. 7045, pp. 763–780. Springer, Heidelberg (2011)
11. Köpke, J., Eder, J.: Logical invalidations of semantic annotations. In: Ralyté, J., Franch, X., Brinkkemper, S., Wrycza, S. (eds.) CAiSE 2012. LNCS, vol. 7328, pp. 144–159. Springer, Heidelberg (2012)
12. Köpke, J., Joham, D., Eder, J.: Path-based semantic annotation for web service discovery. In: Nurcan, S., Pimenidis, E., Pastor, O., Vassiliou, Y. (eds.) CAiSE-Forum-DC 2014, Thessaloniki, June 2014. CEUR Workshop Proceedings, vol. 1164, pp. 81–88. CEUR-WS.org
13. Maßmann, S., Raunich, S., Aumüller, D., Arnold, P., Rahm. E.: Evolution of the coma match system. In: OM (2011)
14. Mukhopadhyay, D., Chougule, A.: A survey on web service discovery approaches. In: Wyld, D.C., Zizka, J., Nagamalai, D. (eds.) ICCSEA 2012. Advances in Intelligent and Soft Computing, vol. 166, pp. 1001–1012. Springer, Heidelberg (2012)
15. Szymczak, M., Koepke, J.: Matching methods for semantic annotation-based XML document transformations. In: New Developments in Fuzzy Sets, Intuitionistic Fuzzy Sets, Generalized Nets and Related Topics: Application, vol. 2, pp. 297–308. SRI-PAS (2012)

A Semantic-Aware Framework for Composite Services Engineering Based on Semantic Similarity and Concept Lattices

Ahmed Abid[1,3][✉], Nizar Messai[1], Mohsen Rouached[2], Thomas Devogele[1], and Mohamed Abid[3]

[1] LI, University Francois Rabelais Tours, Tours, France
ahmed.abid@etu.univ-tours.fr,
{nizar.messai,thomas.devogele}@univ-tours.fr
[2] College of Computers and Information Technology, Taif University, Taif, Saudi Arabia
m.rouached@tu.edu.sa
[3] CES Laboratory, Sfax University, Sfax, Tunisia
mohamed.abid@enis.rnu.tn

Abstract. This paper presents a semantic framework called IDECSE for composite Web services modeling and engineering. This framework uses semantic similarity measures and Formal Concept Analysis formalism to generate classes of similar services that can be composable to satisfy users queries and preferences. A reasoning mechanism is also proposed to produce reliable composite services. By considering semantics for describing, discovering, composing, and monitoring services, IDECSE addresses the challenge of achieving a full governance of the composition process.

Keywords: Semantic web services · Semantic similarity · Formal concept analysis · Web services composition

1 Introduction

Today, business processes are increasingly implemented by dynamically composing Web services seen as the main contribution the Service Oriented Architecture (SOA) brings to enterprise business process automation. Therefore, Web services composition has became an attractive way of developing value added Web services and would lead to substantial gains in productivity in several application domains including e-Enterprise, e-Business, e-Government, and e-Science. However, an important problem with current services compositions concerns their life-cycle and their management, also called their governance. The challenge is how to achieve a full governance of the composition allowing the continuous and dynamic improvement of the composition to support and encourage the adoption of SOA technologies. IDECSE [1] addressed the above challenge and proposed an integrated declarative framework to bridge the gap between the

© Springer International Publishing Switzerland 2015
S. Nurcan and E. Pimenidis (Eds.): CAiSE Forum 2014, LNBIP 204, pp. 148–164, 2015.
DOI: 10.1007/978-3-319-19270-3_10

process modeling, verification and monitoring and thus allowing for self-healing Web services compositions. Another challenge concerns the semantic gaps in the definition of atomic Web services provided by autonomous and different services providers, and therefore composition modeling frameworks should provide support for bridging such semantic gaps. Supporting environment dynamicity is also a critical requirement since available services as well as user requirements change frequently over time. Thus, the environment for service engineering needs to support rapid and dynamic re-design through appropriate and automatic tools for dealing jointly with adaptation at modeling, deployment and run-time.

While numerous composition approaches have been developed, very little has been done towards dealing with these challenges because of their complexity. Consequently, existing frameworks need to be enhanced using new semantic-aware methods and tools. In this paper, we propose to address this issue by enhancing IDECSE approach with semantics in all composition steps. Mainly, improvement of IDECSE consists in considering service similarity measures.

The rest of the paper is organized as follows. Section 2 presents the architecture of the improved IDECSE framework and details its modules. We mainly focus on the Service Classification Module. In Sect. 3, we discuss the current implementation and the ideas to validate the proposed approach. Section 4 exposes literature review. Finally, Sect. 5 concludes the paper and outlines future work.

2 IDECSE Framework

A major problem with current services compositions concerns their life-cycle and their management, also called their governance. The challenge is how to achieve a full governance of the composition allowing the continuous and dynamic improvement of the composition to support and encourage the adoption of SOA technologies. Many SOA management initiatives fail to get off the drawing board once systems architects recognize the scale of integration work to bring the different elements of functionality into play. IDECSE [2] addressed this challenge by proposing an integrated framework to bridge the gap between the process modeling, verification and monitoring and thus allowing for self-healing Web services compositions. This framework aims also to fully integrate semantics in all stages of the composition global life-cycle. First, user requirements are better understood using refinement techniques such as generalization or specification of concepts from a given ontology. IDECSE appeals for data mining techniques for classifying and mining services into Service Registry based on semantic relations. The main components of the IDECSE architecture are depicted in Fig. 1. It consists of five modules covering the global composition life-cycle (i.e. specification, modeling, composition, deployment, and monitoring). These modules are described and detailed in the following sections.

2.1 Service Request Module

The Service Request module (First layer in Fig. 1) translates the user requirements to an internal language to be used by the Service Classification module and

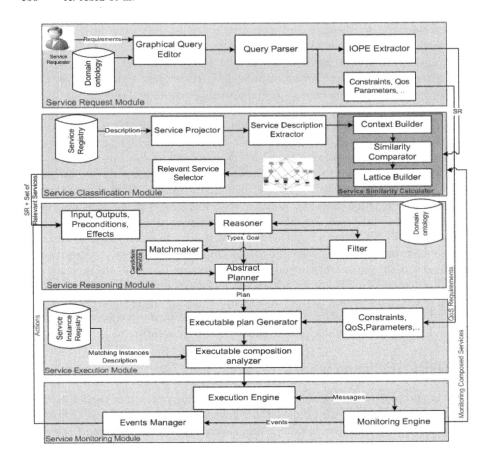

Fig. 1. IDECSE architecture

the Service Reasoning module. The Graphical Query Editor relies on a domain ontology to analyze user requirements before enriching them through adding new ontology concepts based on semantic relations such as generalization, specialization, etc. The query is then parsed to extract functional and non-functional requirements. Functional requirements are modeled using the IOPE Extractor, which extracts the Inputs, Outputs, Preconditions and Effects.

Extracted requirements are then modeled as a new requested service called S_R. Given a domain ontology O, a user query Q, modeled as S_R, consists of a set of provided inputs $S_{R_{in}} \subseteq O$, a set of desired outputs $S_{R_{out}} \subseteq O$, a set of preconditions $S_{R_{pre}} \subseteq O$, a set of effects $S_{R_{eff}} \subseteq O$, and a set of quality of service constraints $S_{R_{qos}} = \{(q_1, v_1, w_1), (q_2, v_2, w_2), ..., (q_k, v_k, w_k)\}$, where $q_{i(i=1,2,...,k)}$ is a quality criterion, v_i is the required value for criterion q_i, and w_i is the weight assigned to this criterion such that $\sum_{i=1}^{k} w_i = 1$, and k the number of quality criteria involved in the query. We can model S_R as $S_R = \sum IOPE + \sum QoS$.

2.2   Service Classification Module

To deal with the important number of Web services and instead of considering the whole Service Registry, this module allows to classify available services semantically into classes according to their similarities. Its second role is to return only relevant services to S_R from the registry. This module contains four main components which are: Service Projector, Service Description Extractor, Service Similarity Calculator, and Relevant Service Selector.

To introduce the functionality of the proposed module for Web service classification, an example of semantic Web services is presented in Table 1.

Table 1. A set of services with their operations

Services	Id	Operations	Id
AUTHOR FINDER	WS_1	Find Author(B)	op_{11}
AUTHOR PRICE FINDER	WS_3	Find Author(B)	op_{21}
		Find Price(B)	op_{22}
SEARCH BOOK	WS_2	Find Book(A)	op_{31}
CURRENCY CONVERTOR	WS_4	Convert (C,C,P)	op_{41}
DOLLAR2EURO	WS_5	Dollar2euro(A)	op_{51}

The role of the Service Classification components is described and illustrated in the following parts.

1. **Service Projector:** The Service Projector selects services capabilities based on syntactical and semantic description for each service into one interface. Different semantic description languages were proposed, OWL-S and WSMO are the most important ones for this purpose. Both WSMO and OWL-S have the aim of providing the conceptual and technical means to realize Semantic Web services. The comparison done in [3] shows that although the aims of both WSMO and OWL-S are the same, they present some differences in the approach they take to achieve their goals especially in the definition of the process model and the grounding of Web services. OWL-S is more mature and is therefore considered in the IDECSE framework. The role of the Service Projector Module is to select service capabilities from OWL-S and WSDL descriptions and transmit them to the Service Description Extractor. In the running example, the operations of each service shown in Table 1 are the results transmitted by the Service Projector.

2. **Service Description Extractor:** Extracting comparator parameters from service capabilities is a mandatory step to measure similarity between services. The Service Classification Module relies on the functional properties of services which will be the parameters to extract from the OWL-S files.

    Semantic and Syntactic functional parameters of services are given in OWL-S description. In fact OWL-S is an ontology for services. Each service class in OWL-S refers to a declared semantic service [4]. Each service description is composed of three main parts: Service Profile, Service Model, and Service Grounding. In the following sections, we select relevant data to be compared from these parts:

a. Functionality Description in the Service Profile: The Service profile consists of four main parts. The first part describes the links between the Service profile and the service and its process model. The second part describes the contact information, intended for human consumption. The third part describes the functionality in terms of Input, Output, Precondition and Effect (IOPE). The last part describes the attributes of a profile. Relevant functional information about services exist in the last two parts. The Profile class defines the following properties for IOPE *hasInput* ranges over the Inputs, *hasOutput* ranges over the Output, *hasPrecondition* specifies a precondition of the service, *hasResult* specifies under which condition outputs are generated.

b. Functionality Description in the Service Model: The Service Model gives a detailed description on how to interact with the service. It can be used to supplement initial similarity measure by giving a more detailed perspective on the service internal workings.

c. Functionality Description in the Service Grounding: The Service Grounding specifies the details of how to access a service. It is not required in measuring service similarity because it can be the same especially for services from the same organization, but it provides a useful way of allowing users to specify the way of using the service.

In the syntactic side, IDECSE relies on the types of inputs and outputs of services. The Service Description Extractor tries to extract those parameters with their attributes and transmits them to the Service Similarity Calculator. Considering the previous example, Table 2 shows the different details of services. We note that the example uses simple services based on input and output functional parameters.

Table 2. Detailed Web services Description

Operations	Input concept	Output concept	Input Type	Output Type
op_{11}	Book	Person	String	String
op_{21}	Book	Person	String	String
op_{22}	Book	Price	String	Float
op_{31}	Text	Book	String	String
op_{41}	Price, Currency	Price	String/Float	Float
op_{51}	Price	Price	Float	Float

3. **The Service Similarity Calculator:** After selecting relevant parameters from services description, the Service Similarity Calculator measures the similarity and uses data mining techniques in order to classify available services

into classes according to their similarity. The main parts of this module and their functionalities are described below:

a. Context Builder: The Context Builder is responsible for preparing the input dataset to the classification module. It selects the main properties of Web services and creates a tabular representation where the rows correspond to the Web services, the columns correspond to the services capabilities (descriptions) such as type of input or the ontology that the input refers to, and finally table cells contain real values of these properties for each service.

b. Similarity Comparator: It can be considered as the main component of this module. The Similarity Comparator relies on a set of formulas and relations used to calculate similarity between services. Two types of formulas are taken into account by the IDECSE framework: the first is for the semantic and the second is for the syntactic Similarity and relatedness.

In the semantic field, and based on the selected parameters in the Service Description Extractor module, IDECSE defines a semantic measure function. Let S be a set of services ($|S| = n \in N$) and let σ be a similarity measure function $\sigma : S \times S \rightarrow [0, 1]$ which verify the conditions below:

$-\ \sigma(S_i, S_i) = 1 \forall\ i \in \{1, .., n\}$,
$-\ \sigma(S_i, S_j) = \sigma(S_j, S_i) \forall\ i \in \{1, .., n\}, \forall\ j \in \{1, .., n\}$.

An OWL-S service similarity can be defined as follows: For $i, j \in \{1, .., n\}$,

$$\sigma(S_i, S_j) = U_1 Sim_P(S_i, S_j) + U_2 Sim_M(S_i, S_j) + U_3 Sim_G(S_i, S_j) \quad (1)$$

where $\sum_{k=1}^{3} U_k = 1$

The functions Sim_P, Sim_M and Sim_G present respectively the similarity function between tow Services Profiles, Models and Groundings. As Service Model and Service Grounding are used to supplement the initial similarity and to specify details of how to access a service, their parameters can be modeled as Quality of services thus more importance is given to the functional similarity.

$$\sigma(S_i, S_j) \approx Sim_P(S_i, S_j) = W_1 Sim_I(S_i, S_j) + W_2 Sim_O(S_i, S_j) + W_3$$
$$Sim_P(S_i, S_j) + W_4 Sim_E(S_i, S_j) \quad (2)$$

where $\sum_{k=1}^{4} W_k = 1$

Sim_I, Sim_O, Sim_P, Sim_E are respectively the similarity function between two services Input, Output, Precondition and Effects. Each parameter is semantically annotated with respect to an OWL concept. Thus, the functional similarity measurement between services is mapped to Ontology-based similarity. Studying ontological concepts, their details are divided into tow types which are: Type of Concept and Relation

of Concept. Otherwise, measuring similarity between services in the
IDECSE framework is based on semantic and syntactic similarity.

Regarding semantics, being machine interpretable and constructed
by experts, ontologies present a very reliable and organized knowledge
source system. For these reasons, ontologies have been extensively exploited in knowledge-based systems and, more precisely, to compute semantic similarity. Measures on the ontology based similarity are divided
into three main categories which are: Edge-counting approaches [5,6],
Features-based approaches [7] and Information Content approaches [8,9].
After surveying different Ontological similarity measures and their application situations and based on experimental results and benchmarks
tests [10,11], the measure proposed in [12] gives pertinent results in our
case. The formula is given below:

Let A and B be two concepts, represented by the nodes a and b in a
predefined is-a semantic taxonomy (ontologies). Let C be a set of concepts of a given ontology, ($\leq$) is defined as a binary relation $\leq: C \times C$. For
two concepts c_i and c_j, $c_i \leq c_j$ is fulfilled if c_i is a hierarchical specialization of c_j or if $c_i \equiv c_j$ (i.e. same concept). The set of taxonomical features
describing the concept a is defined in terms of the relation $\leq$ in (3).

$$\phi(a) = \{c \in C | a \leq c\} \tag{3}$$

[12] defines the semantic similarity between tow concepts as follow:

$$Sim(a,b)_{sanchez} = 1 - \log(1 + \frac{|\phi(a)\backslash\phi(b)| + |\phi(b)\backslash\phi(a)|}{|\phi(a)\backslash\phi(b)| + |\phi(b)\backslash\phi(a)| + |\phi(a) \cap \phi(b)|}) \tag{4}$$

Compared to other measures based on taxonomical knowledge, the
exploitation of the whole amount of unique and shared subsumers seems
to give solid semantic evidences of semantic resemblance. Results show
that the measure proposed by [12] surpasses basic Edge-Counting Features and Information content measures.

Moving to syntactical similarity, [13] proposed a practical measure
between different data types, Table 3 groups different data types and
Table 4 gives the similarity between different data types.

Table 3. Simple DataType groups [13]

Group	Simple Data Types
Integer Group	Integer, Byte, Short, Long
Real Group	Real, Float, Double, Decimal
String Group	String, NormalizedString
Date Group	Date, DateTime, Duration, Time
Boolean Group	Boolean

Table 4. Simple DataType groups similarity [13]

	Int.	Real	Str.	Date	Bol.
Int.	1.0	0.5	0.3	0.1	0.1
Real	1.0	1.0	0.1	0.0	0.1
Str.	0.7	0.7	1.0	0.8	0.3
Date	0.1	0.0	0.1	1.0	0.0
Bol.	0.1	0.0	0.1	0.0	0.1

Finally to compute semantic similarity between services, IDECSE framework combines the tow measures proposed in [12] and in [13]. The first one is used as a semantic measure based on the ontological features of concepts and the second is based on the syntactic measure between inputs and outputs types of services. Based on similarity measure given in (4), we redefine our similarity measure (2) in (5).

$$\sigma(S_i, S_j) = W_1[N_{11}Sim_{I_{[12]}}(S_i, S_j) + N_{12}Sim_{I_{[13]}}(S_i, S_j)] + W_2$$
$$[N_{21}Sim_{O_{[12]}}(S_i, S_j) + N_{22}Sim_{O_{[13]}}(S_i, S_j)] + W_3$$
$$[N_{31}Sim_{Pre_{[12]}}(S_i, S_j) + N_{32}Sim_{Pre_{[13]}}(S_i, S_j)] +$$
$$W_4[N_{41}Sim_{Eff_{[12]}}(S_i, S_j) + N_{42}Sim_{Eff_{[13]}}(S_i, S_j)] \quad (5)$$

where $\sum_{k=1}^{4} W_k = 1$, $\sum_{j=1}^{2} N_{aj} = 1$ and $a \in \{1,2,3,4\}$.

The function σ is used then to calculate similarity between concepts that are referred by functional parameters of services. Finally, this module returns a Similarity Matrix (SimMat) containing similarity measures between available services. The Similarity Matrix generated from the proposed example using (5) is given in Table 5.

From $SimMat$, we can mainly extract several binary contexts using a threshold $\theta \in [0,1]$. Values of SimMat, which are greater or equal to the fixed threshold θ, are scaled to 1 and other values are scaled to 0. The binary context that corresponds to an arbitrary threshold for operations and services are shown in Tables 6 and 7. The SimCxt is a triple (O,O,R_{Sim_θ}), where O is a set of operations and R_{Sim_θ} is a binary relation indicating whether an operation is similar to another operation or not. The Context Matrix (Table 7 in our example) is the result transmitted to the next module to build the Lattice.

c. Lattice Builder: In this sub-module a Lattice of operations is built according to the Formal Concept Analysis (FCA)[14] formalism and its extension to complex data called Similarity-based Formal Concept Analysis (SFCA)[15]. An example of obtained Lattice for a binary context using the ConExp[1] tool is given in Fig. 2. This Lattice shows the grouping of similar operations.

---

[1] http://conexp.sourceforge.net/.

Table 5. The operations SimMat

	op_{11}	op_{21}	op_{22}	op_{31}	op_{41}	op_{51}
op_{11}	1	1	0.40	0.35	0	0
op_{21}	1	1	0.40	0.35	0	0
op_{22}	0.40	0.40	1	0.32	0	0
op_{31}	0.35	35	0.32	1	0	0
op_{41}	0	0	0	0	1	0.45
op_{51}	0	0	0	0	0.45	1

Table 6. The operation SimCxt for $\theta = 0.4$

	op_{11}	op_{21}	op_{22}	op_{31}	op_{41}	op_{51}
op_{11}	X	X	X			
op_{21}	X	X	X			
op_{21}	X	X	X			
op_{31}				X		
op_{41}					X	X
op_{51}					X	X

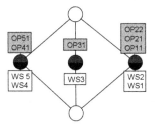

Fig. 2. Generated lattice for (SimCxt) shown in Table 7

4. **Relevant Service Selector:** Once the Lattice of services is built, the Relevant Service Selector identifies the most relevant classes of services from the Lattice. The Relevant Service Selector has two main roles. The first role is to select the most relevant services for the purpose of substitution process and thus to maintain a composite Web service application functionality as much as possible. The second role is about finding equivalent, similar and composable services to S_R requested by users in order to transmit them to the reasoning module.

Table 7. The service SimCxt for $\theta = 0.4$

	op_{11}	op_{21}	op_{22}	op_{31}	op_{41}	op_{51}
WS_1	X	X	X			
WS_2	X	X	X			
WS_3				X		
WS_4					X	X
WS_5					X	X

5. **Example of User Query:** We consider a simple user query Q = "Find an author of a Book based on its title" in order to demonstrate the usefulness of the Service Classification Module in the IDECSE framework.

Table 8. S_R detailed descriptions

Op	Input	Output	In. Type	Out. Type
op_R	Title	Author	String	String

Parsing the query is the role of the Service Request Module. Table 8 details S_R description generated from this module. Then Table 8 is transmitted to the Service Similarity Calculator sub-module. After adding S_R to the existing context, a similarity measure is then calculated between S_R and the rest of available services. We suppose here that available services are those given in Table 1. Results of similarity measures are shown in Table 9.

Table 9. S_R similarity measures

	op_{11}	op_{21}	op_{22}	op_{31}	op_{41}	op_{51}
op_R	0.7	0.7	0.35	0.56	0	0

Now, we add the S_R to the context and build the Lattice to ensure returning relevant results. We fix the threshold θ at 0.45. Table 11 presents the new context builder which will be transmitted to the Lattice Builder.

The Relevant Service Selector is charged then to identify most relevant service to S_R using appropriate algorithms for browsing Lattices. In our case only and according to the generated lattice in Fig. 3 three operations are selected and then transmitted to the Reasoning Module. Those operations are $\{op_{11}, op_{31}, op_{21}\}$. Thus, the composition process is reduced to reason only on three operations in which op_{31} can be composed with op_{11} or op_{21}.

The example illustrates the advantage of the Service Classification Module in anticipating the composition task, maintaining the composition plan

Table 10. The operation SimCxt for $\theta = 0.45$

	op_{11}	op_{21}	op_{22}	op_{31}	op_{41}	op_{51}	op_R
op_{11}	X	X					
op_{21}	X	X					
op_{22}			X				
op_{31}				X			
op_{41}					X	X	
op_{51}					X	X	
op_R	X	X		X			X

Table 11. The service SimCxt for $\theta = 0.45$

	op_{11}	op_{21}	op_{22}	op_{31}	op_{41}	op_{51}	op_R
WS_1	X	X					
WS_2	X	X	X				
WS_3				X			
WS_4					X	X	
WS_5					X	X	
S_R	X	X		X			X

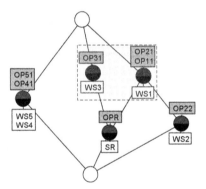

Fig. 3. The generated lattice including S_R

working as much as possible by notifying the reasoner that op_{11} and op_{21} are similar.

2.3 Service Reasoning Module

The Service Reasoning module identifies the candidate composition plans that realize the goal (S_R) based on a logic reasoner. IDECSE relies on a logic Reasoner that takes into account results given from the Service Classification Module.

In order to enable working with large collections of Web services, IDECSE distinguish between Web services types and instances. A Web service type is a set of Web service instances with identical functionality. A Web service type is semantically described by the inputs, outputs, preconditions and effects that capture the functionality offered by this type of services. Web services instances are the actual services that can be invoked. This separation allows reducing the search space, which helps ensuring the scalability of the composition process [16]. The main components of the Service Reasoning Module are:

- Reasoner: is responsible for checking the ontology consistency in addition to handling the maintenance of the state including preconditions and effects application.
- Filter: avoids redundancy from the plan by identifying service types with potential relevance to the goal and checks the dependency relationships between each two consecutive service types.
- Matchmaker: allows querying the Service Registry for available services in order to match the preconditions of a Web service with the effects of another service.
- Abstract planner: can be considered as the main component of this module and is responsible for generating a set of abstract plans.

IDECSE relies on a planning algorithm [1] to create a composition of the available service types by providing an abstract plan that meets the functional requirements. In this algorithm, inputs and outputs are distinguished conditions where inputs are attempted to be achieved before preconditions since preconditions may have arguments consisting of several inputs. A plan of composite services is formalized as a proof of the goal to answer the user query. Thus, a Plan $\{\mathcal{P}\} = \{A_i\}_{i=1..n}$ is a sequence of n actions A_i. Each action applies on a state E_i to produce a state E_{i+1}: $\forall i \in \{0, .., n-1\}, E_i \wedge A_i \models E_{i+1}$. Starting from an initial state E_0 the plan produces the goal G: $E_0 \wedge \{\mathcal{P}\} \models G$. Therefore composite services generated are new services that meet all the query requirements. Finally, generated plans are transmitted to the service execution module.

2.4   Service Execution Module

The Service Execution Module translates the abstract plan into an executable one by associating to each service type its specific instances using the Service Instances Registry. The plan generated by the previous module is considered as a template for the composite service and drives the process of matching each service type to a corresponding service instance. The Service Execution Module is mainly composed of the two following components:

- The Executable Plan Generator considers non-functional requirements of the goal (provided by Service Request Module) and enables to concretize the abstract plan generated by the abstract Reasoning Module.
- The Executable Composition Analyzer generates executable code and invokes the execution engine.

In IDECSE, the Executable Plan Generator implementation is based on the algorithm presented in [17]. This algorithm takes as input a composition plan, the QoS permissible values imposed by the user, and their weights and generates as output a composition plan that satisfies the requirements of the user.

2.5 Service Monitoring Module

Monitoring deals with the actual execution of the composite service and is responsible for monitoring the execution and recording violation of any requirement of the goal service at run-time. For this purpose, we plan to propose an event-based monitoring framework that allows specifying and reasoning about the monitoring properties during composition process execution. Properties to be monitored are specified by the user and added to process specification at both design and execution time. These properties include functional constraints (invocation and execution order), non-functional properties (security, QoS...), temporal constraints (response time, invocations delay), data constraints (data availability, validity and expiry). These properties can be also combined such as monitoring the data validity and access control within specific time frame.

Services providers can also specify additional assumptions about the composition process in terms of events extracted from its specification. Run-time deviations and inconsistencies will be monitored by using a variant of techniques developed for checking integrity constraints in temporal deductive databases. When requirements variations are detected, a deviation notification is sent to the composition manager. This notification indicates: (i) the requirement that has been violated, (ii) the malfunctioning service(s) that violated it, and (iii) diagnostic information regarding the violation. Based on the type of the deviation notification and service monitoring policies, recovery policies will be triggered.

3 Implementation and Validation

The overall architecture for the IDECSE approach is under development as a java application that presents all the functionalities from design phase to monitoring and recovery phases. This application contains a user friendly interface to specify the composition design (services/constraints/ and control/ data flow), to automatically generate the corresponding models, to invoke the reasoner, and show the results returned. The application provides also an assumption editor to specify assumptions and check their correctness.

Once each type in the selected plan is bound to a concrete Web service instance, a generator produces a concrete workflow that can be deployed onto a runtime infrastructure, to realize the composite service. For that, we first generate the WSDL description (name, interface, port types) for the composite service. Then, we define partner link types to link the component services, and proceed to the generation of the composition flow (BPEL flow for instance). The selected plan gives the invocation order. We use an Eclipse Modeling Framework (EMF) model of BPEL (WSDL) that is automatically created from a BPEL

(WSDL) schema. The model provides in-memory representation of constructs and support for persistence to files (serialization) and loading from files (deserialization). BPEL and WSDL manipulation become significantly simplified with the corresponding EMF models. In case of conflicts, the monitoring process is initiated by the monitoring manager after receiving a request to start a monitoring activity as specified by a monitoring policy. First, it checks if the requested constraint or property can be monitored or not. This checking is based on the composition process identified in the policy, and the event reporting capabilities indicated by the type of the execution environment of the composition process. If the requested constraint can be monitored, the monitoring manager triggers an event listener to capture events from the composition execution environment and passes to it the events that should be collected. It also sends to the monitor the specification of the constraint to be checked.

These components are still under refinement and tests. Then, we plan to compare our results with important approaches close to our contribution such as [18]. Also, it will be interesting to measure the performance of the IDECSE framework before and after incorporating the similarity based approach in order to show its added value. To conduct fair experiments, we need a sufficient number of services and ontologies with a variety of sizes. However, it is very hard to collect or manually construct appropriate data. For this reason, we may randomly generate experimental data.

4   Related Work

A considerable number of research efforts have focused on various aspects of Web service compositions ranging from semantic service discovery to service specification, composition, deployment, and monitoring [19–25]. A deep analysis of these efforts shows that some has focused on the execution aspects of composite Web services by considering WSDL to describe Web services and BPEL to compose them, without much consideration for requirements that drive the development process. Some other efforts are concerned by the feasibility of the composition process by considering semantics and AI approaches without taking into account the run-time deployment and execution. However, we believe that these two approaches can be complementary and can be combined for managing the global life-cycle of the composition i.e. specifying, composing, verifying, deploying, monitoring, and analyzing to achieve a full governance of the composition. Semantic classification of services was also investigated. For instance, [26] uses FCA formalism to highlight the relationships between services and permits the identication of different categorizations of a certain service. Lattice of services is built in [27], by extracting keywords from their specification. [28] combines text mining and machine learning techniques for classifying services. This approach improves the performance of Web-service clustering by considering the two main steps in the clustering process. It introduces first a Web-service similarity-measuring approach that uses both ontology learning and IR-based term similarity. Second, it proposes an approach to identifying cluster centers by using similarity values for service names to improve the performance in a second step. Using ant-based algorithm, [29] considers the degree of semantic similarity between services as the main clustering criterion. The semantic description is based on measuring similarity between ontological concepts referred by input and output parameters of the service. A matching method and metrics are used to measure the semantic similarity. Other approaches rely on measuring similarity between service, [13] proposes a novel approach for Web service retrieval based on measuring similarity between services interfaces. The evaluation of the similarity between Web services considers both the semantic and the structure of a WSDL description with a semantic annotation.

5   Conclusion and Future Work

This paper describes IDECSE, a new semantic integrated approach for composite services engineering. Compared to existing approaches, IDECSE considers semantics in all the composition global life-cycle, addresses the challenge of fully automating the composition processes, and proposes and adapts reasoning, monitoring, and adaptation techniques. The main new added values are on the Web services classification level. In fact, we propose to enhance IDECSE with semantic measures and FCA for building Web service Lattices according to functionality domains. Similarity measures are used to calculate semantic and syntactic similarity based on OWL-S. Our work in progress includes the enrichment of service Lattices with QoS aspects and user preferences. We also plan to extend the framework to include additional features such as failure handling, and an interactive visual environment for testing composite services.

References

1. Rouached, M., Messai, N.: SCoME: a web services composition modeling and engineering framework. In: 2013 IEEE/WIC/ACM International Joint Conferences on Web Intelligence (WI) and Intelligent Agent Technologies (IAT), IEEE (2013)
2. Abid, A., Messai, N., Rouached, M., Devogele, T., Abid, M.: IDECSE: a semantic integrated development environment for composite services engineering
3. Lara, R., Roman, D., Polleres, A., Fensel, D.: A conceptual comparison of WSMO and OWL-S. In: (LJ) Zhang, L.-J., Jeckle, M. (eds.) ECOWS 2004. LNCS, vol. 3250, pp. 254–269. Springer, Heidelberg (2004)
4. Martin, D., Burstein, M., Hobbs, J., Lassila, O., McDermott, D., McIlraith, S., Narayanan, S., Paolucci, M., Parsia, B., Payne, T., et al.: OWL-S: semantic markup for web services. W3C member submission, vol. 22 (2004)
5. Rada, R., Mili, H., Bicknell, E., Blettner, M.: Development and application of a metric on semantic nets. IEEE Trans. Syst. Man Cybern. **19**, 17–30 (1989)
6. Wu, Z., Palmer, M.: Verbs semantics and lexical selection. In: Proceedings of the 32nd Annual Meeting on Association for Computational Linguistics, Association for Computational Linguistics (1994)
7. Tversky, A.: Features of similarity. Psychol. Rev. **84**, 327–352 (1977)
8. Resnik, P.: Using information content to evaluate semantic similarity in a taxonomy. arXiv preprint cmp-lg/9511007 (1995)
9. Jiang, J.J., Conrath, D.W.: Semantic similarity based on corpus statistics and lexical taxonomy. arXiv preprint cmp-lg/9709008 (1997)

10. Rubenstein, H., Goodenough, J.B.: Contextual correlates of synonymy. Commun. ACM **8**, 627–633 (1965)
11. Miller, G.A., Charles, W.G.: Contextual correlates of semantic similarity. Lang. cogn. process. **6**, 1–28 (1991)
12. Sánchez, D., Batet, M., Isern, D., Valls, A.: Ontology-based semantic similarity: a new feature-based approach. Expert Syst. Appl. **39**, 7718–7728 (2012)
13. Plebani, P., Pernici, B.: URBE: web service retrieval based on similarity evaluation. IEEE Trans. Knowl. Data Eng. **21**, 1629–1642 (2009)
14. Ganter, B., Wille, R.: Formal Concept Analysis: Mathematical Foundations. Springer, New York (1999)
15. Azmeh, Z., Hamoui, F., Huchard, M., Messai, N., Tibermacine, C., Urtado, C., Vauttier, S.: Backing composite web services using formal concept analysis. In: Jäschke, R. (ed.) ICFCA 2011. LNCS, vol. 6628, pp. 26–41. Springer, Heidelberg (2011)
16. Agarwal, V., Chafle, G., Dasgupta, K., Karnik, N., Kumar, A., Mittal, S., Srivastava, B.: Synthy: a system for end to end composition of web services. Web Semant. Sci. Serv. Agents World Wide Web **3**, 311–339 (2011)
17. Ko, J.M., Kim, C.O., Kwon, I.H.: Quality-of-service oriented web service composition algorithm and planning architecture. J. Syst. Softw. **81**, 2079–2090 (2008)
18. Cugola, G., Ghezzi, C., Pinto, L.S.: DSOL: a declarative approach to self-adaptive service orchestrations. Comput. **94**(7), 579–617 (2012)
19. Xiaoming, P., Qiqing, F., Yahui, H., Bingjian, Z.: A user requirements oriented dynamic web service composition framework. In: Proceedings of the 2009 International Forum on Information Technology and Applications, IFITA 2009, vol. 1, pp. 173–177. IEEE Computer Society, Washington, DC (2009)
20. Hatzi, O., Vrakas, D., Nikolaidou, M., Bassiliades, N., Anagnostopoulos, D., Vlahavas, I.: An integrated approach to automated semantic web service composition through planning. IEEE Trans. Serv. Comput. **5**(3), 319–332 (2012)
21. Marconi, A., Pistore, M.: Synthesis and composition of web services. In: Bernardo, M., Padovani, L., Zavattaro, G. (eds.) SFM 2009. LNCS, vol. 5569, pp. 89–157. Springer, Heidelberg (2009)
22. Rabah, S., Ni, D., Jahanshahi, P., Guzman, L.F.: Current state and challenges of automatic planning in web service composition. CoRR (2011)
23. Kuang, L., Li, Y., Wu, J., Deng, S., Wu, Z.: Inverted indexing for composition-oriented service discovery. In: 2007 IEEE International Conference on Web Services, Salt Like City, USA, pp. 257–264 (2007)
24. Kona, S., Bansal, A., Gupta, G.: Automatic composition of semantic web services. In: ICWS, pp. 150–158 (2007)
25. Lecue, F., Mehandjiev, N.: Towards scalability of quality driven semantic web service composition. In: Proceedings of the 2009 IEEE International Conference on Web Services, ICWS 2009, pp. 469–476. IEEE Computer Society, Washington, DC (2009)
26. Aversano, L., Bruno, M., Canfora, G., Di Penta, M., Distante, D.: Using concept lattices to support service selection. Int. J. Web Serv. Res. (IJWSR) **3**, 32–51 (2006)
27. Bruno, M., Canfora, G., Di Penta, M., Scognamiglio, R.: An approach to support web service classification and annotation. In: Proceedings of the 2005 IEEE International Conference on e-Technology, e-Commerce and e-Service, EEE 2005. IEEE (2005)

28. Kumara, B.T., Paik, I., Chen, W.: Web-service clustering with a hybrid of ontology learning and information-retrieval-based term similarity. In: 2013 IEEE 20th International Conference on Web Services (ICWS). IEEE (2013)
29. Pop, C.B., Chifu, V.R., Salomie, I., Dinsoreanu, M., David, T., Acretoaie, V.: Semantic web service clustering for efficient discovery using an ant-based method. In: Essaaidi, M., Malgeri, M., Badica, C. (eds.) Intelligent Distributed Computing IV. SCI, vol. 315, pp. 23–33. Springer, Heidelberg (2010)

Work Systems Paradigm and Frames for Fractal Architecture of Information Systems

Marite Kirikova[✉]

Department of Artificial Intelligence and Systems Engineering, Riga Technical University,
1 Kalku, Riga 1658, Latvia
marite.kirikova@rtu.lv

Abstract. Contemporary information systems have to satisfy needs of agile and viable enterprises. They shall include mechanisms of business intelligence, business process management, information technology infrastructure management, and alignment between business and computer systems. The mechanisms for business process handling and computer systems handling are similar, and the mechanisms for their continuous integrated improvement also are similar, therefore the architecture of information systems components that support these processes also can have a measure of similarity if considered at a particular level of abstraction. The paper, focusing on aforementioned similarities, uses St. Alter's work systems paradigm for constructing fractal architecture of information systems that can be used for supporting agile and viable enterprises. The architecture includes predefined frames of processes, a frame for virtual agents, frames of information flows in viable systems, and a frame for information flows in the enterprise architecture that help to derive requirements for introducing continuous changes in information systems.

Keywords: Work systems · Fractal systems · Viable systems · Information systems · Continuous change

1 Introduction

Cloud solutions and use of business intelligence tools have transformed the landscape of information systems from relatively rigid internal architectures to more flexible and open structures of information handling [1, 2]. This refers to more flexible distribution of physical devices as well as possibility to acquire real time data that can be used for introducing changes in business and information technology solutions. The question arises how these abilities of information technology solutions can be represented in information systems architectures so that complexity that increases with the introduction of higher variability and flexibility could be embraced and managed.

While business, software, and hardware systems are very different, the mechanisms used in their analysis and management do not differ so much. For instance, similarities can be found in the actor based approaches in business analysis and actor based approaches in parallel programming. Moreover, according to our experience [3, 4] - data acquisition and analysis methods for big data analysis in social networks can be

© Springer International Publishing Switzerland 2015
S. Nurcan and E. Pimenidis (Eds.): CAiSE Forum 2014, LNBIP 204, pp. 165–180, 2015.
DOI: 10.1007/978-3-319-19270-3_11

compared with similar methods in computer networks. These similarities suggest to seek for common architecture patterns that could be used in business and information technology domains, since the information systems processes cross both domains.

In this paper we propose to use the work systems paradigm introduced by St. Alter [5], and several types of architecture frames as the basis for reflecting architecture of information systems. St. Alter has suggested the work systems paradigm after analyzing more than 20 different information systems definitions. He defines a work system as a system in which human participants and/or machines perform work (processes and activities) using information, technology, and other resources to produce specific products and/or services for specific internal or external customers. This paradigm gives an opportunity to focus on common structural features of handling information at business, software application, and technical device levels as well as to use inclusion relationship between work systems belonging to aforementioned levels. These structural commonalities of information handling at different levels of abstraction are rarely addressed in contemporary research of information systems engineering. Therefore the aim of this paper is to discuss usage of them in information systems engineering, especially in the context of information systems for viable enterprises.

The paper is structured as follows. We discuss related work in Sect. 2. In Sect. 3 we propose several frames for analyzing information system issues in viable enterprises. In Sect. 4 we discuss the benefits of viewing information system architecture as a fractal architecture composed of multiple work systems. Brief conclusions and directions of further research are presented in Sect. 5.

2   Related Work

The approach proposed in this paper is based on three main sources of related work, namely, on the work systems theory [5], contemporary applications of viable systems model [6–8], and use of fractal paradigm in information systems development [9, 10].

According to Steven Alter [5] "an information system is a work system whose processes and activities are devoted to processing information, that is, capturing, transmitting, storing, retrieving, manipulating, and displaying information. A work system is a system in which human participants and/or machines perform work (processes and activities) using information, technology, and other resources to produce specific products and/or services for specific internal or external customers". The customers can be external customers of the enterprise as well as internal customers (one sub-work system has produced information valuable for another sub-work system). The work system is embedded in its environment, and depends on organizational strategy and infrastructure (see Fig. 1). The goal(s) of the work system (or the results produced by the work system) depend on the organizational strategy; while the way how they are achieved mainly depends on the enterprise environment and available infrastructure.

Thus, we can state that behind each organizational process there is a work system. From the modeling perspective, there is a real or virtual work system behind of each business process at any level of abstraction or decomposition. On another hand, for each business process there can be identified an information processing sub-process

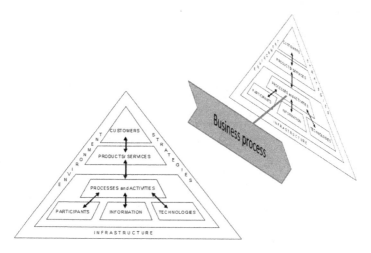

Fig. 1. Work system behind the process (the triangle in the figure is adopted from [5])

(or activities that themselves perform the transformation of inputs into outputs and therefore can be regarded as processes, which produce information). Thus, using Alter's work system paradigm it is possible to identify information systems architecture that consists of work systems that are structured according to the chosen model of representation of business processes. This issue will be discussed in more detail in the next section.

Contemporary applications of viable systems model show that an enterprise has to handle its internal work systems as well as it has to have good environment scanning capabilities [6–8]. For the enterprise to be viable, its internal units have to have a measure of autonomy and it should be organized as fractals [9]. Figure 2 shows traditional outlook of viable systems model consisting of five so-called Systems. Each "ONE" in System 1 corresponds to processes that bring value to enterprise customers. According to viable systems model, the "ONE" recursively can be represented by similar viable systems model of a smaller scale. Such structure enables flexibility that is essential to ensure agility of enterprises. More details about Systems of viable systems model are given in Sect. 3.

Thus, according to the viable systems model, for the value adding (System 1) and strategic processes (System 4) of the enterprise, i.e., processes that are directly related to the external environment, we can distinguish at least three sub-processes: production (transforming given inputs into given outputs), environment scanning, and internal control or management (see Fig. 2). In this paper we extrapolate that such three sub-processes are applicable to any process in an enterprise, because also other processes (e.g., enabling processes and different management processes) have to scan their environment inside the enterprise.

The application of viable systems model for contemporary enterprises is a multidisciplinary research topic, which is out of the scope of this paper. Hereby we just borrow the idea of necessity to be aware of external environment, to produce the value, and to be able to manage itself (quality management, change management, etc.) for each autonomous unit (we regard the process as an autonomous unit here). Another issue is that while the viable systems model has a fractal architecture, the fractal architecture of

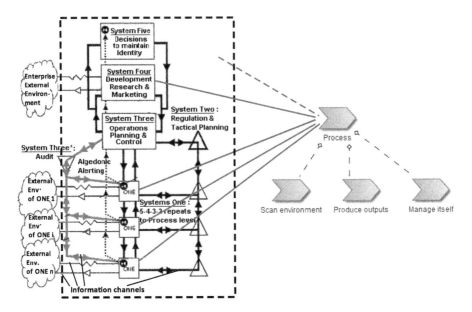

Fig. 2. Viable systems model (adapted from http://www.wikipedia.org): a process perspective. Dotted lines with arrowheads show the algedonic channel in viable systems model. Interrupted lines without arrowheads refer to the highest level of abstraction of viable systems model

information systems proposed in this paper is viewed from the point of view of an information system as a subsystem of an enterprise, not just from the point of view of operational fractals of the viable systems model.

'Fractality' has been introduced as a watchword for a new way of thinking about the collective behavior of many basic but interacting units. Fractality, thus, is regarded as the study of the behavior of macroscopic units that are endowed with the potential to evolve in time. Their interactions lead to coherent collective phenomena, so-called emergent properties that can be described only at higher levels than those of the individual units. Fractal theory is based on relationships, emergence, patterns and iterations [11]. It is used to describe structure and processes of flexible, adaptive and evolving systems. Fractal theory is applied in biomedicine, fractal geometry, mathematics, statistical analysis, signal analysis, image analysis [12], manufacturing [13], product design [14] enterprise development [15–17], software development [18], and other areas. The above-discussed variety of applications of fractal paradigm suggests that it can be suitable for information systems engineering in the context of viable enterprises, on which we focus in this paper [19], because the main peculiarity of information systems is interplay of many different natural and artificial systems that influence each other from various viewpoints and at different levels of scale. Computerized part of the information systems may consist of different software and hardware (sub)systems that are related by supporting various organizational processes and individual requests. This computerized information (sub)system may be directly or indirectly used by other components of the information system, namely, particular human actors and components (software and hardware) of other information systems [18].

The most common properties of fractal systems are self-similarity, self organization, goal-orientation, and dynamics and vitality [13]. These properties well align with the viable systems paradigm.

Self–similarity may manifest in different ways. For instance, fractals are called "self-similar" if they can produce the same (at a particular level of conceptual abstraction) outputs with the same inputs regardless of their internal structure. However, self similarity may be observed also in the architecture of components at different levels of abstraction, e.g., the same architecture patterns can emerge at smaller and larger granularities in information systems architecture. Further in this paper we will not use the concept "pattern" (commonly applied in literature on fractal systems) regarding the architecture. We will use the concept "frame" instead or the concept "pattern" to avoid misunderstandings with respect to the way how particular architecture constructs are derived.

Self-organization means ability to apply methods for controlling processes and workflows within fractals, and optimizing the composition of fractals in the system.

Goal-orientation means that fractals perform a goal-formation process to generate their own goals by coordinating processes with participating fractals and by modifying the goals as necessary. To coherently achieve their goals, goal consistency supported by an inheritance mechanism should be maintained.

Dynamics and vitality is a property that characterizes high individual dynamics and ability to adapt to a dynamically changing environment by cooperation and coordination between self-organizing fractals.

Besides these properties there are some other properties of fractal systems that are essential in the context of information systems of viable enterprises. One of such properties is *emergence*. Information systems depend on user requirements, organizational structure of enterprises, relationships between enterprise partners, suppliers, and clients. All of them are influenced by external environment, therefore requirements change in apparently random rather than planned way which in turn introduces the same type of changes in the information systems. *Requisite variety* is also mentioned among the properties of fractal systems. This property is very important for embracing the variety by providing appropriate variability in information systems services [20]. *Connectivity* is an essential property, too. The very existence of an information system is needed because of information it can provide. The components of the information system are related by physical or virtual information channels. Without these channels the information system does not exist. *Simple rules* is one more property often related to fractal systems. With passing of time we can see how very complex structures and processes (e.g., centralized databases, ERP) are gradually replaced by simpler, more loosely coupled alternatives e.g., data warehouses, distributed databases, service oriented architectures, etc.).

In this paper we focus our discussion to self-similarity issues. And we handle this property from the point of view of structure of processes and architecture components behind of these processes. We use concept "frames" to refer to these structures. The architecture frames and sub-frames here are regarded as work systems that perform different types of processes.

3   Self-similarity via Frames

In this section we discuss several frames that can be used to implement continuous changes in information systems that support viable enterprises. The frames represent structural (self)similarities. We assume, that utilization of these similarities can simplify identification and implementation of changes continuously. We start with information flow frames of viable systems, then proceed to information flow frames using constructs of three level enterprise architecture, and we conclude with process and agent frames for viable systems.

The frames of *information flows in the viable systems model* are identified on the basis of the viable systems model communication channels described in [8]. They represent the minimum of information flows prescribed by the viable systems model. The flows are reflected using ArchiMate enterprise architecture language [21] by dotted lines with arrowheads. Solid lines as well as placement of one box into another one show the aggregation relationships. Two alternative ways of representing aggregation are used to achieve better view on information flows. The representation is made solely from the functional perspective. The information flows here are shown for one only fractal level of the viable systems model. The channels between different fractal levels will not be fully reflected [8]. In the most of cases the representation is limited to one-step flows and one flow in one direction only to keep the models as simple as possible. The content of the flows is not considered in this paper. In the presentation of frames the viable systems model's Systems are briefly described to provide the context for the flows.

System 1 (S1) in the viable systems model is responsible for such functions as production and delivery of the enterprise's goods or services to the pertinent environment. It may consist of several operational units which in turn consist of smaller scale operational and managing units. Figure 3 reflects information flows around the functions of the S1.

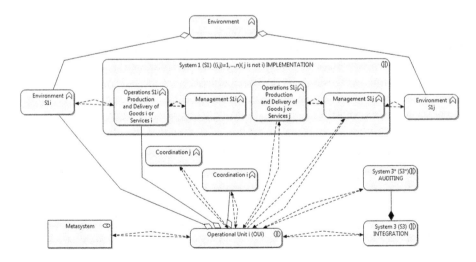

Fig. 3. Frame for flows in System 1 (adopted from [22])

Figure 3 shows that functions of S1 are strongly dependent on various information flows inside and outside the S1 [22]. According to [8] these are information flows that concern the Management System (System 3 (S3) and its information System 3* (S3*) for receiving instructions (from S3 and S3* to Operational Unit i (OU$_i$) of S1), for accountability (from OUi to S3 and S3*), and resource bargaining; the flows to and from specific environment (including market of products and addressees of services of OU$_i$); the flows to and from regulatory units of OU$_i$ from the System 2 (S2) - coordination for OU$_i$ and coordination for other units OU$_j$ of S1; the information flows to and from other operational functions of S1; the flows to and from managerial functions of other operational units of S1; and the flows to and from the Meta-system (the next fractal level). It is essential that all abovementioned units (except of the Meta-system) are represented as functions, i.e., they are performer free at the particular perspective of consideration. This applies also to all other viable systems model Systems, which are discussed in the remainder of this section.

Typical functions of *System 2* (S2) are associated to personnel policies, accounting policies, legal requirements, programming of production, organizational norms, etc. [8]. Here the decisions concerning particular structure of S1 can be made. Information flows for S2 are reflected in Fig. 4.

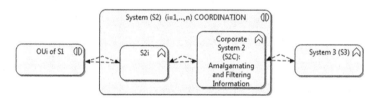

Fig. 4. Frame for information flows for System 2

System 3 (S3) functions as an operational management of the enterprise. System 3* (S3*) supports S3. S3 has to integrate operational units of S1, ensure that S1 functions harmoniously and exploits synergies that might appear in S1. S3 assigns goals for each operational unit of S1 in cooperation with System 4 and in conformity with System 5 [4]. The main function of S3* is ensuring the completeness of information, which reaches S3. Information flows for S3 and S3* are reflected in Fig. 5. S3 is threefold supported by information about S1: directly from S1, via S2, and via S3*. This shows high importance of information completeness in managerial decisions. S3 has also information flows with System 4 and System 5. The information is used in tasks where several management system functions interact.

The principal responsibility of *System 4* (S4) is to identify and carry out, in a timely manner, internal changes necessary for the enterprise to remain viable. This system may exploit different tools for analyzing the environment and the impact of its changes on an enterprise (business intelligence tools, simulation, Delphi studies, etc.). The decisions made by S4 are produced in cooperation with S3 and under the approval of System 5. Functions of *System 5* (S5) possess the highest authority in the enterprise. They must balance the present and future of the enterprise, establish and maintain the "identity" of

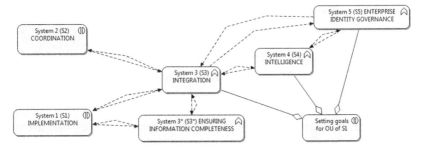

Fig. 5. Frame for information flows for System 3, System 3*, System 4, and System 5

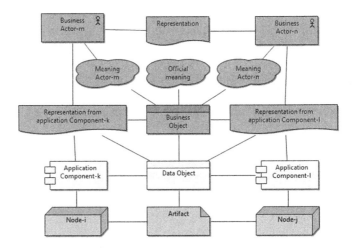

Fig. 6. Frame for reflecting information flows by enterprise architecture (adopted from [22])

the enterprise by, e.g., determining vision, mission, and strategic goals of the enterprise. The information flows for S5 are also reflected in Fig. 5.

The most complex information flows are for S1. Here we have to take into consideration that at the next fractal level the S1, being a viable system, may include all information flows reflected in Figs. 3, 4, and 5. One more issue to be taken into consideration is the necessity to have the information system support for each interaction reflected in Figs. 2, 3, and 4, i.e., specific interaction facilities are to be available to ensure needed exchange of information.

The distinction between different *information flows in the enterprise architecture* is done on the basis of the way of information processing and accessibility of the meaning of the data. The basic architectural constructs used in the frame for the analysis of information flows in the enterprise architecture are represented in Fig. 6.

The frame for flow analysis is represented at three levels of abstraction according to ArchiMate language [21]. It is made for reflecting information flows between any two information processing elements, e.g., from Actor on the left to Actor on the right. At the technology level the information processing elements are Nodes; at the application level – Application Components; at the business level – Actors. The frame shows three Representations – one human and two application made ones, as well as three Meanings, the one for Actor on the left, the one for Actor on the right, and the official meaning which corresponds to organizational ontology, database schemes, or other codified shared organizational knowledge.

When considering any process, which includes information handling activities, there will be information flow between the natural or artificial elements handling the information in each couple of related activities. Depending on the information processing entity substance (human, software, or hardware), the flow will correspond to one of the sub-structures of the frame reflecting information flows (Fig. 6). The application of the frame gives an opportunity to ensure that all relevant architecture elements are in place for each case of information flow inside and between the processes.

As described in previous section, the viable systems model indirectly prescribes that each value producing unit has to handle sub-processes for being aware of its environment, for value production, and self-management. (see Fig. 2). Each of these sub-processes certainly needs information that, in turn, is supported by the information systems sub-processes (see View A in Fig. 7). These *information systems sub-processes* have to be supported by particular human or artificial information handling units that represent a specific part of information systems architecture. Thus there will be an information systems process behind of each business process as its sub-process (View B in Fig. 7). This information systems process may include information system sub-processes for environment scanning, value production, and self-management similarly as processes reflected in Fig. 2.

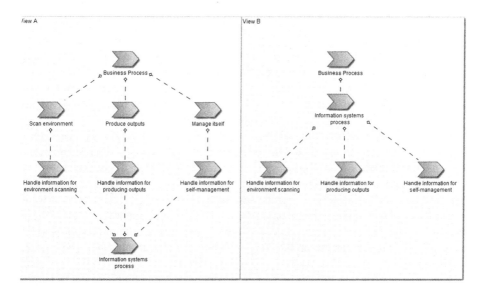

Fig. 7. Frame for information systems process as a sub-process of business process (View A - sub-process level dependency, View B - process level dependency)

The information systems processes are part of work systems that are handling them. Thus behind each information systems process, that supports business process, there is a work system capable of information handling for the particular process (see Fig. 8). The work system in Fig. 8 is a part of work system reflected in Fig. 1.

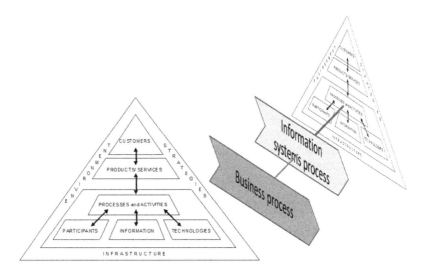

Fig. 8. Information systems work system behind the business process (via corresponding information systems process)

From the process point of view, all work systems behind information system processes are self-similar (according to the definition and explanation of notion 'work system' given at the beginning of Sect. 2); they have to have a measure of autonomy; and they are a part of a whole work system that supports all information processes in a an enterprise. Thus work systems that support business processes form a fractal architecture [7, 9] that can expose a high level of flexibility needed for agile and viable enterprises.

On another hand, information systems management also is a business process, thus the scanning of information systems environment, information production, and management of information system are sub-processes to be supported (recursively) by the information system. This applies to information systems processes at a high level of abstraction as well as to physical processes, such as cloud management or software development process management, or hardware cluster management [1, 2]. In all these cases the same type work system processes are present, just at different levels of scale and using information systems architecture elements of different substance (see Figs. 2, 6, 7, and 8).

The proposed fractal elements of the information systems architecture can be recognized at two dimensions: at the value production dimension and the work systems substance dimension. *At the value production dimension* we consider all business processes including their variants and value production oriented decompositions. Value production oriented decomposition is different from business process sub-process types reflected in Figs. 2 and 7. Value production decomposition means product oriented decompositions, e.g., the process "educate students" can be decomposed into sub-processes "educate students in chemistry" and "educate students in physics" (alternatively these can be viewed as process variants, too), the process "manufacture cars" can be decomposed into sub-processes "manufacture sport cars" and "manufacture city cars", or, alternatively - "manufacture engine" and "manufacture navigation system", etc. We use the value production dimension from the business perspective. From information system perspective, we use *work systems substance dimension*, where the work system can be considered as a *virtual agent* composed from human participants and computer systems: software, and hardware elements (Fig. 9). Thus, using inclusion relationship between systems of different substance, the virtual agent at the business level of enterprise architecture can be represented by a combination of elements of all substances (including different variants and decompositions still reflecting human actors as part of the work system); at the application level - as software (application software and/or systems software) together with hardware systems; as well as it can be represented as pure hardware systems with embedded information handling functions. Systems software (such as operating systems or data base management systems) can be attributed to application level or, as prescribed by enterprise architecture description language ArchiMate [21], at technology level (where hardware entities are considered as information processing elements). In other words, in virtual agent, we can distinguish between two types of sub-agents - human actors and computer systems. Computer systems include all different information handling entities excluding human actors; i.e. application and technology level elements of the frame reflected in Fig. 6.

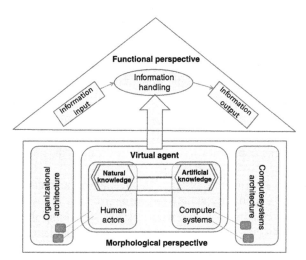

Fig. 9. Frame for virtual actor: the related performers in the work system behind the process

Thus the virtual agent is composed of arbitrary structured human actors and computer systems. We assume that each human actor possesses at least partly identifiable natural knowledge and each computer system (arbitrary network of application and systems software, and hardware) possesses artificial knowledge. Artificial knowledge can be (1) built-in artificial knowledge that is transferred from human being to software or hardware component, e.g., by programming; and (2) artificially learned artificial knowledge, as computer systems with built-in machine learning capabilities can obtain knowledge without human assistance. Combination of this natural and artificial knowledge is an emergent knowledge of a virtual agent, which performs a process. Virtual agent that possesses particular emergent knowledge is capable to perform a particular information handling activity if it can do the following: It can perceive (recognize) input information; it can extract data from the input information; it can interpret the extracted data (turn it into the internally interpreted information); it "knows", what information is expected to be produced; and it is able to produce output information in case relevant input information is available.

At the given level of abstraction the model presented in Fig. 9 does not prescribe any methods for detecting knowledge models of human actors and computer systems. We acknowledge also that obtaining models of human knowledge is only partly possible. However, the frame in Fig. 9 clearly shows that it is necessary to consider knowledge models built into computer systems to understand the capabilities of virtual agents. The frame has morphological flexibility, as it can represent any combinations of enterprise human actors and computer systems. It is applicable also in situations where the virtual agent consists of human actors only or computer systems only. The frame is applicable for use in fractal and viable systems, as the frame of virtual agent supports autonomy and self-organization and it does not change due to scaling or switching to another viewpoint of modeling [7].

4   Discussion

There are the following benefits from viewing information systems architecture as a fractal architecture composed of multiple work systems:

- This helps to ensure that all business processes are supported by information system services (sub-processes for environment scanning, value production, and self-management). These services or sub-processes are essential for agile and viable companies as these companies have to cope with unpredictable changes in their environments.
- Consideration of information systems architecture as a fractal system of work systems gives an opportunity to, at least, recognize (and if possible - manage) all actual virtual information system's work systems supporting the business system regardless of ownership of software and hardware and regardless of functional boundaries of the enterprise.
- Since the work system can be considered as a virtual system, the changes in the architecture can be introduced on a regular basis by combining the work systems or introducing their new versions at the needed level of abstraction or granularity, based on self-similarity principles of fractal systems [7].
- While the particular concept of work system is introduced on the basis of viable systems model (Fig. 2) by considering its operational and strategic processes that

have to directly analyze the external environment of an enterprise, still the concept is applicable also for business processes that do not belong to two abovementioned categories. Such approach enables to look beyond not only functional boundaries of an enterprise, but also to consider customers of the enterprise as partners and switch between physical and virtual boundaries of enterprises in modeling of information systems.

On the basis of frames discussed in the previous section it is possible to define the procedure for requirements acquisition for continuous changes of information systems (Fig. 10). The procedure consists of the following steps:

1. *Identify all Systems prescribed by viable systems model (VSM) in the enterprise.* This mainly concerns analysis of organizational functions and processes. Usually enterprises have at least part of functions prescribed by VSM. It is necessary to map these processes to VSM systems explicitly. Further the processes have to be classified according to the process frame reflected in Fig. 7. This is done in order to ensure that viable systems properties are preserved in the smaller granularity sub-processes.
2. *Check information flows* in the identified processes and identify existing or potential information processing elements that relate to these information flows. For this purpose the enterprise architecture frame reflected in Fig. 6 can be used.
3. *Identify virtual agents behind of each System of VSM.* The processes corresponding to each System of VSM have to be performed by human actors and/or software and hardware systems. These performers not necessarily belong to one and the same structural unit of the enterprise. The virtual agents can be represented using the frame reflected in Fig. 9.
4. *Check whether the virtual agents are capable to handle the information prescribed by frames of information flows in viable systems* (Figs. 3, 4 and 5). As we assume that the virtual agent possesses some emergent knowledge; each human actor possesses at least partly identifiable natural knowledge; and each computer system (arbitrary network of application and systems software and hardware) possesses built-in and possibly also artificially learned knowledge; it is essential that the agent can receive and handle all information flows inside the agent and among the agent and other related agents. For each two information processing elements the information flows may be identified using the frames for information flows in viable systems and enterprise architecture (Figs. 3, 4, 5 and 6) [22]. If any flow cannot be identified it is necessary to perform Step 5.
5. *Define new requirements for information systems development* [23].

Currently the proposed approach of considering information systems architecture as a fractal system of work systems is applied to two library processes at Riga Technical University. Library processes do not directly belong to System 1 or System 4, which are related to the external environment in viable systems model. Nevertheless the library processes may have a direct relationship with external environment of the library and the external environment of the university. Therefore frames of processes discussed in previous section are applicable in this situation. We consider two processes - book ordering and acquisition of electronic resources. The information system's work systems for both processes cross several functional units of the university and for both processes

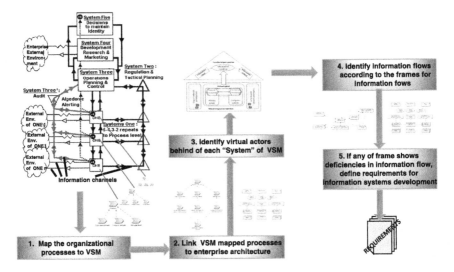

Fig. 10. Use of frames for requirements identification (VSM - viable systems model)

environment scanning, value production, and self-management sub-processes are relevant. Similar information technology support is used for external environment scanning and internal environment scanning (e.g., acquisition of usage statistics and acquisition of popularity statistics).

The analysis of information flows in identified processes and related elements of enterprise architecture uncovered new information requirements and necessity to cooperate between different organizational units to handle the information in order to improve the process behavior. Actually the need for changes in the network of activities in book ordering and acquisition of electronic resources was identified. Information flows were analyzed with respect to the to-be network of the activities. The perspective taken in the analysis did not identify the library as a System 1 of viable systems model. Therefore frames of flows in viable systems model reflected in Figs. 3, 4 and 5 could not be fully utilized. The frame for information flow analysis in enterprise architecture (Fig. 6) was applied and found to be useful for identification of the virtual agents and for identification of new information systems requirements.

The results obtained so far show that a specific, organizational processes and work systems based, information systems architecture management system is needed to fully benefit from the application of work systems based fractal information systems architecture. The results also show also that the approach can be extended to the processes, which do not correspond to specific Systems of VSM, i.e., it can be used in enterprises, which do not fully operate according to viable systems model.

5   Conclusions

The paper proposes to use the concept of a work system for designating virtual and physical components of fractal information systems architecture. The proposal roots in related work on work systems by St. Alter [5] and contemporary applications of viable systems model [6–8]. Fractality of an enterprise and information systems is considered from the point of view of the value production dimension and the work systems substance dimension. The value production dimension concerns value for external customers as well as value for internal customers. The approach allows to consider customers as partners and switch between physical and virtual boundaries of enterprises in modeling of information systems. The work systems paradigm supports fractality as it allows to view the basic information system sub-processes at the level of virtual agents composed of human actors and computer systems; as well as at the levels of business, applications, and systems software and hardware by using inclusion relationship.

The work system is suggested to be considered as an architectural component that for each given business process supports environment scanning, value production, and self-management processes. The main contributions of the paper are the following:

- The paper integrates work systems, viable systems, and fractal systems concepts
- The paper proposes several frames for handling continuous changes in viable enterprises
- The paper proposes simplified method for information systems requirements identification based on the proposed frames and viable, fractal, and work systems paradigms

The paper is limited to the introduction of the concepts and methods at a high level of abstraction. The fractal properties are mainly analyzed only regarding structural self-similarity, connectivity, and emergence. Two experiments are currently in progress to clarify the details and prepare the ground for defining requirements for work systems based fractal information systems architecture management system. A number of case studies in varieties of contexts is a part of further research for providing domain specific guidelines for application of the proposed approach.

Acknowledgment. This work is partly supported by the research grant of Latvian Council of Science, Project No. Z12.0342.

References

1. Cloud Transforms IT, EMC2 (2013). http://www.emc.com/campaign/global/cloud/emc-cloud-services.htm
2. Big Data Transforms Business, EMC2 (2013). http://www.emc.com/campaign/bigdata/index.htm
3. Rudzajs, P.: Towards automated education demand-offer information monitoring: the system's architecture. In: Niedrite, L., Strazdina, R., Wangler, B. (eds.) BIR Workshops 2011. LNBIP, vol. 106, pp. 252–265. Springer, Heidelberg (2012)
4. Asnina, E.: Essentiality of changes in business models. In: Kirikova, M., Lazdane, G., Grabis, J., Lace K. (eds.) Proceedings of the 2nd International Business and System Conference BSC 2013, pp. 44–51. RTU Press (2013). https://bsc2013-journals.rtu.lv/issue/current/showToc
5. Alter, St.: Defining information systems as work systems implications for the IS field. Eur. J. Inf. Syst. **17**, 448–469 (2008)

6. Hoverstadt, P.: The Fractal Organization: Creating Sustainable Organizations with the Viable Systems Model. Wiley, Chichester (2008)
7. Espejo, R., Reyes, A.: Organizational Systems. Managing Complexity with the Viable System Model. Springer, Berlin (2011)
8. Rios, J.P.: Design and Diagnosis for Sustainable Organization. Springer, Berlin (2012)
9. Kirikova, M.: Towards flexible information architecture for fractal information systems. In: Kusiac, A., Lee, S. (eds.) The Proceedings of the International Conference on Information, Process, and Knowledge Management, eKNOW, pp. 135–140. IEEE Computer Society (2009)
10. Kirikova, M.: Towards multifractal approach in is development. In: Barry, C., Conboy, K., Lang, M., Wojtkowski, G., Wojtkowski, W. (eds.) Information Systems Development: Challenges in Practice, Theory and Education, vol. 1, pp. 295–306. Springer, New York (2009)
11. Fryer, P., Ruis, J.: What are fractal systems: a brief description of complex adaptive and emerging systems (2006). http://www.fractal.org. Accessed 14 April 2007
12. Klonowski, W.: Signal and image analysis using chaos theory and fractal geometry (2000). http://www.fractal.org. Accessed 14 April 2007
13. Tharumarajah, A., Wells, A.J., Nemes, L.: Comparison of emerging manufacturing concepts. Syst. Man Cybern. 1, 325–331 (1998)
14. Chiva-Gomez, R.: Repercussions on complex adaptive systems on product design management. Technovation 24, 707–711 (2004)
15. Ryu, K., Jung, M.: Fractal approach to managing intelligent enterprises. In: Gupta, J.N.D., Sharma, S.K. (eds.) Creating Knowledge Based Organizations, pp. 312–348. Idea Group Publishers, Hershey (2003)
16. Ramanathan, Y.: Fractal architecture for the adaptive complex enterprise. Commun. ACM 48(5), 51–67 (2005)
17. Hongzhao, D., Dongxu, L., Yanwei, Z., Chen, Y.: A novel approach of networked manufacturing collaboration: fractal web based enterprise. Int. J. Adv. Manuf. Technol. 26, 1436–1442 (2005)
18. Gabriel, R.P., Goldman, R.: Conscientious Software. In: Proceedings of OOPSLA 2006, pp. 433–450. ACM (2006). 1-59593-348-4/06/0010
19. Sprice, R., Kirikova, M.: Feasibility study: new knowledge demands in turbulent business world. In: Nilsson, A.G., Gustas, R., Wojtkowski, W., Wojtkowski, W.G., Wrycza, S., Zupancic, J. (eds.) Advances in Information Systems Development: Bridging the Gap Between Academia and Industry, vol. 2, pp. 131–142. Springer, Heidelberg (2006)
20. Ashby, W.R.: Requisite variety and its implications for the control of complex systems. Cybernetica 1(2), 83–99 (1958)
21. ArchiMate 2.1 Specification. http://pubs.opengroup.org/architecture/archimate2-doc/ (2014)
22. Kirikova, M., Pudane, M.: Viable systems model based information flows. In: Catania, B., et al. (eds.) New Trends in Databases and Information Systems. AISC, vol. 241, pp. 97–104. Springer, Heidelberg (2014)
23. Kirikova, M.: Viable systems model based requirements engineering. In: Proceedings of REFSQ-2014 Workshops, Doctoral Symposium, Empirical Track, and Posters, co-located with the 20th International Conference on Requirements Engineering: Foundation for Software Quality (REFSQ 2014), Essen, Germany, vol. 1138, pp. 143–144. CEUR-WS.org (2014)

Towards Ontology-Based Information Systems and Performance Management for Collaborative Enterprises

Barbara Livieri[1][(✉)] and Mario Bochicchio[2]

[1] Department of Economic Sciences, University of Salento, Lecce, Italy
barbara.livieri@unisalento.it
[2] Department of Innovation Engineering, University of Salento, Lecce, Italy
mario.bochicchio@unisalento.it

Abstract. Much of the research on Performance Management (PM) for collaborative enterprises (CE) is based on qualitative considerations and does not consider the impact of modern Information Systems both on the collaborative/competitive dimension of firms and on the PM process. The peculiarities of the different types of CEs are not clearly addressed and managed in literature, and the performance measurements are often oriented to specific aspects rather than to assess the overall quality of business. Moreover, in several proposals, the skills and the time required to the managers of CEs are far from those available in the largest part of existing SMEs. In this scenario the objective of the paper is to discuss how conceptual modeling techniques, and namely ontologies and performance modeling, can contribute to better manage collaborative enterprises.

Keywords: Information systems · Enterprise modelling · Performance evaluation · Collaborative enterprises · Ontologies

1 Introduction

Collaboration among enterprises is gaining ever more importance due to globalization, which has forced businesses to rearrange their organizational structures. In this work, we focus on collaboration from a systemic perspective [1,2]; in order to emphasize this view on collaboration and to abstract from the specific forms that it can assume (e.g., strategic alliances, networked organizations, etc.), we use the term collaborative enterprise (CE).

In the last twenty years, organizational relationships have moved from intra-organizational to inter-organizational ones (i.e., collaboration among enterprise, also defined as cross-organizational) and are moving towards trans-organizational relations (i.e., collaboration among collaborative enterprises), with a prediction of a speed for value creation never seen before [3]. Nonetheless, it is known that globally between 50 % and 70 % of CEs fails [4,5], often due to the lack of a comprehensive analysis that combine strategic goals and KPIs, whereas performance

© Springer International Publishing Switzerland 2015
S. Nurcan and E. Pimenidis (Eds.): CAiSE Forum 2014, LNBIP 204, pp. 181–196, 2015.
DOI: 10.1007/978-3-319-19270-3_12

measurement is a key element in achieving business goals [6]. In fact, although, as outlined in a review of literature [7], several authors studied the role of management accounting in inter-organizational environments, to our knowledge no one applied these results in order to quantitatively analyze the performance of CEs, of involved firms and of their linkage [3,8,9] for governance purposes. Moreover, in several proposals, the skills required to managers are far from those available in the largest part of existing SMEs, which are the most numerous actors in CEs. In this context, organizations would benefit from methodologies and tools allowing them to better link desired objectives and achieved results in an inter-organizational environment. This requires a more structured and systematic approach to evaluate not only the individual organizations' performance but also how it compares with partners and competitors [10], even in different CEs. In practical cases, this kind of interrelated performance evaluation and comparison cannot be conceived and realized without a set of suitable IS elements and procedures, which becomes not neutral with respect to the measured performance and to type of collaboration, as well as a music instrument is not neutral with respect to the played music.

In this perspective, Information Systems (IS) have to face the new challenge offered by collaboration among enterprises [11,12] and Information Technology (IT) concepts, such as online databases, information modeling, ontologies and Semantic Web techniques, become relevant to CEs for their operational life.

The aim of this paper is (a) to identify the challenges for IS deriving from the collaboration among organizations and the existing gaps in literature, (b) to elicit a set of requirements, starting from the gaps in existing literature and (c) to propose a IS architecture for CEs that can satisfy these requirements.

The paper is organized as follows: in Sect. 2 the research method is defined as a foundation for the explorative research; in Sect. 3, the research problem is outlined and the high-level requirements for the architecture are elicited; in Sect. 4, the related works on the modeling of performance and collaborative enterprises are presented. In Sect. 5 the high-level architecture of the IS for collaborative enterprises is presented, while in Sect. 6 we discuss a use case. The last section is for concluding remarks.

2   Method

The research method here adopted is based on the Design Science Research methodology proposed in [13,14]. This methodology implies the identification and motivation of the problem, the definition of the possible solution (Relevance cycle), the adoption of grounding theories and methods at the state of the art (Rigor Cycle) and the design of the artefact and its evaluation (Design cycle). In particular, this work is concerned with the with the identification of the problem and with the proposition of a suitable architecture for an information system able to satisfy the characteristics and the need of collaborative enterprises and of the participating organizations.

As a first step, we outline the general problem in order to motivate our proposal. In order to follow a technology-enabled enterprise-driven approach, as recommended by [11], we elicited the requirements towards the IS architecture starting from the management literature on collaboration among organizations. As a second step we analyze and compare the existing literature and its compliance whit the above defined general requirements. Finally, we propose a set of guidelines and a high-level architecture and we discuss its compliance towards the requirements, in order to evaluate whether our proposition is suitable to face the challenges posed by the collaboration among enterprises.

3 Problem Definition

In this section, we analyze both the literature on performance management for CEs and on cross-organizational information systems, in order to outline which challenges arise from the collaboration among organizations and are still open. Furthermore, we elicit the high-level requirements related to performance measurement.

3.1 Domain Outline

Whilst we are going towards a network-SMEs-driven society, new challenges arise for performance measurement systems, since they have to be developed and used across the traditional organizational boundaries. Indeed, the key element in the future seems to be cooperation [12], thus IS should "enable new forms of participation and collaboration, catalyze further the formation of networked enterprises and business ecosystems [...] ushering in a new generation of enterprise systems" [11]. Indeed, according to contingency theory, a change in the organizational structure implies a change in the IS. In this sense, IS usually distinguish and oppose relations within a firm, from those across it, whilst in an inter-organizational setting it is necessary to broaden data sources so to include partners and to consider them as beneficiary of the information [15].

One of the roles of information systems is to allow performance measurement, which is a key function in the assessment of the collaborative enterprises and of how the CE is affecting the individual organizations. At the Enterprise System level, this can be achieved through shared databases, data warehouses, workflow management systems, web services, SOAs or cross-organizational ERP [16], which are used from several independent firms whom cooperate in an inter-organizational environment [17]. In particular, cross-organizational Information Systems can assure a flow of information among and within organizations [16], thus permitting the coordination among partners, which is essential in order to define and to achieve shared goals. However, the use of cross-organizational ERP systems can lead to a lost on flexibility because it implies processes standardization which is not easy to achieve in CEs, being the collaborative relations not always stable. Anyway, most of the IS adopted are not cross-organizational; thus, they focus on a single enterprise with some supports towards sharing performance information with external parties [3]. On the other hand, there are also non IS-based enforcement methods, such as Open Book Accounting (OBA), which allows firms to share accounting information. Nonetheless, they are sometimes seen as formal control mechanism that damages trust [18].

In this scenario, there is the need to manage both the performance of CEs and of organizations (SMEs or big enterprises) [3]: it is necessary to modify existing tools for inter-organizational settings, overcoming the clear-cut between external and internal environment. Indeed, whilst it is possible to use the same performance measurement frameworks used for firms, it is still necessary to structurally and operatively change the measurement system [19]. Therefore, the question is how to design and develop IS, allowing a monitoring at two levels of granularity (i.e., the collaborative enterprise level and the organizational level), with a guarantee of comparability between KPIs and perspectives of the two levels, providing also suggestions for KPIs and dashboards.

3.2   High Level Requirements for the IS Architecture

Research and empirical studies [4,5] suggest that collaborative enterprises need specialized tools to support performance management and decision-making processes, by enabling a clear linkage between strategic goals and Key Performance Indicators (KPIs). Indeed, the continuous monitoring of the fulfillment of goals is a critical factor in determining the success of CE [20,21]. This can be achieved by designing and implementing suitable information architectures, as defined in [22], based on appropriate models and right technologies. Staring from the papers on collaboration available in literature, it is possible to define some high-level requirements. In the following, we will outline the most relevant ones in connection to performance measurement issues.

When the performance measurement is related to inter-organizational aspects, interoperability issues need to be accounted for. Indeed, different organizations often use different terms to describe the same concept or the same term to refer to different concepts (semantic heterogeneity), use different data structures in their information systems [23] (structural heterogeneity) or apply diverse data formats (syntactic heterogeneity). This is sometimes due to different accounting standards and methods or to a different calculation and interpretation of KPIs.

Requirement 1. Interoperability issues should be accounted for.

Collaborative enterprises that differ for type, goals or other characteristics, require different KPIs [24] in order to measure the achievement of the business goals. However, the definition of relevant KPIs and dashboards is particularly difficult in CEs, due to the implicit complexity of the collaboration. This is even more difficult for SMEs, which often lack of the know-how needed to perform these kinds of analyses. Therefore, it can result particularly useful the automatic suggestion of relevant KPIs and dashboards, based on the context. In order to achieve this result, there is the need to also precisely define the context and the domain-specific KPIs.

Requirement 2. It should be possible to automatically suggest, based on the context, domain-specific KPIs and dashboards.

Requirement 2.1. It should be available a comprehensive analysis of the context, taking into account CEs type, organizational structures, roles and goals.

Requirement 2.2. It should be possible to derive domain-specific KPIs, i.e., KPIs specific for the specific context.

Furthermore, the organizations participating in a CE can establish some policies and governance rules that define their constraints on the behavior over time, which sometimes are embedded in contracts. Some of these policies can be easily re-used by others, creating general patterns (i.e., useful for all kinds of collaborations) or patterns specific to a particular type of collaboration (e.g., rules on the supply of raw materials).

Requirement 3. It should be possible to store the information on the contracts and on the specific type of CEs that used them and assist in the contract drawing and enactment by means of contractual patterns.

Finally, among the organizations of a CE, there is usually a certain degree of information asymmetry. On one hand, this is sometimes an unwanted effect of the difficulty to communicate (e.g., interoperability issues). On the other hands, it can also results from a choice of partners, who prefer to keep private the information concerning, for instance, revenues and costs, because they are afraid of potential opportunistic behaviors.

Requirement 4. The information disclosure should be balanced with the degree of privacy defined from each organization.

4 Related Works

Enterprise Modeling is a set of formal, semi-formal and non-formal languages able to model, represent and describe important aspects of the structure and of the operational life of an enterprise. The research on enterprise modelling has several topics. Some authors focus on the analysis of business processes [25–27], others on the information architecture [28] of firms, some others on the modeling of strategic an organizational aspects as well [29,30], of the collaboration between enterprises, or of performance indicators, by means of domain-specific modeling languages (DSML) and ontologies.

Performance Modeling. Domain specific modeling languages (DSML) have been used in order to offer models able to support the creation and the interpretation of performance measurement systems effectively and efficiently by providing differentiated semantics of dedicated modeling concepts and corresponding descriptive graphical symbols [29]. Some of these works model performance for business processes, describing, e.g., the meta-types `Indicator` and `Indicator Group` with the aim of aggregating different KPIs and to offer different views to the users [31]. In [29] other concepts, e.g., formula, unit of measurement, time horizon, and the inter-relation between KPIs are accounted for. Moreover, in [6] causal, correlation and aggregation relations are defined, as well as the high-level relation between the concepts of KPI, task, goal, process, role and agent. Another approach has been used with the Business Intelligence Model (BIM) [32,33], which provides high level concepts that can be used in order to model the strategy and the related goals, indicators and potential situations (Strengths, Weaknesses, Threats and Opportunities). In other works, the modeling of performance is achieved by means of ontologies, which can be very effective to represent shared conceptualizations of specific domains and to infer new knowledge, as outlined in [34]. In particular, some authors [35] focus on Process Performance Indicators (PPIs) and on the computation methods, such as the use of base measures, the use of aggregation functions (e.g., min, max) or of mathematical functions. An interesting work has been done in [36] where an ontology of KPIs with reasoning functionalities for Virtual Enterprises is presented. In more detail, the main reasoning functionalities concerns the formula manipulation, used to derive relation between indicators and to rewrite a formula; the equivalence checking, used in order to check for duplicates; the consistency checking and the extraction of common indicators. Both the works on DSML and on ontologies still lack of some characteristics which are particularly desirable when it comes to developing IS for collaborative enterprises. Even though the works on DSML and semi-formal frameworks offer a broad analysis of performance indicators and of their relations, it is not possible to add reasoning functionalities. On the other hand, these works offer high-level models; therefore, the concrete use of these models requires too much work for the users and it is seldom feasible in SMEs. Moreover, for what concerns ontologies, most of the works do not take properly into account reasoning functionalities, they are seldom available online, existing ontologies are rarely re-used and no pattern is presented, as discussed in [37]. In general, there are still few works that analyze ontologies of KPIs and a lack of works that simultaneously take into account KPIs, goals and CEs, which are entities far more complex than individual enterprises.

Collaborative Enterprise Modeling. Ontologies and taxonomies have been used as well to model the collaboration among enterprises. An ontology for Collaborative Networks has been proposed in [38], where the organizational structure and the domain specific knowledge of Virtual Breeding Environments (VBEs) are represented. In particular, each VBE has some assets and have some participants. Each VBE participant has a VBE Role and to each role some tasks are associated. Also, a VBE has some business opportunities related to the development and commercialization of products and services. VBEs are defined as organizations, to which are connected competencies and processes. In turn, each Process uses some resources and produce or use as inputs other products and services. Although this ontology provides a general representation of CNOs and VBEs and it is possible to analyze the roles of participants, it is not possible to understand CEs types, since the ontology is focused on VBE. Moreover, in [39,40], a taxonomy of Collaborative Networks (CNs) is provided. The authors start from a definition of CNs in order to classify 26 types of CNs, among which digital ecosystems. The study is quite interesting and takes into account criteria such as the time perspective, however, the analysis is not enough broad and deep and accounts for a limited subset of collaboration forms. Also, the lack of a formal language does not allow the semi-automatic classification of instances (CEs) nor the suggestion of relevant KPIs for the type of collaboration. In [41] the IDEON ontology is proposed in order to support the design and the management of collaborative and distributed enterprises. To this aim, the authors take into account four views of the collaboration, namely, (a) Enterprise Context View; (b) Enterprise Organizational View; (c) Process View; and (d) Resource/Product View. Finally, in [42] a model for supply chain is presented with the aim of enabling the semantic integration of Information Systems. In order to do so, some basic concepts, such as the supply chain structure (`SC_Structure`), the participants (`Party`), their roles (`Role`), the purpose of the alliance (`Purpose`), the `Activity`, the `Resource`, the `Performance` and the `Performance_Metric`. However, not even in these two cases there is a classification of the types of collaborative enterprises, although the basic concepts used in these ontology can be borrowed.

5 A High-Level Description of an Ontology-Based Information System for CEs

5.1 Functionalities of the Information System

From the requirements outlined in Sect. 3.2, it emerges that the Information System of a collaborative enterprise should have four aims, as outlined in the following. Conceptual models in general, and ontologies in particular, play a central role [43] both to understand the business and organizational domain of CEs (which is essential in the IS design phase) and to support a number of important services at runtime (data and information integration, knowledge sharing, reasoning), which represents the collaborative hearth of any good IS for CEs.

Performance Monitoring of Organizations and CEs and Benchmarking, through the creation of personalized dashboards, KPIs evaluation and information sharing. Through benchmarking it is possible to compare firms or CEs with similar ones, without the necessity to provide analytic data on costs and revenues and, thus, overcoming one of the main limits of management accounting solutions such as open book accounting (OBA). In this case, interoperability issues need to be accounted for. Indeed, different organizations often use different terms to describe the same concept or the same term to refer to different concepts (semantic heterogeneity), use different data structures in their information systems [23] (structural heterogeneity) or apply diverse data formats (syntactic heterogeneity). This is sometimes due to different accounting standards and methods.

Context-Aware Recommender System. In order to better link strategic goals to KPIs, a context-based recommender system for performance indicators could facilitate the decision of which performance to use, thus offering a more comprehensive perspective and, based on the achieved performance, help managers in taking strategic decisions. The recommender system should suggest relevant KPIs and possible dashboards starting from the information on the collaborative enterprise's and the participants' goal system and from the collaboration type. Indeed, each actor and CE has a goal system - explicitly or implicitly formulated - and can use a set of metrics to monitor the goal achievement. These metrics should also be linked with the role of each participant and to the resources used to perform the required activities. On the other hand, the performance measurement system cannot abstract from the peculiarities of collaborative enterprises and from the specific types of collaboration. The system should help organizations and collaborative enterprises to understand and manage the collaborative aspects. In this way, Requirement 1 and Requirement 3 of Sect. 3.2 should be satisfied. Examples of domain specific KPIs for a supply chain with an informal-technical based connection at the early stages of the CE and with the goal of cost reduction are the following:

1. Overall production costs variation, for a given firm, between t0 (before entering a given CE) and t1 (after entering the CE), since the comparison between two periods of time is an effective indicator [19];
2. Overall transportation costs variation, for a given firm, between t0 and t1;

This approach enables the representation of the linkage between the goals and KPIs of collaborative enterprises and individual organizations and makes it possible to track which KPIs are used from firms with specific goals of a specific type and with a certain maturity, so that this information is stored and used to suggest to not expert users which KPIs to choose (Requirements 1–5). The effective availability of this information for the above mentioned layers, and the creation of an online repository with a suitable set of access rights to preserve confidentiality, could facilitate the search for partners (individual organizations or CEs), thus supporting and simplifying the partner selection process (Requirement 6). In short, this approach can facilitate firms also in the choice of which KPIs to include in the dashboard, thus which KPIs are relevant for their specific goals, CE type and maturity. Indeed, through data visualization tools and KPIs ontologies it is possible to develop an interpretative framework able to understand KPIs and to offer information on relevant variables, depending on the typology of partnership. This is particularly useful for SMEs, who lack of the skills to develop and maintain adequate performance measurement systems.

Repository of Templates. Contracts or agreements and organizational structures, whereas available, can be furthermore processed, in order to make available an online repository of domain-specific templates for CEs, such as those provided by the Legal-IST project (http://cordis.europa.eu/project/rcn/71925_en.html), for organizations that decide to formalize or change the collaboration and organizational structures.

Information Sharing, in order to better collaborate with partners and to have more detailed benchmarks, with different level of privacy. This is coherent with the interest in techniques such as open-book accounting (OBA) [44], which allows for the exchange of financial information. In this case, it would be useful to have more information than the one on financial aspects. Indeed, organizations that cooperate need to exchange information (e.g., on their transactions, goals), since this can increase their performance [45]. Also, in case they decide to share more data not only with partners but also with other organizations, this can increase the effectiveness of benchmarking. In the collaborative IS firms should be able to share information, in order to better collaborate with partners and to have more detailed benchmarks, with different level of privacy. This means that each firm can decide to be a grey box, a white box or a black box for each other firm. In more detail, it is (a) a white box if choose to be completely transparent for other firms, e.g., disclosing its processes and organizational structures, (b) a black box if the firm choose to disclose to other firms only external parameters (e.g., financial statements, information on web sites); (c) a gray box if the firm choose to disclose only partial information.

These features can be offered through a collaborative, ontology-based Information System delivered online. As stated in [3], IS are essential for the development and use of Performance Measurement Systems. In order for the information system to operate in an inter-organizational setting, it has to be Interned-based, thus being easily accessible by all firms. In this scenario, as we will discuss in Sect. 5.2, ontologies are particularly useful due to both the reasoning functionalities that they enable and for their ability to offer a shared conceptualization of both performance measurement and collaborative enterprises.

In order to exploit these functionalities, it is useful to see a collaborative enterprise as a system [24] composed by three layers: the *CE structural layer*, the *organization structural layer* and the *dynamic layer*. The CE structural layer is about information on the CE (e.g., objectives, activities, program) and on its performance (e.g. results achieved) as described in financial statements, web sites and other available sources. The organizational structural layer is for information on firms participating in CEs, such as firm objectives, activities, business sector, characteristics, organizational structure and performance. Finally, the dynamic layer is for information on formal and informal strategic agreements among firms and between each firm and the CE, on partnership contracts, on their governance, duration, obligations and expected outcomes.

5.2 The Role of Ontologies

In our proposal, the main role of ontologies is to provide a description of the context used by the recommender system, enabling also the use of reasoning functionalities [46]. Indeed, ontologies are often used in recommender systems [47]. In this case, they are particularly useful, since the recommender system should deal with different domains, such as KPIs, goals, organizational aspects and collaborative types and features that should be considered simultaneously. Indeed, without the use of domain ontologies, the system might return non-accurate suggestions [46].

For example, let us suppose we have two collaborative enterprises (Alpha and Beta), both among organizations operating in the same business sector. The CE Alpha is made up by manufacturing companies that want to increase their performance through the reduction of the distribution costs. On the other hand, the CE Beta, is made up by manufacturing companies that want to increase their performance through innovation, thus investing in research. In both cases, we have the same structure of collaboration with an horizontal integration, the same general goal, the same business sector, but the performance needs to be measured in different ways. In the first case, we have to look at costs indicators and profits indicators, whilst in the latter what matters is the potential increase of incomes or the potential cost reduction, since the financial effects can only be visible after years.

A first step towards this goal, is to provide a shared understanding on what collaboration is and what types of collaboration exist. However, the literature on collaboration is vast and multidisciplinary, thus it sometimes lacks of coherence in the definition and understanding of collaboration. In particular, this is due to two issues:

1. Sometimes the same term is used to describe different concepts or, on turn, the same concept is described by means of different terms. For instance, the term *alliance* is sometimes referred indistinctly to both horizontal or vertical partnerships [48], while it is often used only to describe vertical alliances and sometimes only dyadic relations, which accordingly to [49] should not be considered as alliances. The same goes for the term *joint venture*, which sometimes is regarded as one of the possible types of alliances [48,50] and sometimes as a different concepts [51].
2. In order to classify the collaboration types, different authors refers to different perspectives (e.g., temporal, geographical, integration type, goal-related and so on). Even when the same perspective is used, it can result in a different classification or in a classification that refers to different meaning of the term *collaboration*, as above mentioned.

In this sense, ontologies are particularly useful when there is a lack of a shared knowledge on a specific domain.

Moreover, for what concerns the modeling of indicators and their conjunct use among the organizations participating in the collaborative enterprise, as outlined by Diamantini et al. (2013) *"the formal representation and manipulation of the structure of a formula is essential in Virtual Enterprises to check inconsistencies among independent indicator definitions, reconcile indicators values coming from different sources, and provide the necessary flexibility to indicators management"* [36]. Indeed, bot semi-formal and rigorously formal ontologies [52] are well known as a solution to heterogeneity issues [53], which can originate when dealing with indicators.

Finally, complex information systems rely on robust and coherent, formal representations of their subject matter. In this sense, ontologies can provide models of different aspects of a business entity contributing to intra- and inter-enterprise information systems. By committing to the same ontological specification, different applications share a common vocabulary with a formal language and clear semantics. Also, by representing knowledge with a well-established formalism [54], internal consistency and compliance checking can be performed in order to determine content adequacy.

5.3   High-Level Architecture

The block diagram of a software architecture implementing the above-mentioned functions and satisfying the requirements specified in Sect. 3.2 is depicted in Fig. 1.

The system is composed by two type of nodes, namely Base and Aggregator. The internal structure of the Base Nodes is represented in the upper part of Fig. 1. Base Nodes are replicated for each CE and, for confidentiality reasons, the access to each base node is reserved only to the members of the belonging CE. For the same reason Base Nodes can be deployed and managed directly by CE members or on the Cloud. Organizations data is stored in three databases, namely the ORG database for organizational structures, the PPI database for inter-organizational processes and their performance indicators, and the ADM database for financial data and the related indicators. Each CE member can work only on its own data and on partners data for which it has been explicitly authorized. Dashboards for the whole CE and for each one of its participants are managed by the DSB module and by its components named CEC and SFC. The DSB module is also in charge of receiving recommendations from the Aggregator Node and to notify them to the proper users according to their state and to the context. User models and context models are managed locally by the LOM (Local Ontology Manager) Module. The non-private data and indicators representing

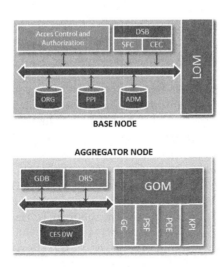

Fig. 1. High-level architecture

each organization and each CE (e.g. financial statements and public reports) is then brought to the Aggregator Node, represented in the lower part of Fig. 1, where acquired data is stored in a global repository (CES-DW). In this Node, a Global Dashboard module (GDB) summarizes the main indicators representing the whole set of CEs adopting the system. Moreover, the GDB module allows organizations and collaborative enterprises to benchmarks their performance.

One of the role of the Aggregator Node is to gather data from the Base Nodes and to enrich KPI models with user-preferences for the collaborative filtering part of the recommender system. The ontological model of the global context is built by the GC module, also based on the information coming from the public information available on CEs (PCE module) and on single organizations (PSF module). All the above-mentioned ontological models are based on the Global Ontology Manager (GOM) module. The ORS component collect contextualized recommendation data and send it to the Base Nodes. To summarize, the aggregator node retrieves information from different sources on component organizations, financial and non-financial data, contracts, KPIs, etc. and stores them in the respective databases. The Ontology-based modeling of both single organizations and CEs easily permit to classify CEs and their organizational structures. Other context data comes from sources, such as public data (e.g., financial statements, publicly available in several countries, web pages, collaboration agreements), organizations internal data (e.g., business plan, business processes, etc.).

6 Use Case

The detailed design of the software system includes several use cases. Here, we present one of these use cases as an example. The main actor is the agent whose role is to monitor the performance of the collaborative enterprise. In order to do so, the CE must be already defined in terms of participants, goals and temporal perspective. The requirements defined in Sect. 3.2 is satisfied if the classification of the CE type is correct and the suggestion of the KPIs is compliant with the type and the goals.

In order to classify the collaboration, the system needs some basic information regarding the CE. The information can be divided in information regarding the individual organizations and information regarding the collaborative enterprise. The information on individual enterprises concerns the geographical area in which the organizations operate, the business sector; the business sector of the activities on which the individual organizations collaborate, the shared resources, the main goals, the role that the organization play inside the collaboration. The information on the collaborative enterprise concerns the expected years of collaboration, the number of participants, the main goals, the joint activities. This data is also used in order to determine other relevant information, such as the temporal horizon (short, medium or long term), the CE size, the organizational structure (from the roles), the integration type (from the business sectors), etc. Based on this, it is possible to determine the type of collaboration and to check its compliance with the main goals. This information, compared with the goals, is then used to derive domain-specific KPIs.

Let us suppose that we have a CE made up by 81 organizations (bathing establishments), which aim is to increase the overall competitiveness of the participants, by means of the increase of security on the beaches, the improvement of environmental sustainability and the coordination in the supply of services. Since all organizations are operating in the same business sector, we know that it is a big (81 members) horizontal alliance, with a long term perspective (no term defined). From this input, the system will return some domain-specific KPIs, such as the total occupancy of umbrellas, the space between umbrellas (to account for the quality of the service) and the % of recycled garbage. These KPIs are relevant for both the type of alliance and for the goals. Indeed, if we had known only the goals of the CE, it would not have been possible to eliminate KPIs such as, for instance, the reduction of the supply costs, the investment in research and so on.

7 Conclusions

In this paper, through the analysis of existing literature, we discussed how the research on Information Systems (IS) can contribute to reshape the performance measurement process to better integrate it in the management cycle. In this perspective, Information Systems (IS) have to face the new challenge offered by a networked society. Starting from the literature analysis, we elicit a set of high level requirement for the IS architecture and propose an approach to develop a comprehensive service, based on ontologies, for CEs governance and analysis, through the creation of a collaborative IS and of repositories. In particular, in the present work, we analyze the functionalities required to the IS, the role of ontologies and the high-level architecture. Finally, we discuss a use case in order to clarify how the recommender system functionality works. Indeed, the designed architecture is useful for understanding KPIs in relation to CEs goals, types and maturity signaling promptly anomalies and offering information on relevant variables, depending on the typology of CEs. The application of this approach is particularly useful when SMEs comes into play, since they often lack of the financial and the know-how required to enforce a complex and heterogeneous performance measurement system. Future research should move towards the development of cloud based IS designed for collaboration among SMEs.

References

1. Von Bertalanffy, L.: General system theory. Gen. Syst. 1(1), 11–17 (1956)
2. Schneider, M., Somers, M.: Organizations as complex adaptive systems: implications of complexity theory for leadership research. Leadersh. Quart. 17(4), 351–365 (2006)
3. Bititci, U.S., Garengo, P., Dörfler, V., Nudurupati, S.: Performance measurement: challenges for tomorrow. Int. J. Manag. Rev. 14(3), 305–327 (2012)

4. Bititci, U.S., Butler, P., Cahill, W., Kearney, D.: Collaboration: a key competence for competing in the 21st century (2008)
5. Kaplan, R.S., Norton, D.P., Rugelsjoen, B.: Managing alliances with the balanced scorecard. Harv. Bus. Rev. **88**, 114–121 (2010)
6. Popova, V., Sharpanskykh, A.: Modeling organizational performance indicators. Inf. Syst. **35**(4), 505–527 (2010)
7. Caglio, A., Ditillo, A.: A review and discussion of management control in inter-firm relationships: achievements and future directions. Acc. Organ. Soc. **33**, 865–898 (2008). Elsevier Ltd
8. Krathu, W., Engel, R., Pichler, C., Zapletal, M., Werthner, H.: Identifying inter-organizational key performance indicators from EDIFACT messages. In: 2013 IEEE 15th Conference on Business Informatics, pp. 276–283, July 2013
9. Bochicchio, M.A., Livieri, B., Longo, A., Di Cagno, P.: DsNA: a database for strategic network analysis in Italy. In: Baglieri, D., Metallo, C., Rossignoli, C., Iacono, M.P. (eds.) Information Systems, Management, Organization and Control, pp. 153–161. Springer, Heidelberg (2014)
10. Parmenter, D.: Key Performance Indicators (KPI): Developing, Implementing, and Using Winning KPIs. Wiley, Hoboken (2010)
11. FInES Research Roadmap Task Force: Future Internet Enterprise Systems (FInES)- Research Roadmap. Technical report, June 2010
12. Missikoff, M.: The future of enterprise systems in a fully networked society. In: Ralyté, J., Franch, X., Brinkkemper, S., Wrycza, S. (eds.) CAiSE 2012. LNCS, vol. 7328, pp. 1–18. Springer, Heidelberg (2012)
13. Hevner, A.R.: A three cycle view of design science research. Scand. J. Inf. Syst. **19**(2), 4 (2007)
14. von Alan, R.H., March, S.T., Park, J., Ram, S.: Design science in information systems research. MIS Q **28**(1), 75–105 (2004)
15. Håkansson, H., Lind, J.: Accounting and network coordination. Acc. Organ. Soc. **29**(1), 51–72 (2004)
16. Eckartz, S., Katsma, C., Daneva, M.: The inter-organizational business case in ES implementations: exploring the impact of coordination structures and their properties. In: Quintela Varajão, J.E., Cruz-Cunha, M.M., Putnik, G.D., Trigo, A. (eds.) CENTERIS 2010. CCIS, vol. 110, pp. 188–197. Springer, Heidelberg (2010)
17. Daneva, M., Wieringa, R.: Cost estimation for cross-organizational ERP projects: research perspectives. Softw. Qual. J. **16**(3), 459–481 (2008)
18. Windolph, M., Möller, K.: Open-book accounting: reason for failure of inter-firm cooperation? Manag. Acc. Res. **23**(1), 47–60 (2012)
19. Bititci, U.S., Martinez, V., Albores, P., Parung, J.: Creating and managing value in collaborative networks. Int. J. Phys. Distrib. Logistics Manag. **34**(3/4), 251–268 (2004)
20. Estanyol, F.: The SME co-operation framework: a multi-method secondary research approach to SME collaboration. In: International Conference on E-business, Management and Economics IPEDR, vol. 3, pp. 118–124 (2010)
21. Hoffmann, W., Schlosser, R.: Success factors of strategic alliances in small and medium-sized enterprises–an empirical survey. Long Range Plann. **34**, 357–381 (2001)
22. Resmini, A., Rosati, L.: Pervasive Information Architecture: Designing Cross-Channel User Experiences. Elsevier, Burlington (2011)
23. Laurier, W., Poels, G.: An enterprise-ontology based conceptual-modeling grammar for representing value chain and supply chain scripts. In: ICEIS 2013, p. 95 (2013)

24. Parung, J., Bititci, U.S.: A conceptual metric for managing collaborative networks. J. Modell. Manag. **1**(2), 116–136 (2006)
25. Comuzzi, M., Vonk, J., Grefen, P.: Measures and mechanisms for process monitoring in evolving business networks. Data Knowl. Eng. **71**(1), 1–28 (2012)
26. Comuzzi, M., Vanderfeesten, I., Wang, T.: Optimized cross-organizational business process monitoring: design and enactment. Inf. Sci. **244**, 107–118 (2013)
27. Pan, Y.C., Tang, Y., Gulliver, S.R.: Artefact-oriented business process modelling-an ontological dependency approach. In: ICEIS (3), pp. 223–230 (2013)
28. Kulkarni, V., Roychoudhury, S., Sunkle, S., Clark, T., Barn, B.: Modelling and enterprises-the past, the present and the future. In: MODELSWARD, pp. 95–100 (2013)
29. Strecker, S., Frank, U., Heise, D., Kattenstroth, H.: MetricM: a modeling method in support of the reflective design and use of performance measurement systems. Inf. Syst. e-Business Manag. **10**(2), 241–276 (2012)
30. Frank, U.: Multi-perspective enterprise modeling: foundational concepts, prospects and future research challenges. Softw. Syst. Model. (2012)
31. Pourshahid, A., Amyot, D., Peyton, L., Ghanavati, S., Chen, P., Weiss, M., Forster, A.J.: Business process management with the user requirements notation. Electron. Commer. Res. **9**(4), 269–316 (2009)
32. Maté, A., Trujillo, J., Mylopoulos, J.: Conceptualizing and specifying key performance indicators in business strategy models. In: Proceedings of the 2012 Conference of the Center for Advanced Studies on Collaborative Research, pp. 102–115. IBM Corp. (2012)
33. Barone, D., Jiang, L., Amyot, D., Mylopoulos, J.: Composite indicators for business intelligence. In: Jeusfeld, M., Delcambre, L., Ling, T.-W. (eds.) ER 2011. LNCS, vol. 6998, pp. 448–458. Springer, Heidelberg (2011)
34. Bertolazzi, P., Krusich, C., Missikoff, M.: An approach to the definition of a core enterprise ontology: CEO. In: OES-SEO 2001, International Workshop on Open Enterprise Solutions: Systems, Experiences, and Organizations, pp. 14–15. Citeseer (2001)
35. del-Río-Ortega, A., Resinas, M., Ruiz-Cortés, A.: Defining process performance indicators: an ontological approach. In: Meersman, R., Dillon, T.S., Herrero, P. (eds.) OTM 2010. LNCS, vol. 6426, pp. 555–572. Springer, Heidelberg (2010)
36. Diamantini, C., Potena, D., Storti, E.: A logic-based formalization of KPIs for virtual enterprises. In: Franch, X., Soffer, P. (eds.) CAiSE Workshops 2013. LNBIP, vol. 148, pp. 274–285. Springer, Heidelberg (2013)
37. Livieri, B., Bochicchio, M.: Performance modeling for collaborative enterprises: review and discussion. In: Johansson, B., Andersson, B., Holmberg, N. (eds.) BIR 2014. LNBIP, vol. 194, pp. 57–71. Springer, Heidelberg (2014)
38. Plisson, J., Ljubic, P., Mozetic, I., Lavrac, N.: An ontology for virtual organization breeding environments. IEEE Trans. Syst. Man Cybern. Part C: Appl. Rev. **37**(6), 1327–1341 (2007)
39. Camarinha-Matos, L.M., Afsarmanesh, H.: Collaborative Networks: Reference Modeling. Springer, Heidelberg (2008)
40. FInES Task Force on Collaborative Networks and SOCOLNET: Taxonomy of Collaborative Networks Forms. Technical report (2012)
41. Madni, A.M., Lin, W., Madni, C.C.: IDEONTM: an extensible ontology for designing, integrating, and managing collaborative distributed enterprises. Syst. Eng. **4**(1), 35–48 (2001)

42. Ye, Y., Yang, D., Jiang, Z., Tong, L.: An ontology-based architecture for implementing semantic integration of supply chain management. Int. J. Comput. Integr. Manuf. **21**(1), 1–18 (2008)

43. Guarino, N.: Formal ontology in information systems. In: Proceedings of the First International Conference (FOIS 1998), Trento, Italy, 6–8 June, vol. 46. IOS Press (1998)

44. Kajüter, P., Kulmala, H.I.: Open-book accounting in networks: potential achievements and reasons for failures. Manag. Account. Res. **16**(2), 179–204 (2005)

45. Essa, S.A.G., Dekker, H.C., Groot, T.: The influence of information and control on trust building in buyer-supplier negotiations. In: Management Accounting Section (MAS) Research and Case Conference (2014)

46. Costa, A., Guizzardi, R., Filho, J.G.P.: Cores: context-aware, ontology-based recommender system for service recommendation. In: Workshop on Ubiquitous Mobile Information and Collaboration Systems, 19th International Conference on Advanced Information Systems Engineering (2007)

47. Middleton, S.E., De Roure, D., Shadbolt, N.R.: Ontology-based recommender systems. In: Staab, S., Studer, R. (eds.) Handbook on Ontologies, pp. 779–796. Springer, Heidelberg (2009)

48. Todeva, E., Knoke, D.: Strategic alliances and models of collaboration. Manag. Decis. **43**(1), 123–148 (2005)

49. Caglio, A., Ditillo, A.: Interdependence and accounting information exchanges in inter-firm relationships. J. Manag. Gov. **16**(1), 57–80 (2012)

50. Gulati, R.: Alliances and networks. Strateg. Manag. J. **19**(4), 293–317 (1998)

51. Dussauge, P., Garrette, B., et al.: Cooperative strategy-competing successfully through strategic alliances (1999)

52. Gómez-Pérez, A., Fernandez-Lopez, M., Corcho, O.: Ontological Engineering: with examples from the areas of Knowledge Management, e-Commerce and the Semantic Web. Advanced Information and Knowledge Processing, 1st edn. Springer, London (2010)

53. Hakimpour, F., Geppert, A.: Resolving semantic heterogeneity in schema integration. In: Proceedings of the International Conference on Formal Ontology in Information Systems, vol. 2001, pp. 297–308. ACM (2001)

54. Guarino, N.: Understanding, building and using ontologies. Int. J. Hum. Comput. Stud. **46**(2), 293–310 (1997)

Innovative Tools and Prototypes

Conciliating Model-Driven Engineering with Technical Debt Using a Quality Framework

Fáber D. Giraldo[1,2]([✉]), Sergio España[2], Manuel A. Pineda[1],
William J. Giraldo[1], and Oscar Pastor[2]

[1] System and Computer Engineering, University of Quindío, Quindio, Colombia
{fdgiraldo,mapineda,wjgiraldo}@uniquindio.edu.co
[2] PROS Research Centre, Universitat Politècnica de València, Valencia, Spain
{fdgiraldo,sergio.espana,opastor}@pros.upv.es

Abstract. The main goal of this work is to evaluate the feasibility to calculate the technical debt (a traditional software quality approach) in a model-driven context through the same tools used by software developers at work. The *SonarQube* tool was used, so that the quality check was performed directly on projects created with Eclipse Modeling Framework (EMF) instead of traditionals source code projects. In this work, XML was used as the model specification language to verify in SonarQube due to the creation of EMF metamodels in XMI (XML Metadata Interchange) and that SonarQube offers a plugin to assess the XML language. After this, our work focused on the definition of model rules as an XSD schema (XML Schema Definition) and the integration between EMF-SonarQube in order that these metrics were directly validated by SonarQube; and subsequently, this tool determined the technical debt that the analyzed EMF models could contain.

Keywords: Model-driven engineering · Technical debt · EMF · SonarQube

1 Introduction

Two representative trends for the software development industry that appeared in the nineties were the *model-driven* initiative and the *technical debt* metaphor. Both trends promote software quality each in its own way: high abstract levels (models) and software process management (technical debt). However, despite the wide exposition of these trends in the literature, there are not more indications about the combination of them into software development scenarios; each initiative is implemented in a separated way.

More than 20 years ago, the *technical debt* term was introduced as a way to describe the long-term costs associated with problems of software design and implementation. Some typical examples of technical debt exposed in [17] include: *glue* code, code done and fixing it after release, hundreds of customer-specific branches on same code base, *friendly* additions to interfaces, multiple codes for

© Springer International Publishing Switzerland 2015
S. Nurcan and E. Pimenidis (Eds.): CAiSE Forum 2014, LNBIP 204, pp. 199–214, 2015.
DOI: 10.1007/978-3-319-19270-3_13

the same problem, and so on. The technical debt approach has been used as a control mechanism for projects to lower maintenance costs and reduce defects.

In traditional software development projects (those involving manual programming), technical debt is mainly focused in quality assurance processes over source code and related services (e.g., common quality metrics are defined over source code). However, model-driven engineering (MDE) promotes for modelling instead of programming [3]. A review of the literature reveals that there is currently no application of the technical debt concept to environments outside the traditional software development. There exist approaches to the measurement of model quality [11,13,15,18], but these do not include technical debt calculus. Therefore, we claim that dealing with technical debt in MDE projects is an open problem.

Two issues pose challenges to the inclusion of technical debt into MDE. *(i)* Different authors provide conflicting conceptions of quality in model management within MDE environments [7]. *(ii)* The MDE literature often neglects techniques for source code analysis and quality control[1]. Therefore, in model-driven developments it is difficult to perform an analysis of the state of the project that is important for technical debt management: establishing what has been done, what remains to be done, how much work has been left undone. Also, other specific issues that belong to model theory such as: number of elements in the metamodel, coverage for the views, complexity of the models, the relationship between the abstract syntax and the concrete syntax of a language, quantity of OCL verification code, among others, contribute to increase the technical debt in model-driven projects.

Similar to software projects, model-driven projects could be affected by events that impact the quality of the conceptual models and its derived artifacts. The technical debt incidents for model-driven contexts come mainly from the software development inherent practices and model specific issues. Also, the lack of a standardized definition about quality in models increase the complexity of modelling tasks, so that, the bad modelling practices become specific according to the kind of modelling project that is performed.

The main contributions of this paper are the following:

1. A discussion about the importance of considering the technical debt calculus in model-driven projects, as part of a model quality initiative.
2. A demonstration of a integration between model-driven and technical debt tools for supporting a technical debt calculus process performed over conceptual models.
3. The operationalization of a recognized framework for evaluating models.

In this work, we used the principles of research in quality over models to generate quality metrics that can be useful to validate these models with a technical debt focus. This work is organized as follows: Sect. 2 introduces the motivation of

---

[1] Neglecting the code would seem sensible, since MDE advocates that the model is the code [4]. However, few MDE tools provide full code generation and manual additions of code and tweakings are often necessary.

our idea, Sect. 3 presents the technical solution implemented, Sect. 4 exposes a preliminary validation process around of our proposal, Sect. 5 presents the state of the art; and finally, the conclusions and further works derived of our proposal are presented.

2 Motivations

The technical debt definition was originally focused on source code; but as shown in [12], this concept could be extended to other activities and artifacts belonging to the software construction process. Technical debt focuses on the management of the consequences of anything that was not done intentionally or unintentionally, and subsequently, it is materialized as bugs or anormal situations that affect a software project or product. Currently, it is possible to evidence how software companies have assimilated the importance of technical debt control in its software projects, highlighting the use of tools like SonarQube[2], responsible for assessing the presence of technical debt through evidence of malpractices embodied on software artifacts like source code. Also from a technical viewpoint, these kind of tools support project management very close to code and low-level artifacts.

The technical debt practice has become an important strategy in current quality assurance software processes. Its application can help to identify problems over the artifacts quantifying the consequences of all the work that was not done in order to contrast it regarding the budgetary constraints of the project.

Despite the several particular approaches involved in software quality assurance, it has certain maturity levels due to the effort of software quality practitioners for encompassing these approaches around the fulfillment of expectations, requirements, customer needs, and value provisions [9]. It is supported by descriptive models and standards that define the main issues of software quality. In this way, activities such as defect detection and correction, metric definition and application, artifact evolution management, audits, testing, and others, are framed into these software quality definitions. Software quality involves a strategy towards the production of software that ensures user satisfaction, absence of defects, compliance with budget and time constraints, and the application of standards and best practices for the software development.

Instead, it is possible to identify a proliferation of model quality definitions in the model-driven context with multiple divergences, different motivations and additional considerations due to the nature of the model artifacts. Quality in the MDE context is particularly defined according to the specific proposals or research areas developed by the MDE practitioners. In [7], authors note that the *quality in models* term does not have a consistent definition and it is defined, conceptualized, and operationalized in different ways depending on the discourse of the previous research proposals. The lack of consensus for the model quality definition produce empirical efforts for verifying quality over specific features of models.

---

[2] http://www.sonarqube.org/.

Within the MDE literature is possible to find proposals which extrapolate particular approaches for evaluating software quality at model levels (supported by the fact that the MDE is a particular focus to the software engineering), such as the use of metrics, defect detection over models, application of software quality taxonomies (in terms of characteristic, sub-characteristic and quality attributes), best practices for implementing high quality models and model transformations; and even, it is possible to see a research area oriented to the usability evaluation of modelling languages [23], where the usability is prioritized as the main quality attribute.

Most of the model quality frameworks proposed act over specific model artifacts, generally evaluation of notations or diagrams. These frameworks do not consider the implications around the performed activities over models in terms of the consequences of the good practices that were not made. This is a critical issue because the model-driven projects have the same project constraints with respect to software projects. The only difference is the high abstract level of the project artifacts and the new roles with respect to domain experts and languages users.

Notations and diagrams are the main way of interaction for the final users of a language, and in this sense, most of the model quality proposals are around specific attributes of interaction, cognition, readability, usage and comprehensibility. The evaluation of the global quality of a conceptual model is a very complex task. A first important attempt is the quality evaluation based on notations used by the model, avoiding the incorrect combinations of conceptual constructs and ambiguous situations that could violate the principles and rules of the language and its associated constructs. Notations in a key aspect for the evaluation of model quality. However, we claim that model-driven activities can contribute to establishing a technical debt for modelling projects beyond a notation perspective, because it considers both modelling issues and software practices involved. The technical debt for model-driven projects could be more complex than software technical debt. Also, the use of technical debt at the model-driven context could help to manage and evaluate the employed process over a model-driven specific context.

The main concern of the technical debt is the consequence of poor software development [27]. This is a critical issue not covered in model-driven processes whose focus is specific operation over models such as model management or model transformations. A landscape for technical debt in software is proposed in [12] in terms of evolvability challenges and external/internal quality issues; we think that model-driven iniatives cover all the elements of these landscapes taking into account that authors like [20] suggest models as elements of internal quality software due to its intermediate nature in a software development process. Integration between model-driven and technical debt have not been considered by practicioners of each area despite the enormous potential and benefits for software development processes.

3   Our Proposal

3.1   Proposal in a Nutshell

In order to demonstrate the feasibility to calculate technical debt over models in a model-driven working environment, we performed the following steps:

1. We operationalized a quality framework for models to derive technical debt evidences w.r.t. a previous quality reference (Sect. 3.2).
2. An integration of a MDE working environment with an instance of a Sonar-Qube server (the selected technical debt tool) was implemented. This was made through a plugin that automatically invokes the SonarQube tool (Sect. 3.3).
3. A technical debt verification process is performed over a model sample. Since the models workspace the Sonarqube instance is invoked. This instance uses the operationalization of the quality framework to find technical debt over the model sample under evaluation (Sect. 3.4).

3.2   Definition of an XSD for SonarQube

One of the most critical issues in a technical debt program is the definition of metrics or procedures for deducting technical debt calculations; in works like [6,10] it is highlighted the absence of technical debt values (established and accepted), and features such as the kinds of technical debt. Most of the technical debt calculation works are focused on software projects without an applied model-driven approach; some similar works report the use of high level artifacts as software architectures [22], but they are not model-driven oriented. Emerging frameworks for defining and managing technical debt [24] are appearing, but they focus on specific tasks of the software development (not all the process itself).

From one technical perspective, the SonarQube tool demands an XSD (XML Scheme Document) configuration file that contains the specific rules for validating the code; or in this case, a model. Without this file, the model could be evaluated like a source code by default. In order to define these rules, we chose one of the most popular proposals for validating models (*Physics of notations - PoN -* of Moody [21]) due to its relative easiness to implement some of its postulates in terms of XSD sentences.

In the case of this work, visual notation was taken as the textual information managed by XMI entities from EMF models (text are perceptual elements too), focusing that each item meets syntactic rules to display each information field regardless about what is recorded as a result of the EMF model validation. The analysis does not consider the semantic meaning of the model elements to be analyzed.

The operationalization of Moody principles over the XSD file posteriorly loaded in SonarQube was defined as follows:

- *Visual syntax - perceptual configuration*: in the XSD file, it is ensured that all elements and/or attributes of the modelled elements are defined according to the appropriate type (the consistence between the values of attributes and its associated type is validated).
- *Visual syntax - attention management*: a validation order of the elements is specified by the usage of order indicators belonging to XML schemes.
- *Semiotic clarity - redundant symbology*: a node in the model can only be checked by an XSD element.
- *Semiotic clarity - overload symbology*: an XSD element type only validates a single model node type.
- *Semiotic clarity - excess symbolism*: a metric to validate that there are no blank items was implemented (for example, we could create several elements of *Seller* type, but its data does not appear).
- *Semiotic clarity - symbology deficit*: a validation that indicates the presence of incomplete information was made (e.g., we could have the data of a *Customer* but we don't have his/her name or identification number). For this rule, we made constraints with occurrence indicators to each attribute.
- *Perceptual discriminability*: in the XML model, nodes must be organized in a way that they can be differentiated, e.g., one *Seller* element does not appear like a *Location* element. This is ensured by reviewing in the XSD that it does not contain elements exactly alike, and in the same order.
- *Semantic transparency*: this was done by putting restrictions on the names of the tags, so that the tags correspond to what they must have, e.g., a *data* label must be of *data* type.
- *Complexity management*: this was done by the *minOccurs* and *maxOccurs* occurrence indicators. With these indicators it is possible to define how many children one node can have.
- *Cognitive integration*: this was done using namespaces in the XSD file, so that it is possible to ensure the structure for the nodes independent from changes in the model design.
- *Dual codification*: this was done by measuring the quantity of commented code lines with respect to the XML lines that define the elements of the model.
- *Graphic economy*: we established a limit for different items that can be handled in the XSD, and reporting when different elements are found marking the mistake when these data types are not found in the schema.
- *Cognitive fit*: this was done by creating several XSD files where each one is responsible for reviewing a specific view model.

Figure 1 exposes a portion of the XSD code implemented for some Moody principles.

3.3   Implementation of a Technical Debt Plugin for EMF

We implemented an Eclipse plugin for integrating the EMF environment with SonarQube; so that, results of the technical debt can be shown directly on the Eclipse work area instead of changing the context and opening a browser with

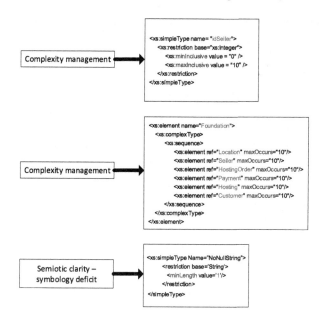

Fig. 1. Mapping between some Moody principles to XSD code.

the SonarQube report. Figure 2 exposes main issues of the developed plugin. We used configuration options belonging to EMF *XMIResource* objects to export the XMI file as an XML without the specific XMI information tags (Fig. 2, part *C*). Also, the integration with the Eclipse IDE was done by a button and a menu as it can be seen in part *A* and *B* of the same figure.

3.4   Verification of Technical Debt from EMF Models

In order to demonstrate the integration of both tools (EMF-SonarQube), a sample metamodel (Fig. 3) was made in EMF. This model is extracted from the case study formulated in [8], and it is complemented with data patterns exposed in [2] such as *Location, Client, Payment* and *Master/Detaill*. Regarding to the rules specified in the Sect. 3.2 we introduce some errors like *no valid options, date format* and *specific quantity of elements*, to evidence abnormalities not covered with model conceptual validation approaches like OCL.

Once the validation option had been chosen (by the SonarQube button or menu), we obtain a report similar to Fig. 4. Part *A* indicates the number of lines of code that have been tested, comment lines, and duplicate lines, blocks or files. Also, part *B* of this figure reports the total of errors that contain the project (in this case the EMF model), as well as the technical debt graph (part *C*), which shows the percentage of technical debt, the cost of repair, and the number of men needed to fix errors per day (this information was not configured for this case).

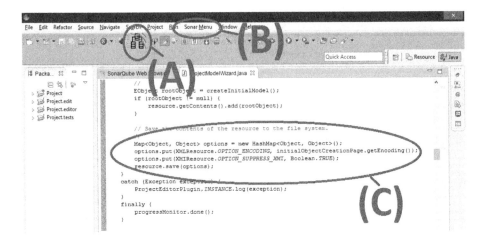

Fig. 2. Supressing XMI tags to analyze the EMF model as a XML document.

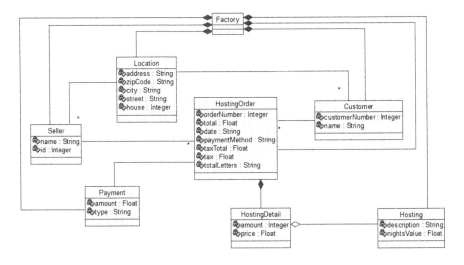

Fig. 3. Sample metamodel implemented over EMF.

SonarQube offers an *issues* report where it indicates the number of errors found; and consequently, the error list distributed in order of importance from highest to lowest:

- *Blocker*: they are the most serious errors; they should have the highest priority to review.
- *Critical*: they are design errors which affect quality or performance of the project (model errors can be classified in this category).
- *Major*: although these errors do not affect performance, they require to be fixed for quality concerns.

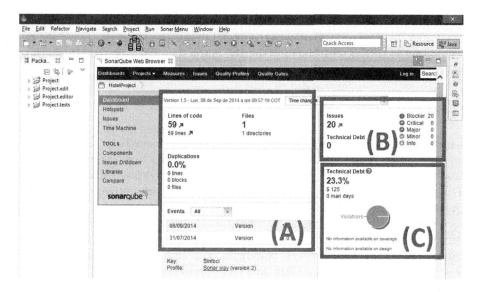

Fig. 4. SonarQube screen report loaded into EMF work area

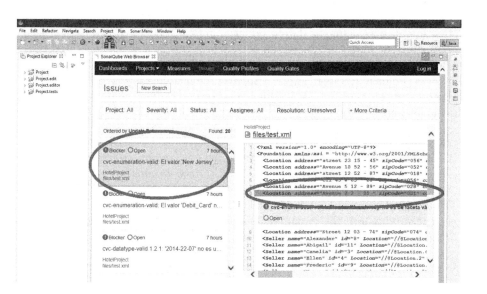

Fig. 5. Example of error (issue) detected by SonarQube over the EMF model.

– *Minor:* they are minor errors that do not affect the operation of the project.
– *Info:* they are reporting errors, not dangerous.

Figure 5 present the reports about technical debt errors detected over the sample model. In the first place, an error category was chosen. For the respective category, the error list associated is show in detail posteriorly. Intentionally, we introduced errors over the XML information of the model to test the respective detection by SonarQube according with the rules defined in the XSD file from the Moody proposal.

4   Validation

A first validation of our proposal was performed using some basic usability testing procedures. The main goal of these validation was to identify interaction issues associated to the Eclipse EMF-SonarQube integration. Also, the utility of this integration (from a model-driven practioners perspective) was checked. The participant population were students from software engineering courses that work with conceptual models and structural data models in Eclipse EMF, and software engineering researchers (experts) who work with EMF in real software projects using the model-driven paradigm. The chosen public was invited by their previous knowledges in EMF and data productions with EMF. The total population was 17 participants.

4.1   Test Design and Procedure

In first instance we defined a data production for the model exposed in the Fig. 3. Intentionally we have introduced ten defects over the data of the generated EMF model production. These defects are related to rules configured in a XML schema previously defined and associated to SonarQube instance server. These rules are derived from some Moody PoN principles (Sect. 3.2). The employed rules over the model were the following:

- Accepted payment types are *Cash*, *Credit_Card* and *Bank_Check*.
- Cities that are permitted for the data model are *London*, *Medellin*, *SaoPaulo*, *NewYork*, *Washington*, *Valencia*, *Madrid*, *Paris*, *Bogota*.
- Seller ID must be a number between 0 to 10.
- Valid date format is YYYY-MM-DD.
- In the production, the maximum number of elements type *Location*, *Seller*, *HostingOrder*, *Payment*, *Hosting* and *Customer* are ten elements for each one.

These rules were accesible for all participants during the test execution.

For the usability test a Tobii X2-30 Eye Tracker[3] device was employed in order to precisely capture and determine where the participants are looking when we shown them the Eclipse enviroment with the EMF-SonarQube integration mechanisms. Figure 6 presents the test scenario with the hardware and software used with each participant. Figure 7 presents the software testing scenario (supported by the Tobii Studio Eye Tracking Software).

This test was split into three parts or *momentums* as follows:

---

[3] http://www.tobii.com/en/eye-tracking-research/global/products/hardware/tobii-x2-30-eye-tracker/.

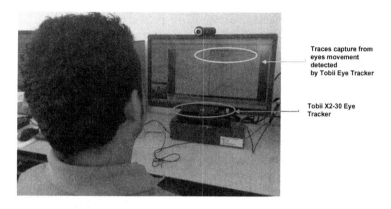

Fig. 6. Test enviroment used for the validation.

- *Momentum 01:* for each participant he/she was asked about evidenciable defects over the EMF production directly. The main goal of this part is *to check if the participant can detect the defects intentionally introduced in the production using the information given by EMF.*
- *Momentum 02:* in this section of the test researchers request to each participant to validate the model in SonarQube using the provided mechanism (button or menu). The main goal of this was detect if *the participants could recognize the graphical elements (plugin) that link the EMF with SonarQube.*
- *Momentum 03:* each participant was asked about how *to access to the defects reported by SonarQube using the user interface provided for this tool and loaded into Eclipse.*

Finally, a *Retrospective Think Aloud* (RTA) procedure was performed with each participant. Using the recordings of the previous usability test researchers asked to the participants about their actions during the usability test. The RTA activity considered these issues:

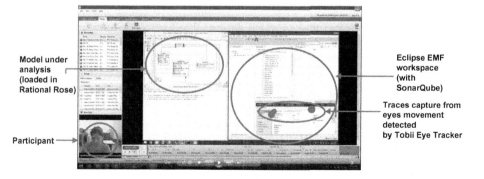

Fig. 7. Test software environment supported by the usability testing tool.

- The identification of defects over the EMF production directly.
- The easiness for identifying defects directly from the EMF production.
- The easiness to invoke the SonarQube validation over the EMF model.
- The sufficiency of the information provided by SonarQube in order to find defects in the EMF production.
- The usefulness of the EMF-SonarQube integration.

4.2   Results

Results of the usability test are exposed in Table 1. It is splited in the three *momentums* described above. For the *momentum 01 - the participant detected defects over the production* - the percentage of participants that report defects directly over the EMF production is high but the defects reported (in average) is too low with respect to the total of defects intentionally introduced (15 % in average). This reflects that finding defects directly over the EMF production is a hard task, and the probability of accidently discard defects are representative.

Table 1. Results of the usability test over the EMF-SonarQube integration.

	Momentum 01			Momentum 02		Momentum 03		
	No	Yes	Def. Av.	Button	Menu	No	Yes	Time Av.
Experts	16,67 %	83,33 %	1,80	66,67 %	33,33 %	16,67 %	83,33 %	83,00
Students	18,18 %	81,82 %	1,33	90,91 %	9,09 %	45,45 %	54,55 %	89,83
Participants	**17,65 %**	**82,35 %**	**1,50**	**82,35 %**	**17,65 %**	**35,29 %**	**64,71 %**	**86,73**

For the *momentum 02 - Can the user validate the model in SonarQube from Eclipse EMF?-* all the participant reports that they did this, mainly through the button exposed in the Fig. 2-A. EMF experts users have found the new graphical elements associated with SonarQube so that they access directly to these elements to make the validation. However, in the case of the students, 45,45 % of them request an additional explanation to researchers in order to identify the elements and make the validation. It's due to the low contact of the students with quality platforms in their software engineering courses.

Finally, in the *momentum 03 - Do the participant access to the reported defects in SonarQube?* - we found a representative percentage of participants who reported no access to the defects of the model reported by SonarQube. This is consequence of the native navigation model of SonarQube (no considered in the scope of our validation process as such).

Main findings from the RTA procedure were: *(i)* The relative big size of the proposed button proportional to the Eclipse tools area. This in particularly important due that this feature let to users (mainly experts) to identify the new proposed tool. *(ii)* The image icon used in the SonarQube button does not associate it to the model validation process itself. Most of the users request a new icon that express the model validation more natively from Eclipse EMF. *(iii)* A new requirement from the participants that exist a doble via navigation between the defects of the model reported in SonarQube and the EMF model/production in order that the context of the validation does not disappear when the Sonar-Qube browser is invoked. All these findings promote a second version of our proposal.

5   State of the Art

There are not major reports about the integration of technical debt with model-driven works; it is evident the works where technical debt is applied jointly with specific methods of software quality [14]. A closer work is reported in [16] where a technical debt evaluation framework was proposed, and it was applied over the EMF project for determining the technical debt of this Eclipse project based on all the versions of it. EMF was chosen because it contains some features expected by the framework (popularity, maturity, proficiency and open source), but the quality assessment was made with a tool different to SonarQube.

The main challenge of this kind of work is the derivation of quality metrics or rules from model quality frameworks. High abstraction and specific model issues influence the operationalization of model quality frameworks, so that quality rules or procedures could no be full implemented by operational mechanisms such as XSD schemas. Authors in [26] expose an attempt to make operational the *Physics of notations* evaluation framework, but this operationalization (and any similar proposal) could be ambiguous as consequence of the lack of precision and detail of the framework itself. Also, they suggest the need of a guideline for the evaluation framework prior to the production of its associated metrics.

Regarding the usage of the SonarQube platform to evaluate models a similar work is exposed in [25] where a SonarQube plugin was implement in order to support the evaluation of business process models described in the event-driven process chains language. This plugin uses the software quality model ISO 9126 (in terms of characteristics and subcharacteristics) and other measures previously formulated.

An example of model quality assurance tools as reported in [1] where it is presented an operational process for assessing the quality through static model analysis to check model features like consistency (with respect of language syntax), conceptual integrity, and the conformity with modelling conventions. Instead of having an operational model quality framework, we can see how a quality framework like *6C* [19] has been used as a conceptual basis for derivating a quality assurance tool.

6   Conclusions

In this work we show the technical feasibility to integrate a technical debt tool like SonarQube with a model-driven development enviroment such as the Eclipse modelling framework. We present an example of technical debt validation applied over a sample metamodel implemented for testing purposes. Thereby, we demonstrate the technical feasibility for measuring any artefact used in an model-driven engineering process [5]. However, the main challenge is the definition of the model quality metrics and the operationalization of the model quality frameworks reported in terms of expressions that can generate metrics, and its association with a model-driven development process.

A plethora of model quality frameworks are proposed, but their operationalization is very incipient and these are used as reference frameworks. A metric/rules derivation process from quality frameworks is needed taking into account its operationalization in order to support a model quality assurance process by tools. An important further work is the applicability of technical debt to the visual quality of diagrams because these are the most representative quality proposals for models; it means, evaluting the quality of diagrams in a similar way as SonarQube evaluates quality at the source code. Also, the implementation of automatic checks over the OCL code could be an important strategy to verify quality issues over models.

From a technical perspective, as another further work, we propose to use SonarQube plugins that offer technical debt evaluation through specific approaches like the SQALE Methodology (software quality assessment based on lifecycle expectations)[4] [14]. The main challenge of this proposed work is the extrapolation of the particular technical debt method to the model-driven context; this could be supported by the quality taxonomy of characteristics/sub-characteristics/metrics or quality attributes common employed in model quality proposals.

Acknowledgments. F.G, thanks to Colciencias (Colombia) for funding this work through the Colciencias Grant call 512-2010. F.G. and M.P. thanks to David Racodon (david.racodon@sonarsource.com) and Nicla Donno (nicla.donno@sonarsource.com) for their suppport with the SQALE plugin for SonarQube. This work has been supported by the Spanish MICINN PROS-Req (TIN2010-19130-C02-02), the Generalitat Valenciana Project ORCA (PROMETEO/2009/015), the European Commission FP7 Project CaaS (611351), and ERDF structural funds.

References

1. Arendt, T., Taentzer, G.: A tool environment for quality assurance based on the eclipse modeling framework. Autom. Softw. Engg. **20**(2), 141–184 (2013)
2. Blaha, M.: Patterns of Data Modeling. CRC Press, Boca Raton (2010). ISBN 1439819890
3. Brambilla, M., Cabot, J., Wimmer, M.: Model-Driven Software Engineering in Practice. Synthesis Lectures on Software Engineering. Morgan & Claypool Publishers, San Rafael (2012)

---

[4] http://www.sonarsource.com/products/plugins/governance/sqale/installation-and-usage/.

4. Embley, D.W., Liddle, S.W., Pastor, O.: Conceptual-model programming a manifesto. In: Embley, D.W., Thalheim, B. (eds.) Handbook of Conceptual Modeling, pp. 3–16. Springer, Heidelberg (2011). ISBN 978-3-642-15864-3
5. Bertoa, M.F., Antonio, V.: Quality attributes for software metamodels. In: Proceedings of 13th TOOLS Workshop on Quantitatives Approaches in Object-oriented Software Engineering, QAAOSE 2010, 2 July, Málaga, Spain, February 2010
6. Falessi, D., Shaw, M.A., Shull, F., Mullen, K., Keymind, M.S.: Practical considerations, challenges, and requirements of tool-support for managing technical debt. In: 2013 4th International Workshop on Managing Technical Debt (MTD), pp. 16–19 (2013)
7. Fettke, P., Houy, C., Vella, A.-L., Loos, P.: Towards the reconstruction and evaluation of conceptual model quality discourses – methodical framework and application in the context of model understandability. In: Bider, I., Halpin, T., Krogstie, J., Nurcan, S., Proper, E., Schmidt, R., Soffer, P., Wrycza, S. (eds.) EMMSAD 2012 and BPMDS 2012. LNBIP, vol. 113, pp. 406–421. Springer, Heidelberg (2012)
8. Giraldo, W.J.: Framework for the development of interactive groupware systems based on the integration of process and notations. Ph.D. thesis (2010)
9. ISO/IEC. ISO/IEC 9126. Software engineering - Product quality. ISO/IEC (2001)
10. Izurieta, C., Griffith, I., Reimanis, D., Luhr, R.: On the uncertainty of technical debt measurements. In: 2013 International Conference on Information Science and Applications (ICISA), pp. 1–4 (2013)
11. Krogstie, J.: Quality of models. In: Krogstie, J. (ed.) Model-Based Development and Evolution of Information Systems, pp. 205–247. Springer, London (2012). ISBN 978-1-4471-2935-6
12. Kruchten, P., Nord, R.L., Ozkaya, I.: Technical debt: from metaphor to theory and practice. IEEE Softw. **290**(6), 18–21 (2012)
13. Lange, C.F.J., Chaudron, M.R.V.: Managing model quality in UML-based software development. In: 2005 13th IEEE International Workshop on Software Technology and Engineering Practice, pp. 7–16 (2005). LCCN 0029
14. Letouzey, J., Ilkiewicz, M.: Managing technical debt with the sqale method. IEEE Softw. **29**(6), 44–51 (2012)
15. Marín, B., Giachetti, G., Pastor, O., Abran, A.: A quality model for conceptual models of mdd environments. Adv. Soft. Eng. **2010**, 1:1–1:17 (2010)
16. Marinescu, R.: Assessing technical debt by identifying design flaws in software systems. IBM J. Res. Dev. **56**(5), 9:1–9:13 (2012)
17. McConnell, S.: Managing technical debt. In: Fourth International Workshop on Managing Technical Debt in conjunction with ICSE 2013 (2013)
18. Mohagheghi, P., Dehlen, V.: Developing a quality framework for model-driven engineering. In: Giese, H. (ed.) MODELS 2008. LNCS, vol. 5002, pp. 275–286. Springer, Heidelberg (2008)
19. Mohagheghi, P., Dehlen, V., Neple, T.: Definitions and approaches to model quality in model-based software development - a review of literature. Inf. Softw. Technol. **51**(12), 1646–1669 (2009)
20. Moody, D.L.: Theoretical and practical issues in evaluating the quality of conceptual models: current state and future directions. Data Knowl. Eng. **55**(3), 243–276 (2005)
21. Moody, D.L.: The 'physics' of notations: Toward a scientific basis for constructing visual notations in software engineering. IEEE Trans. Softw. Eng. **35**(6), 756–779 (2009)

22. Nord, R.L., Ozkaya, I., Kruchten, P., Gonzalez-Rojas, M.: In search of a metric for managing architectural technical debt. In: 2012 Joint Working IEEE/IFIP Conference on Software Architecture (WICSA) and European Conference on Software Architecture (ECSA), pp. 91–100 (2012)
23. Schalles, C.: Usability Evaluation of Modeling Languages: An Empirical Research Study, vol. 1, p. 197. Springer Gabler, Heidelberg (2013). ISBN 978-3-658-00051-6
24. Seaman, C., Guo, Y.: Chapter 2 - Measuring and Monitoring Technical Debt. Advances in Computers, vol. 82. Elsevier, London (2011)
25. Storch, A., Laue, R., Gruhn, V.: Measuring and visualising the quality of models. In: 2013 IEEE 1st International Workshop on Communicating Business Process and Software Models Quality, Understandability, and Maintainability (CPSM), pp. 1–8, September 2013
26. Störrle, H., Fish, A.: Towards an operationalization of the "physics of notations" for the analysis of visual languages. In: Moreira, A., Schätz, B., Gray, J., Vallecillo, A., Clarke, P. (eds.) MODELS 2013. LNCS, vol. 8107, pp. 104–120. Springer, Heidelberg (2013)
27. Tom, E., Aurum, A., Vidgen, R.: An exploration of technical debt. J. Syst. Softw. **86**(6), 1498–1516 (2013)

Towards Supporting the Analysis of Online Discussions in OSS Communities: A Speech-Act Based Approach

Itzel Morales-Ramirez[1,2]($\boxtimes$), Anna Perini[1], and Mariano Ceccato[1]

[1] Software Engineering Research Unit, Fondazione Bruno Kessler - IRST,
Via Sommarive 18, 38123 Trento, Italy
{imramirez,perini,ceccato}@fbk.eu
[2] University of Trento, Trento, Italy

Abstract. Open-Source Software (OSS) community members report bugs, request features or clarifications by writing messages (in unstructured natural language) to mailing lists. Analysts examine them dealing with an effort demanding and error prone task, which requires reading huge threads of emails. Automated support for retrieving relevant information and particularly for recognizing discussants' intentions (e.g., suggesting, complaining) can support analysts, and allow them to increase the performance of this task. Online discussions are almost synchronous written conversations that can be analyzed applying computational linguistic techniques that build on the speech act theory. Our approach builds on this observation. We propose to analyze OSS mailing-list discussions in terms of the linguistic and non-linguistic acts expressed by the participants, and provide a tool-supported *speech-act* analysis method. In this paper we describe this method and discuss how to empirically evaluate it. We discuss the results of the first execution of an empirical study that involved 20 subjects.

Keywords: Online discussions · Intentions extraction · Speech act theory

1 Introduction

The increasing participation of stakeholders to online discussions of Open-Source Software (OSS) is turning these discussions into an attractive source of information, although still costly to exploit. OSS is usually produced by distributed collaborative communities composed of heterogeneous and diverse stakeholders (including users, developers, and analysts [1]). Such stakeholders extensively rely on online communication channels such as open forums or mailing lists, to elaborate solution design, code writing, software deployment, maintenance and evolution. Mailing-list discussions are highly exploited by all kind of stakeholders to provide bug reports, feature requests or simply to ask for clarifications. Wherein discussants express their arguments mainly as unstructured natural

© Springer International Publishing Switzerland 2015
S. Nurcan and E. Pimenidis (Eds.): CAiSE Forum 2014, LNBIP 204, pp. 215–232, 2015.
DOI: 10.1007/978-3-319-19270-3_14

language (NL) text. The immediacy that email offers to its users makes it the preferred channel of communication, as reported in [2]. But this can result in huge threads of emails that the analysts need to carefully check in order to identify information that could be important for software development tasks. Similarly, open forum is a communication channel typically chosen by users of software applications to discuss about tips, bugs or features related to such an application, still using unstructured NL text.

Analysts who aim at recognizing feature requests or bug identification by reading the resulting huge threads of messages or emails, face an effort demanding and error prone task. This motivates research on techniques for automating the extraction of relevant information from online discussions. Our research has the ultimate goal of lighten the burden of analyzing online discussions related to software development by supporting developers or requirements analysts to identify discussants' intentions (such as suggesting or complaining). We take the inspiration from the Speech Act Theory (SAT), originally formulated by Austin and Searle [3,4], whose core idea is captured in the following quotation: "by saying something, we react by doing something". Indeed, a speaker may aim at persuading, inspiring or getting a hearer to do something. Concretely, speech acts are classified according to specific performative verbs, such as *suggest, recommend*, and *advise*, among other verbs. Since online discussions are considered almost synchronous written conversations, we propose to analyze them in terms of *speech-acts* including linguistic acts, which corresponds to the *speech-act* types as per the SAT, and non-linguistic acts that are commonly used in such type of discussions, e.g. log files or URL links. We define a tool-supported method at use of analysts during the processing of online discussions. This tool aims at facilitating the recognition of *speech-acts* frequently used in sentences that describe bug identifications, features or clarifications requests, by supporting *speech-acts* annotation of online discussions. The tool builds on a natural language processing (NLP) framework [5] and the SAT along with its application in computational linguistic [6].

In this paper, we describe our method and the first phase of an empirical evaluation plan, which aims at providing evidences about the method's effectiveness. Indeed, to empirically evaluate the approach we designed a three-phase plan: the first phase is devoted to the investigation of how non-trained humans perform the activity of annotating sentences; the results are used in the second phase as ground truth, as well as input for improving the classification rules exploited by the tool; and the third phase is aimed at evaluating if the tool-supported identification of bug and feature requests will be effective in a realistic setting with expert analysts. As said before, here we focus on the first phase whose research question is: *RQ: How difficult is for non-trained human annotators to recognize speech-acts in online discussions?* We present the design of an empirical study and report the results of the analysis of the first execution with 20 subjects, who were requested to annotate 20 OSS online discussions containing 1685 sentences in total. The results allow us to estimate the effort required to manually annotate sentences. Moreover, the study provided interesting suggestions on how to improve the study design towards building a ground truth to be used for evaluating the performance of our proposed tool-supported method.

The remainder of the paper is structured as follows. In Sect. 2 we give some background on SAT and on the NLP framework used in our approach. In Sect. 3 our tool-supported approach for analyzing online discussions is presented. The design of an empirical study for the first phase of the evaluation plan is presented, together with a description of its execution in Sect. 4. The discussion of the results is given in Sect. 5. The related work is presented in Sect. 6 and the conclusion in Sect. 7.

2 Background: Speech Act Theory and the NLP Framework

The Speech Act Theory (SAT) was developed by Austin and Searle in the field of philosophy of language [3,4]. In a nutshell, the theory claims that when a person says something she/he attempts to communicate certain things to the addressees, which affect either their believes and/or their behavior. So, for instance, if I say "I'll bring you a chocolate", this utterance expresses my intention (technically named *illocutionary act*) to make you aware that I'm committing to bring you a chocolate, and the effect (technically named *perlocutionary act*), is that you get convinced about my intention and expect to receive a chocolate. According to the classification proposed by Bach and Harnish in [7], this type of *speech-act* is called *Commissives* since it expresses the speaker's intention to commit to do something for the benefit of the hearer. Other types are: the *Constantives* type, which expresses the speaker's belief and her intention or desire that the hearer forms a like belief; the *Directives* type, which expresses the speaker's attitude toward some prospective action that should be performed by the hearer; and the *Acknowledgements* type that expresses the speaker's intention to satisfy a social expectation.

The NLP framework used is GATE (General Architecture for Text Engineering) which is a Java suite of tools [5], developed by the University of Sheffield in UK, for building and deploying software components to process human language. GATE can support a wide range of NLP tasks for Information Extraction (IE). IE refers to the extraction of relevant information from unstructured text, such as entities and relationships between them, thus providing facts to feed a knowledge base [8]. GATE is widely used both in research and application work in different fields (e.g. cancer research, web mining, law). This tool is composed of three main components for performing language processing tasks, namely the *Language Resources* component that represents entities such as lexicons, corpora or ontologies; the *Processing Resources* component, which contains a library of executable procedure, such as parsers, generators or ngram modelers; and the *Visual Resources* component that provides visualization and editing functions that are used in GUIs.

3 Approach to Analyse Online Discussions

In order to analyze online discussions through mailing lists, as those used in OSS development, we apply the concepts related to SAT and a communication ontology that we have described in a previous work [9]. Specifically, we first identify which linguistic and non-linguistic acts can be used to model such online discussions, we define a suitable *speech-act* taxonomy and, based on it, a proposal for analyzing online discussions.

The concepts are: a *sender*, a *receiver* and an expression (typically a *sentence* or *proposition*). The expression is written in a given language and within certain context that is determined by a *topic*. For example, by analyzing the directive *speech-act* - "Open the door, please!"- results in: the *sender* is me; the *receiver* is you; the *sentence* or *proposition* is "Open the door, please!"; in English; and the context could be a situation in which we are exiting the office and I'm carrying a heavy box.

Mailing-list discussions are organized as emails threads. A thread is initiated by a member of the mailing list, who proposes a topic to be discussed (i.e., the field *Subject:* of such an email). The discussion develops as a thread of replies by interested people who give their contribution, writing NL text. Different behaviors of the participants emerge in a conversation: someone asks about a topic, or states problems related with it; others provide suggestions, answer questions or simply add details.

To analyze these conversations we first apply the concepts mentioned previously, as shown in the excerpt depicted in Fig. 1: the *sender* corresponds to the *writer* who is specified in the field *From*; the *receiver* is the *addressee* who is the person in the field *To* (it can be also addressees); each *proposition* is a *sentence* in the email body; the language is English, with terms that may be typically used in the context; and the context is determined by the *topic* in the field *Subject*.

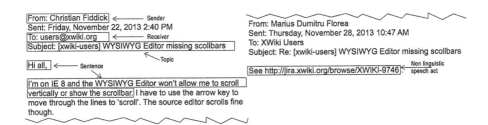

Fig. 1. Excerpt of an online discussion in OSS.

In terms of SAT concepts we can characterize emails of discussion threads as a set of linguistic acts (*speech-acts*) and non-linguistic acts, such as email attachments, URL links, fragments of code, etc. For the sake of simplicity we will use the term *speech-act* to name both types of acts. We find that *speech-acts*, hence, are composed of verbal, syntactic and semantic aspects that reflect the *intention* of a writer. In this paper we consider that an intention is found in a sentence and it is reified by a sequence of specific words, e.g. the sentence "Please help me ..." makes an addressee recognize the speaker's *intention* of requesting something. In the right part of Fig. 1 the sentence in the rectangle shows a non-linguistic *speech-act* with the *intention* to make the addressee give a look at an URL link.

3.1 Taxonomy of Speech Acts

We have elaborated a taxonomy[1] of categories and subcategories of *speech-acts*, shown in Table 1. Column *Category* refers to the main types of *speech-acts* found in the literature, the column *Subcategory* refers to the specific types of *speech-acts*. The column *Analysis category* is the aggregation of *speech-acts* in a reduced number of categories. Finally, the column *Some definitions* presents some *speech-acts* definitions and examples. For instance, the category *Constantives* is specialized into seven subcategories, from which *Assertives*, *Confirmatives* and *Concessives* are aggregated into the analysis category *Assertives*. The *speech-act Assertives* is considered as a strong belief and intention by a sender who maintains his/her belief about something.

Table 1. Categories of *speech-acts*.

Category	Subcategory	Analysis category	Definition (excerpt)(see Footnote 1)
Constantives	Informatives	Not used	*Assertives: speech-act* that is considered as having a strong belief and intention by a sender who maintains his/her belief about something, e.g., "I know the chocolate is good for your health...". *Suppositive: speech-act* conveying that is worth considering the consequences of something regardless of whether it is true, e.g. "I suppose the configuration file ..." *Requestive: speech-act* expressing sender's intention that the receiver take the expressed desire as reason to act, e.g., "I kindly ask you to provide me ..."
	Assertives	Assertives	
	Confirmatives		
	Concessives		
	Suggestives	Responsives	
	Suppositives		
	Responsives		
Directives	Requestives	Requestives	
	Questions		
	Requirements		
Expressives	Thank	Not used	
	Accept	Accept	
	Reject	Reject	
	Negative opinion	Negative opinion	
	Positive opinion	Positive opinion	
Attach (non-linguistic)	URL link	Attach	
	Code line		
	Log file		

3.2 Automated Tagging of Speech Acts

The procedure we followed to build our method includes a gathering of seed words and the computation of their frequencies. This was done in order to have evidence of a presence of performative verbs in messages of OSS community

---

[1] Taxonomy and definitions have been adapted from the work of Bach and Harnish [7].

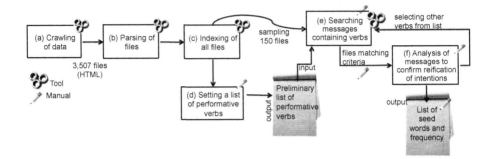

Fig. 2. Process to select the seed words.

discussions. The resulting seed words compose sets of words that are used later to elaborate rules for tagging *speech-acts*. In the following we explain the steps of the procedure.

Selection of Seed Words for the OSS Context. To find out what are the words reifying the intentions that we want to identify, we examined crawled messages from Apache OpenOffice bugzilla[2] to find regularities in written messages. We analyzed empirical data from other OSS project to not be biased in defining the kind of words regularly used by participants in online discussions. Following a supervised selection of seed words, we executed the process depicted in Fig. 2, from step (a) to (f):

(a) Crawling of data: we used a tool for crawling data, called Teleport Ultra[3]. We first executed a simple search on Apache OpenOffice bugzilla platform using a single word, i.e. *feature*, in the searching box. Then we took the web link appearing and used it for the crawling tool.

(b) Parsing of data: we applied an algorithm to parse them into files with the extension *properties*, by using Jsoup[4]. We obtained 3,507 files.

(c) Indexing files: we indexed all the files, using Lucene[5], to have a corpus of messages.

(d) Setting a reference list or verbs: we then elaborated a preliminary reference list of performative verbs taken from the suggested list described by Bach and Harnish [7].

(e) Searching messages containing verbs: for this step we sampled 150 files that we selected randomly and we took the reference list to search for the performative verbs contained in the messages, using Lucene. The output is a set of messages that were analyzed.

(f) Analyzing messages: we read each one of the messages from the resulting set of files matching the searched verbs (output from step (e)). By reading and

---

[2] https://issues.apache.org/ooo/.
[3] http://www.tenmax.com/Teleport/ultra/home.htm.
[4] http://www.jsoup.org.
[5] http://lucene.apache.org/core/.

interpreting the whole message wrt. the intentions described in our taxonomy, see Table 1, we classified the sentence containing the verb in the corresponding subcategory. A given set of seed words accompanying the verbs that appear in the message become candidate indicators for the identified subcategory if we found at least three occurrences of the same set of seed words in the same subcategory. We returned to step (e) till we finish the reference list of verbs.

For example, the final list of seed words and their occurrence contains the intention *Requirements*, whith the following three instances of seed words: "I want" with a frequency of 11 messages, "I would like to have" found in 7 messages, and "It would be nice" in 65 messages.

Design of the Speech-Acts Tagging Tool. Our tool is based on a knowledge-heavy approach [10], this means the use of a part-of-speech (POS) tagger, java annotation patterns engine (JAPE) rules, a tokenizer, a lemmatizer and gazetteers (list of performative verbs). Gazetteers and JAPE rules have been tailored to annotate the intentions applying some tags. These tags are used to annotate fragments of text, the tags are the subcategories of *speech-acts* defined in Table 1. To adapt the JAPE module we have formulated lexico-syntactic rules, by using a set of words inspired from the examples given by Jurafsky [11] and by the obtained seed words from the previous step. The Gazetteers used in our approach are the lists of verbs and seed words for each subcategory of *speech-act*. Some JAPE rules use the Gazetteers to annotate intentions. The linguistic analysis is executed on discussion threads in the format of TXT files, which are the input. The tool is used to annotate sentences on the text messages of each thread. After this, the files annotated with intentions are parsed to extract the intentions found in each message. Finally, an analysis of intentions is performed, following an analysis model that we are elaborating.

Examples of design of JAPE rules are illustrated below in Table 2, the full set of rules are available online[6]. The first column, *Category*, refers to the category of *speech-act*. The second column, *Tag*, refers to the name for tagging sentences. The third column, *Rule*, shows the rule for tagging the *speech-act*, for example, the category *Constantives* has two tags, namely, *Suggestives* and *Responsives*. Along these lines, the tag *Suggestives* presents two rules to annotate. As it can be seen there are POS tags and seed words that are used by the tool to annotate the *speech-acts*. The POS tags $< PRP >$ and $< MD >$ refers to the initial set of words to annotate, the $< Keyword >$ refers to the list of verbs or seed words defined in the Gazetteer[7] modules and that are used by the JAPE rules.

We manually designed the rules considering some characteristics for extracting the intentions, such as preceding and succeeding words, length of the words, root of the words, special types of verbs, using the seed words, syntax and the

---

[6] JAPE files are available at http://selab.fbk.eu/imramirez/JAPErulesSep2014/files.zip.

[7] Gazetteer files are available at http://selab.fbk.eu/imramirez/GazetteerSep2014/files.zip.

Table 2. Example of rules for tagging *speech-acts Directives* and *Constantives*.

Category	Tag	Rule
Directives	Questions	$< WRB > + < PRP > + < content > +$ "?"
		$< MD > + < PRP > + < content > +$ "?"
Constantives	Suggestives	$< PRP > + (< MD >)* + ($ "try" $\|$ "check" $)$
		$< PRP > + (< MD >)* + ($ "suggest" $\|$ "recommend" $)$
	Responsives	$(< PRP >)* +$ "[Hh]ope" $ + < content > +$ "help"

codification of the POS tagger used by GATE. The tag is used to label a text fragment when one of the corresponding rule matches it. Each rule is formulated as a regular expression. The regular expressions $< content >$, $(< MD >)*$ and [Hh], for example, make reference to a set of words in the middle of two keywords or POS tags, to the presence or absence of the POS tag and to the uppercase or lowercase of the first letter of a word, respectively. More details can be found our previous work [12].

Analysis Model. We are building an analysis model of the intentions in a discussion thread that can be performed at different levels of granularity, see Table 3. At the sentence level we can identify single and nested *speech-acts*.

Table 3. Granularity of analysis.

Granularity level	Aggregation of intentions	Example
Sentence	Single intention	*Suggestives* "*I suggest you*"
	Nested intentions	*Questions* "*Why don't you try?*"
Message	Compound intentions	Bug indicator = $\begin{cases}\end{cases}$ *Suggestives* "*There is a problem*" *Negative opinion* "*Can anyone help me?*" *Questions*
		Feature indicator = $\begin{cases}\end{cases}$ "*I really like the application*" *Positive opinion* "*It would be nice*" *Requirement*

For instance, in the sentence "I suggest you to make a copy of your data", the single intention of suggesting is triggered by the sequences of words "I suggest you...", which refers to the *speech-act Suggestives*. An example of nested intentions is expressed in the sentence "Why don't you try to use the wizard?". In this case there are two *speech-acts*, one is "Why...?", and the other one is "don't you try", representative of the intentions of questioning and suggesting, respectively. At the message level the occurrences of pairs of intentions is analyzed, called compound intentions, and we claim can be indicators of *Bug*, *Feature*, or *Clarification* requests. For example, a combination of *speech-act Negative opinion* ("There is a problem") and *Question* ("Can anyone help me?") can be an indicator of a bug. Therefore, a set of nested or compound linguistic and non-linguistic acts can be considered as indicators of bugs, features, etc.

4 Empirical Evaluation Phase 1: Human Annotation of *Speech-Acts*

4.1 Overall Plan

Our plan for empirically evaluating the proposed approach consists of three phases. In the first phase we investigate how non-trained humans perform when annotating *speech-acts*, for which we have formulated the following research question: *RQ1. How difficult is for non-trained human annotators to recognize speech-acts in online discussions?* For the second phase we would use part of the annotated database for improving the rules of our tool and to evaluate the performance of it. Then, we want to investigate *RQ2. What is the accuracy of the tool for annotating speech-acts in terms of precision and recall?* The third phase is aimed at evaluating if the tool-supported identification of bug and feature requests will be effective in a realistic setting, possibly with the participation of expert analysts. In the following subsections we describe the details of the first execution of phase one.

4.2 Context

The context of the study is the following: the *subjects* are people playing the role of a receiver of messages that must interpret the predominant intention in each sender's sentence. The *objects* are 20 discussions from an OSS project, namely the XWiki project whose data is publicly available[8]. The 20 discussions are split into 1685 sentences in total. We sent email invitations to 38 people to participate in the empirical study. The people invited have a position either as a PhD student, Post-doc or technician. Their field of expertise is in Computer Science, Software Engineering or Biology. All of them are from different countries (e.g., China, The Netherlands, Mexico, Brazil, Germany, among others). We informed them that the activity should have been performed through an online platform and that it should have required approximatively 1 hour and 30 min to be completed. We did not specify time constraints, although we expressed our expectation to collect data after a week. Only 20 subjects accepted the invitation, we grouped them in pairs (labeled as $G_1 \ldots G_{10}$) but they worked individually. The members of a group were selected randomly. Each group was assigned with two online discussions to annotate.

---

[8] XWiki is an OSS generic platform for developing collaborative applications, http://www.xwiki.org/xwiki/bin/view/Main/WebHome.

4.3   Metrics

Given the research question *RQ1. How difficult is for non-trained human annotators to recognize speech-acts in online discussions?* We collect these (dependent) metrics:

- $Time_i$ = seconds spend by subject to annotate the sentence i;
- $Effort_p = sum(Time_i)/\#\ of\ sentences$ [for the participant p];
- $AgreementN$ = Kappa(i,j) between subject i and j (on the same discussion) with N number of classes.

The first two metrics measure respectively the *Time* required to annotate a single sentence, and the *Effort* to annotate an entire session, as the average time per sentence in the session. The last metric represents the *Agreement* between a pair of subjects in annotating the same sentences, computed with the statistical measure Cohen's Kappa (see Analysis, Sect. 4.5).

Moreover, based on a profiling questionnaire, we also measure independent factors that possibly influence our dependent metrics, such as:

1. *Working field:* we have classified the annotators according to three fields, namely, Biology, Computer Science and Software Engineering.
2. *Years of experience:* according to the answers we created 4 ranges of years of experience (i.e., 1–3, 4–5, 6–8, 9–15).
3. *Current position:* another possible factor could be if the participant is a PhD student, Post doc or technician.
4. *Distributed collaboration:* we have asked to the participants their experience in working collaboratively in a distributed setting.
5. *Channel of communication:* we also wanted to know which is their preferred channel of communication.
6. *Knowledge about OSS:* the participants' knowledge about OSS is also one possible factor.

4.4   Experiment Material and Procedure

In this first execution we exploited an online platform that allows us to set up annotation tasks on preprocessed sets of OSS online discussions, involving distributed annotators[9]. We gave the subjects instructions about how to perform the assigned task, by sending individual emails including: a password and a URL link to access the online platform; and a PDF document containing a short guide about the *speech-act* annotation. The guide briefly introduces the goal of the annotation task, it lists *speech-acts*, gives some hints of what is meant by the speaker's intention expressed through a *speech-act*, and illustrates some screenshots of the platform they would have been presented along the basic steps. A screenshot is depicted in Fig. 3. Each text box, from the top to the bottom, shows a sentence in a discussion. Above each text box there is a drop down

---

[9] Similar to crowdsourcing platforms, such as CrowdFlower http://www.crowdflower.com/.

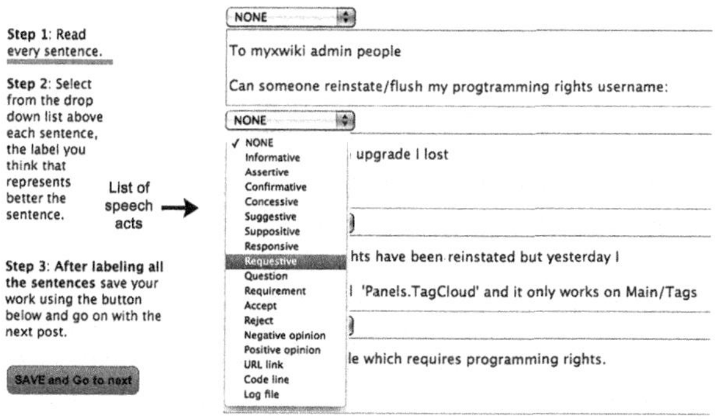

Fig. 3. Interface of the online platform to annotate sentences.

menu containing the list of the labels for the different *speech-act* subcategories. After reading each sentence the subjects should select the *speech-act* label that represents the intention of the sentence. The annotation session is saved by clicking the button *SAVE* before being given a new set of sentences (varying the # of sentences).

The list of *speech-acts* labels to be used for the annotation study was reduced from the 18 presented in Table 1, column *Subcategory*, to 17. Indeed, the *speech-act Thank* was ignored since it is trivially identifiable by the word "thank" and its variants. We added a label "NONE" to describe a nonsense sentence in case the participants were not satisfied with any other label. However, we did not consider it as well as the default *speech-act Informative* in the analysis of the data, reported below.

4.5   Analysis

For the analysis we have used descriptive statistics and ANOVA tests to make our interpretations of how difficult is for human annotators to identify expressed intentions in online discussions. Since each group was assigned with different number of sentences, for the purpose of our analysis, and taking into account space limits, we have selected the first 100 sentences that each participant annotated[10]. We have computed descriptive statistics such as the mean, median and standard deviation. We have applied the ANOVA test of time and ANOVA test of time by participant profile to analyze possible influencing factors. We present some plots for cases where the statistical significance is reached with a confidence of 95%, i.e. with a p-value < 0.05. We have used the R tool to compute the descriptive statistics and ANOVA tests.

We computed the Cohen's Kappa coefficient [13] to obtain the percentage of agreement of a pair of annotators. There is a perfect agreement when $k = 1$ and no agreement when $k = 0$. We interpret the quality of agreement, thereby quality

---

[10] The complete analysis is described in the technical report available at http://selab. fbk.eu/imramirez/TR_CAiSEDec2014.pdf.

of the data, according to two different scales, namely Landis and Koch [14] and Green [15].

Eventually, in order to understand how difficult is for non-trained human annotators to recognize *speech-acts* in online discussions, we present our interpretations based on the empirical evidence.

5 Results

In this section we describe the results of the measurements applied and the interpretation of the ANOVA tests.

Analysis of Time. We observed that the time for annotating has the following distribution: a mean of 35 s, a median of 18 and a standard deviation of 56 s.

The ANOVA test of time shows that the time for annotating a sentence is influenced by the order of the sentences, i.e. there is a learning effect. Another factor that influences the time is the participant profile, whose ANOVA test is shown in Table 4 (see Footnote 10).

Table 4. ANOVA of time by participants' profile.

	Df	Sum Sq	Mean Sq	F value	Pr(>F)
Field	1	28461.79	28461.79	9.72	**0.0019**
Years	3	180122.91	60040.97	20.50	**<0.01**
Position	1	16577.79	16577.79	5.66	**0.0175**
Distributed	1	156474.19	156474.19	53.43	**<0.01**
Channel	1	11737.71	11737.71	4.01	**0.0455**
OSS	1	4165.79	4165.79	1.42	0.2332
Residuals	1454	4257992.54	2928.47		

As it can be observed the participant's field of expertise, years of experience, position (PhD vs. Post-doc), the past experience in working with a distributed team and the preferred communication channel are co-factors that influence the time to annotate a sentence. Therefore, the difficulty (in terms of time) that each participant experienced during the annotation of sentences varies according to these factors. Focusing on the years of experience, we see that for experienced participants it took 25 s per sentence, while for participants with less experience it took 10 s per sentence. Our interpretation is that with more years of experience, participants become more meticulous in analyzing something, paying more attention in performing the assigned tasks. Instead, less experienced participants take risks and act more by instinct or common sense. However, we cannot exclude that participants who spent more time in annotating just experienced a higher difficulty.

Analysis of Effort. While the analysis of time is focused on the answers of the questionnaire, the analysis of effort involves the complete annotation session. Regarding the distribution of effort spent by subject, we observed a mean of 36 s per sentence, a median of 33 and a standard deviation of 19 s. We computed the ANOVA of effort with factors such as the participant's group, the kappa agreement for 8-type *speech-act* categories and the agreement for 16-type *speech-act* categories. Also, we computed the ANOVA of effort by participant profile. We found in the ANOVA of effort that the agreement for 16-categories has a slight influence on the effort, and that the experience in working in a distributed setting can be a factor on the effort. Figure 4 shows that participants who exchange many emails per day have spent around 10 s per sentence, which can be interpreted as the annotation task is less difficult due to their high experience in working collaboratively, differently from other participants who exchange emails less frequently.

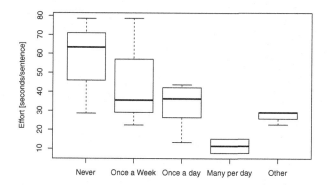

Fig. 4. Boxplot of effort by collaborative working frequency.

Analysis of Agreement. The third metric refers to the Cohen's Kappa value, we computed the k-values by considering the 16-categories (called *Subcategory* in Table 1) and the 8-categories, shown in Table 5. The first column reports the number of types of *speech-acts* . The following 10 columns present the k-value of each group $(G_\#)$. The second row reports the k-value computed on the 16-categories and the third row on the 8-categories. These 8-categories correspond to the aggregated subcategories of *speech-acts*, ignoring Default and Thank; and including the single categories Accept, Reject, Negative and Positive opinion.

According to the Landis scale, values of k from 0.0 to 0.2 correspond to *Slight*, from 0.2 to 0.4 to *Fair*, from 0.4 to 0.6 to *Moderate*, from 0.6 to 0.8 to *Substantial* and from 0.8 to 1.0 to *Perfect*. While for Green's scale values of k ranging from 0.0 to 0.4 are considered *Low*, from 0.4 to 0.75 *Fair/Good*, and from 0.75 to 1.0 *High*. The best agreement is between the participants of group G_6 with 0.51 for 16-categories and 0.66 with 8-categories. The interpretation are *Moderate* and *Substantial* on the Landis scale and *Fair/Good* for both cases in the Green scale. The slight correlation between the agreement on 16-categories

Table 5. k-value per group for the *speech-acts* subcategory and analysis category (*#speech-act*). Gray-colored cells are the highest k-values.

#speech-act	G_1	G_2	G_3	G_4	G_5	G_6	G_7	G_8	G_9	G_{10}
16	0.38	0.31	0.15	0.33	0.22	0.51	0.41	0.28	0.29	0.28
8	0.49	0.44	0.29	0.34	0.23	0.66	0.48	0.43	0.38	0.39

and effort can be seen in the plot of their correlation in Fig. 5. This can be interpreted as the participants who put more effort in annotating sentences, indeed, take more time to analyze the sentences. Therefore, there is an increase in the agreement and probably the quality of the task also increases. Thus the annotation task becomes difficult because there could be a cognitive overload while understanding all the categories and select only one for a given sentence.

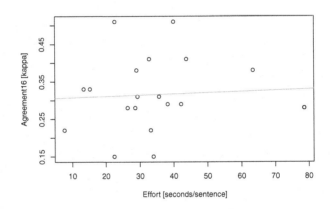

Fig. 5. Correlation of effort and kappa agreement for the 16-type *speech-act* categories.

5.1 Threats to Validity and Observations

We discuss the threats to validity as recommended by the literature in empirical software engineering [16]. *Conclusion validity* threats concern issues that affect the ability to draw the correct conclusion on the observed phenomenon. The evidence obtained so far does not show a trend, thus we need replications and more data to confirm the difficulty experienced by the human annotators. *Internal validity* threats concern the possible confounding elements that may hinder a well performed experiment. On one side, since the participants did not receive any training we consider that they were not biased while performing the activity. On the other side, variables as different background, not enough attention or low understanding of the task and that participants are non-native English speakers could have affected the results. *Construct validity* threats concern the relationship between theory and observation. As we requested to participants to annotate sentences using 16 *speech-acts* labels (based on the theory) and then for the analysis we aggregated the classes and reduced them to 8, we see that there might not be a clear disambiguation of all the classes and for further experiments we will reduce the number of labels. *External validity* threats concern extending the validity of observations outside the context. *Speech-acts* are not limited to a certain domain and are expressed by people mainly in spoken language, but the NLP research field exploits transcripts of telephone conversations to find *speech-acts*. We claim that *speech-acts* can be found in any type of written document, specially but not uniquely, in archives of online discussions.

Observations. The execution of the empirical evaluation brought to our attention important aspects to be considered in future empirical evaluations, which did not emerge in a pilot execution with one of the authors acting as annotator. We shortly discuss them in the following. We need to consider *speech-acts* as an aggregated category. Indeed, we have recognized that there were misunderstandings between *speech-acts* such as Question and Requestive. Some participants were labeling as a Requestive act a Question act that other participant was annotating. For example, the participants 19 and 20 with the sentences: *Is SQL Server 2005 a hard requirement?* and *Which errors do you meet?* Based on this, we acknowledge that the tool will likely fail since we rely on a lexico-syntactic approach for annotating. We need to train people in this matter for the software domain, in line with what reported by Plaza [17], where a similar recommendation is discussed with reference to the maritime domain. The tutorial must be revised to include feedback from the annotators in order to improve their understanding of the task and increase their motivation to perform it at best. We are planning to increment the number of annotators per group, i.e. by having at least three annotators per group.

6   Related Work

The analysis of NL text messages in online forums, bug-tracking systems or mailing lists has been addressed by research works in HCI, computer-mediated business conversation analysis, and more recently in software engineering. We briefly recall relevant works in the following. Ko et al. [18] perform a linguistic analysis of titles of bug reports to understand how people describe software problems. In their approach they use a part-of-speech tagger to identify nouns, verbs, adjectives, etc. and obtain their frequency. They make reference to an intent of a sentence or *grammatical mood* that is indicated by the verbs, which can help in classifying problem reports from requests, but they only analyze the titles and conclude that the use of such a mood concepts need further investigation. Contrary, we analyze speech acts in the body of the emails of a discussion thread. An automated identification of intentions is presented by Twitchell et al. [19]. This investigation proposes a tool that is based on SAT, dialogue acts and fuzzy logic to analyze transcripts of telephone conversations. The goal of this research is to derive participant profiles based on a map of the intentions expressed in the conversation. Our work aims at supporting automated identification of discussants' intentions in OSS communities, such as requesting for features, reporting bugs, or others. The classification of emails using speech acts is investigated by Carvalho et al. [20]. They are interested in classifying emails regarding office-related interactions as negotiation and delegation of tasks. They introduce the term *email acts* which follows a taxonomy of verbs and nouns and they highlight the fact that sequential email acts in a thread of messages contain information useful for a task-oriented classification. Moreover they consider non-linguistic acts as *deliver*. Analogously, we define speech acts to characterize the communication actions in the context of mailing-list discussions in OSS development and consider non-linguistic acts as attachments. The investigation of speech acts by Ravi et al. [21] on thread of discussions in student forum aims at identifying unanswered questions, to be assigned to an instructor for their resolution. They present some patterns of interaction found in the threads, the patterns correspond to the acts *Responsive* and *Question*.

With reference to Requirements Engineering tasks, Knauss et al. [22] analyze discussion threads for requirements elicitation purposes. They focus on the content of communication between stakeholders to find patterns of communication used by stakeholders when they are seeking clarification on requirements. Their approach is based on a Naive Bayesian classifier, a classification scheme of clarification and some heuristics, with interesting results. Worth mentioning is the work of Galvis Carreño et al. [23] that aims at analyzing messages, or *comments*, from users of software applications. Information extraction techniques and topic modeling are exploited to automatically extract topics, and to provide requirements engineers with a user feedback report, which will support them in identifying candidate new/changed requirements. A similar approach is the one of Guzman et al. [24] where App reviews are the input of an automated tool that supports the tasks of filtering, aggregating and analyzing the reviews by applying topic modeling and sentiment analysis. All the above mentioned research works in the area of Requirements Engineering use NL text messages or documents to discover patterns, relevant topics or identify domain key terms, but none of the them consider SAT based techniques to understand stakeholders' intentions behind their messages. We consider that the application of SAT in Requirements Engineering can be a powerful strategy to understand stakeholder's intentions, thus supporting the analysis of the messages they exchange in current distributed collaboration and deriving requirements knowledge.

7   Conclusion

In this paper we proposed a tool-supported method approach to analyze OSS mailing-list discussions in terms of linguistic and non-linguistic acts. We described how the method builds on the idea that the recognition of *speech-acts* expressed in these conversations is key to reveal discussants' intentions, such as suggesting, or complaining. We introduced a three-phase plan to empirically evaluate it and discussed a first execution of phase one, which involved 20 human annotators that were doing the activity of annotating sentences with intentions. The result of this execution gave us a first dataset of *speech-acts* annotations in the domain of OSS online discussions, which may represent a valuable resource for the research community in itself. So far, the interpretation of the results indicates that human annotators might have experienced difficulties when identifying intentions in sentences, mainly if their expertise is not in Software Engineering. But a replication of the experiment must be performed to draw a stronger conclusion. We are working on improving the study design to build a ground truth. This data would be used for evaluating the effectiveness of the proposed method, which is part of the second phase of our empirical evaluation. We are also using the dataset with machine learning algorithms to identify patterns of speech acts. The long-term objective is to use our tool for supporting the classification of messages as bug reports, feature requests or clarifications. We are also considering to collect online discussions of non OSS projects to evaluate the generalizability of the proposed approach in different distributed development settings.

References

1. Castro-Herrera, C., Cleland-Huang, J.: Utilizing recommender systems to support software requirements elicitation. In: RSSE, pp. 6–10. ACM (2010)
2. Camino, B.M., Milewski, A.E., Millen, D.R., Smith, T.M.: Replying to email with structured responses. Int. J. Hum. Comput. Stud. **48**(6), 763–776 (1998)
3. Searle, J.R.: Speech Acts: An Essay in the Philosophy of Language, vol. 626. Cambridge University Press, Cambridge (1969)
4. Wilson, D., Sperber, D.: Relevance theory. In: Horn, L., Ward, G. (eds.) Handbook of Pragmatics. Blackwell, Oxford (2002)
5. Cunningham, H., Maynard, D., Bontcheva, K., Tablan, V., Aswani, N., Roberts, I., Gorrell, G., Funk, A., Roberts, A., Damljanovic, D., Heitz, T., Greenwood, M.A., Saggion, H., Petrak, J., Li, Y., Peters, W.: Text Processing with GATE (Version 6) (2011)
6. Stolcke, A., Coccaro, N., Bates, R., Taylor, P., Van Ess-Dykema, C., Ries, K., Shriberg, E., Jurafsky, D., Martin, R., Meteer, M.: Dialogue act modeling for automatic tagging and recognition of conversational speech. Comput. Linguist. **26**(3), 339–373 (2000)
7. Bach, K., Harnish, R.M.: Linguistic Communication and Speech Acts. MIT Press, Cambridge (1979)
8. Cowie, J., Lehnert, W.: Information extraction. Commun. ACM **39**(1), 80–91 (1996)
9. Morales-Ramirez, I., Perini, A., Guizzardi, R.: Providing foundation for user feedback concepts by extending a communication ontology. In: Yu, E., Dobbie, G., Jarke, M., Purao, S. (eds.) ER 2014. LNCS, vol. 8824, pp. 305–312. Springer, Heidelberg (2014)
10. Ahrenberg, L., Andersson, M., Merkel, M.: A knowledge-lite approach to word alignment. In: Véronis, J. (ed.) Parallel Text Processing. Text, Speech and Language Technology, vol. 13, pp. 97–116. Springer, Dordrecht (2000)
11. Jurafsky, D., Shriberg, L., Biasca, D.: Switchboard SWBD-DAMSL shallow-discourse-function annotation coders manual, draft 13. Technical report, University of Colorado at Boulder Technical Report 97–02 (1997)
12. Morales-Ramirez, I., Perini, A.: Discovering speech acts in online discussions: a tool-supported method. In: Proceedings of the CAiSE 2014 Forum, pp. 137–144 (2014)

13. Cohen, J.: A coefficient of agreement for nominal scales. Educ. Psychol. Measur. **20**(1), 37–46 (1960)
14. Landis, J.R., Koch, G.G.: The measurement of observer agreement for categorical data. Biometrics **33**, 159–174 (1977)
15. Green, A.M.: Kappa statistics for multiple raters using categorical classifications. In: Proceedings of the Twenty-Second Annual SAS Users Group International Conference (online), March 1997
16. Wohlin, C., Runeson, P., Höst, M., Ohlsson, M., Regnell, B., Wesslén, A.: Experimentation in Software Engineering - An Introduction. Kluwer Academic Publishers, Norwell (2000)
17. Plaza, S.M.: Teaching performative verbs and nouns in eu maritime regulations. Procedia Soc. Behav. Sci. **141**, 90–95 (2014)
18. Ko, A.J., Myers, B.A., Chau, D.H.: A linguistic analysis of how people describe software problems. In: VLHCC 2006, pp. 127–134. IEEE Computer Society (2006)
19. Twitchell, D.P., Nunamaker, J.F.: Speech act profiling: a probabilistic method for analyzing persistent conversations and their participants. In: International Conference on System Sciences, p. 10. IEEE Computer Society Press (2004)
20. Carvalho, V.R., Cohen, W.W.: On the collective classification of email speech acts. In: ACM SIGIR Conference on Research and Development in Information Retrieval, pp. 345–352. ACM (2005)
21. Ravi, S., Kim, J.: Profiling student interactions in threaded discussions with speech act classifiers. Front. Artif. Intell. Appl. **158**, 357–364 (2007)
22. Knauss, E., Damian, D., Poo-Caamano, G., Cleland-Huang, J.: Detecting and classifying patterns of requirements clarifications. In: RE, pp. 251–260. IEEE (2012)
23. Carreño, L.V.G., Winbladh, K.: Analysis of user comments: an approach for software requirements evolution. In: ICSE, pp. 582–591. IEEE (2013)
24. Guzman, E., Maalej, W.: How do users like this feature? a fine grained sentiment analysis of app reviews. In: RE, pp. 153–162. IEEE (2014)

Visual and Ontological Modeling and Analysis Support for Extended Enterprise Models

Sagar Sunkle[(✉)] and Hemant Rathod

Tata Research Development and Design Center, Tata Consultancy Services,
54B, Industrial Estate, Hadapsar, Pune 411013, India
{sagar.sunkle,hemant.rathod}@tcs.com
http://www.tcs.com

Abstract. To remain competitive in dynamic environment, enterprises need to make effective and efficient decisions in response to changes. Good modeling tools and analysis support is a necessity in this regard. Such modeling and analysis tools should to be able to visually model and programmatically analyze several descriptive and prescriptive modeling languages in concert. We recount our experience with visual modeling editor and ontological representation for both descriptive and prescriptive models for enterprise decision making. Starting with purposive modeling tools, we shifted to integrated modeling environment where all relevant models of enterprise coexist and are analyzed together. Our ongoing research suggests that apart from integrated modeling environment, scalable modeling facilities for better interaction between modelers and domain experts are also necessary to make modeling and analysis of enterprise models more streamlined.

Keywords: Enterprise modeling · Intentional models · Visual modeling · Enterprise analysis · ArchiMate · Adex

1 Introduction

Modern enterprises face external change drivers such as evolving market conditions, pressure from competitors' innovation, technology obsolescence and advance, dynamic supply chains and complying with increasingly strict regulations. While external change drivers often demand enterprise transformation [1], internal policies within enterprises tend to be targeted at improvement of enterprise's business as usual (BAU) situation [2]. To remain competitive, enterprises need to respond to changes in an efficient and effective manner. Current state of the art and practice in enterprises rely extensively on expert knowledge with much of the artifacts being document-oriented [1]. We take the stance that responding to changes requires a model-based treatment of four tasks- creating the AS-IS enterprise architecture (EA), coming up with possible TO-BE EAs, devising a way to evaluate TO-BE EAs based on some criteria, and enabling the operationalization of the desired TO-BE EA.

© Springer International Publishing Switzerland 2015
S. Nurcan and E. Pimenidis (Eds.): CAiSE Forum 2014, LNBIP 204, pp. 233–249, 2015.
DOI: 10.1007/978-3-319-19270-3_15

Using purpose-specific, machine-processable models to capture AS-IS and TO-BE EAs, it becomes possible to lessen the reliance on experts by constructing meaningful analyses on such models. The ability to model enterprise change contexts along with rationale is required to be able to relate reasons behind design decisions with on-ground actions of enterprise in both transformation and BAU improvement scenarios. For this we chose ArchiMate [3] and i* [4] as respective modeling languages [5] and Archi [6] and OpenOME [7] as respective modeling tools.

Since the EA and intentional models existed in separate tools, it was not possible to construct combined EA- and intentional modeling-specific analyses. This created problems in terms of traceability between intentional models and elements of TO-BE EA, as it was not preserved in this approach [5]. We had to adopt an ad-hoc process in enacting desired TO-BE EA model presuming that concerns expressed in intentional models are represented completely and consistently in TO-BE EA model.

In accordance with these pointers, we extended Archi to enable integrated visual modeling of EA models as descriptive models and intentional and motivation models (called IM models henceforth) as prescriptive models. We also extended our EA ontology [1], originally containing only EA modeling elements, similarly to carry out various analyses required in terms of prescriptive courses of actions from AS-IS to TO-BE EAs. Our ongoing model building effort with real world case studies suggests that integrated visual modeling support simplifies and streamlines modeling process. At the same time, integrated ontological modeling support enables expressing requisite analyses with ease.

Yet, we perceive the need to be able to carry out both modeling and analysis of EA and IM models using single modeling framework that is capable of providing metamodeling, visualization, and programming support. In practical implementation of EA and IM models, there would be other needs in terms of scalability as well as support for a method for EA and IM modeling and analysis. For this, we propose to use our own reflexive (meta-) modeling framework [8,9] which includes all the above necessary components as well as scalability features.

This paper recounts our experience from our experiments with explicit intentions in EA change response from using separate visual modeling environments to carrying out the visual modeling in integrated modeling environment [10]. Sections 2 and 3 discuss the requisite elements for modeling change response in enterprise context and transition to integrated visual and ontological modeling environment respectively. In Sect. 4, we outline the proposal for knowledge transfer to our modeling environment which has proven scalability features. Section 5 discusses related work and several observations. Section 6 concludes the paper.

2   Modeling Enterprises with Explicit Intentions

With more than 15 years of experience in delivering 70+ large business-critical enterprise applications, we know that the cost of incorrect decisions is prohibitively high in building and evolving these applications, especially in the face

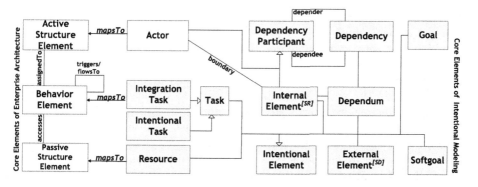

Fig. 1. Mapping EA and intentional modeling elements [5]

of imminent changes. In this regard, we investigated an approach for modeling EA with explicit intentions of enterprise actors. Such a treatment would enable modeling and analyzing strategic alternatives available to enterprise in response to change. We chose ArchiMate for its economy of core concepts and coverage of concepts pertaining to various aspects of enterprise [5]. We chose i* for representing strategic alternatives because of its actor-orientation and availability of evaluation algorithms for ranking strategic alternatives.

We represented AS-IS enterprise architecture (EA) models using Archi [6]. Intentional models were treated as models of the problems an enterprise is trying to solve [5]. These were modeled using OpenOME [7]. We came up with a metamodel mapping between ArchiMate metamodel and intentional metamodel, enabling us to derive intentional models from AS-IS EA models. We represented strategic alternatives in given change situation in OpenOME and evaluated them with label propagation algorithm [11]. Only a single alternative from amongst the optimum alternatives was then chosen to be realized on top of AS-IS EA [5]. The next section describes the elements necessary to model and analyse enterprise rationale using the mapping between EA and intentional modeling elements shown in Fig. 1.

2.1 Requisite Elements for Modeling and Analyzing Explicit Rationale

The ArchiMate generic metamodel defines active structure elements (ASEs) as the entities that are capable of performing behavior. These are assigned to behavior elements (BEs), which indicate units of activity. The passive structure elements (PSEs) are the objects on which behavior is performed [3].

The i* metamodel from [12] considers actors performing tasks as means to ends that are captured as (soft) goals [13]. Resources may be used or created by actor while performing tasks. Actors may depend on each other to perform a task and/or to use or create a resource to achieve a goal or soft goal. Two kinds of models are used in i* namely, strategic dependency (SD) and strategic rationale

(SR) models, to capture dependencies between actors and to model the intentions of actors in performing their appointed tasks respectively. SR models describe reasoning that actors employ in determining the merit in organizing their tasks one way or the other. SD models describe an enterprise in terms of dependencies that enterprise actors have on each other in accomplishing their work.

We mapped the active structure entities (ASEs) such as business actors, application components, hardware and system software, as well as interfaces to actors in i*. The behavioral entities (BEs) such as business processes, and business, application, and infrastructure services were mapped to tasks in i*. The passive structure entities (PSEs) were mapped to resources in i*, which are essentially informational or physical entities used or created by actors. Via this mapping, it was possible for us to model facts of enterprise summarized by *ASEs use or create PSEs while performing BEs as means to ends that are goal(s) or soft goal(s)*.

2.2   Using Explicit Rationale

We used this metamodel mapping in a case study in which we re-imagined our Model-driven Engineering-based software development unit as an enterprise and presented two distinct stages in its evolution as current and future states in retrospect [5]. The EA models of this enterprise were developed using Archi [6] and the intentional models were developed using OpenOME [7]. This consisted of the following steps:

1. Obtain/create AS-IS models of the enterprise using Archi.
2. Using these, create intentional models devoid of goals via metamodel mapping using OpenOME.
3. Represent the problems in the change context in terms of goals to be achieved.
4. Model new tasks for original actors and new actors with tasks that might be necessary for achievement of goals modeled in earlier step.
5. Model the dependencies between actors.

The process that an enterprise would follow to go from AS-IS EA to TO-BE EA is shown in Fig. 2. Using the metamodel mapping it was possible for us to represent ASEs, PSEs, and BEs in EA models modeled in Archi in terms of actors, resources, and tasks in intentional models in OpenOME. Using OpenOME's in built alternative evaluation mechanism based on satisfaction label propagation [11], the optimum alternative would be decided.

This alternative existed in the intentional model. The new set of actors and their dependencies would be then transferred back on top of AS-IS EA model via metamodel mapping, thus giving a specific TO-BE model. This TO-BE model would dictate what needs to be operationalized on ground to reach desired response to change under consideration.

This arrangement worked as far as a specific TO-BE model was to be built. As we applied the same process to create considerably larger models [14], we found that:

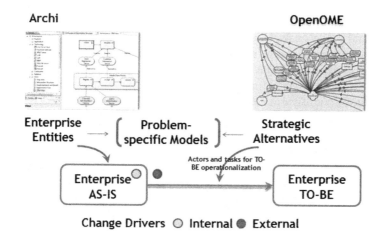

Fig. 2. Using explicit rationale for transition to desired TO-BE EA [5]

- For really large enterprise models containing thousands of entities, keeping the EA and intentional models in sync in two different modeling tools became nearly impossible as models started to grow in size.
- In our original approach, the transformation of intentional models from EA models and the other way round was manual because of the independent tools.
- This also meant that only a single TO-BE EA model could be obtained at a time. Ideally, it should be possible to derive any TO-BE EA model corresponding to selected optimum strategic alternative.

In short, we needed a way to be able to visually model both EA and intentional concerns together. Our ongoing efforts in this regard are discussed in the next section.

3   Modeling EA and IM with Integrated Visual Modeling Support

As explained at the end of last section, we needed both visual modeling and analysis support for combined EA and intentional models. Furthermore, the process of capturing AS-IS had to be more guided as otherwise domain experts were found to be at loss as to what it is that modelers wanted to model in a particular change context. Finally, the analysis had to make a way for preserving the information about specific alternatives in the TO-BE EA models.

3.1   Adding Motivation Elements to Intentional Models

In spite of the fact that ArchiMate motivation extensions provide goal related elements already [15], we chose intentional modeling for capturing goals for the following reasons:

1. Actors should own the tasks that are used as means to achieve certain ends. Intentional models take the actor/agent-oriented view in SR models whereas ArchiMate's treatment in motivation extensions is more generic as well as implicit via *associated with* links.
2. Dependencies between actors are captured in intentional models in SD models; ArchiMate motivation extensions do not provide any specialized elements for capturing dependencies.
3. Qualitative aspects of a solution to problem in enterprise change context are not explicitly captured in motivation extensions as opposed to soft goals and their semantics in intentional modeling.
4. Finally, motivation extensions do not provide any evaluation mechanism for strategic alternatives similar to satisfaction label propagation in intentional modeling [11].

As we started modeling EA and intentional models of various problems in real world case studies, we found that domain experts were more at home with elements like *internal* and *external drivers (motivations), stakeholders, assessment,* and so on, although they agreed that sharp goal definitions with qualitative aspects were also used in change scenarios. Drivers, both within an enterprise and from the enterprise's environment, influence rest of the IM elements. Generally, a stakeholder becomes interested in assessment of a driver and it is this assessment that leads to formulation of a goal. From thereon, intentional modeling begins in terms of actor who is responsible for achieving the goal and actions that need to be taken by that actor, in most cases depending on other actors. Reader is redirected to some of our case studies presented in [2,16] for further details.

We needed to amend the intentional metamodel with motivation related elements for better articulation in interaction between modelers and domain experts. Also, earlier approach consisted of including additions and modifications to EA elements of AS-IS model to represent the TO-BE model. Instead of this ad hoc process, a model-based process would be more helpful where for a given strategic alternative, the corresponding TO-BE model could be obtained without manual adjustment to the AS-IS EA model.

Figure 3 shows the extended enterprise metamodel with motivation modeling elements. This mapping enabled us to specify that *key stakeholders' assessments of external and/or internal drivers of enterprise lead to goals and soft-goals that active structure entities are motivated to achieve by performing behavior (entities) and using or creating passive structure entities.*

To streamline this kind of articulation of problems in enterprise change context as well as to overcome limitations of independent modeling environments, we created integrated visual modeling support. We chose Archi as it already supports modeling the business, application, and infrastructure layers of ArchiMate [6] and we would have to add only the IM elements to it. The next section describes how we created the integrated visual modeling environment.

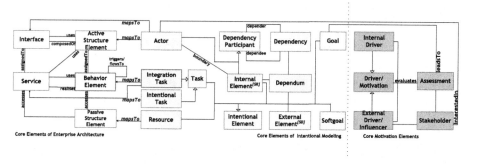

Fig. 3. Extending enterprise metamodel in Fig. 2 with motivation elements

3.2 Enabling Integrated Visual Modeling Environment

Archi is based on Eclipse Modeling Framework (EMF). The process of adding IM elements and relations to base EA metamodel in Archi consisted of adding IM element- and relation-specific classes and then specifying permitted relations between specific elements.

After this, visualization aspects of elements and relations need to be defined. By defining all the elements required by EA and IM models and sets of allowed relations between various elements, EA and IM models can be drawn as shown by ③ in Fig. 4. The models panel in Fig. 4 enlists AS-IS EA models as well as IM models of these problems we refer to as global views. ④ shows such a global view of products and services rationalization problem. Current version of Archi

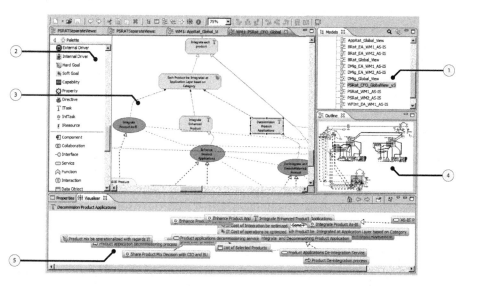

Fig. 4. Extended Archi for EA and IM modeling

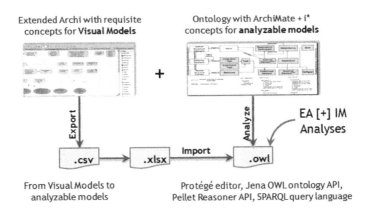

Fig. 5. Architecture of integrated EA and IM modeling environment

supports visualization of a selected model element in terms of all other elements that it is related to as shown by ⑤ in Fig. 4.

In Fig. 4, ① shows list of integrated models enterprise under consideration with the facility to model both EA and IM elements. The extended Archi elements based on the extended enterprise metamodel in Fig. 3 are shown by ② in Fig. 4. With the core metamodel of Archi extended to metamodel in Fig. 3, it became possible to visually model both EA and IM elements together.

The architecture of integrated tooling is shown in Fig. 5. We were already using ontological representation of EA models for easier specification of EA-specific analyses. While extended Archi enabled visual modeling, constructing analyses in EMF would require considerable boilerplate coding which could be easily done away by extending EA ontology with IM elements and then specifying various analyses using ontology APIs as shown in Fig. 5. Archi enables export to CSV files which retain EA element type and name of both source and target nodes along with relation and documentation if any. The next section describes how the ontological representation is leveraged for EA- and IM-specific as well as combined analyses.

3.3   Extended Enterprise Ontology for Purposive Analysis

We presented an ontological representation that captures ArchiMate's core meta-model as well as layer specific metamodels. This is shown in Fig. 6. The relations between generic elements reflect in each of business, application, and infrastructure layers. This is shown in the middle of Fig. 6 with two example elements each in business and application layers. An active structure element is assignedTo a behavior element. In the business layer, a BusinessRole is assignedTo a BusinessProcess. A behavior element accesses a passive structure element. In the application layer, an ApplicationFunction accesses an ApplicationDataObject. This representation was versatile enough for conducting change impact and landscape mapping analyses. For a more complete elaboration of these analyses, reader is requested to refer to [1].

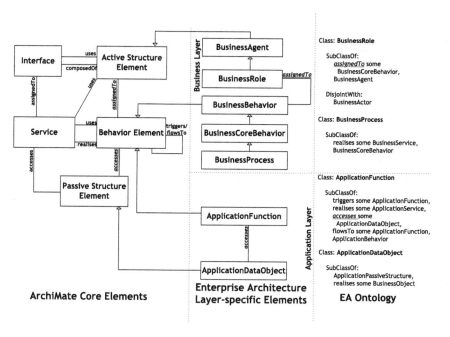

Fig. 6. EA-based ontology [1]

We extended the EA ontology presented in [1], with intentional elements as shown in Fig. 7. We found that all of the relations in intentional model namely, means-ends (MELink), task decomposition (TDLink), contribution (CTLink), and strategic dependency (SDLink) relations, benefit from being represented as *reified* relations [17]. For instance, a contribution link indicates not only which element contributes to a soft goal but also what that contribution is. This ontology also includes motivation elements shown in Fig. 3.

The model exported from Archi is easily read into ontology model by first constructing the dictionary, leveraging the type information of instances and then constructing the data in terms of relations.

We import an important convention introduced in the ArchiMate motivation extensions to connect requirements of goals with behavior of active structure entities [3, ArchiMateSpecification 10.2.5]. This convention is captured in the ontology in the definition of EABehavior class which realizes some IntegrationlTask element from IM models. Integration tasks essentially represent leaf tasks in SR models which are not dependent on any other elements. These are treated as *primitively workable* elements [4] and used in defining operationalization models of TO-BE EA via connecting elements which are instances of sub-classes of EABehavior class.

3.4   Conducting Combined EA and IM Model Analysis

We have implemented the bottom-up label propagation algorithm in [11] to compute satisfaction level of the root goal. The ontological representation easily

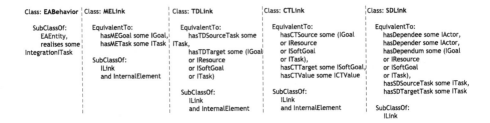

Fig. 7. Extending EA ontology with IM elements and relations [2]

enables implementing the label propagation as well as computation of specific routines in terms of ontology APIs. The concept of actor's routine is central in computing optimum alternatives. It is the set of tasks an actor needs to carry out to achieve a goal which may also include set of tasks of other actors via dependency links. Both label propagation and actors' routine computation is carried out by recursively traversing down the intentional graph starting with the root goal and using queries to traverse over means-ends, task decomposition, contribution, and strategic dependency links.

Leaf tasks in IM models are related to EA elements that will operationalize them from TO-BE EA perspective. It is possible that in some cases some of the AS-IS elements could be reused, mostly by reference through a relation between newly added element and existing AS-IS element. In order to preserve which elements were added for specific leaf tasks, we tag them in the ontological representation. With this tagging, the EA elements that are added anew in contrast to AS-IS elements are identified. Using this combined analysis, both EA and IM models can be refined such that they capture the reality to the satisfaction of domain experts [10].

3.5 Toward Industry Strength Modeling and Analysis for Enterprises

With ontological representation we have been able to apply various decision making analyses to EA and IM models thus created. Yet, our experience in development of model-driven applications suggests that for practical implementation of EA and IM modeling and analyses, we need scalable tooling [18]. In the next section, we propose to use our proprietary reflexive (meta-) modeling framework called **Adex** which we have successfully used in over 70+ applications in multiple domains for organizations spread across the globe.

4 Scalable Modeling and Analysis for Enterprise Decision Making

Our current tooling for modeling and analysis is based mainly on visual modeling of EA and IM elements enabled by extended Archi and ontological representation to which extended Archi models are exported. We are using this tooling for experimenting with various EA and intentional decision making modeling and analyses. Eventually though, EA and IM modeling and analysis will need to be supported in industry strength tooling with proven scalability characteristics. We propose to implement the EA and IM modeling support showcased so far in proprietary (meta-) modeling framework Adex [8].

4.1   Enabling EA and IM Modeling and Analysis in Adex

The process of creating purpose-specific metamodel in Adex is similar to EMF. Visualization functionality is provided with Adex through *symbol designer* as shown on the right of Fig. 8. Visual aspects of elements and relations can be defined not unlike in EMF-based Archi. The minor difference is that symbols and connectors for elements and relations can be defined separately and then mapped to existing elements and relations, whereas in Archi, specific classes related to defined elements and relations have to be extended in specific ways manually to construct visual representations.

The ontological representation to which Archi models are exported enables flexible analysis implementation with various ontology APIs [1]. A similar support is provided in Adex with *OMGen* language, which is a (meta-) model-aware language [8]. OMGen scripts can be used to perform desired actions such as initialization of instances, value computation and propagation to related instances, performing validations, and triggering external actions. Scripts can interface with external C programs, allowing custom software and third-party utilities to be linked in. Adex's scripting feature can be effectively utilized to integrate modeling activity with analysis building.

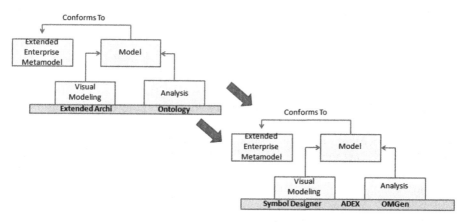

Fig. 8. Shifting modeling and analysis for EA and IM models from extended Archi to Adex

Table 1. Modeling and analysis features for EA and IM models [2]

Modeling and/or Analysis Feature	Archi	Adex
Metamodeling	Yes	Yes
Visual Modeling	Yes	Yes
Scripting for flexible code and report generation	No	OMGen
Domain-specific checks for model consistency	Predefined	Predefined + configurable
Manage work units	No	Packages
Data File/DB support	Stored in XML, export to CSV available	File, in memory, MySQL, Oracle, etc.
Multi-user/role support	No	Yes
Versioning	No	Yes
Diff/Merge	No	Yes

Italic Font- Common features, *Italic Bold Font*- Adex-specific features

While SPARQL[1] query language provides SQL-like syntax and functionality that is declarative in nature, OMGen is an imperative language. We may need to provide a declarative wrapper over imperative scripts, as we have found SPARQL like syntax to be quite effective in building EA [1] and intentional analyses.

4.2 Scalability Features for EA and IM Models

As shown in Fig. 8, both visual modeling and analysis can be supported out of the box using Adex. But Adex provides substantially different functionality beyond representation and manipulation of (meta-) models that is a must for highly scalable modeling activity including EA and IM modeling and analyses.

Table 1 distinguishes between such requisite features from the common ones between Adex and (extended) Archi. There are set of features that Adex supports which we have found to be absolutely critical for scalable model-driven development and we think that these features will also be needed to scale EA and IM models of enterprises. We discuss these features in brief here. For detailed explanations, reader is directed to [8,18]. Note that the lack of scripting over Archi models is balanced by ontological representation in our ongoing approach. Ontological representation can be used also to include domain-specific consistency checks. In Adex, this can be done with OMGen.

While Adex's metamodel is similar to OMG's metaobject facility, Adex provides much richer set of constructs that enable model consistency checks, work units partitioning, database, multi-user/role support, versioning and diff-merge abilities [8].

Adex uses *components* for partitioning given models. Versioning of models is carried out at component level. *Configurations* are provided as containers for assembling different versions of components. A configuration is what represents the notion of a *work unit*. Inter-component associations (between objects

---

[1] http://www.w3.org/TR/rdf-sparql-query/.

belonging to different component versions) provide a mechanism to establish and enforce compatibility semantics between two component versions.

When a component is developed concurrently by independent teams, diff-merge operations can be used to do so in a non-interfering way at configuration, component, or object level. Both metamodels and models are stored in separate repositories. Together these features have been and are being used in several active assignments with model size often rising to many gigabytes and several teams with differing roles across the globe using these models.

We believe that in the context of combined EA and IM modeling and analysis, such features will become essential and with Adex we are poised to transfer our ongoing efforts to a unified and scalable modeling and analysis environment.

5 Related Work

Elements for Explicit Intentions, Motivation, and Operationalization. ArchiMate provides essential elements for modeling business, application, and infrastructure layers of an enterprise. Further extensions such as ArchiMate motivation extensions add motivation/goal related elements [15]. As discussed earlier in Sect. 3.1, from strategic analysis point of view, we preferred to use intentional modeling while adding some elements from motivation extensions as well as referring to business motivation model (BMM) for better understanding of motivation elements. We tried to keep new elements less in number as similar studies related to requirements modeling languages such as ARMOR language [19], have indicated that adding several elements from different goal modeling languages is not useful from practitioners' perspective [20].

Our focus in selecting additional elements on top of regular intentional modeling elements was to make the process of modeling EA and intentional aspects of enterprise easier for modelers and domain experts. At the same time, we found it necessary to record assessments of drivers because assessments and assumptions influence the rest of decision making. Our ongoing research with regards directives, policies, and regulations compliance makes use of these concepts and follows BMM's logical progression in reaction to change [21, Fig. 7.2]. With regards specific elements, our internal surveys revealed that domain experts are often exposed to notions of drivers or influencers as well as sharply defined goals (internally we use balanced scorecard for capturing goals). Some of our observations are contrary to other studies such as [20], which found goal and motivation elements like means-ends relationship, distinction between hard and soft goals, and assessment did not make much sense to practitioners. We believe that every enterprise should decide on the set of elements that all the key actors in that enterprise agree on as to what they mean and how useful they are for capturing AS-IS and TO-BE EAs for decision making.

Failure of strategic response to changes is found to be rooted in the lack of strategy operationalization [22]. Still goal modeling approaches for enterprises tend to focus only on strategy making, often referred to as problem of constructing design/solution alternatives, and evaluation of strategic alternatives

[20,23,24]. Operationalization, if at all, is considered from business perspective as in strategy maps [25] or from IT perspective [26]. Also operationalization is either presumed to just happen or it is generally just a set of guidelines. We have borrowed the notion of goal requirements realized by behavior entities in EA from ArchiMate. We treat this as the glue between suggested alternatives and TO-BE EA. In future, we intend to investigate the ways in which TO-BE EA is operationalized via human resources and IT systems. We have presented some initial work in this regards with respect to operationalizing internal policies by persisting suggested alternatives to business processes [2], which is in line with ArchiMate's implementation and migration extensions [3].

Visualization of EA and other Models. An approach is suggested in [27], which enables visualization of purposive analyses upon EA model. This EA modes conforms to metamodel that incorporates elements from ArchiMate, BMM, and Business Process Modeling Notation, etc. Their modeling environment visualizes purposive analyses like business-IT alignment in terms of paths between motivation and IT elements using visualization techniques like sunburst. In contrast our work focuses on using visual environment for modeling alone, whereas analyses are always conducted using ontological representation.

For capturing enterprise transformation to TO-BE states, graphical viewpoints on TO-BE states are suggested in [28,29], whereas [30] proposes to visualize migration roadmap. As shown earlier, our approach so far has been to use visual modeling for creating the models and then using ontological representation for coming up with TO-BE states as well as paths to TO-BE states. The models used in these are also EA models without other purposive models like intentional models.

Analysis of EA and Other Models. Most research in EA analysis focuses on analysis of EA models themselves, e.g., change impact analysis of EA models [31], quantitative analysis of EA models [32], and analysis of various non-functional properties in EA while incorporating treatment of uncertainty in EA models [33–35]. In contrast, we treat EA models as descriptive models and use intentional models [5] and system dynamic models [36] as prescriptive models upon which to base decision making. The modeling and analysis need to be supported by tooling environment that supports visual modeling of purposive modeling languages and also programmable analysis.

6   Conclusion

Our ongoing explorations with visual modeling support for extended enterprise models suggests that integrated visual modeling streamlines the enterprise modeling activity while integrated ontology modeling support enables implementing requisite analyses. Visual models are imported into ontology because of which, models and analysis results remain in sync. While visual modeling support explained in the paper is working as desired, we suspect that when many modelers are simultaneously modeling various problem-specific IM and enterprise models in multiple interactions with domain experts, a more robust distributed enterprise and IM modeling environment will be necessary. We have outlined how current support for enterprise and IM modeling can be shifted from open source Archi to our own (meta-) modeling framework Adex. Our long term goal in this regard is to make enterprise and purposive modeling and analysis as simple and effective as it is when it comes to code generation.

References

1. Sunkle, S., Kulkarni, V., Roychoudhury, S.: Analyzing enterprise models using enterprise architecture-based ontology. In: Moreira, A., Schätz, B., Gray, J., Vallecillo, A., Clarke, P. (eds.) MODELS 2013. LNCS, vol. 8107, pp. 622–638. Springer, Heidelberg (2013)
2. Sunkle, S., Kholkar, D., Rathod, H., Kulkarni, V.:Incorporating directives into enterprise TO-BE architecture. In: [37], pp. 57–66
3. Iacob, M., Jonkers, D.H., Lankhorst, M., Proper, E., Quartel, D.D.: Archimate 2.0 Specification. The Open Group, Van Haren Publishing, Reading (2012)
4. Yu, E.S.K.: Modelling strategic relationships for process reengineering. Ph.D. thesis, Toronto, Ontario, Canada (1996). UMI Order No. GAXNN-02887 (Canadian dissertation)
5. Sunkle, S., Kulkarni, V., Roychoudhury, S.: Intentional modeling for problem solving in enterprise architecture. In: Hammoudi, S., Maciaszek, L.A., Cordeiro, J., Dietz, J.L.G. (eds.) ICEIS (3), pp. 267–274. SciTePress (2013)
6. Institute, E.C.: Archi Developer Resources. http://archi.cetis.ac.uk/developer. html. Accessed 16 Mar 2014
7. Horkoff, J., Yu, Y., Yu, E.S.K.: OpenOME: an open-source goal and agent-oriented model drawing and analysis tool. In: de Castro, J.B., Franch, X., Mylopoulos, J., Yu, E.S.K. (eds.) iStar. CEUR Workshop Proceedings, vol. 766, pp. 154–156. CEUR-WS.org (2011)
8. Reddy, S., Mulani, J., Bahulkar, A.: Adex – a meta modeling framework for repository-centric systems building. In: 10th International Conference on Management of Data (COMAD) (2000)
9. Kulkarni, V., Reddy, S.: Integrating aspects with model driven software development. In: Al-Ani, B., Arabnia, H.R., Mun, Y. (eds.) Software Engineering Research and Practice, pp. 186–197. CSREA Press (2003)
10. Sunkle, S., Rathod, H.: Visual modeling editor and ontology API-based analysis for decision making in enterprises - experience and way ahead. In: [37], pp. 182–190
11. Horkoff, J., Yu, E.S.K.: Evaluating goal achievement in enterprise modeling – an interactive procedure and experiences. In: Long, M. (ed.) World Congress on Medical Physics and Biomedical Engineering May 26-31, 2012 Beijing, IFMBE Proceedings, vol. 39, pp. 145–160. Springer, Heidelberg (2013)
12. Ayala, C.P., Cares, C., Carvallo, J.P., Grau, G., Haya, M., Salazar, G., Franch, X., Mayol, E., Quer, C.: A comparative analysis of i*-based agent-oriented modeling languages. In: Chu, W.C., Juzgado, N.J., Wong, W.E. (eds.) SEKE, pp. 43–50 (2005)
13. López, L., Franch, X., Marco, J.: Making explicit some implicit i^* language decisions. In: Jeusfeld, M., Delcambre, L., Ling, T.-W. (eds.) ER 2011. LNCS, vol. 6998, pp. 62–77. Springer, Heidelberg (2011)

248 S. Sunkle and H. Rathod

14. Sunkle, S., Kulkarni, V., Rathod, H.: (Multi-) modeling enterprises for better decisions. In: Combemale, B., DeAntoni, J., France, R.B., Barn, B., Clark, T., Frank, U., Kulkarni, V., Turk, D. (eds.) GEMOC+AMINO@MoDELS. CEUR Workshop Proceedings, vol. 1102, pp. 69–78. CEUR-WS.org (2013)
15. Quartel, D., Engelsman, W., Jonkers, H.: ArchiMate ® Extension for Modeling and Managing Motivation, Principles and Requirements in TOGAFT™, October 2010
16. Sunkle, S., Rathod, H., Kulkarni, V.: Practical goal modeling for enterprise change context: a problem statement. In: Indulska, M., Purao, S. (eds.) ER Workshops 2014. LNCS, vol. 8823, pp. 139–144. Springer, Heidelberg (2014)
17. Group, W.W.: Defining N-ary Relations on the Semantic Web. http://www.w3.org/TR/swbp-n-aryRelations/. W3C Working Group Note, 12 April 2006. Accessed 16 Mar 2014
18. Kulkarni, V., Reddy, S., Rajbhoj, A.: Scaling up model driven engineering – experience and lessons learnt. In: Petriu, D.C., Rouquette, N., Haugen, Ø. (eds.) MODELS 2010, Part II. LNCS, vol. 6395, pp. 331–345. Springer, Heidelberg (2010)
19. Quartel, D.A.C., Engelsman, W., Jonkers, H., van Sinderen, M.: A goal-oriented requirements modelling language for enterprise architecture. In: EDOC, pp. 3–13. IEEE Computer Society (2009)
20. Engelsman, W., Wieringa, R.: Goal-oriented requirements engineering and enterprise architecture: two case studies and some lessons learned. In: Regnell, B., Damian, D. (eds.) REFSQ 2011. LNCS, vol. 7195, pp. 306–320. Springer, Heidelberg (2012)
21. OMG: Business Motivation Model - Version 1.2., May 2014
22. Ross, J.W., Weill, P., Robertson, D.: Enterprise Architecture As Strategy: Creating a Foundation for Business Execution. Harvard Business School Press, Boston (2006)
23. Yu, E.S.K., Strohmaier, M., Deng, X.: Exploring intentional modeling and analysis for enterprise architecture. In: Tenth IEEE International Enterprise Distributed Object Computing Conference (EDOC) Workshops, p. 32 (2006)
24. Bryl, V., Giorgini, P., Mylopoulos, J.: Supporting requirements analysis in tropos: a planning-based approach. In: Ghose, A., Governatori, G., Sadananda, R. (eds.) PRIMA 2007. LNCS, vol. 5044, pp. 243–254. Springer, Heidelberg (2009)
25. Giannoulis, C., Zdravkovic, J., Petit, M.: Model-driven strategic awareness: from a unified business strategy meta-model (UBSMM) to enterprise architecture. In: Bider, I., Halpin, T., Krogstie, J., Nurcan, S., Proper, E., Schmidt, R., Soffer, P., Wrycza, S. (eds.) EMMSAD 2012 and BPMDS 2012. LNBIP, vol. 113, pp. 255–269. Springer, Heidelberg (2012)
26. Frank, U.: Multi-perspective enterprise modelling as a foundation of method engineering and self-referential enterprise systems. In: Hammoudi, S., Maciaszek, L.A., Cordeiro, J., Dietz, J.L.G. (eds.) ICEIS (1), pp. IS-9. SciTePress (2013)
27. Naranjo, D., Sánchez, M.E., Villalobos, J.: Connecting the dots: examining visualization techniques for enterprise architecture model analysis. In: Grabis, J., Kirikova, M., Zdravkovic, J., Stirna, J. (eds.) Short Paper Proceedings of the 6th IFIP WG 8.1 Working Conference on the Practice of Enterprise Modeling (PoEM 2013), Riga, Latvia, 6–7 November 2013. CEUR Workshop Proceedings, vol. 1023, pp. 29–38. CEUR-WS.org (2013)
28. Lankhorst, M.: Enterprise Architecture at Work: Modelling, Communication and Analysis. Springer, Heidelberg (2005)
29. Niemann, K.D.: From Enterprise Architecture to IT Governance. Elements of Effective IT Management, 1st edn. Vieweg+Teubner, Wiesbaden (2006)

30. Kim, H., Lee, R.Y. (eds.): 10th ACIS International Conference on Software Engineering, Artificial Intelligences, Networking and Parallel/Distributed Computing, SNPD 2009, in conjunction with 3rd International Workshop on e-Activity, IWEA 2009, 1st International Workshop on Enterprise Architecture Challenges and Responses, WEACR 2009, Catholic University of Daegu, Daegu, Korea, 27–29 May 2009. IEEE Computer Society (2009)

31. de Boer, F.S., Bonsangue, M.M., Groenewegen, L., Stam, A., Stevens, S., van der Torre, L.W.N.: Change impact analysis of enterprise architectures. In: Zhang, D., Khoshgoftaar, T.M., Shyu, M.L. (eds.) IRI, pp. 177–181. IEEE Systems, Man, and Cybernetics Society (2005)

32. Iacob, M., Jonkers, H.: Quantitative analysis of enterprise architectures. Proceedings of the First International Conference on Interoperability of Enterprise Software and Applications (INTEROP-ESA), February 2005

33. Buschle, M., Ullberg, J., Franke, U., Lagerström, R., Sommestad, T.: A tool for enterprise architecture analysis using the PRM formalism. In: Soffer, P., Proper, E. (eds.) CAiSE Forum 2010. LNBIP, vol. 72, pp. 108–121. Springer, Heidelberg (2011)

34. Ekstedt, M., Franke, U., Johnson, P., Lagerström, R., Sommestad, T., Ullberg, J., Buschle, M.: A tool for enterprise architecture analysis of maintainability. In: Winter, A., Ferenc, R., Knodel, J. (eds.) CSMR, pp. 327–328. IEEE (2009)

35. Franke, U., Johnson, P., Ericsson, E., Flores, W.R., Zhu, K.: Enterprise architecture analysis using fault trees and MODAF. In: Proceedings of CAiSE Forum 2009, vol. 453, pp. 61–66, June 2009. ISSN 1613–0073

36. Sunkle, S., Roychoudhury, S., Kulkarni, V.: Using intentional and system dynamics modeling to address WHYs in enterprise architecture. In: Cordeiro, J., Marca, D.A., van Sinderen, M. (eds.) ICSOFT, pp. 24–31. SciTePress (2013)

37. Grossmann, G., Hallé, S., Karastoyanova, D., Reichert, M., Rinderle-Ma, S. (eds.): 18th IEEE International Enterprise Distributed Object Computing Conference Workshops and Demonstrations, EDOC Workshops 2014, Ulm, Germany, 1–2 September 2014. IEEE (2014)

Unified Process Modeling with UPROM Tool

Banu Aysolmaz[(⌧)] and Onur Demirörs

Informatics Institute, Middle East Technical University, Ankara, Turkey
banu@aysolmaz.com, demirors@metu.edu.tr

Abstract. UPROM tool is a business process modeling tool designed to conduct business process and user requirements analysis in an integrated way to constitute a basis for process automation. Usually, business process models are not utilized systematically to develop related artifacts, specifically when a process-aware information system is to be developed to automate those processes. This results in completeness, consistency and maintainability problems for those artifacts. Unified business process modeling methodology, UPROM, is developed to integrate process modeling and practices. Enabling the application of UPROM, the tool provides editors for six different diagram types based on a common metamodel. It offers features so that modelers can develop a cohesive set of models. Using these models, UPROM tool can be used to automatically generate artifacts of user requirements document, COSMIC based software size estimation, process definition document and business glossary.

Keywords: Business process modeling · User requirements analysis · Software functional size estimation · Business glossary · Process documentation · Artifact generation

1 Introduction

Business process models (or shortly process models) represent the organizational processes in an abstract way including at least the activities, control flow between the activities, roles, events and artifacts [1]. Process models are utilized for pure organizational purposes such as process improvement and communication between stakeholders; and for many other practices such as project management, requirements specification, conformance to regulations and knowledge management [2, 3].

We frequently observe in the organizations that process models are not utilized in a systematic manner to develop artifacts of related practices that can benefit from this knowledge. This increases the development effort and makes it hard to achieve completeness for those artifacts, as process analysis is repeated for each artifact. The separate development of artifacts also results in broken traceability between the artifact and business processes. Later, as business process definitions and artifacts are updated separately, they may become unrelated and conflicting; and high amount of effort is spent for maintenance. The problem is more critical if the organization plans to automate its processes by a process-aware information system (PAIS) [4]. In this case, process models are essential for the design of PAIS [5] and many artifacts are developed in

© Springer International Publishing Switzerland 2015
S. Nurcan and E. Pimenidis (Eds.): CAiSE Forum 2014, LNBIP 204, pp. 250–266, 2015.
DOI: 10.1007/978-3-319-19270-3_16

software development life cycle (SDLC) based on business process knowledge. Failing to use process models systematically in SDLC means that the knowledge captured in business domain cannot be transferred to technological domain, thus it becomes difficult to meet business needs by the PAIS.

To overcome the problems, we developed a unified BPM methodology, UPROM. UPROM components include notation, process, guidelines and artifact generation principles. UPROM notation and process guide the users to analyze business processes and user requirements in an integrated way [6]. When the methodology is followed, the following artifacts can be generated automatically: user requirements document and COSMIC software functional size estimation [7] for the PAIS, and process documentation including process definition document and business glossary.

UPROM tool is a graphical BPM tool that supports UPROM methodology and automatically generates the mentioned artifacts. Model driven approach is followed based on Eclipse Modeling Framework (EMF) [8] and Eclipse Graphical Modeling Framework (GMF) [9]. Diagram editors are developed as Eclipse plugins. All editors are based on a meta-model. Some plugins were reused from bflow* Toolbox [10], thus inheriting its specific features such as continuous verification.

UPROM tool provides editors for six diagram types in conformance with the notation: Value Chain (VC), Function Tree (FT), Event Driven Process Chain (EPC), Organization Chart (OC), Conceptual Entity Relationship (ER) and Function Allocation (FA). Diagrams represent different business process perspectives which are functional (VC and FT), behavioral (EPC), organizational (OC) and data (ER and FA). The core diagram of the notation is EPC which is known with the ARIS framework [11].

The objective of the UPROM tool is to provide a modeling environment to analyze and model business processes and user requirements in an integrated way. The modeling environment provides editors for six diagram types; together with the features to enrich the diagram objects for analysis, form a coherent modeling project structure and generate artifacts that can be utilized as input to software design and development.

UPROM tool is used by process modelers for analysis of processes in the business domain. End users utilize it to review and validate the models. The tool provides functionality for modelers to integrate business process and user requirements analysis. There are tools that can generate process documentation, but we did not encounter a BPM tool generating also textual user requirements and functional size estimation. UPROM tool was utilized in various projects, including two e-government projects for Company and Trademark Central Registration Systems, Public Investment Analysis of Ministry of Development, Integrated Information System Project of METU Campus and three small internal applications.

In this paper, we present the features particular to UPROM tool to support the methodology and generate the artifacts. In Sect. 2, UPROM methodology is briefly presented. Section 3 describes the tool features and the generation of artifacts. Section 4 provides related work with a brief comparison with other tools. Section 5 provides the conclusion, summarizes the findings from the applications and presents the future work.

2   UPROM Methodology

UPROM methodology aims to integrate the practices of business process analysis and user requirements analysis By unifying analysis activities, a set of models can be developed that embeds all information to generate artifacts related to user requirements, software size estimation and process documentation practices. The methodology includes the notation, meta-model, process, guidelines and artifact generation procedures. The artifacts that can be generated by UPROM methodology are: textual user requirements document, COSMIC software functional size estimation, process definition document and business glossary. As all of these artifacts are based on a single source of model set, completeness and consistency of them are improved, they become traceable to business processes and maintainability is enhanced. More information on UPROM methodology and outputs of case studies can be found in [6, 12]. UPROM process consists of three main activities as shown in Fig. 1.

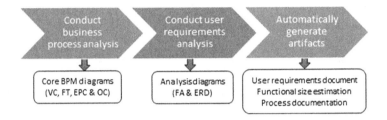

Fig. 1. UPROM high level process and related outputs

2.1   Developing Core BPM Diagrams

This step includes the analysis of business processes by developing core BPM diagrams. Initially, the scope of BPM studies is defined. Then, highest level decomposition of processes is identified as *process modules* and modeled in a *process map* (as a VC, FT or EPC diagram). The processes are decomposed further into lower level process modules. Detailed business process analysis is then conducted for process modules. The process shown in Fig. 1 can be conducted in parallel for multiple process modules by different teams in an iterative manner. Alternatively, process modules can be analyzed one by one with a waterfall-like approach.

Functional, behavioral, and organizational perspectives of business processes are analyzed in this step. Process information is elicited through workshops. Available process documents, legislations and laws applicable to the domain are also important sources of information. The modelers depict the decomposition of processes by using VC and FT, and model control flow by means of EPC diagrams. A VC diagram represents high level value added activities to obtain products and services. Other VC or EPC diagrams can be assigned as sub-diagrams for value chain symbols. A FT diagram depicts decomposition of related activities. Functions in FT diagrams can have other FT or EPCs as sub-diagrams. EPC is the core of the notation to analyze the control flow [13].

Another EPC, FT or FA can be assigned to a function; and an EPC or FT diagram can be assigned to a process interface in an EPC diagram. In parallel, all organizational elements placed in EPCs and their relations are modeled in an OC diagram.

2.2 Developing Analysis Diagrams Associated to BPM Diagrams

In this step, each leaf function in EPC diagrams is analyzed to identify if that function is required to be automated in the PAIS to be developed. If so, an FA diagram is created as a sub-diagram of that function. Leaf functions in EPCs are the functions in the lowest level of the hierarchy, which have no further EPC or FT sub-diagram assigned. FA diagram serves the purpose of analyzing user requirements for the related function. An FA diagram is used to analyze the responsibilities to conduct the function, related entities, operations on entities, related applications and constraints. In parallel to FA analysis, entities that are placed on FA diagrams and their relations are modeled in conceptual ER diagram. An ER diagram provides an overview of all entities in the system, together with generalization, aggregation and named relations between them. Further features provided by UPROM tool are described in Sect. 3.

2.3 Generating Artifacts

Upon completion of business process and user requirements analysis steps, artifacts can be generated automatically by using UPROM tool. Artifact generation principles are detailed in Sect. 3. Generated artifacts can be utilized as inputs to subsequent phases of software design and development. User requirements, core business process and analysis models and process documentation are inputs to the detailed requirements analysis, testing and acceptance phases. Functional size estimation is critical for software development planning in early phases. Process definition document and business glossary are used by different stakeholders types in the operation phase of the software.

3 UPROM Tool

UPROM tool provides an integrated environment to develop six different diagram types based on a meta-model. A snapshot of the modeling environment with EPC diagram editor can be seen in Fig. 2. In conformance with the tool's objectives, the tool features described in the following sections enable users to apply the methodology. The feature described in Sect. 3.1 is on the structure of the modeling project. This feature helps the user to organize core BPM and analysis diagrams in a structured way in the form of a coherent modeling project. Independent of the complexity of the models, the user can understand the process hierarchy. This structure also helps to generate artifacts in a standard form. Feature in Sect. 3.2 forces the users to develop diagrams conforming to the meta-model. Section 3.3 is about defining unique objects. This feature helps to establish conceptual connections between the business process and analysis concepts. The same concepts in the project, independent of being used in business process or requirements analysis, become cohesive. It enables business processes and generated artifacts become consistent and traceable to each other. Section 3.4 is on additional attributes. This feature is used to enrich the diagrams and the objects so that extra information required for detailed business process and user requirements analysis can be trapped all in the same set of models. The extra information is then utilized in artifact generation. Section 3.5 includes artifact generation procedures.

3.1   Structure of the Modeling Project

The repository in which the set of diagrams in the same BPM scope is maintained is called *modeling project*. Within a modeling project, all functional and behavioral diagrams of types VC, EPC and FT must be connected to each other by sub-diagram relations. The folder structure of the modeling project is established in conformance with its sub-diagram decomposition. Each sub-diagram of type VC, EPC or FT shall be placed under a folder with the same location with the higher level diagram this sub-diagram is referenced to. There can be no FA diagrams in the top level hierarchy, as they can only exist as a sub-diagram of a function in an EPC diagram.

UPROM tool checks if the folder structure conforms to the hierarchical structure of the modeling project. An example modeling project structure is shown on the left part of Fig. 2. Only one diagram of type VC, FT or EPC exists at the top level, which is the process map (e.g. Company.ftd). For each sub-diagram referenced from the process map, the sub-diagram file is placed inside a folder. The same rules apply for lower level diagrams. FA diagrams are placed inside the folder of their related EPC. ERD and OC diagrams can be placed anywhere, preferably in the highest level to be easily accessible.

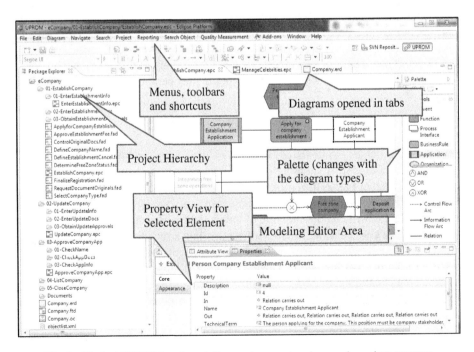

Fig. 2. Typical UPROM tool modeling environment and example project structure

3.2 Diagram Editors and Relation Constraints

UPROM tool editors run in conformance with the meta-model. VC diagram comprises value chain, risk, objective and product objects. FT diagram has only the function object. EPC diagram include event, function, process interface, logical operators (and, or, xor), business rule, application, organizational elements (position, organizational unit, group, internal and external person), information carriers (document, list, log, file, reference), key performance indicator (KPI), risk and improvement objects [14]. OC diagram notation has organizational element objects. FA diagram has organizational elements, function, entity, application and constraint objects. ER diagram covers entity, cluster, attribute, generalization, aggregation and relationship objects. Simplified meta-model of the most distinguishing diagram types of UPROM, EPC and FA, are provided in Fig. 3. Inheritance relations and connection types (control flow, information flow and relation) are not shown. An EPC diagram can contain any number of these objects, but must at least have two events (start and end) and a function. An FA diagram can contain one and only one function, and must have at least one application and entity.

UPROM tool prevents formation of a connection not allowed in the meta-model. Predefined connection names are assigned between some constructs. An organizational element and a function can be connected via a relation named as: *"carries out, approves, supports, contributes to, must be informed"*. A function can be connected to an entity with a relation named as: *"reads, changes, lists, creates, deletes, views, uses"*.

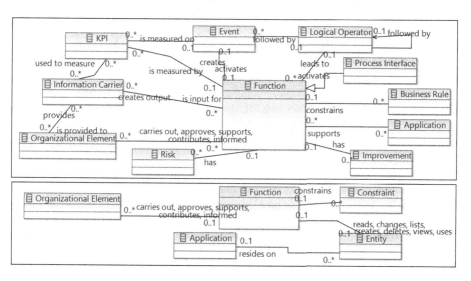

Fig. 3. Simplified UPROM meta-model for EPC (up) and FA (down) diagrams

3.3 Unique Object Assignment

The objects in the same modeling project are assigned to be unique if they are assigned the same name and they are of the same object type or group. Instances of the same object can exist in any diagram. Objects from these groups can be assigned to be unique:

- Information carriers, entity, cluster, attribute, key attribute.
- Function, process interface, value chain.

When a new object is added, if there is already an object with the same name and type (or one of the object group types) in the project, the user is asked if the new object is the same with existing object(s). If the user approves that they are the same, attribute values of the objects are assigned to be the same. When attributes of any instance of the unique object are updated, all other instances also have the updated values. Users can search for the occurrences of unique objects and see the list of instances.

3.4   Process and Object Attributes

A set of attributes representing meta-data of a process can be assigned to each diagram. The meta-data of a process include description, model name, purpose, scope, status and version. All objects have the attributes of name, id, description, incoming and outgoing connections. In addition, some object types have specific attributes. Organizational elements, information carriers, application, entity, cluster, KPI and attribute type objects can be assigned a technical term attribute. Information carriers, entity, cluster, business rule and constraint type objects can have document link attribute. Sub-diagrams can be assigned to function, process interface and value chain objects.

3.5   Generation of Artifacts

Utilizing the information embedded in the modeling project which is developed by using the features explained in the above sections, UPROM tool can be used to automatically generate artifacts. As a characteristic of EMF and GMF libraries; files for six diagram types and related attributes are all saved in a standard XML format by UPROM. The only information used by UPROM to generate the artifacts are the folder structure (to find the diagram files) and the files in XML format. UPROM tool finds the diagram files under the selected project by using the folder structure, parses these XML diagram files to obtain variables for each diagram and object (using *dom4j* libraries); and generates the artifacts in PDF format using iText library [15].

When a user reads the diagrams by using the tool, she can dynamically navigate through the hierarchy, jump between the diagrams using sub-diagram relations and examine the attributes on will. The problem with the static reports in PDF format is that, the information is provided to the users in a static and non-navigable way. To present a report where the user can still have the feeling of the hierarchy, we arranged the diagrams so that they are initially ordered through the lower levels of the hierarchy, then go back to the upper levels in conformance with the placement of objects in the process models. For all reports except business glossary, the information presented is grouped under headings for functional diagrams (VC, FT or EPC). In all these reports, the placement of the diagram in the hierarchical structure is written in the heading.

When the report is to be prepared using the information only from a single diagram, such as business process models report, generating the related section of the report is easy. But in most of the reports, we need to parse information regarding diagrams in the whole project, and interpret the cross-relations across diagrams. Two examples of this are identification of external applications (on which no entities are created, changed or deleted in any of the FA diagrams) and identification of the processes that triggered an EPC diagram (which requires examining all other EPC diagrams that have the same end event(s) of that EPC's start event). Such reports are more complex and requires accurate analysis algorithms. However, they add value by providing extra information to the user which cannot be directly observed by reading the diagrams.

Business Process Models Report and *Analysis Models Report* present pictures of the diagrams in pdf format so that the users can read the diagrams independent of the tool. In business process models report, VC, FT, EPC and OC diagrams in the modeling project are reported. Diagrams are placed under headings with name and address of the related process. FA and ER diagrams are listed in Analysis Models Report. For FA diagrams, model name, address, and the related EPC process are placed as the heading.

User requirements document, functional size estimation report, process definition document and business glossary require detailed generation procedures and formatting. Generation details are explained in the following sections based on example diagrams in Figs. 4 and 5. A partial EPC diagram is depicted in Fig. 4. Figure 5 is the FA diagram for the function named "Identify company director" in this EPC. Complete versions of the artifacts in four different case studies can be seen in [12].

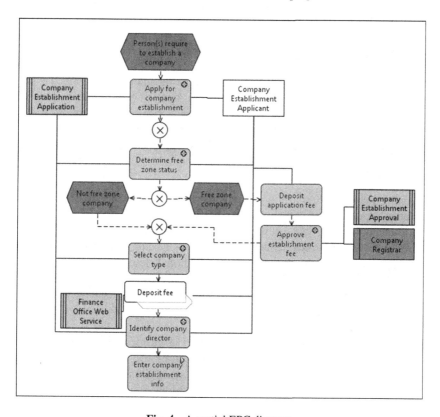

Fig. 4. A partial EPC diagram

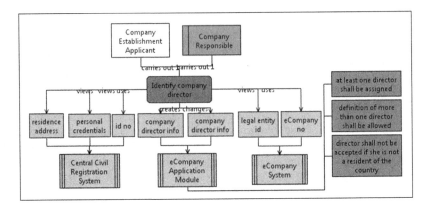

Fig. 5. An example FA diagram for "Identify company director" function of the above EPC

User requirements document, functional size estimation report, process definition document and business glossary require detailed generation principles and formatting. The details for generating these artifacts are explained in the following sections based on example diagrams in Figs. 4 and 5. A partial EPC diagram is depicted in Fig. 4. Figure 5 is the FA diagram for user requirements analysis of the function named "Identify company director" in the EPC. The complete versions of the artifacts generated in four different case studies can be seen in [12].

User Requirements Document: User requirements statements are generated using FA diagrams. Requirements derived from an FA diagram are for the function in focus. A requirement is related to the EPC diagram which carries this function. Each FA diagram is utilized to generate three types of natural language sentences [16]. Example user requirements sentences generated for the FA diagram in Fig. 5 are provided below:

Type 1: Organizational Element – Function:

- Company Establishment Applicant or Company Responsible shall *carry out* the operation of identifying company director.

  This requirement type specifies the role(s) to execute the function. The name of the connection type can be selected from: "carries out, approves, supports, contributes to, must be informed". More than one organizational element can be connected to a function with the same or different connection types. If the connection is labeled with a number as in Fig. 5, either of the organizational elements can conduct the function.

Type 2: Function – Entity – Application:

- During entering company director, by using id no residence address and personal credentials shall be viewed on Central Civil Registration System; by using eCompany no legal entity id shall be used on eCompany System; company director info shall be created and updated on eCompany Application Module.

  This type of requirement specifies the entities involved and the operations conducted on those entities during the execution of the function, and also the applications related to those entities. The type of operations can be chosen from the list: "uses, views, creates, changes, reads, deletes, lists". Each operation has a meaning in terms of defining the user requirement for the function [16]. As seen in the example, parts of this sentence are formed for each application on the FA diagram, then joined as a single sentence.

Type 3: Application – Constraint:

- During entering company director, at least one director shall be assigned.
- During entering company director, definition of more than one director shall be allowed.
- During entering company director, director shall not be accepted if she is not a resident of the country.

Constraints to be considered by the applications during the execution of the function are stated in this sentence type. Constraints can include state changes, limitations on attributes of entities, time and other limitations. The formation of this sentence is relatively straightforward, as constraints are already defined in the models in natural language form. Still, constraint object is helpful as analysts are guided to identify the related constraints during their analysis specific to the function.

The textual requirement statements identified according to the algorithms above are placed in a user requirements document. The organization of the statements in the document is important to enhance readability of the document. A new heading is put in the document for each VC, FT and EPC diagram. Requirements formed by all FA diagrams referenced from an EPC are placed under the heading of the related EPC. When there is an EPC sub-diagram in that VC, FT or EPC diagram, a subheading is placed for that EPC diagram and related requirements are placed under that heading. A hierarchical

---

1. Process Name: Company.ftd. Process address: eCompany

1.1. Process name: EstablishCompany.epc. Process address: eCompany/01-EstablishProcess

1.1.1. REQ1. Company Establishment Applicant shall cary out the operation of applying for company establishment.

1.1.2. REQ2. During applying for company establishment, application status and company records shall be created on Company Establishment Application System.

1.1.3. REQ3. During applying for company establishment, company status shall be assigned as "data entrance".

1.1.4. REQ4. Company Establishment Applicant shall cary out the operation of determining free zone status.

...

1.1.11. REQ11. During selecting company type, company type shall be selected from a list of types determined in the legislation.

1.1.12. REQ12. Company Establishment Applicant or Company Responsible shall carry out the operation of identifying company director.

...

1.1.1. Process name: EnterEstablishmentInfo.epc.
Process address: eCompany/01-EstablishProcess/01-EnterEstablishmentInfo

1.1.1.1. REQ17. Company establishment Applicant shall carry out the operation of entering company communication info. ....

Fig. 6. Excerpt from user requirements document for the example EPC diagram.

number and a unique ID is assigned to each statement. An excerpt from the generated user requirements document can be seen in Fig. 6. This document includes sample statements from the same EPC in Fig. 4, but this time for the functions of: "Apply for company establishment" and "Select company type". The details of user requirements analysis and generation in UPROM can be found in [16].

COSMIC Functional Size Estimation Report: FA diagrams which serve the purpose of user requirements analysis are also utilized to generate an early functional size estimation of the software to be automated. The estimation is based on COSMIC standard [7]. COSMIC method defines the size of a software as the total number of data movements (DM), which is added up to calculate the size in function points (FP). DM types are: Entry, Read, Write, eXit [7]. According to COSMIC method, DMs are identified from software requirements. In this early phase where we do not yet have the software requirements, we utilize the user requirements to establish an early size estimation of the system. For this, we convert operations defined in FA diagrams to DMs, as it is a high level way of expressing data manipulations in the system. Functional size estimation is achieved by, first converting operations to DMs; then applying various rules. In the first step, for each operation, the following conversion is applied to identify DMs:

Create, Delete: 1 Entry + 1 Write   **View, List**: 1 Entry, 1 Read, 1 eXit
Change: 1 Entry, 1 Read, 1 Write, 1 eXit   **Use, Read**: 1 Read

Following the conversion step, four rules are applied to fine-tune estimated DMs identified for each application in an FA diagram. Then, two rules are further applied by scanning the overall modeling project. At the end, for each FA diagram, total size is identified separately for each module in the diagram that is to be developed to automate the processes. For example, for "Identify company director" diagram (in Fig. 5), there is no FP assigned to "Central Civil Registration System" (shown in Fig. 7-right). This is because it is an external system and is not to be developed as part of the process automation. The details of the rules can be found in [17].

In functional size estimation report, a heading is placed for each EPC diagram numbered in conformance with its hierarchical position as in the user requirements document. For an EPC diagram, each FA diagram referenced from that EPC is placed in a subheading, given a unique ID. DMs for each application in that FA diagram are listed. An excerpt from the functional size estimation report can be seen in Fig. 7. This figure includes the estimated FP values for the functions: "Apply for Company Establishment", "Determine Free Zone Status", "Identify Company Director" which are all part of the EPC in Fig. 5, and "Enter Company Communication Info" function which is in another EPC. The total FP size of each application is calculated and provided in the summary section of this report.

Process Definition Document: This document presents natural language definitions of processes in a predefined template format. VC, FT and EPC models are utilized to generate the document conforming to a template. A separate numbered section is generated for each VC, FT and EPC diagram in the project. Those sections are concatenated to form the whole document. Sections of the document for an EPC diagram are as follows:

1. Process Name: Company.ftd	
Process address: eCompany	
1.1. Process name: EstablishCompany.epc	...
Process Address: eCompany/01-EstablishCompany	MSR5. IdentifyCompanyDirector
MSR1. ApplyforCompanyEstablishment	Company Establishment Application:
Company Establishment Application:	Entry Function Point: 5
Entry Function Point: 1	Read Function Point: 6
Read Function Point: 0	Write Function Point: 2
Write Function Point: 2	Exit Function Point: 4
Exit Function Point: 1	Total: 17 FP
Total: 4 CFP	**1.1.1 Process name: EnterEstablishmentInfo.epc**
MSR2. DetermineFreeZoneStatus	**Process Address: eCompany/01-EstablishCompany/**
Company Establishment Application:	**01-EnterEstablishmentInfo**
Entry Function Point: 2	MSR6. EnterCompanyCommInfo
Read Function Point: 1	Company Establishment Application:
Write Function Point: 2	Entry Function Point: 2
Exit Function Point: 1	Read Function Point: 1
Total: 6 FP	Write Function Point: 2
...	Exit Function Point: 1
	Total: 6 FP

Fig. 7. Excerpts from a functional size estimation report

- Process Information: Process purpose, scope, status, version, author, description.
- Process Responsibilities (table): Responsible name, type (e.g. organizational unit, position, etc.) and responsibility types.
- Inputs (table): Name, type, source (if input is provided by another role), link.
- Outputs (table): Name, type, target (if outputs are handed to another role), link.
- Entrance criteria (table): Event, processes that exit with this event, their address.
- Exit criteria (table): Event, processes that start with this event, their address Activities (listed in the order of vertical placement on the diagram): Responsibilities of that activity, inputs and outputs, application, risks, sub-diagrams/external processes, description, business rules.
- Business rules: Name, related activity.
- External processes and sub-processes utilized by the process.
- KPIs: related activity, information sources used, measurement period, target.

Some fields of the process definition document are filled by using the attributes described in Sect. 3.4. These are all fields under process information heading, link for inputs and outputs and description of activities. Some fields are identified by examining inter-relations between diagrams. For entrance criteria, "other processes that exit with this event" is achieved by scanning all EPC diagrams in the modeling project and identifying other processes that have the same event as the exit event. The same applies for the corresponding field of exit criteria. In this way, the user can, at a glance, obtain cross-process information that she could only achieve by examining the whole project. The excerpt shown in Fig. 8 provides an example for the partial EPC given in Fig. 4.

---

2. Establish Company

/01-EstablishCompany/EstablishCompany.epc/

1 Process Information

Purpose: Define the high level process to establish a company
Scope: All companies to be registered as general and free zone company
Status: Approved by customer
Version: 1.0

2 Responsibilities

Responsible	Type	Responsibility Type			
		R	A	S	C	I
Company Establishment Applicant	External Person	X				
Company Registrar	Position	X				

3 Inputs

Name	Type	Source	Link
declaration of registry	Document	Company Establishment Applicant	Documents\Ek4-6.ms1.pdf
clearance record	Document	Company Establishment Applicant	

4 Outputs

Name	Type	Target	Link
Approval of documents	Log		

5 Entrance Criteria

Event	Processes that exit with this	Address
Person(s) require to establish a company		

6 Exit Criteria

Event	Processes that start with this	Address
Applicant is informed for the inappropriate documentation		
Company establishment completed	Obtain Establishment Approvals	

7 Activities

7.1 Apply for company establishment
Responsibles: Company Establishment Applicant - carries out

Application System: Company Establishment Application System
Any citizen registering as a user of e-Company system with ID info can apply for the company establishment. For a private company two or more people shall apply.

...

7.8 Enter company establishment info
Responsibles: - (sub process)
Sub process: /01-EstablishCompany/01-EnterEstablishmentInfo/EnterEstablishmentInfo.epc
Company Establishment Applicant shall enter all information regarding the establishment of the company in separate screens. Details are described in the sub process.

Fig. 8.   Excerpt from process definition document

Business Glossary: Business glossary is a supplementary document to ensure common understanding of the terminology used in the processes. This report also requires scanning of the modeling project to find out distinct terms. All definitions in the project are obtained from the models by using technical term attributes of organizational element, information carrier, application, entity, cluster and attribute objects. By means of unique object property, an object has a single definition regardless of the number of its instances. Easy maintenance is also ensured, as the terminology definitions can be updated on any instance of an object. As exemplified in Fig. 9, the report is composed of three parts: organizational, application and general definitions. The ER diagram is utilized to organize general definitions. An aggregate entity is placed at the top of the general organization list, left indented. The components of the aggregate entity are grouped under that item and indented right. Indentation is used in a similar manner for relationships and generalizations. In this way, a business user can get an understanding of the entities in the system and their relations with each other by reading the document.

1 Organizational Definitions		
Name	Abbreviation	Definition
Company Registrar Office	RKMMD	
Company Registrar		Officer responsible for registering and maintaining company registrations
Company Establishment Applicant		The person who applies for company establishment. She shall be the shareholder, director or lawyer of the company.

2 Application Systems	
Name	Definition
Company Establishment Application	The system on which application for a new company establishment is conducted, updated and status updates viewed.

3 General Definitions	
Name	Definition
Company	Any company established and registered as 1949 Company Law.
company communication info	Address of main and branch office, web address, phone, GSM, e-mail
company fundamental info	all fundamental info regarding the company
business domains	domains selected from NACE codes.
application no	
company name	
free zone status	

Fig. 9. Excerpt from business glossary

4   Related Work

BPM tools provide a software environment to develop business process model diagrams. They are usually more comprehensive than just a drawing tool. These are named as "suite" providing many other functionalities to the users, including model object data-bases, model checkers, various modeling techniques, guidance for users, creation of reports, support for customization and process execution environments.

UPROM tool is developed specifically to apply UPROM methodology. Before developing this tool in our research group, we tailored diagrams in ARIS Business Architect [14] to meet meta-model needs and develop scripts to generate the artifacts. Thus, ARIS Business Architect or any other tool which has a tailorable meta-model and produce custom reports can be used to apply UPROM methodology. However, ARIS and similar suites provide abundant notation alternatives. On the contrary, diagram types of UPROM tool are limited and focused on integrated analysis of process models and user requirements as defined by the methodology.

As an alternative to Eclipse, we could also use a modeling language creation tool such as MetaEdit+ [18] to design and use the diagrams based on the meta-model. Meta-Edit+ already provides many notations including business process notation. If tailored to include the diagram types of UPROM and generate the artifacts in the same manner, MetaEdit+ environment, instead of Eclipse, can as well be used. Moreover, MetaEdit+ can also be utilized to generate code for the diagrams; which is not a functionality provided and aimed by UPROM tool. However, we preferred an Eclipse based tool as we were able to reuse plugins from the open source bflow* Toolbox. bflow* Toolbox provides EPC and VC diagram editor plugins that are similar to UPROM notation and an integrated environment for multiple diagram editors; together with continuous validation for EPC.

There are other BPM tools with process documentation and glossary functionality such as Signavio [19], Bizagi [20], ARIS and Visual Paradigm [21]. These tools could be used as well, if tailored, to generate similar process documentation. However, although value is observed in generating textual requirements from models, approaches do not exist to generate textual requirements from business process models [22]. We cannot also find any tools to support such approaches. As the measurement procedure for functional size requires too much effort, many researchers worked on automating the measurement from software models, mostly using UML models such as use cases, sequence and class diagrams [17]. But we observe no tool to automate the estimation by using process models. Thus, to our knowledge, there are no tools that can generate textual user requirements and functional software size estimation for process automation together with the process documentation.

5   Conclusion and Future Work

In this paper, we presented a unified BPM tool. UPROM tool is based on EPC for control flow modeling, and supports five other diagram types. It provides an integrated modeling environment for business process and user requirement analysis. Using the diagrams developed, the tool can automatically generate textual user requirements document, software size estimation and process documentation that can be used as input to software design and development phases.

UPROM was used in two e-Government projects (Company and Trademark Central Registration Systems) and Public Investment Processes of Ministry of Development. The first two projects included 3 analysts from the main contractor, 3 analysts from organization and 2 domain experts. These projects aimed to automate the establishment of new companies and trademarks, and manage them through their lifetime. The first phase covered the analysis of processes and user requirements, and preparation of the technical contract to automate the processes. 3 analysts and 70 domain experts were involved in the third project. The scope was the analysis of the development and publishing of the governmental investment programs.

Generated artifacts were used as project deliverables and acceptance is completed by the users [12]. The results collected by observations and interviews revealed that completeness, consistency and maintainability of the generated artifacts were improved. Another case study was conducted in a retrospective manner to compare business process and requirements analysis outputs of the Integrated Information Systems project for our university campus with the ones developed by applying UPROM. Ninety seven percent of the items in the existing documents were covered and 40 % of these items were improved by the artifacts generated by UPROM. A case study set of three internal business applications was conducted to evaluate size measurement estimation capability of the method. The results deviated at most by 5.6 % compared to formal COSMIC measurement results.

We observed various benefits in these projects by applying UPROM [6]. Apart from the benefits achieved by means of the methodology, which is out of scope of this paper, many of the benefits were enabled by the tool. The analysts reported that integrated modeling environment for six diagram types supported them to smoothly move from process to user requirements analysis and transfer the process knowledge to analysis phase. The analysts mostly enjoyed the automated artifact generation. In three of the projects, the analysts needed to develop these artifacts manually if they were not generated. Another important point mentioned was the reduced maintenance effort. The customer required many changes (specifically in the Public Investment Processes). The analysts emphasized the ease of regeneration instead of manual update of documents. The artifacts were traceable to the models. However, the generated statements did not cover all possible requirements. The analysts needed to manually add non-functional and general system requirements to prepare the technical contract (for two projects). Moreover, specifically for process definition document, different templates were required in different projects, so we needed to tailor the code generation.

The users in our projects, being nontechnical, were not confident in analyzing the requirements. However, they mentioned that they were able to understand and review the generated requirements. Process documentation was favored by many domain experts of different backgrounds. Both domain experts and analysts found the business glossary helpful to ensure a common understanding of the concepts. In the organizations, project managers were using subjective methods to estimate the project effort. The availability of an objective estimation without the need of an expert and even an extra effort, was highly appreciated by them.

The artifacts generated by UPROM tool only cover analysis results in the business domain and create an opportunity to transfer this knowledge to the technical domain. Additionally, traceability to the process models is limited only to the artifacts, whereas the big challenge is achieving traceability to the implementation. The project team needs to design necessary methods to directly utilize these artifacts as direct inputs to software requirements analysis, design and development, and complete traceability until implementation. We will work on such methods in the following phases of the mentioned projects.

For future versions, we plan to develop a functionality to enable users design the format and content of the artifacts and add new process documents presenting process information from different perspectives like RACI charts. At the moment, requirements sentences are generated in Turkish and generation of English sentences are planned for future versions. BPM tools supporting EPC notation are rather restricted in number. EPC is commonly accepted as a good notation for analyzing processes with end users. We believe that similar functionality can be achieved for also BPMN and plan to implement the methodology in a similar way also based on BPMN.

References

1. Curtis, B., Kellner, M.I., Over, J.: Process modeling. Commun. ACM **35**, 75–90 (1992)
2. Becker, J., Rosemann, M., von Uthmann, C.: Guidelines of business process modeling. In: van der Aalst, W.M.P., Desel, J., Oberweis, A. (eds.) Business Process Management. LNCS, vol. 1806, pp. 30–49. Springer, Heidelberg (2000)
3. de Oca, I.M.-M., Snoeck, M., Reijers, H.A., Rodríguez-Morffi, A.: A systematic literature review of studies on business process modeling quality. Inf. Softw. Technol. **58**, 187–205 (2014)

4. Dumas, M., van der Aalst, W., ter Hofstede, A.: Process-Aware Information Systems: Bridging People and Software Through Process Technology. Wiley, New Jersey (2005)
5. Sánchez-González, L., García, F., Ruiz, F., Mendling, J.: Quality indicators for business process models from a gateway complexity perspective. Inf. Softw. Technol. **54**, 1159–1174 (2012)
6. Aysolmaz, B., Demirörs, O.: Modeling business processes to generate artifacts for software development: a methodology. In: 2014 ICSE Workshop on Modeling in Software Engineering (MISE), Hyderabad, India (2014)
7. Abran, A., Desharnais, J.-M., Oligny, S., St-Pierre, D., Symons, C.: The COSMIC Functional Size Measurement Method Version 3.0.1 Measurement Manual (2009)
8. The Eclipse Foundation: Eclipse Modeling Framework Project (EMF). http://www.eclipse.org/modeling/emf/
9. The Eclipse Foundation: Graphical Modeling Project (GMP). http://www.eclipse.org/modeling/gmp/
10. Kühne, S., Kern, H., Gruhn, V., Laue, R.: Business process modeling with continuous validation. J. Softw. Maint. Evol. Res. Pract. **22**, 547–566 (2010)
11. Scheer, A.-W.W.: Aris-Business Process Frameworks. Springer, New York (1998)
12. Aysolmaz, B.: Unified Business Process Modeling Methodology (UPROM) Application: Case Study Results METU/II-TR-2014-32, Ankara, Turkey (2014)
13. Fettke, P., Loos, P., Zwicker, J.: Business process reference models: survey and classification. In: Bussler, C.J., Haller, A. (eds.) BPM 2005. LNCS, vol. 3812, pp. 469–483. Springer, Heidelberg (2006)
14. Davis, R., Brabander, E.: ARIS Design Platform Getting Started with BPM. Springer, London (2007)
15. iText Software Corp.: ITEXT PDF Library. http://itextpdf.com/
16. Aysolmaz, B., Demirörs, O.: Deriving user requirements from business process models for automation: a case study. In: 2014 IEEE 1st International Workshop on the Interrelations Between Requirements Engineering and Business Process Management (REBPM), pp. 19–28. IEEE, Karlskrona, Sweden (2014)
17. Aysolmaz, B., Demirörs, O.: Automated functional size estimation using business process models with UPROM method. In: Abran, A., Braungarten, R., Dumke, R., Cuadrado-Gallego, J., Brunekreef, J. (eds.) Software Process and Product Measurement. Springer, Heidelberg (2014)
18. Tolvanen, J., Pohjonen, R., Kelly, S.: Advanced tooling for domain-specific modeling: MetaEdit+. In: Object-Oriented Programming Systems, Languages, and Applications (OOPSLA) (2007)
19. BPM Academic Initiative: Signavio Process Modeler. http://academic.signavio.com/p/explorer
20. Bizagi: Bizagi Process Modeler. http://www.bizagi.com/products/bizagi-process-modeler
21. Visual Paradigm: Visual Paradigm Process Modeling Tools for In-Depth Process Analysis. http://www.visual-paradigm.com/features/business-process-modeling/
22. Nicolás, J., Toval, A.: On the generation of requirements specifications from software engineering models: a systematic literature review. Inf. Softw. Technol. **51**, 1291–1307 (2009)

Case Study Report

Requirements for IT Governance in Organizations Experiencing Decentralization

Jelena Zdravkovic[1(✉)], Irina Rychkova[2], and Thomas Speckert[1]

[1] Department of Computer and Systems Sciences, Stockholm University, Forum 100,
16440 Kista, Sweden
{jelenaz,thsp7525}@dsv.su.se
[2] Centre de Recherche En Informatique, Université Paris 1 Panthéon - Sorbonne,
90 Rue Tolbiac, 75013 Paris, France
irina.rychkova@univ-paris1.fr

Abstract. Decentralization of organizations and subsequent change of their management and operation styles require changes in organization's processes and heavily involve IT. Enterprise Architecture (EA) frameworks fit to primarily centralized organizational structures, and as such have shortcomings when used in decentralized organizations. We illustrate this idea on the example of one organization in the Higher Education sector that faces decentralization of its structure and has to adapt to it. Overcoming these challenges requires some new principles to be introduced and incorporated into the EA knowledge. In particular for IT governance, in this study we argue that peer-to-peer principles can offer more suitable governance over current EA frameworks as they are able to better align with decentralized components of an organizational structure.

Keywords: Enterprise modeling · Enterprise architecture · IT governance

1 Introduction

Enterprises have traditionally implemented formal, centralized forms of organizational structure [1], such as hierarchical or matrix structures. In these structures, communication patterns, roles and decision rights are strictly defined. This allows for management to have a high degree of control over the enterprise and therefore enforce compliance with standards, procedures and policies which results in a highly stable enterprise. However, this comes at the expense of agility; it is difficult for these organizations to quickly adapt to a changing environment. While centralized structures were appropriate for the business environments of the past, modern business environments demand a high level of agility [2].

The objective of EA methodologies created in early 1990s was to align IT capabilities with business needs via IT centralization. The main price to pay was the loss of flexibility and the inertia in decision making for IT. By that time, however, this was much less critical than to make the IT "disciplined" and to justify the investments in IT. Today, the flexibility in IT becomes more and more strategic. For modern organizations with transparent boundaries, loose business units and agile processes, it is impossible to

© Springer International Publishing Switzerland 2015
S. Nurcan and E. Pimenidis (Eds.): CAiSE Forum 2014, LNBIP 204, pp. 269–285, 2015.
DOI: 10.1007/978-3-319-19270-3_17

centralize IT. On the other hand, it is still crucial to maintain "disciplined" approach in IT evolution using appropriate IT governance principles so that the organizational units not only remain independent but could also efficiently work together as a whole [3, 4].

Rapidly changing business conditions and structures have been identified as an important problem in EA [5, 6]. For these reasons, ensuring suitability of EA frameworks for decentralized organizational structures and IT governance which are highly dynamic, are increasingly relevant [7].

Our research has envisioned to addresses the problem of suitable EA and IT governance principles for decentralized organizations. The three concepts in focus interrelate - EA should be compliant with IT governance by including its principles or correlating with them, and in the way to reflect a given Organizational Structure.

Upon the described challenge, we have defined the following research question: *Do, and if yes - how existing EA frameworks need to be extended in order to support IT Governance in decentralized organizations?* Using a Design Science research method [8, 9], including literature studies, interviews and document studies from an empirical case for data collection, and a qualitative approach for data analysis, we propose the artifacts summarizing shortcoming of current EA frameworks and formulating the requirements for IT governance for decentralized environments.

The paper is organized as follows: Sect. 2 gives an overview of different organizational structures; in Sect. 3 a brief description of the research method and proposed artifacts is given; in Sect. 4, we describe the deficiencies of conventional EA frameworks for providing decentralization support; Sect. 5 illustrates misalignment between EA principles, organizational structure, and IT governance principles on the example of one organization in Higher Education sector; based on that study, in Sect. 6, we revisit the IT governance principles defined by Weill and Ross in [4] and provide explicit requirements for IT governance to support decentralization. Discussion, conclusions and directions of future work are presented in Sect. 7.

2   From Centralized to Decentralized Organizations

The organizational structure defines the rules according to which allocation of responsibilities and resources, coordination and supervision, is made for an organization. In order to differentiate between centralized and decentralized organizations, we consider three organizational properties: *geographical dispersion*, *coordination*, and *communication patterns* [10–12].

On the continuum from centralized to decentralized structures, *federated organizations* have emerged combining characteristics of centralized organizations, such as centralized authority, planning and regulations, with for example local leadership, as well as competitive local objectives of including business units (decentralized aspects) (Table 1).

Table 1. Organizational properties of centralized vs. decentralized organizations.

Property	Centralized	Decentralized
Geographical dispersion	Single location	Geographically distributed with a reliance on IS to work together
Coordination: authority, decision rights, and regulations	Vertical coordination: decision rights are strictly defined and act down from the top; strict governance and control by the upper management; rigid structuring of accountability, roles and responsibilities; standardized methods and procedures; homogeneous goals set by high-level authorities	Lateral coordination: authority and decision making rights are pushed down to the level of business units, groups, or even individuals; individuals can define their own roles and responsibilities; heterogeneous goals; individual entities in the organization are collaboratively working towards some common or complementing goals
Communication patterns	Communication patterns follow the hierarchy; direct interactions and communications are not practiced	Informal communication lines; flexible, constantly changing communication lines; fluid, project-oriented teams.

3   Research Method

Having the desire in our research to combine literature and empirical research to develop novel artifacts addressing the problem emphasized in Introduction, we have followed Design Science (DS) research method [8], also presented in [9] In a nutshell, the method is composed of five research activities with input-output relationships: *explicate problem, outline artifact and define requirements, design and develop artifact,* and *evaluate artifact.* These activities are commonly carried out in an iterative and incremental manner to enable changes and improvements of intermediate results, as well as of final research artifacts.

Adhering to space limitations of this paper, we will in our presentation mostly pay attention to the content of the artifacts and not to the DS process of achieving them; for details of the application of DS to our research, the reader can refer to [23].

The research has aimed to develop several artifacts. The first artifact presents conclusions obtained from the literature study on potential deficiencies of current EA to support decentralized organizations. The artifact has been in details elaborated in [13], while in Sect. 4 we present its summary. The second artifact is the result of the empirical case study presented in Sect. 5, proposing EA principles supportive for decentralized organizations [14]. The third artifact, making the use of the previous one, followed by an additional literature study, proposes a set of IT governance principles for a decentralized organizational context; it is presented in Sect. 6.

4   Deficiencies of EA Frameworks to Support Decentralization

EA frameworks include artifacts to specify the current state of a company's architecture ("as-is"), the target architecture ("to-be"), identify how to best cross the gap between them (architectural roadmap), and to set up the standards and rules to follow during this transformation (EA principles). These elements are often addressed in literature as *EA description*; the process that an organization has to execute in order to obtain its EA description is called *EA method*. To assure that the organization will continuously follow the EA principles and achieve the designated goals (architecture "to-be") a third element has to be defined: *EA engine*. The presence of this reflects the fact that EA is not static: it makes the organization to change while changing itself over time.

In our research effort, the first task was to investigate how existing EA frameworks are supportive for decentralized organizations. The three key organizational properties from Sect. 2 – geographical dispersion, coordination, and communication patterns were used to assess three wide-known frameworks - TOGAF [15], FEA [16], and Zachman Framework [17].

While the analysis [13] revealed some support for decentralization, the main conclusion drawn was that the EA frameworks of TOGAF, Zachman, and FEA are primarily supportive of centralized organizational structures, and therefore fail to address the demands of decentralized. A summarized view is provided in Table 2:

Table 2.   Existing support of decentralization by EA frameworks.

EA Component	Existing support for centralized organizations	Existing support for decentralized organizations
EA Method	Approval process is based on hierarchy; architecture development is coordinated, supervised and evaluated by well-defined roles in a company; EA teams coordinate architectural work and communicate results; results are controlled and evaluated centrally.	Federated architectures; possibility to adapt ADM for specific organizations; architecture development process involves multiple stakeholders.
EA Description	Strategic level architectures; hierarchy Of architecture principles; a common set of reference models; hierarchical organization of EA artifacts with explicitly defined roles and domains.	Architecture partitions; architecture reference models; segment architecture; the concept of "shared vision".
EA Engine	Architecture board; formal governance framework; common principles for entire organization (global commitment is taken for granted); centrally managed architecture repository.	Integration of various (segment) architectures is assured by (centralized) management and governance.

The important properties of a decentralized business environment that need to be supported by EA are *horizontal coordination* and *lateral communication patterns*. However, the three EA frameworks primarily support vertical coordination in their governance styles and top-down/bottom-up formal communication patterns.

5 Case Study

We have analyzed a prominent university for higher education in Sweden. Our objective was to investigate the alignment between the organizational structure (including the organization of IT functions), and the EA and IT Governance rules in use. As common, the university includes a number of entities - faculties, faculty departments, and units. Nowadays, the entities are becoming more independent than before, due to several factors:

- Geographical dislocation. Some faculty departments have been moved out of the main university campus. An example is the Computer and Systems Sciences department located in Kista, the leading Swedish IT cluster. This proximity enables cooperation between IT companies and students through mentoring programs, internships, graduate work opportunities, guest lectures, etc.
- Decentralization of management. Decision rights are of the type "push-down" delegated by the principal to the faculty boards and deans, and some to the faculty departments and their units.
- Both formal and informal communication patterns. Formal hierarchical communication from the faculty to its departments, and informal direct communication between and within the departments are present. For example, the administrative tasks (such as registration for graduate courses, or postgraduate research, etc.) are primarily formal, whereas course curriculum can be established between departments cooperatively, using informal communication links.

Hence, the university is seen as having high decentralization tendencies. The study was to analyze the aspects of organization's EA and IT governance in order to assess the decentralization support provided, to reveal the deficiencies and to formulate the guidelines for an EA and IT governance in order to overcome these deficiencies.

This case is representative for the Higher Education sector: universities adopt more agile forms of organization including virtual research labs, scientific interest groups in research, joint master programs in education, and so on. As in the studied university, these examples involve geographical dislocation, decentralization of management, virtualization of communication, and use of informal communication patterns.

5.1 Approach

Four separate interviews were conducted in one of university's departments in order to get a holistic view of the way of work across the whole university. The roles of the interviewees were chosen to cover the major business activities of the institution – management, research, education, and IT support: vice division lead, head of postgraduate studies, head of undergraduate studies, and head of IT support. The interviews were conducted face-to-face in a semi-structured manner, starting with a set of open-ended questions that promote the interviewees to elaborate on their views to organization's processes, decision making, coordination, etc.; for details of the interviews, the reader is referred to [23]. In addition, many official documents on the organizational structure are available, thus making a document study viable. The documents that formed this study are described in Table 3:

Table 3. Documents used in the documentation study

Document	Description
Institution's homepage	Contains descriptions of different topic areas of the institution as well its organizational structure
Authority delegation documents	Publicly available documents specify authority and delegations of said authority of the insinuation's organizational units
Rule book	The official rule book of the institution detailing the rules and decisions that must be followed by the institution

5.2   Results

During our study, we found that despite an evident decentralization, EA principles used by the studied organization largely rely upon centralized coordination and vertical communication patterns. On the other hand, IT governance mechanisms currently used by this organization often adhere to decentralization and thus represent a mismatch with the existing EA. This problem is a serious constraint for successful evolution of organizational IT. For the purpose of this study, we illustrate our findings on the example of one established EA principle:

– Integrated IT systems across the university.

Owing to a federated organizational structure, and as in more details uncovered during the interviews, some decision rights are pushed down to the operational level, which for the IT-related organizational structure has resulted in highly *decentralized* governance:

The IT governance mechanisms described in the table are in a non-alignment with the established EA principle to *integrate IT systems*. As a consequence, IT governance initiatives typically fail, and decisions about IT become inefficient.

An example of immediate consequence of this is wasted financial resources: we consider a situation outlined in the interview with the head of IT of the department which concerned the acquisition of a software system with the objective of integrated facility management across departments (i.e. "integrated IT systems" principle). Following the principle, a software system has been bought for university-wide use; since the principle holds for the whole organization, the purchase was the decision of the university-board, i.e. the departments were not involved in the decision making process. In contrast, following the decentralized IT governance in-place for the use of "non-essential" software systems (Table 4), a subset of them consequently refused to shut down their local systems and switch to the global one. As a consequence, the principle of integration failed; the departments were able to protect their interests (local, decentralized systems tailored for their needs), but were still charged for the acquired system they never used. To improve the situation, the following problems need to be resolved:

• EA principles have to be aligned with the evolving organizational structure by acknowledging novel modes of coordination and communication;

Table 4. In-place IT governance mechanisms

Name	Org. Property / Centralization	Description
Authority structure	Coordination / Decentralized	The department and the university have separate IT and the departmental IT does not report to the university.
IT adoption (department)	Coordination / Decentralized	Department IT does not dictate all IT used in the department; research projects and centers; for example, units can develop and use their own IT systems should they desire.
Approval (department)	Coordination / Mixed	IT projects are run independently by groups, though they sometimes need approval from the department if they are expensive.
IT collaboration	Coordination / Decentralized	Any decision to cooperate with other departments or with the university IT is made by the departmental IT itself and is based on cooperation resulting in mutual benefit.
Management of "essential" central IT systems	Coordination / Centralized	"Essential" systems (e.g. administrative systems such as HR) for the whole university are controlled by the university board. The department is required to pay for, and use these systems.
Management of "non-essential" central IT systems	Coordination / Mixed	"Non-essential" systems (such as course portals and schedules) are centrally budgeted, but departments are not required to use them.
Use of IT systems (department)	Communication / Decentralized	Informal communication patterns are used, i.e. when changes are performed on systems, they are informally spread to those who use the systems.

• As a part of the EA engine, the IT governance has to be transparent and aligned with the established EA principles; in particular, it has to adequately support decentralization and to ensure efficient coordination and communication between organizational center and its sub-entities.

5.3 Recommendations: Peer-to-Peer Principles

Drawing parallels between the domains of peer-to-peer systems used to provide a mechanism and architecture for organizing peers in such a way so that they can cooperate to provide a useful service to a community of users [18] and decentralized organizations, we think that the peer-to-peer concept may be a source of the principles forming a basis for evolving current centralization-focused EA frameworks into ones that are supportive of decentralization.

Peer Production: we see organizations as being composed of peers (a peer could be individual, or an organizational unit), For example, TOGAF relies on an Architecture Board responsible for high-level decisions and governance. Instead of a central board responsible for making decisions, a model based on the principle of peer production [19] for creation and evaluation of EA artifacts could be used instead. This would better support decentralization as decision making would then be distributed amongst the peers that make the organization. In the university case, departments' members could produce strategy, or budget, using peer production (such as for use of information systems). Eventually, faculty or university boards could have control/advisory roles.

Peer Trust Management: TOGAF employs the idea of an approval process grounded on the presence of centralized authority. This is to ensure that the presented architectural material is in fact valid for the enterprise. According to peer trust management [20], whether some content proposed by a peer is of a sufficient quality to be included in the overall architecture, is determined by other peers. In the studied case, this principle could provide a formal mechanism for communication among peers when needed, hence avoid the situations when other peers are not informed about a new proposal (such as a change in IS use).

The suggested peer-to-peer principles will seek to maintain the departmental independence becoming prevalent at the university, while addressing the incompatible architecture components this results in. This would be accomplished through a cooperative classification of essential and non-essential software systems by the departments, for example by giving each department a vote. Systems classified as essential are required to be used or integrated by the departments, while departments have the option to choose if they want to utilize systems classified as non-essential. These changes would help at reconciling differences between the architecture principles emphasized in the case without actually changing it. Decision rights are still pushed down, and IT systems are still integrated throughout the organization; this change in IT governance at the university level addresses the conflict that can arise when a decision is made to use a decentralized system that the rest of the organization is integrating (as occurs in the current state).

6 IT Governance Principles in Federated and Decentralized Organizations

We have emphasized in the beginning that the notions of Organizational Structure, IT governance, and EA are interrelated: EA specifies architecture principles according to which both business and IT environment of the organization will evolve. Thus, it has to reflect the style of organizational structure. IT governance ensures that these architecture principles are respected by handling the everyday IT operations within the organization. In [21], the authors acknowledge that the organizational structure of a company (centralized, federated, decentralized) and its IT functions in particular affect the IT governance; the IT governance mechanisms hence need to be selected or designed taking this structure in to account. As a result of an extensive study of different organizations, in [4], Weill and Ross define 10 generic principles of IT Governance. Practice-inspired, these principles do not consider the organizational structure in-place.

Upon an analysis, we concluded that some of the principles refer to structures and mechanisms adhering only to centralized organizations and require hence adaptation for federated and decentralized organizations. In particular, adaptation is needed for *coordination mechanisms and communication patterns* on which IT governance relies upon.

Our proposed adaptations are mainly based on the concepts defined by peer-to-peer domain, i.e. peer production and peer trust management (Sect. 5): *distributed content production, peer production of relevance and accreditation, peer review process and moderation, peer produced rating, peer trust management, decentralized decision making or group decision-making* [19, 20].

The objective we pursue is twofold: first, we want to formulate requirements for IT governance in order to better support decentralization in organizations and, second, to provide relevant recommendations about tools to use in order to facilitate the coordination and communication (Sect. 2).

Principle 1: *Actively Design Governance.* According to [4], management should actively design IT governance around enterprise's objectives and performance goals. Actively designing governance involves senior executives taking the lead and allocating resources, as well as for support to business processes.

Decentralized Organizations: Due to management decentralization, senior executives do not play the leading role in the process coordination and resource allocation. Instead, *coordination* has to be grounded on the principles such as distributed content production and group decision-making. Traditional reporting/approval process used in centralized organizations can be replaced by peer review processes and peer produced rankings. Senior executives can play the role of moderators during the content creation. Lateral *communication patterns* (e.g. on-line and off-line informal discussions, content sharing) have to be employed replacing formal top-down/bottom-up communication patterns based on a hierarchy. Use of social software for communication and production of relevant content is an important requirement for IT governance in decentralized organizations: traditional meetings or workshops devoted to IT governance design can be highly inefficient as they assume centralized planning and require physical presence of assigned specialists in a given location, and at a given time.

In the studied case, IT governance principles supporting peer review of design are well recognized - one example is a by a unit proposed software system for thesis management; reviewed by the other units in iterations of system's development. Hence, a next step could be to extend good practices of coordination and communication patterns for reviewing to facilitate peer production as well. To summarize:

RQ1	With a lack of centralized coordination, governance design process should adhere to principles of distributed content creation and management. **Recommendation**: group decision-making and peer reviewing can be seen as an alternative to centralized approval process for coordination.
RQ2	IT governance should encourage collaborative design, where each entity can easily benefit from and contribute to a common organizational knowledge. **Recommendation**: adoption and systematic use of IT and non-IT knowledge management tools.
RQ3	Mechanisms supporting lateral communication patterns (informal social exchange, semi-formal discussions) have to be encouraged replacing vertical (hierarchy-based) communication patterns. **Recommendation**: lateral communication can be facilitated using social software platforms.

Federated Organizations: IT governance has to be designed at multiple levels: at the unit level, to support the autonomy of each unit, and at the *corporate level*, to maintain the consistency and foster cooperation between units. Successful *coordination* mechanisms should involve both elements of centralized coordination (e.g. centralized definition of objectives and performance goals, hierarchical assignment of tasks from the corporate level to the unit level), and decentralized elements based on the peer production principles (as defined for decentralized organizations). Both lateral *communication patterns* (i.e. from a unit to a unit) and top-down/bottom-up communication patterns (from a unit to the corporate level, and vice versa) have to be used. Efficiency in communication and content creation for both decentralized and federated organizations can be gained using commenting tools, on-line discussions, ranking and many other features provided by social software. Possibility to easily and instantaneously evaluate the content, to see evaluation of the others, and to get/receive feedbacks, guarantees a massive user involvement and fosters relevant content creation.

RQ4	IT governance needs to support the synergy of units at the corporate level, and units' autonomy at the unit level, by combining centralized coordination with distributed (peer) production. See also RQ1.
RQ5	Mechanisms combining lateral and vertical (top-down/bottom-up) communication patterns have to be adopted (e.g. peer reviewing, moderation) See also RQ3.

Principle 2: Know When to Redesign. According to [4], rethinking the whole governance structure requires that individuals learn new roles and relationships. Learning takes time. Thus, governance redesign should be infrequent. The recommendation is that a change in governance is required with a change in desirable behavior.

Decentralized Organizations: Compared to centralized organizations, where the governance structure is global and its change impacts the whole organization, entities in decentralized organizations can redesign the IT governance locally. Thus, on the smaller scale, the organizational learning takes less time and the changes can be made more frequently, allowing for more agility and flexibility. The whole organization can benefit from the experience of each of its business units by reusing their best practices. By sharing best practices and lessons learned, units contribute to the common pool of knowledge and foster the organizational learning.

In the studied case, a unit specialized for technology-enabled learning (TEL) is capable to propose redesign, such as use of new IT solutions and principles for "flexible learning" (spanning from off- to on-line) to improve organization's business. However, at the present time, neither a systematic coordination is installed, nor the TEL unit has real communication mechanism in place to share its knowledge for redesign.

RQ6	IT governance needs to encourage shorter cycles of organizational learning for more flexibility and agility.
RQ7	Systematic sharing of practice and lessons learned has to be an integrated part of any governance redesign. **Recommendation**: communities of practice, social networks, and document libraries are examples of tools facilitating knowledge sharing.

Federated Organizations: Organizational learning process consists of both short cycles when business units redesign their governance locally, and long cycles when the corporate IT governance is reorganized. The local redesigns have to be aligned with the corporate governance. IT governance evolution strongly depends on the capacity of units to share and reuse their local practices. Both lateral *communication patterns* (from unit to unit) and top-down/bottom-up communication patterns (from unit to the corporate level, and vice versa) have to be used.

RQ8	IT governance needs to support short cycles of organizational learning at the unit level and long cycles at the corporate level. See also RQ7.

Principle 3: Involve Senior Managers. In [4] it is argued that organizations with more effective IT governance have more of senior management involvement. For example, CIOs must be effectively involved in IT governance for success. Other senior managers must participate in the committees, the approval processes, and performance reviews.

Decentralized/Federated organizations: It is important to involve both senior management and local (unit) management in IT governance by forming committees, boards, and expert groups. *Communities of practice (COP)* can be seen as an alternative for "assigned" groups of senior managers to steer the IT governance. A COP refers to a group of people who share a concern or a passion for something they do and has an objective to share and create common skills, knowledge, and expertise. These groups are formed on the volunteer basis and not by a hierarchical assignment; they also gain trust and reputation within the community of by professionals where they exist. Due to the lack of central authority, an approval process has to be grounded on the principles of group decision-making. In *communication*, an accent has to be made on knowledge sharing and cooperation over authority and hierarchy.

Due to a lack of appropriate coordination mechanisms, in the discussed case, there is a problem of non-involving units in management of the IT governance on the corporate level. The example in Sect. 5.2 is an illustration of that.

RQ9	Units have to be involved in IT governance management via boards and expert groups. **Recommendation**: COPs as an alternative to centrally assigned boards/ groups.
RQ10	Combination of centralized approval process and distributed decision-making has to be adopted for federated organizations. **Recommendation**: Performance review can be done using peer-reviewing principles.

Principle 4: Make Choices. According to [4], governance can and should highlight conflicting goals for debate. As the number of tradeoffs increases, governance becomes more complex. Top-performing enterprises handle goal conflicts with a few clear business principles."

Some of the most ineffective governance observed in [4] was the result of conflicting goals. The unmanageable number of goals typically arose from not making strategic business choices and had nothing to do with IT. It is observed that good managers trying diligently to meet all these goals became frustrated and ineffective.

Decentralized Organizations: Having maximum autonomy, units can have different (event conflicting) goals. Peer ranking, peer trust management, peer reviewing and group decision-making are examples of the mechanisms to be adopted for *coordinating* conflict solving and decision-making. Social software platforms are indispensable instrument to support these mechanisms within the organization. Lateral *communication* patterns replace the traditional approval process.

In the case illustrated in Sect. 5, this principle has not been yet implemented adequately: at the present time choices/goals are either determined centrally, or solely by the units, i.e. without communication to other units (i.e. goals are not shared).

RQ11	IT governance needs to support local units' goals supporting group decision making. **Recommendation**: peer reviewing, peer ranking, peer trust management are examples of mechanisms that can support "democratic choice" in decentralized organizations.

Federated Organizations: The goals and priorities are set up at different levels (corporate, and unit). Unit level goals have to be compliant with the corporate level goals. Between the units, the same coordination mechanisms and communication patterns as for decentralized organizations can be used to negotiate and to resolve the local conflicts.

RQ12	IT governance needs to support both centralized and decentralized mechanisms for decision making: "democratic choice" (see also RQ11) on the unit level, and compliance with few high level business principles.

Principle 6: Provide the Right Incentives. Following [4], a common problem encountered in studying IT governance was a misalignment of incentive and reward systems with the behaviors the IT governance arrangements were designed to encourage. If IT governance is designed to encourage business unit synergy, autonomy, or some combination, the incentives of the executives must also be aligned.

Decentralized Organizations: Decentralized organizations support maximum of units' autonomy. In a number of situations, however, the benefits from the "whole" produced collectively, by units' synergy, exceed the benefits from components contributed by individual units. With the lack of central authority, these synergies can hardly be "encouraged" using regular market incentives. Their formation, however, can result from application of peer production principles and creation of production system based on collaboration among business units who cooperate without relying on either market pricing or managerial hierarchies to coordinate their common enterprise [22]. In this case, the incentives can include status, benefits to reputation, value of innovation to themselves [13]. Motivations can be cooperation are characterized by a combination of a will to create and to communicate with others [19].

Federated Organizations: The challenge of federated organizations is to encourage units' synergy at the corporate level and units' autonomy - locally. To do so, an organization has to promote the culture of *collaboration* rather than *competition* between units. Collaborative environments pave the road to peer production systems; here the individual units are much more sensitive to non-market incentives and are willing to form synergies more than in the competitive environments based on "survival of the fittest" principles.

Contradictory incentives can represent a problem in Higher Education organizations like the one we studied: encouraging interdisciplinary Master programs on the university level (synergy) in exchange to reputation and recognition will not be efficient until each department is evaluated and financially rewarded based on its individual performance.

RQ13	IT governance needs to encourage cooperation instead of competition. **Recommendation**: use of nonmarket incentives (e.g. status, reputation)

Principle 8: Design governance at Multiple Organizational Levels. The authors of [4] argue that in large multi-unit organizations, it is necessary to consider IT governance

at several levels. The starting point is enterprise-wide IT governance driven by a small number of enterprise-wide strategies and goals. Enterprises with separate IT functions in divisions, business units, or geographies require a separate but connected layer of IT governance. Assembling the governance arrangements matrixes for the multiple levels in an enterprise makes explicit the connections and pressure points. This principle explicitly refers to IT governance with a complex organizational structure, and proposes multi-level governance.

Decentralized Organizations: Governance arrangements for decentralized organizations can vary from a set of autonomous "silos" to a single, distributed IT governance resulted from collaborative efforts of individual units. In both cases, only one governance level is explicitly defined.

In the discussed case, IT governance has been defined at multiple levels (department level, faculty level); its design, however, was not systematic as no coordination within level or between levels was provided.

RQ14	Distributed IT governance can be encouraged in the organizations with cooperative culture; For highly competitive environments, governance "in silos" needs to be supported.

Federated Organizations: For federated organizations that support both units' synergy (on the corporate level) and units' autonomy (locally, at the unit level), at least two IT governance levels have to be defined. The special attention has to be paid for adoption of collaborative software for facilitating lateral communication between units.

RQ15	IT governance needs to be defined at (at least) two levels: corporate and unit.

Principle 9: Provide Transparency and Education. According to [4], transparency and education often go together - the more education, the more transparency, and vice versa. The more transparency of the governance processes, the more confidence in the governance. Also, the less transparent the governance processes are, the less people follow them. Communicating and supporting IT governance is the single most important IT role of senior leaders.

Decentralized Organizations: Communication and knowledge sharing supported by social software is extremely important for providing transparency and education in IT governance. Adopting technique and tools for distributed content production and collaborative content management, an organization can easily and naturally involve its employees into design of the IT governance process, thus guaranteeing its transparency for the users. *Lateral communication* patterns should be used - facilitated by senior experts, virtual or live, structured, semi-structured (e.g. webinars, workshops) or informal discussions (e.g. forums, chats, knowledge cafes) on the existing IT governance practice contribute to education and foster the organizational learning.

In the given case, this principle is enabled through the means of internal social software, however its broad use is typically ensured only in the situations when a higher level has provided the approval of a "knowledge" and has given recommendations for its use (.i.e. lateral communication is not in place).

RQ16	IT governance needs to ensure employees involvement into the IT governance design process. **Recommendation**: distributed content production and management, social software.
RQ17	To foster the education and organizational learning, IT governance needs to extensively use lateral communication patterns

Federated Organizations: Techniques and tools for distributed content production and collaborative content management play equally important role in achieving transparency in the IT governance process as in decentralized organizations. The role of senior leaders is to setup learning objectives, to supervise the education process, and to evaluate its outcomes.

7   Discussion, Conclusion and Future Work

In this study we have addressed the challenge of suitable EA and IT governance principles for decentralized organizations arguing that existing frameworks offer a limited support, and that new principles are needed in order to make them to fully support decentralized organizational structures.

While technology serves as a catalyst for organizational transformations, it is important to utilize right IT resources, and in a supportive manner. To accomplish this in decentralized organizations, adequate EA processes, principles and concepts need to be employed to both handle the IT resources and to foster business/IT co-evolution.

We have used an institution of Higher Education in Sweden as an illustrative case study. This case was chosen as an example of an organization that exhibits many decentralized properties (in particular with respect to IT governance). The focus was on analyzing the state of its EA in order to assess the decentralization support provided, in contrast with what is needed; and proposing features of an EA and in particular IT governance principles, that could provide the needed support. Our proposed recommendations are mainly based on the 2 principles defined by peer-to-peer domain – peer production and peer trust management. These principles were evaluated by a demonstration to the interviewees in the case; and argumentatively seen as applicable /valid to "university" contexts, which are shifting more and more to decentralization; however no validation on this issue was conducted for other organization types. Hence, the current work is based on a single case study that illustrated the argued limitations of current EA and non-alignment with IT governance in-place, and thus gave us a foundation for proposing new principles for EA and IT governance; however the case study did not validate the proposed principles.

To generalize and stream-forward our foundations from the case, we have in Sect. 6 revisited the IT governance principles defined by Weill and Ross in [4], and following them defined a set of requirements for IT governance in supporting the specifics of federated and decentralized organizations. We believe that they may be of interest to three groups: the case organization, researchers in the field of EA, and, potentially, other organizations with decentralized structures interested in implementing some form of EA. For the case organization, the proposed mechanism of peer production, reviewing and trust, also embedded into requirements for adequate IT governance, might be important as their application could offer some improvements to their governance structure. For researchers, this study work might be of interest as it highlights some potential issues with traditional EA knowledge, while giving guidelines on how they could be solved. This work may be of interest to organizations that have adopted, or are interested in adopting a decentralized structure and are looking for the insights into how governance can be successfully done in this environment.

For the future work, our short term objective is to evaluate our conclusions in the given case context, and then to extend our study and in other organizations. In long terms, we envisage to in more details analyze mechanisms for coordination (decision making) as well as communication patterns, in centralized, decentralized and mixed (federated) organizations, and to see how they can be transformed into IT governance-type patterns, and how to merge them into exiting EA methodologies.

References

1. Pearlson, K.E., Saunders, C.S.: Strategic Management of Information Systems, 4th edn. Wiley, Chichester (2009)
2. Fulk, J., DeSanctis, G.: Electronic communication and changing organizational forms. Organ. Sci. **6**(4), 337–349 (1995)
3. Rockart, J., Earl, M., Ross, J.: Eight imperatives for the new IT organization. Sloan Manag. Rev. **38**, 43–56 (1996)
4. Weill, P., Ross, J.W.: IT Governance: How Top Performers Manage IT Decision Rights for Superior Results. Harvard Business School Press, Boston (2004)
5. Lucke, C., Krell, S., Lechner, U.: Critical issues in enterprise architecting - a literature review. In: Proceedings of AMCIS 2010 (2010). http://aisel.aisnet.org/amcis2010/305
6. Bente, S., Bombosch, U., Langade, S.: Collaborative Enterprise Architecture: Enriching EA with Lean, Agile, and Enterprise 2.0 Practices. Morgan Kaufmann, Waltham (2012)
7. Ross, J.W., Weill, P.: Enterprise Architecture As Strategy: Creating a Foundation for Business Execution. Harvard Business Review Press, Boston (2006)
8. Hevner, A.R., March, S.T., Park, J., Ram, S.: Design science in information systems research. MIS Q. **28**(1), 75–105 (2004)
9. Johannesson, P., Perjons, E.: A Design Science Primer, 1st edn. CreateSpace, Boston (2012). http://designscienceprimer.wordpress.com
10. Luthans, F.: Organizational Behavior. McGraw-Hill/Irwin, New York (2006)
11. Ahuja, M.K., Carley, K.M.: Network structure in virtual organizations. J. Comput.-Mediated Commun. **3**(4), 1–31 (1998)
12. Bolman, L.G., Deal, T.E.: Reframing Organizations, 4th edn. Wiley, San Francisco (2008)

13. Speckert, T., Rychkova, I., Zdravkovic, J., Nurcan, S.: On the changing role of enterprise architecture in decentralized environments: state of the art. In: Proceedings of 8th International Workshop on Trends in Enterprise Architecture Research (TEAR), Vancouver, BC, Canada, 9–13 September (2013) (to appear)

14. Zdravkovic, J., Rychkova, I., Speckert, T.: IT governance in organizations facing decentralization – case study in higher education. In: Proceedings of the 26th CAiSE 2014 Forum (2014). http://ceur-ws.org/Vol-1164/

15. The Open Group, TOGAF Version 9.1. The Open Group (2011)

16. Federal Enterprise Architecture Program Management. FEA Practice Guidance (2007)

17. Zachman, J.A.: John Zachman's Concise Definition of the Zachman Framework (2008). http://www.zachman.com/about-the-zachman-framework

18. Saroiu, S., Gummadi, P.K., Gribble, S.D.: Measurement study of peer-to-peer file sharing systems. In: El. Imaging, International Society for Optics and Photonics, pp. 156–170 (2001)

19. Benkler, Y.: The Wealth of Networks: How Social Production Transforms Markets and Freedom. Yale University Press, London (2006)

20. Aberer, K., Despotovic, Z.: Managing Trust in a Peer-2-Peer Information System. In: Proceedings of the 10th International Conference on Information and Knowledge Management ACM, pp. 310–317 (2001)

21. De Haes, S., Grembergen, V.W.: IT governance and its mechanisms. Inf. Syst. Control J. **1**, 27–33 (2004)

22. Benkler, Y.: Coase's penguin, or Linux and the nature of the firm. Yale Law J. **112**, 369–446 (2002)

23. Speckert, T.: Enterprise architecture for decentralized environments. Master thesis (2013). https://daisy.dsv.su.se/fil/visa?id=104520

Author Index

Abid, Ahmed   148
Abid, Mohamed   148
Ahmed, Naved   20
Anton Fröschl, Karl   68
Aysolmaz, Banu   250

Bochicchio, Mario   181

Ceccato, Mariano   215
Cleve, Anthony   85

Dahman, Karim   3
Demirörs, Onur   250
Devogele, Thomas   148
Dunkl, Reinhold   68

Eder, Johann   133
España, Sergio   199

Gateau, Benjamin   3
Giraldo, Fáber D.   199
Giraldo, William J.   199
Godart, Claude   3
Goettelmann, Elio   3
Grambow, Gregor   52
Gross, Daniel   102
Grossmann, Wilfried   68

Joham, Dominik   133

Kirikova, Marite   165
Kolb, Jens   52
Kop, Christian   116
Köpke, Julius   133

Leopold, Henrik   36
Livieri, Barbara   181

Malinova, Monika   36
Matulevičius, Raimundas   20
Mayr, Heinrich C.   116
Mendling, Jan   36
Messai, Nizar   148
Morales-Ramirez, Itzel   215
Mori, Marco   85
Mundbrod, Nicolas   52

Nalchigar, Soroosh   102
Noughi, Nesrine   85

Pastor, Oscar   199
Perini, Anna   215
Pineda, Manuel A.   199

Rathod, Hemant   233
Reichert, Manfred   52
Rinderle-Ma, Stefanie   68
Rouached, Mohsen   148
Rychkova, Irina   269

Shekhovtsov, Vladimir A.   116
Speckert, Thomas   269
Sturm, Arnon   102
Sunkle, Sagar   233

Wang, Jian   102

Yu, Eric   102

Zdravkovic, Jelena   269

Printed in the United States
By Bookmasters